Brides of Christ

BRIDES OF CHRIST
Women and monasticism in medieval and early modern Ireland

Martin Browne OSB, Tracy Collins, Bronagh Ann McShane and
Colmán Ó Clabaigh OSB

EDITORS

FOUR COURTS PRESS

Typeset in 10pt on 12.5pt BemboPro by
Carrigboy Typesetting Services for
FOUR COURTS PRESS LTD
7 Malpas Street, Dublin 8, Ireland
www.fourcourtspress.ie
and in North America for
FOUR COURTS PRESS
c/o IPG, 814 N Franklin St, Chicago, IL 60610.

A catalogue record for this title is available
from the British Library.

ISBN 978-1-80151-022-6

Printed in England
by CPI Antony Rowe, Chippenham, Wilts.

Contents

Illustrations

FIGURES

COLOUR PLATES

(between pages 80 and 81)

Abbreviations

AH	*Archivium Hibernicum*
Beach and Cochelin, *CHMMLW*	Alison I. Beach and Isabelle Cochelin (eds), *The Cambridge history of medieval monasticism in the Latin West*, 2 vols (Cambridge, 2020)
Begley, *Limerick*	J. Begley, *The diocese of Limerick ancient and modern*, (Dublin, 1906, repr. Limerick, 1993)
Browne and Ó Clabaigh, *Benedictines*	Martin Browne OSB and Colmán Ó Clabaigh OSB (eds), *The Irish Benedictines: a history* (Dublin, 2005)
Browne and Ó Clabaigh, *Households*	Martin Browne OSB and Colmán Ó Clabaigh OSB (eds), *Households of God: the regular canons and canonesses of Saint Augustine and of Prémontré in medieval Ireland* (Dublin, 2019)
CLAHJ	*County Louth Archaeological and Historical Journal*
Collins, *Female monasticism*	Tracy Collins, *Female monasticism in medieval Ireland: an archaeology* (Cork, 2021)
CPL, 1 [etc.]	*Calendar of entries in the papal registers relating to Great Britain and Ireland: papal letters* (London & Dublin, 1893–)
DIB	*Dictionary of Irish biography*
Flanagan, *Charters*	Marie Therese Flanagan, *Irish royal charters: texts and contexts* (Oxford, 2005)
Flanagan, *Transformation*	Marie Therese Flanagan, *The transformation of the Irish church in the twelfth century* (Woodbridge, 2010)
Gwynn and Gleeson, *Killaloe*	Aubrey Gwynn and Dermot Gleeson, *A history of the diocese of Killaloe* (Dublin, 1962)
Hall, *Women*	Dianne Hall, *Women and the church in medieval Ireland*, c.1140–1540 (Dublin, 2003)
HBS	Henry Bradshaw Society
IHS	*Irish Historical Studies: the Joint Journal of the Irish Historical Society and the Ulster Society for Irish Historical Studies*
JCHAS	*Journal of the Cork Historical and Archaeological Society*
JCKAHS	*Journal of the County Kildare Archaeological and Historical Society*
JMMS	*Journal of Medieval Monastic Studies*
JRSAI	*Journal of the Royal Society of Antiquaries of Ireland*
Kenney, *Sources*	*The sources for the early history of Ireland (ecclesiastical): an introduction and guide* (New York 1929, repr. Dublin, 1979)
MGH	*Monumenta Germaniae Historica*
Milne, *CCCD*	Kenneth Milne (ed.), *Christ Church Cathedral Dublin: a history* (Dublin, 2000)

MRHI	A. Gwynn and R.N. Hadcock, *Medieval religious houses: Ireland* (Dublin, 1970 [repr. Dublin, 1988])
NLI	National Library of Ireland, Dublin
NMAJ	*North Munster Antiquarian Journal*
Ní Dhonnchadha, 'Caillech'	Máirín Ní Dhonnchadha, '*Caillech* and other terms for veiled women in medieval Irish texts', *Éigse*, 26 (1994–5), 71–96
Ó Riain, Dictionary	Pádraig Ó Riain, *Dictionary of Irish saints* (Dublin, 2011)
PRIA	*Proceedings of the Royal Irish Academy*
trans.	translation/translated by
TCD	Trinity College Dublin
UCD	University College Dublin
UJA	*Ulster Journal of Archaeology*

Contributors

MARTIN BROWNE is a monk of Glenstal Abbey and former headmaster of the abbey school. He currently serves as an official of the Dicastery for Promoting Christian Unity in Rome.

TRACY COLLINS is a state archaeologist with the National Monuments Service. She completed her PhD in 2016 at University College Cork and in 2018 held an Irish Research Council Post-Doctoral Fellowship there. Her monograph entitled *Female monasticism in medieval Ireland: an archaeology* was published by Cork University Press in 2021.

ANNE DYER is the Anglican bishop of Aberdeen and Orkney, in the Scottish Episcopal Church. She is the first and only female bishop in Scotland. Previously she was the principal of an Anglican seminary in England, the first woman to hold such a position. Anne's research interest is the interface between theology and fine art, particularly the visual and material culture of women.

MÁIRE HICKEY is a Benedictine nun based at Kylemore Abbey, Connemara, since 2008. After studying Classics at Cambridge, she entered the monastery of St Scholastika at Dinklage, Germany, where she served as abbess from 1983 to 2007. From 1997 to 2006 she was leader of the *Communio Internationalis Benedictinarum* – the International Communion of Benedictine Women.

ELVA JOHNSTON lectures in the School of History, University College Dublin. Her monograph, *Literacy and identity in early medieval Ireland* (Woodbridge, 2013), was awarded the Irish Historical Research Prize. She is the editor of *Analecta Hibernica* and a member of the Irish Manuscripts Commission.

COLM LENNON is professor emeritus of history at Maynooth University. He has researched society and religion in early modern Ireland and the history of Dublin. Among his publications are *The lords of Dublin in the Age of Reformation* (Dublin, 1989) and *Confraternities and sodalities in Ireland: charity, devotion and sociability* (Dublin, 2012).

MARY ANN LYONS is professor of history at Maynooth University. She has published on Franco-Irish relations, Irish migration to continental Europe, the Kildare dynasty, women, and religion in late medieval Ireland, and professional medicine in early modern Ireland. Her recent publications include (with Jacqueline Hill) *Representing Irish religious histories: historiography, ideology and practice* (Cham, Switzerland, 2017), 'The onset of religious reform: 1460–1550' in *The Cambridge history of Ireland*, I. *600–1550* (Cambridge, 2018) and (with Brian Mac Cuarta), *The Jesuit mission in early modern Ireland, 1560–c.1760* (Dublin, 2022).

BRONAGH ANN MCSHANE, FRHistS, teaches at the University of Limerick and specializes in the history of women, gender and religion. She is the author of *Irish women in religious orders, 1530–1700: suppression, migration and reintegration* (Woodbridge, 2022) and a guest editor of *Irish Historical Studies*, 'A New Agenda for Women's and Gender History in Ireland' (2022).

COLMÁN Ó CLABAIGH is a monk of Glenstal Abbey and a specialist in the history of monastic and religious orders in medieval Ireland. He is the author of *The friars in Ireland, 1224–1540* (Dublin, 2012).

DAGMAR Ó RIAIN-RAEDEL studied German, English and Celtic philology at the University of Bonn and was a member of the Department of History, UCC, specializing in medieval history and on the connections between Ireland and Europe from the Middle Ages to the eighteenth century. Her monograph on relations between Ireland and imperial Germany during the eleventh and twelfth centuries is forthcoming.

YVONNE SEALE (PhD Iowa, 2016) is an associate professor of history at SUNY Geneseo in western New York state. She is the co-editor of *The cartulary of Prémontré* (Toronto, 2023), and the author of several works on women in reformed religious orders, particularly in medieval France.

CATHERINE SWIFT teaches medieval life and culture at Mary Immaculate College, Limerick. She did her M.Phil. at Durham on the archaeological evidence for early Hebridean monasticism and a D.Phil. at Oxford on Tirechán's Life of Patrick. She holds another M.Phil. in Old Irish (TCD) and is the author of *Ogam stones and the earliest Irish Christians* (Maynooth, 1997).

Acknowledgments

This volume represents the proceedings of the Fifth Glenstal History Conference that took place in Glenstal Abbey from 2 to 4 July 2021. Given the restrictions resulting from the COVID pandemic this was primarily an online event and we are especially grateful to the contributors who rose to the challenge of delivering presentations and producing papers under such difficult circumstances. We thank Martin Fanning and all at Four Courts Press for their patient and supportive expertise in seeing the volume through to publication.

Neither the conference nor this book would have been possible without the generous support of several individuals and institutions. We are particularly grateful to Abbot Brendan Coffey OSB and the monastic community at Glenstal who hosted the conference; to Frank Coyne, Aegis Archaeology, who produced the maps, and to Emmaus O'Herlihy OSB, who designed the conference programme and the book cover.

Likewise, we gratefully acknowledge the financial support received from Aegis Archaeology; the Institute of Archaeologists of Ireland; the Trustees of Glenstal Abbey; the History of Women Religious of Britain and Ireland Network, and the National University of Ireland.

We also wish to the acknowledge the moral and practical support we received from individual friends and colleagues: Edel Bhreathnach, Frank Coyne, Christopher Dillon OSB, Thomas Franklin, Attracta Halpin, Artie and Mena Kenny, Gillian Kenny, Ultan Lally, Columba McCann OSB, Con Manning, Rachel Moss, Gaelán Ó Comáin, and Didier Piquer.

Finally, this volume is affectionately dedicated to Dr Dagmar Ó Riain-Raedel in recognition of her outstanding contribution to Irish and European medieval history and in particular to the study of medieval Irish-German monastic relations.

MARTIN BROWNE
TRACY COLLINS
BRONAGH ANN McSHANE
COLMÁN Ó CLABAIGH

10 February 2023
Feast of St Scholastica

Foreword

ABBESS MÁIRE HICKEY OSB

As a Benedictine nun, it is indeed more than an honour for me to contribute a foreword to this wonderful volume. I say this because the topic touches me existentially: the 'Brides of Christ' are nowadays a rare breed – considered by many almost as an endangered species. As a living member of that species, I am glad to be able to assure you that we are not on the verge of extinction. Right now, at the beginning of the twenty-first century, we are rather in a process of evolution, and I for one am passionately interested in all that can be learned about our origins and how our predecessors survived and flourished for almost two millennia. Like the rest of the human family, nuns and female religious are moving into an uncharted future, and a healthy sense of continuity with our forebears is a helpful balance to the necessary openness about what is to come.

The present volume constitutes the proceedings of the Fifth Glenstal History Conference that took place from 2 to 4 July 2021. The restrictions imposed by the COVID pandemic meant that this was primarily a virtual event. Paradoxically, these restrictions meant that over 800 participants from Alaska to New Zealand and from Uppsala to Uruguay were able to attend online, testimony indeed to the fascination of the topic and the excellence of the papers.

The resulting volume provides a showcase for the work both of established and emerging scholars. The contributions range from the archaeological evidence for the location of nunneries to the various expressions of quasi-religious life that characterized Irish female monasticism. Other essays explore the experience of the mainstream orders of religious women such as Augustinian canonesses, Benedictines, Carmelites, Dominicans and Poor Clares, in addition to the ecclesiastical structures that controlled or supported them. Several contributions examine the social and economic aspects of the life of women religious through the centuries. Gender-related questions are also explored, along with the phenomenon of how Irish women religious adapted themselves to different circumstances, such as the medieval Irish women who moved to Bavaria as part of the Irish Benedictine presence there, or the *emigré* communities that emerged in Spain, Portugal, France and Belgium in the wake of the persecution of the Catholic Church in early modern Ireland.

Brides of Christ is of course an apposite title for a volume on this subject given that the spirituality of medieval women's monasticism in Europe is largely characterized by the bridal imagery of the Bible as meditated and interpreted by the Fathers and Mothers of the church. But apart from its inclusion in the title, the spirituality of the nuns does not figure largely in this work. There are some very good reasons for this, the most obvious one being the lack of substantial spiritual writings by Irish women of the Middle Ages. Hildegard, Gertrude, Mechthild and Teresa do not seem to have had counterparts in Irish history. We may hope that future research on Irish women's monasticism in the Middle Ages will include some consideration of its spiritual profile in relation to the rest of Europe.

This volume is dedicated to a special person, Dr Dagmar Ó Riain-Raedel. A native of Germany, living and working for many years in Ireland, mainly in University College Cork, she has over four decades enriched scholarly activity with the profound knowledge and insights of a German academic on our country and its history. A specialist in the history of medieval Irish missionaries in Europe, she helped to launch the first Glenstal History Conference in 2005 with a comprehensive survey of the *Schottenklöster* – the medieval Irish Benedictine foundations in southern Germany. Within the broad sweep of medieval European history, she has written extensively about medieval manuscripts, saints, kings and pilgrimages. She has a talent for discovering and elucidating connections between Ireland and places all over the continent of Europe: between Cashel, Regensburg and Cologne, between Vienna and Christ Church, Dublin, between Ireland and Scandinavia, Cork and France. She loves movement in history as in life, drawing us into the fascinating connections that often lurk behind the litanies and pilgrimages, the buildings and manuscripts. Above all, her warmth, energy and capacity for friendship has enabled her to share the fruit of her research with a wide variety of audiences in Ireland and further afield. *Liebe verehrte Dagmar, Möge Gott Ihr Wirken unter uns reichlich segnen und es weiterhin fruchtbar machen.*

Like the scribe in the Gospel, the contributors to this volume have brought out of their storehouses treasures both old and new. They have shed light on a fascinating if somewhat neglected topic and we are deeply indebted to them for their efforts. I am confident that they have laid solid foundations on which other scholars will continue to build.

Introduction

TRACY COLLINS & BRONAGH ANN McSHANE

'Brides of Christ', the title of this volume, encapsulates the wide variety of women religious who have existed within and around the church since the early Middle Ages until the present day. The term itself is multi-dimensional and of long-standing. First, it relates to the church as bride to Christ, a biblical metaphor from the Book of Revelation.[1] The term was used throughout the later Middle Ages when it was coupled with the exchange in the *Song of Songs* between the bride and her groom, at a time when bridal imagery became very popular in literary genres ranging from poetry to sermons.[2] Second, 'Bride of Christ' could relate to Mary as a heavenly bride and representative of the church. Finally, but by no means least – and the meaning portrayed in the title – nuns were referred to as Brides of Christ, as a variation of a sacred marriage. Indeed, the precise phrase 'Bride of Christ' was used in the consecration liturgy for the profession of nuns.[3]

The study of women religious of the medieval and early modern periods, however, is sometimes easier-said-than-done.[4] It has been noted by Marie Therese Flanagan that recovering information about the role of women religious in the medieval period can be notoriously difficult, due to the overall paucity of evidence.[5] The earliest descriptions of medieval female religious communities were in lists of monastic and religious houses in Ireland, many written in the seventeenth century; others followed later.[6] Subsequent works included female religious communities as part of wider religious and monastic house accounts rather than in their own right, or as part of edited primary sources.[7] *Medieval religious houses Ireland* (Dublin, 1970) listed information from primary sources on communities of nuns, including the medieval periods and some houses dating to the early modern period.[8] It noted the relative lack of

---

[1] Revelation 21:9–10. [2] See Song of Songs, passim; Isaiah 54:4–7; Jeremiah 2:23; Revelation 19:7; Psalm 45:10–17. This popularity owes much to the influence of the Cistercian Order; see U. Wiethaus, 'Bride of Christ imagery' in M. Schaus (ed.), *Women and gender in medieval Europe: an encyclopaedia* (London, 2006), pp 94–5. [3] Ibid. For background see, C. Walker Bynum, *Jesus as Mother: studies in the spirituality of the high Middle Ages* (Berkley, 1982). [4] The division of the Middle Ages in Ireland into 'early' medieval and 'later' medieval is somewhat arbitrary with the early period traditionally ranging from *c.*AD 400–1169 and the later period from *c.*AD 1169–1540. This study uses *c.*AD 1100–1540 for the later medieval period while the early modern period spans the seventeenth and eighteenth centuries. [5] Flanagan, *Transformation*, p. 73. [6] For example, J. Ware, *De Hibernia et Antiqitatibus Ejus* (London, 1654); J. Morrin (ed.), *Calendar of the Patent and Close Rolls of Chancery in Ireland in the reigns of Henry VIII, Edward VI, Mary and Elizabeth* (Dublin, 1861); P.F. Moran (ed.), *Monasticon Hibernicum, or, A history of the abbeys, priories and other religious houses in Ireland, by Mervyn Archdall*, 2 vols (Dublin, 1873, 1876). [7] For example, E. Hogan, *Onomasticon Goedelicum* (Dublin, 1910); N.B. White, *Extents of Irish monastic possession 1540–41. Manuscripts held in the Public Record Office London* (Dublin, 1943). [8] *MRHI*, pp 20–46, 307–26.

documentary evidence relating to female houses. This, coupled with their reuse
through time, limited their identification both in history, and archaeologically.[9] Despite
some criticism, *Medieval religious houses Ireland* remains a good starting point for
uncovering information about medieval religious communities and ecclesiastical sites
in Ireland, although it has now been superseded by several online resources.[10]

After many years of women religious being in the shadow of male monastic orders
and clerics, their own rich histories are finally emerging in academic disciplines such
as archaeology, history and literary studies. The lack of attention to women religious
in past scholarship has been justified by claims about the relative paucity of
documentary evidence; the absence of upstanding structural remains; as well as the
poverty and perceived mismanagement of women's religious communities. But,
historical accounts relating to medieval and early modern Ireland suggest that there
was a substantial population of female religious active on the island through the ages.[11]
In the case of early modern Ireland, several scholars have put the history of women
religious firmly on the agenda, among them, Marie-Louise Coolahan, Bernadette
Cunningham and Andrea Knox.[12]

Britain as a region has fared better than most, with eminent scholars such as Janet
Burton and Roberta Gilchrist pioneering research on women's monastic communities

---

9 *MRHI*, p. 307.   **10** For example, K. Nicholls, 'Towards a new *Monasticon Hibernicum*', *Peritia*,
3 (1984), 330–3. See now Monasticon https://monasticon.celt.dias.ie/; Monastic Matrix
https://arts.st-andrews.ac.uk/monasticmatrix/home [accessed 15 September 2022]; CIRCLE
https://chancery.tcd.ie/content/welcome-circle [accessed 15 September 2022].   **11** D. Ó Corráin,
'Women in early Irish society' in M. Mac Curtain and D. Ó Corráin (eds), *Women in Irish society:
the historical dimension* (Dublin, 1978), pp 1–14; L. Bitel, 'Women's monastic enclosures in early
Ireland: a study of female spirituality and male monastic mentalities', *Journal of Medieval History*,
12 (1986), 15–36; M. Mac Curtain, M. O'Dowd and M. Luddy, 'An agenda for women's history
in Ireland, 1500–1900', *IHS*, 28 (1992), 1–37; J. McNamara, *Sisters in arms: Catholic nuns through
two millennia* (Harvard, 1996); C. Harrington, *Women in a Celtic church: Ireland 450–1150* (Oxford,
2002); D. Hall, *Women and the church in medieval Ireland, c.1140–1540* (Dublin, 2003); G. Kenny,
Anglo-Irish and Gaelic women in Ireland, c.1170–1540 (Dublin, 2007); Flanagan, *Transformation*.
12 M.L. Coolahan, *Women, writing and language in early modern Ireland* (Oxford, 2010), especially
chapter one; eadem, 'Archipelagic identities in Europe: Irish nuns in English convents' in C.
Bowden and J.E. Kelly (eds), *The English convents in exile*, pp 211–28; B. Cunningham, 'The Poor
Clare Order in Ireland' in E. Bhreathnach, J. MacMahon and J. McCafferty (eds), *The Irish
Franciscans* (Dublin, 2009), pp 159–74; eadem, '"Bethlehem": the Dillons and the Poor Clare
convent at Ballinacliffey, Co. Westmeath', *Áitreabh: Group for the Study of Irish Historic Settlement
Newsletter*, 17 (2012–13), 5–9; eadem, 'Nuns and their networks in early modern Galway' in S.
Ryan and C. Tait (eds), *Religion and politics in urban Ireland, c.1500–c.1750: essays in honour of Colm
Lennon* (Dublin, 2016), pp 156–72; J. Goodrich, 'The rare books of the Galway Poor Clares', *The
Library*, 22:4 (2021), 498–522; A. Knox, 'The convent as cultural conduit: Irish matronage in
early modern Spain', *Quidditas: The Journal of the Rocky Mountain Medieval and Renaissance
Association*, 30 (2009), 128–40; eadem, 'Nuns on the periphery?: Irish Dominican nuns and
assimilation in Lisbon' in F. Sabate i Curull and L. Adno da Fonseca (eds), *Catalonia and Portugal:
the Iberian peninsula from the periphery* (Berlin, 2015), pp 311–26; eadem, 'Her book-lined cell: Irish
nuns and the development of texts, translation and literacy in late medieval Spain' in V. Blanton,
V. O'Mara and P. Stoop (eds), *Nuns' literacies in medieval Europe: the Kansas City dialogue* (Turnhout,
2015), pp 67–86; eadem, *Irish women on the move: migration and mission in Spain, 1499–1700*

which has in turn promoted interest among those engaged in the study of medieval Britain.[13] For the early modern period, there have been a plethora of publications on English nuns in recent years, sparked largely through the work of the ground-breaking 'Who were the nuns?' project, led by Caroline Bowden at Queen Mary University of London.[14]

Nevertheless, despite these seminal publications, there remains a lack of syntheses on medieval and early modern women generally, and in particular, women religious. This lack of attention is a legacy of past scholarship and is not unique to Britain and Ireland.[15] Moreover, a bias towards medieval male religious communities is still clearly manifest in the published literature; this is slowly being corrected with a number of new publications emerging.[16] Furthermore, there has been a lack of discussion around why women chose to be nuns or holy women. This is understandable, in the main due to a lack of contemporary source material to inform the debate. In past scholarship, there has been a tendency to dwell on the negative reasons why a woman might have become a nun: ranging from family pressures to confinement against her will. But it is reasonably suggested that many looked at their vocation as Brides of Christ in a more positive way, with a strong sense of personal vocation, and a desire to live a form of life that enabled a close relationship with God, characterized by prayer, contemplation and service to others. This volume is an attempt to address lacunas in existing scholarship, as well as to showcase the potential and future directions for research in this emerging and growing field of scholarly enquiry.

Terminology in respect of women religious in both the medieval and early modern eras can sometimes be confusing, especially when several disciplines intersect.[17] The term 'nunnery' implies a religious female community living enclosed under a rule, with a particular style of dress. This term fits well with the current evidence for female religious communities of the later medieval period in Ireland, but some early medieval

(Bern, 2020). **13** For example: J. Burton, 'Looking for medieval nuns' in J. Burton and K. Stöber (eds), *Monasteries and society in the British Isles in the later Middle Ages* (Woodbridge, 2008), pp 113–23; R. Gilchrist, *Gender and material culture: the archaeology of religious women* (London, 1994); R. Gilchrist, *Contemplation and action: the other monasticism* (London, 1995). **14** https:// aschresources.org/who-were-the-nuns-a-prosopographical-study-of-the-english-convents-in-exile-1600-1800/ [accessed 23 October 2022]; C. Bowden and J.E. Kelly (eds), *The English convents in exile, 1600–1800: communities, culture and identity* (Farnham, 2013). **15** See J. Burton and K. Stöber (eds), *Women in the medieval monastic world* (Turnhout, 2015), pp 1–4. **16** For example, T. Collins, *Female monasticism in medieval Ireland: an archaeology* (Cork, 2021). See also, eadem, 'An archaeology of Augustinian nuns in medieval Ireland' in Browne and Ó Clabaigh (eds), *Households*, pp 87–102; eadem, 'Unveiling female monasticism in later medieval Ireland: survey and excavation at St Catherine's, Shanagolden, Co. Limerick', *PRIA*, 119C (2019), 103–71; B.A. McShane, *Irish women in religious orders, 1530–1700: suppression, migration and reintegration* (Woodbridge, 2022); eadem, 'Negotiating religious change and conflict: female religious communities in early modern Ireland, c.1530–c.1641', *British Catholic History*, 33:3 (2017), 357–82; eadem, 'The pre-profession examination record of Sister Catherine Browne (in religion Sister Catherine of St Francis), Poor Clare convent, Bethlehem, Co. Westmeath, 1632' *AH*, 70 (2017), 284–93; K. Curran and J. Burton (eds), *Medieval women religious, c.800–c.1500: new perspectives* (Woodbridge, 2023). **17** For the difficulties with terminology in an early medieval context see S. Foot, *Veiled women: the disappearance of nuns from Anglo-Saxon England,* 2 vols (Aldershot, 2000).

female religious communities were likely much more flexible in their organization. Recent publications favour 'female religious house/community' rather than nunnery for the medieval period as a whole since it provides female communities with a comparable description to those of their male religious contemporaries. Moreover, with increasing frequency, religious houses are described by their relative status, for example, abbey or priory, and a description that establishes the gender of the religious community is not used.[18]

In this book the term 'women/female religious' is used to denote the entire spectrum of holy women across the ages.[19] This volume considers the lives of women religious in medieval and early modern Ireland, examining both the nature of their experiences in Ireland, and their wider European connections (Plates 1 and 2). The time period under consideration is framed by what might be considered processes rather than events: Ireland's conversion to Christianity, which is thought to have started early in the fifth century, through to the dissolution of religious houses during the reign of King Henry VIII in the 1530s and 1540s, down to the onset and consolidation of the Catholic Counter-Reformation in the later sixteenth and seventeenth centuries.[20]

In the opening chapter of this volume, Tracy Collins considers the current archaeological evidence of early medieval female religious and their foundations and proposes a classification through which they might be better understood. Elva Johnston follows with a novel exploration and comparison of Irish female saints named in three martyrologies: Tallaght, Óengus and Gorman. She demonstrates how Irish martyrologies are an under-utilized resource in respect of women, and how they can provide a large database of place and personal names on a scale that makes them amenable to a variety of analyses. Catherine Swift widens the scope to the European continent in her chapter, comparing the charism of two Irish female saints, St Brigit, associated with Co. Kildare, and St Íte, and her foundation at Kileedy, Co. Limerick, with their contemporary St Macrina of Cappadocia, situated in central Anatolia in modern Turkey. She concludes that the Irish female saints have more in common with the Roman Mediterranean than other jurisdictions, closer to home, such as Italy or southern France. In Ireland and Anatolia there was an emphasis on enclosed women living under the rule of family relatives, with episcopal oversight, public veiling ceremonies, fasting and night prayers, focusing on charity, neighbourly love, and service to others.

---

18 See also, Curran and Burton, *Medieval women religious.*   **19** E. Makowski, '*A pernicious sort of woman': quasi-religious women and canon lawyers in the later Middle Ages* (Washington, DC, 2005). For this terminology in an Irish medieval context see Collins, *Female monasticism*, pp 5–9; and for the early modern period see McShane, *Irish women in religious orders, 1530–1700*, pp 1–2. For a list of relevant terms and explanations see https://arts.st-andrews.ac.uk/monasticmatrix/ vocabularium [accessed 13 October 2022].   **20** E. Bhreathnach, *Ireland in the medieval world AD 400–1000: landscape, kingship and religion* (Dublin, 2014); Bradshaw, *The dissolution of the religious orders in Ireland.* Places associated with women religious mentioned in this volume are mapped on Plates 1 and 2.

Dagmar Ó Riain-Raedel, the dedicatee of this volume, expands her exploration of Irish-German connections by considering the case of Irish pilgrim nuns in late medieval Regensburg. As she reveals, these women are likely to have hailed from the province of Munster in Ireland. This connection is explained by the Irish Benedictine community's presence in the city of Regensburg from the second half of the eleventh century onwards, during what is considered the final wave of Irish monastic expansion abroad, of which, as Ó Riain-Raedel demonstrates, women religious were a part. Yvonne Seale shifts attention from medieval Germany to medieval France, where she makes a detailed comparison of the female religious communities of Ballymore-Loughsewdy, Co. Meath, with that of Prémontré, France, through the lens of order affiliation. The Loughsewdy community was thought to have followed the Cistercian rule (though this is far from certain), while that of Prémontré followed the Premonstratensian way of life (based on the Rule of St Augustine). She concludes that when considering women's religious communities, their 'official' order affiliation may be less important than other considerations, such as their local benefactors and political contexts.

Family and familial connections is a thread running through this entire volume. Mary Ann Lyons encapsulates this theme in her chapter on the current historical evidence of medieval women religious in Ireland and their familial networks. Lyons suggests that the deliberately 'permeable cloisters' of women's religious communities encouraged close ties with local gentry from whom they recruited new postulants and solicited donations, sometimes over several generations. Relationships were not always positive, however, particularly when external political tensions might affect the religious community within its cloister walls.

Colmán Ó Clabaigh's contribution to the volume widens the definition of what it is to be a woman religious. His chapter explores the nature of the various forms of 'quasi-religious' life known to have existed in medieval Ireland. These included the vocations of vowesses, anchoresses, tertiaries and nursing sisters. Unlike enclosed nuns, vowesses did not live communally or renounce rights to property or income. An anchoress was a person who was formally enclosed in a confined space attached to a church or religious house, known as an anchorhold, whose lifestyle was maintained by benefactors in the surrounding community. Tertiaries were lay associates of male religious orders, particularly the mendicant friars, who lived intense Christian lives under their direction while nursing sisters provided healthcare and administrative services in the hospitals and hospices of medieval Ireland.

Colm Lennon continues in the vein of 'other' medieval religious women. His chapter focuses attention on a little-known group of medieval religious women; those who were active members of the cathedral priory confraternity of Christ Church, or Holy Trinity, Dublin. A medieval confraternity was an association of lay women and men who gathered together as members, and endowed chapels usually in their parish churches or local religious houses, funding the maintenance and ornamentation of the ecclesiastical spaces and the living expenses of chaplains, who ministered at fraternity altars, in chapel or nave, for the benefit of the members' souls.

The late sixteenth and seventeenth centuries was an era of tumultuous upheaval on the island of Ireland. It encompassed unprecedented religious, political and social change that was punctuated by rebellions, plantations and frequent and violent warfare; the Nine Years War (1593–1603), the Confederate wars (1641–53), the Cromwellian campaigns (1649–53) and the Williamite wars (1688–91). In addition, this period witnessed the dispersal of thousands of Irish migrants to continental Europe. In her contribution, Bronagh Ann McShane offers a comprehensive overview of the nature of female religious life in Ireland during this era. She explores female religious communities in Ireland and Irish female religious activities in Europe, highlighting the nuns' use of existing networks to establish monastic foundations across Ireland and their ability to forge new connections in Europe by founding or joining communities in Portugal, Spain, and the Spanish Netherlands. In addition, McShane highlights the rich material and literary culture of early modern Irish female religious communities, revealing their engagement in textual production, consumption and circulation, identifying this as a subject worthy of much more extensive investigation.

In a responsive and thought-provoking epilogue, Bishop Anne Dwyer summarizes and broadens the discussion to key emerging themes. These include identity, family networks, the control of women, women's own power and agency, motivation, enclosure, gender relations, spirituality, and community. All these themes have resonance in the past, but perhaps even more so in the present and future of the communities of women religious in Ireland and globally.

This volume is the culmination of papers given at or inspired by the Fifth Glenstal History Conference in 2021, dedicated to exploring the various ways in which women responded to the monastic and ascetic vocation in medieval and early modern Ireland. Whether as practitioners or as patrons, women found creative and dynamic ways to pursue their calling as 'Brides of Christ' between the fifth and the seventeenth centuries, often in the face of tremendous difficulties and challenges. Their lives of prayer and service are sometimes hard to glimpse but the combined perspectives offered by this collection of interdisciplinary essays brings them into sharper focus. Furthermore, the essays demonstrate clearly the current vitality of research on this topic and include contributions by both established and emerging scholars.

The 2021 conference was also a fitting opportunity to remember the eminent historian and Dominican sister, Margaret MacCurtain (1929–2020). A reflection moderated by Bronagh Ann McShane featured contributions by Margaret's colleagues and friends, Maighread Gallagher OP, Colm Lennon and Mary O'Dowd, which highlighted Margaret's enormous and indelible contribution to the study of women in the past, her kindness and friendship, and her encouragement and mentorship of scholars who followed in her footsteps.[21] *Ar dheis Dé go raibh a hanam.*

---

21 https://www.irishtimes.com/life-and-style/people/margaret-maccurtain-obituary-pioneering-historian-and-campaigner-1.4373446 [accessed 23 October 2022].

'On the brink of the wave': towards an archaeology of female religious in early medieval Ireland

TRACY COLLINS

Religious women of various types are known throughout the written sources dating to the early medieval period and later.[1] But what of their places in the early medieval landscape, their buildings of worship and habitation, and, where and how they might have lived? This chapter outlines what is currently known, and highlights what is not known, of the archaeology of these religious women and provides a background context for the chapters that follow.[2]

The title of this chapter alludes to a legendary episode between the female St Canir and St Senan of Scattery Island in the river Shannon estuary, which possibly occurred sometime in the sixth century and is recounted in the vernacular *Life of Senan*.[3] It provides an appropriate and interesting starting point to consider early female saints and women religious. The legend recounts that Canir had a vision at her home near Bantry, Co. Cork, that all the churches of Ireland were lit with a pillar of fire. The fire of the monastic settlement on Scattery Island was the largest (Fig. 1.1).[4]

Canir decided that she should be buried there, and after walking for three days and finally walking across the water of the Shannon, she arrived at the island's shore. But no woman was allowed to land on Senan's island monastery. After a protracted debate with Senan, where Canir eloquently defended the equality of women and men in the eyes of God, she was given the Eucharist by Senan, and immediately died. But to stay true to his own edicts, he waited until low tide to bury Canir on 'the brink of the wave' in the intertidal zone of Scattery. Although this liminal location was not officially part of the island monastery, it still fulfilled Canir's wish to be buried there, while not breaking Senan's own principles. This interesting episode highlights numerous issues of monastic female–male relations and gender hierarchies in early Ireland, excellently explored by Johnston, and more recently by Callan.[5]

---

1 See C. Harrington, *Women in a Celtic church: Ireland, 450–1150* (Oxford, 2002). For a critique of some of her theses see E. Johnston, 'Review of *Women in a Celtic church: Ireland, 450–1150*, by Christina Harrington', *The English Historical Review*, 119:483 (2004), 1025–6.   **2** This chapter summarizes Collins, *Female monasticism*, pp 28–58.   **3** Senan's Life is recounted in the fifteenth-century *Book of Lismore*. W. Stokes (ed.), *Lives of the saints from the* Book of Lismore (Oxford, 1890), pp 54–74, 201–21. For a full historiography of Senan (Irish Senán) see P. Ó Riain, *Dictionary*, pp 557–60.   **4** Scattery Island, Co. Clare, is also known by its Irish form – Inis Cathaigh.   **5** E. Johnston, 'Transforming women in Irish hagiography', *Peritia*, 9 (1995), 197–220; M. Callan, *Sacred sisters: gender, sanctity and power in medieval Ireland* (Amsterdam, 2020).

1.1 Scattery Island, Co. Clare, associated with St Canir. Image © Photographic Archive, National Monuments Service, Government of Ireland.

It could be argued that early medieval female religious continue to inhabit this position, in the liminal, peripheral and metaphorical '*intertidal* zone' of early monasticism. This is particularly true in the current archaeologies of early medieval monasticism in Ireland. In order to provide a context for a discussion and overview of the archaeological evidence and current evidential issues, it is first necessary to briefly consider women and early society in Ireland. From the sum of the archaeological and historical evidence, it is slowly emerging that female religious were found in a variety of situations that were connected to the church and secular society in early Ireland.[6]

WOMEN AND SOCIETY IN EARLY IRELAND

For Ireland, the early medieval period – broadly the fifth to the twelfth centuries AD – is considered transformational as literacy and Christianity were first introduced,

6 For example: T. Ó Carragáin, *Churches in early medieval Ireland: architecture, ritual, and memory* (New Haven, 2010); T. Ó Carragáin, *Churches in the Irish landscape AD 400–1100* (Cork, 2021); L. Bitel, 'Monastic identity in early medieval Ireland' in Beach and Cochelin, *CHMMLW*, pp 297–316. For recent overviews of the history and archaeology of the early medieval period see

through processes of acculturation.[7] There are limitations in the evidence on early medieval women as sources are patchy, difficult to date, and often written to a traditional formula.[8] Moreover, sometimes terminology used can appear inconsistent or contradictory, and specific groups, for example, women, female religious, children and older people, are not easily identified in either documentary sources or the archaeological record.[9] Despite such limitations, some light can be shed on women in this period.[10] Archaeological studies are now revealing the varied character of the church in early Ireland – traditionally considered more monolithic – from the large ecclesiastical complexes such as Glendalough, Co. Wicklow, to many lesser ecclesiastical sites with pastoral roles and proprietary or family churches, which include those associated with female religious.[11]

Society in early Ireland was based on principles of kinship, land tenure and clientship.[12] Women had their rights protected by law in property, marriage, divorce

E. Bhreathnach, *Ireland in the medieval world AD 400–1000: landscape, kingship and religion* (Dublin, 2014); M. Stout, *Early medieval Ireland, 431–1169* (Dublin, 2017).   **7** C. Thomas, *Christianity in Roman Britain to AD 500* (Berkeley, 1981); C. Thomas, *Christian celts: messages and images* (Stroud, 1998); C. Swift, *Ogham stones and the earliest Irish Christians* (Maynooth, 1997); E. Johnston, *Literacy and identity in early medieval Ireland* (Suffolk, 2013). M. Callan, 'Líadain's *Lament*, Darerca's *Life*, and Íte's *Isucán*: evidence for nuns' literacies in early Ireland' in V. Blanton, V. O'Mara and P. Stoop (eds), *Nuns' literacies in medieval Europe* (Turnhout, 2015), pp 209–27; N. Edwards, 'The archaeology of early medieval Ireland, *c.*400–1169: settlement and economy' in D. Ó Cróinín (ed.), *A new history of Ireland;* i, *Prehistory and early Ireland* (Oxford, 2005), pp 235–300; T.M. Charles-Edwards, *Early Christian Ireland* (Cambridge, 2000); Bhreathnach, *Ireland in the medieval world*; A. O'Sullivan, F. McCormack, T. Kerr and L. Harney, *Early medieval Ireland AD 400–1100: the evidence from archaeological excavations* (Dublin, 2014); M. Stout, *Early medieval Ireland.*   **8** See the contribution by Johnston below.   **9** K. Hughes, *Early Christian Ireland: introduction to the sources* (London, 1972), p. 17; Harrington, *Women in a Celtic church*, pp 16–19; T. Ó Carragáin, 'Is there an archaeology of lay people at early Irish monasteries?' *Bulletin du Centre D'études Médiévales d'Auxerre BUCEMA*, 8 (2015), 2–17.   **10** Harrington, *Women in a Celtic church*, p. 19; Ó Carragáin, *Churches in early medieval Ireland*, pp 12–3; H. Oxenham, *Perceptions of femininity in early Irish society* (Woodbridge, 2016).   **11** R. Sharpe, 'Churches and communities in early Ireland: towards a pastoral model' in J. Blair and R. Sharpe (eds), *Pastoral care before the parish* (Leicester, 1992), pp 81–109; C. Etchingham, *Church organization in Ireland AD 650 to 1000* (Maynooth, 1999); Charles-Edwards, *Early Christian Ireland*, pp 586–99; Harrington, *Women in a Celtic church*, pp 112–18; T. Ó Carragáin, 'A landscape converted: archaeology and early church organization on Iveragh and Dingle, Ireland' in M. Carver (ed.), *The cross goes north: processes of conversion in northern Europe, AD 300–1300* (Woodbridge, 2003), pp 127–52; T. Ó Carragáin, 'Church buildings and pastoral care in early medieval Ireland' in E. FitzPatrick and R. Gillespie (eds), *The parish in medieval and early modern Ireland: community, territory and building* (Dublin, 2006), pp 91–123; P. MacCotter, *Medieval Ireland: territorial, political and economic divisions* (Dublin, 2008), pp 23, 82–5; T. Ó Carragáin, 'The architectural setting of the Mass in early medieval Ireland', *Medieval Archaeology*, 53 (2009), 119–54; Ó Carragáin, *Churches in early medieval Ireland*, pp 225–8; T. Ó Carragáin, 'The view from the shore: perceiving island monasteries in early medieval Ireland', *Hortus Artium Medievalium*, 19 (2013), 21–33 at p. 21; Bhreathnach, *Ireland in the medieval world*, pp 152–213.   **12** Charles-Edwards, *Early Christian Ireland*, pp 71–80; T. Bolger, 'Status inheritance and land tenure: some thoughts on early medieval settlement in the light of recent archaeological excavations' in C. Corlett and M. Potterton (eds), *Settlement in early medieval Ireland in the light of recent archaeological excavations* (Dublin, 2011), pp 1–10 at pp 4–7; Bhreathnach, *Ireland in the medieval*

and the family, but their status was almost always in reference to the men in their lives.[13] In such a society it made sense for women to marry, as it forged alliances and brought with it a substantial bride-price for the woman's family. So, if marriage was the main kin group strategy, what advantages would there be to follow a religious life? Three broad reasons have been proposed: church alliances; containment of surplus women; and the maintenance of kin's status and property. Added to these, it can be reasonably suggested that another important reason was the sense of personal vocation, a desire to live an intense Christian life characterized by prayer, contemplation, service of others, particularly, service of the poor. While personal vocation is not explicitly stated in the *vitae*, it is acknowledged implicitly through the stories relayed in many of the female saints' lives.

By taking up a religious life a woman might forge ambitious alliances with the church, which brought kudos, protection and perhaps political success to her kin group.[14] Additionally, with the practice of bride-price and later dowry payments, entry to the religious life may have been an economic saving, though it does remain unclear if payments were made in this period upon entering a religious community.[15] Not being legally independent, women may also have been 'donated' to religious foundations, equating to a transfer from father to church, and 'the legal parallel to marriage in this practice is obvious'.[16]

The second advantage proposed was that entering a religious community solved the issue of surplus women, when there were too many to be married off. This strategy may have also limited the number of prospective heirs in a particular kin group.[17] These scenarios, noted elsewhere, have not yet been evidenced in Ireland. There is nothing to suggest that religious provision was made for surpluses of eligible aristocratic women; women in early Ireland were considered a precious resource, which may have worked against their choice of religious life.[18] St Patrick's *Confessio* noted that several fathers were displeased with their daughters' decision to enter religious life.[19] Finally, a kin group may have established a proprietary or family church in which a religious woman might live and work, perhaps only for her lifetime, while the family maintained control over its offices and property.[20] Indeed, on occasion women themselves may have established churches or made donations.[21]

---

world, pp 40–129.   **13** F. Kelly, *A guide to early Irish law* (Dublin, 1988); D. Ó Crónín, *Early medieval Ireland* (London, 1995), pp 125–34; T.M. Charles-Edwards, 'Early Irish law' in D. Ó Crónín (ed.), *A new history of Ireland; i, Prehistoric and early Ireland* (Oxford, 2005), pp 331–70. **14** Harrington, *Women in a Celtic church*, p. 132.   **15** T.M. Charles-Edwards, *Early Irish and Welsh kinship* (Oxford, 1993), p. 463; Charles-Edwards, *Early Christian Ireland*, p. 112; Harrington, *Women in a Celtic church*, p. 133.   **16** L. Bitel, 'Women's monastic enclosures in early Ireland: a study of female spirituality and male monastic mentalities', *Journal of Medieval History*, 12 (1986), 15–36 at p. 21.   **17** S. Foot, *Veiled women: the disappearance of nuns from Anglo-Saxon England*, 2 vols (Aldershot, 2000), p. 43.   **18** Flanagan, *Transformation*, p. 201; Bitel, 'Women's monastic enclosures', pp 23, 27.   **19** https://www.confessio.ie/etexts/confessio_english#01. Accessed 23 April 2022. Stout has provided a very accessible translation of the text; see Stout, *Early medieval Ireland*, pp 34–40, at p. 38.   **20** D. Ó Corráin, *The Irish church, its reform and the English invasion* (Dublin, 2017); Harrington, *Women in a Celtic church*, pp 112–22.   **21** L. Bitel, 'Women's donations to the churches in early Ireland', *JRSAI*, 114 (1984), 5–23; J. Ní Ghrádaigh, '"But what

At least fifty-one sites of female religious communities dating to the early medieval period can be identified in the archaeological record. This is a minimum number as many more sites exhibit inconclusive evidence, such as a dedication to a female saint or an association with early female religious.[22] These early female religious establishments can be divided into three very broad categories. First are the major communities: by far the most well-known and important was Kildare, but there are other regionally important sites. The second group comprises those satellite communities that were positioned adjacent to but at a remove from larger ecclesiastical sites.[23] Finally, the third category is what might be termed lesser or other stand-alone communities. The distinction between this relatively large group and the first group of major sites is somewhat arbitrary, as some of these third-tier sites had important roles within their local regions. Furthermore, it is likely that their importance ebbed and flowed through time. For example, Faughart, Co. Louth, is included in this group, as it is neither a major nor satellite community, but archaeological research has shown that it was very important in its local and regional sphere.[24] But many of these third-tier sites were never more than a small church that may have had a female religious function at some point in time.[25]

Major female religious communities

There are seven major large female religious communities which were regionally, if not nationally, important at some stages of their use: Ballyvourney, Co. Cork;[26] Clonbroney, Co. Longford;[27] Cloonburren, Co. Roscommon;[28] Kildare, Co.

exactly did she give?": Derbforgaill and the Nuns' Church at Clonmacnoise' in H. King (ed.), *Clonmacnoise studies, volume 2* (Dublin, 2003), pp 175–207. **22** See, e.g., Ó Riain, *Dictionary*, which includes an extensive list of female saints. For ecclesiastical settlements in Ireland from the fifth to the twelfth century see https://monasticon.celt.dias.ie/. Accessed 23 April 2022. For the early medieval female religious sites mentioned here see the online catalogue at http://doi.org/10.5281/zenodo.5035404. Accessed 23 April 2022. Harrington, *Women in a Celtic church*, p. 185. Many religious women are mentioned in early martyrologies and texts related to St Patrick. Most are not associated with a specific location and little is known of them. Available at: https://confessio.ie/#. Accessed 23 April 2022. For context see, R. Bleier, 'Re-examining the function of St Patrick's writings in the early medieval tradition', *PRIA*, 116C (2016), 95–117. **23** Elsewhere these are termed twin or affiliated houses, or double houses in an English context. See J. Luecke, 'The unique experience of Anglo-Saxon nuns' in J. Nichols and L. Thomas Shank (eds), *Peace weavers: medieval religious women, volume 2* (Kalamazoo, 1987), pp 55–66. **24** G. Boazman, 'The material culture of self-promotion: the Conaille Muirthemne kings and the ecclesiastical site of Faughart, Co. Louth', *CLAHJ*, 28 (2015), 327–50. **25** E.g. the many churches associated with the female saint Rígnach, see T.M. Charles-Edwards, 'Early Irish saints' cults and their constituencies', *Ériu*, 54 (2004), 79–102; Ó Riain, *Dictionary*, pp 536–7. **26** Ballyvourney is thought to have been founded by St Abban and given to St Gobnait (Gobnaid) in the sixth century; *MRHI*, p. 313; Ó Riain, *Dictionary*, pp 368–9; Callan, *Sacred sisters*, pp 170–4. **27** Clonbroney was founded sometime in the later seventh or early eight century. It is usually associated with St Samthann, d. 739; *MRHI*, p. 314; Ó Riain, *Dictionary*, pp 545–6; Callan, *Sacred sisters*, pp 135–55. **28** Cloonburren was established sometime in the sixth century. Its founder

Kildare;[29] Killaraght, Co. Sligo;[30] Killeedy, Co. Limerick (Plate 3);[31] and Killevy, Co. Armagh.[32] Oughterard, Co. Kildare, could be added as its round tower, dated to the eleventh century, suggests a site of status, at least in the latter part of the period.[33] Of this group, Clonbroney, Killaraght, Killeedy and Kildare have little, if any, upstanding early medieval remains.

Kildare, associated with St Brigit, was the premier female religious community of the period, and is unusual, in that it is the only women's house to appear with frequency in the Annals.[34] It has little early medieval fabric upstanding; the date of its 'fire house' structure is uncertain. Like other contemporary ecclesiastical sites, it was presumably enclosed by several concentric enclosures with the most sacred at its centre, which contained the primary church, the position of which probably lies beneath the later cathedral and close to the round tower. The street pattern at Kildare is thought to retain the outline of its enclosures. None of the other sites in this group retain any surface expression of their original enclosing elements.

Of the remaining sites, Cloonburren, associated with St Caoireach Dheragáin, is important due to its assemblage of fragmentary cross slabs.[35] Ballyvourney, associated with St Gobnait, is the only example in this group where a research excavation has taken place and it remains an important regional pilgrimage destination to the present day.[36]

Cairech Dergen (Caoireach Dheragáin) d. 577–8; *MRHI*, p. 315; Ó Riain, *Dictionary*, pp 150–1. **29** Kildare was founded by St Brigit (Brigid) possibly in the late fifth century, though its zenith (as with many early ecclesiastical foundations) was in the seventh century; Callan, *Sacred sisters*, pp 85–112. *MRHI*, pp 319–20; N. Kissane, *Saint Brigid of Kildare: life, legend and cult* (Dublin, 2017); Ó Riain, *Dictionary*, pp 123–5; C. Swift, 'Brigid, Patrick and the kings of Kildare AD 640–850' in W. Nolan and K. McGrath (eds), *Kildare: history and society* (Dublin, 2006), pp 97–128. **30** Killaraght, associated with St Attracta (Athracht), may have been founded in the fifth century, due to her mention in Tirechan's *Life of St Patrick*; *MRHI*, pp 320–1; L. Bieler (ed.), *The Patrician texts in the Book of Armagh* (Dublin, 1979). Ó Riain, *Dictionary*, pp 81–2; Callan, *Sacred sisters*, pp 164–7. **31** Killeedy was founded by the sixth century by St Íte (Íde); d. 570–1; *MRHI*, p. 392; Ó Riain, *Dictionary*, pp 375–8; Callan, *Sacred sisters*, pp 113–34. **32** Killevy was founded in the early sixth century by St Monenna (Moninne, Darerca), d. 517 or 519. *MRHI*, p. 321; I. Sperber, 'The Life of St Monenna or Darerca of Killevy' in A.J. Hughes and W. Nolan (eds), *Armagh: history and society* (Dublin, 2001), pp 63–97; Ó Riain, *Dictionary*, pp 495–7; Callan, *Sacred sisters*, pp 61–84. **33** Oughterard is thought to have been founded in the sixth or seventh century by St Brigit (but not of Kildare). *MRHI*, p. 400; Ó Riain, *Dictionary*, p. 121. **34** Bitel, 'Women's monastic enclosures', p. 26; E. Breathnach, 'Abbesses, minor dynasties and kings *in clericatu*: perspectives of Ireland 700–850' in M. Brown and C. Farr (eds), *Mercia: an Anglo-Saxon kingdom in Europe* (Leicester, 2001), pp 113–25; E. Breathnach, 'The genealogies of Leinster as a source for local cults in Leinster' in J. Carey, M. Herbert and P. Ó Riain (eds), *Studies in Irish hagiography: saints and scholars* (Dublin, 2001), pp 250–67; Swift, 'Brigid, Patrick and the kings of Kildare', pp 100–23. For the Annals on-line see https://celt.ucc.ie/publishd.html; http://www.irish-annals.cs.tcd.ie/ accessed 23 April 2022. **35** R.A.S Macalister, *The memorial slabs of Clonmacnoise, King's Co.* (Dublin, 1909); R.A.S Macalister, 'Some cross-slabs in the neighbourhood of Athlone', *JRSAI*, 42 (1912), 27–31; H.S. Crawford, 'A descriptive list of early cross slabs and pillars [3 parts]', *JRSAI*, 43 (1913), 151–69, 261–5, 326–34, at p. 160; R.A.S. Macalister, *Corpus inscriptionum insularum Celticarum*, vol. I (Dublin, 1945), pp 18–19; Ó Riain, *Dictionary*, pp 150–1. **36** M.J. O'Kelly, 'St Gobnet's house, Ballyvourney, Co. Cork', *JCHAS*, 57 (1952), 18–40; Callan, *Sacred*

Killevy, associated with Saint Moninne/Monenna, is the only major female religious house to clearly retain early fabric.[37] Two churches are extant, once about eleven metres apart but now conjoined. The western example is considered the older of the two and not later than the eleventh century. The eastern church is likely later medieval in date.

Satellite communities

There are perhaps ten larger ecclesiastical complexes where there is some evidence of attached communities of female religious. Satellite community most accurately describes the position of those upstanding female houses that can be considered archaeologically, such as at Clonmacnoise, Co. Offaly; Glendalough, Co. Wicklow; and Lemanaghan, Co. Offaly (Fig. 1.2).[38] From the evidence, it can be concluded that female religious communities were likely in proximity to ecclesiastical complexes traditionally considered to be male monasteries. The women had their own discrete enclosures, and importantly were considered legitimate constituents of the religious population of those complexes.[39] Other such sites include: Annaghdown, Co. Galway;[40] Temple-na-Ferta and St Brigit's, Armagh;[41] Finglas and Tallaght, Co. Dublin;[42] Lismore, Co. Waterford,[43] and perhaps Mayo.[44] For most of these

sisters, pp 170–4.   **37** See T. Ó Carragáin, 'Habitual masonry styles and the local organization of church building in early medieval Ireland', *PRIA*, 105C (2005), 99–149; C. Manning, 'A suggested typology for pre-Romanesque stone churches in Ireland' in N. Edwards (ed.), *The archaeology of the early medieval Celtic churches* (Leeds, 2009), pp 265–79; Ó Carragáin, *Churches in early medieval Ireland*, p. 223.   **38** C. Manning, 'Some early masonry churches and the round tower at Clonmacnoise' in H. King (ed.), *Clonmacnoise studies, volume 2* (Dublin, 2003), pp 63–95 at pp 82–3. C. Doherty, L. Doran and M. Kelly (eds), *Glendalough: city of God* (Dublin, 2011); M. Seaver, C. McDermott and G. Warren, 'A monastery among the glens', *Archaeology Ireland*, 32:2, (2018), 19–23. A church at Lemanaghan is associated with Mella (Mealla), the reputed mother of St Manchán, and may have been founded in the seventh century. *MRHI*, p. 40; E. FitzPatrick and C. O'Brien, *The medieval churches of Co. Offaly* (Dublin, 1988), pp 12–15; M. Quinlan and R. Moss, *Lemanaghan Co. Offaly conservation plan* (Kilkenny, 2007); Ó Carragáin, *Churches in early medieval Ireland*, p. 312; Ó Riain, *Dictionary*, pp 429–30.   **39** See Johnston, this volume. **40** Founded by St Brendan of Clonfert for his sister Brige. *MRHI*, p. 312; O. Alcock, K. De hÓra, and P. Gosling *Archaeological inventory of Co. Galway, vol. II – North Galway* (Dublin, 1999), pp 292–3.   **41** *MRHI*, p. 310; C. Lynn, 'Excavations in 46–48 Scotch Street, Armagh, 1979–80', *Ulster Journal of Archaeology*, 51 (1988), 69–84. Temple na Ferta is also known as the Church of the Repository. For a recent discussion of Armagh's layout see E. FitzPatrick, 'Rethinking settlement values in Gaelic society: the case of cathedral centres', *PRIA*, 119C (2019), 69–102 at pp 84, 86–7.   **42** St Máel Ruain is associated with the ecclesiastical sites of Finglas and Tallaght, known as the 'two eyes of Ireland'; see Ó Riain, *Dictionary*, pp 445–6. Tallaght dates to the eighth century and was associated with the *Céli Dé* movement. Finglas was probably established by the end of the sixth century. The *Customs of Tallaght* indicate that female religious communities were present at both sites and were considered a vital part of the ecclesiastical complexes there; E. Gwynn and W. Purton, 'The monastery at Tallaght', *PRIA*, 29C (1911–12), 115–79; *MRHI*, pp 45, 384; Harrington, *Women in a Celtic church*, pp 107–8, 177, 187, 208; W. Follett, *Céli Dé in Ireland* (Woodbridge, 2006).   **43** In the seventh century, a female community was reputedly established at Lismore. See S. Sanderlin, 'The monastery of Lismore AD 638–1111' in W. Nolan and T. Power (eds), *Waterford: history and society* (Dublin, 1992), pp 27–48; Harrington, *Women*, pp 109, 229; Ó Riain, *Dictionary*, pp 470–3.   **44** This is a putative early community of female

1.2 Lemanaghan, Co. Offaly, associated with Mella mother of St Manchán. Image © Frank Coyne.

(Annaghdown, Finglas, Tallaght, Armagh and Lismore) there is no upstanding archaeological evidence of the precise location of the female religious communities, though there is some excavated evidence from Armagh.[45]

And despite the caution of St Samthann, abbess of Clonbroney (d. 739), to Máel Ruain of Tallaght on the counselling of women, the *Céli Dé* sites of Finglas, Tallaght and Lismore do have historical evidence of female religious in proximity.[46] Tallaght possessed an oratory known as Cell-na-ingen and a female community lived around this church. These religious women were part of the religious *familia* there and were sympathetically accommodated. They were mentioned in the Tallaght monastic rules, which stipulated that menstruating nuns were free from certain vigils and could eat a special gruel.[47] The female community at Finglas was mentioned in the Customs of Tallaght in an anecdote that has been interpreted as showing that female religious were not permitted into the inner (most sacred) enclosure but retained their own enclosure within the larger ecclesiastical complex.[48] Early female religious seem to have been at Lismore before the establishment of the male monastery there, as in the Life of Saint

religious. Collins, *Female monasticism*, p. 38; Ó Riain, *Dictionary*, p. 190.   **45** Lynn, 'Excavations in 46–48 Scotch Street, Armagh'.   **46** Gwynn and Purton, 'The monastery at Tallaght', pp 149–50; Harrington, *Women in a Celtic church*, pp 182–4; Follett, *Céli Dé*, pp 4, 98–9.   **47** Harrington, *Women in a Celtic church*, p. 108.   **48** Ibid., p. 109.

Carthach, the virgin Coemell donated her small church to him. Female religious subsequently reused Coemell's site but were not permitted to enter the monastic enclosure at Lismore.[49]

The locations of the two female communities at Armagh are known. Temple-na-Ferta was situated outside the ecclesiastical complex to the south-east, while St Brigit's was also to the south-east of the centre. Temple-na-Ferta's circular enclosure is shown on Barlett's map dated to 1602.[50] A third church possibly associated with female religious at Armagh, Temple Muire, was located to the north-west within the Trian Mór.[51]

The best-preserved evidence of satellite female religious communities is at the Nuns' Church, Clonmacnoise; St Mary's, Glendalough; and St Mella's, Lemanaghan. Their churches show a diversity of form, though they are all situated some distance outside the main ecclesiastical complex within their own discrete enclosures. The enclosing element in all three cases is now rectilinear rather than the more typical circular enclosures of the period but without archaeological investigation it cannot be verified if this represents later re-modelling of the perimeters. These female religious communities were outside but connected to the main ecclesiastical complexes by routeways.[52]

Lesser female religious communities

The historical evidence has numerous examples of holy women and female religious attached to churches, some of which likely had a laity-serving function, and these are termed the lesser female religious communities. These thirty-three sites – and many more could be added – are represented by the various remains of smaller churches and ecclesiastical enclosures. The nature of these female religious' communities at these places is considered very fluid. For instance, ten are included on the basis of a historical reference alone, which, in many cases relates to the writings of St Patrick, from which sites have been tentatively identified, such as Carricknahorna, Co. Sligo, and Kilreekil, Co. Galway. Killabuonia, Co. Kerry, may also have housed a female religious community, and could be included here, as St Buonia was a reputed sister of Patrick (Fig. 1.3).[53]

Of this group, only Kilreekil and Molough, Co. Tipperary, have possible remains of early circular enclosures, both being preserved in the roadways around the sites. Other sites with remains of enclosing elements are Cam, Co. Roscommon, and Kilglass, Co. Longford. Other possible early female religious sites are based solely on

49 Ibid., p. 229.   **50** C. McCullough and W.H. Crawford, *Irish historic towns atlas, no. 18: Armagh* (Dublin, 2007), map 4.   **51** Ó Carragáin, *Churches in early medieval Ireland*, p. 62.   **52** D. Murphy, 'Excavation of an early monastic enclosure at Clonmacnoise' in H. King (ed.), *Clonmacnoise studies, volume 2* (Dublin, 2003), pp 1–33 at p. 21; Quinlan and Moss, *Lemanaghan*, p. 21; R. Ó Floinn, '"The market cross" at Glendalough' in C. Doherty et al. (eds), *Glendalough: city of God* (Dublin, 2011), pp 80–111 at p. 95.   **53** Killabuonia (Cill Buaine), a putative female religious site, is interesting. There are two ecclesiastical sites in the townland, a larger better-known one and a second smaller site, approximately 500m to the south-west. This arrangement is similar to the satellite female religious houses mentioned previously. See Ó Riain, *Dictionary*, pp 133, 502.

1.3 Killabuonia, the Glen, Co. Kerry, associated with St Buonia. Image © Frank Coyne.

local memory and tradition, like Kilteel, Co. Kildare.[54] The majority of these lesser sites now manifest in the landscape as holy wells, or later churches and graveyards, for example, Aghavea, Co. Fermanagh (St Lasair);[55] Clenor, Co. Cork (St Cránaid);[56] or Faughart, Co. Louth (Sts Brigit and Monenna).[57]

ARCHAEOLOGICAL INVESTIGATION

Considering the wealth of archaeological evidence from the early medieval period in Ireland as a whole, the current dearth of material culture relating to female religious

54 Lord Killanin and M.V. Duignan, *The Shell guide to Ireland*, 2nd edition (London, 1967), p. 87; M. Herity (ed.), *Ordnance Survey letters Kildare: letters containing information relative to the antiquities of the county of Kildare collected during the progress of the OS in 1837–1839* (Dublin, 2002), p. 21. **55** *MRHI*, p. 372; Ó Riain, *Dictionary*, pp 393–4; R. Ó Baoill, 'Excavations at Aghavea, Co. Fermanagh' in C. Corlett, and M. Potterton (eds), *The church in early medieval Ireland, in the light of recent archaeological excavations* (Dublin, 2014), pp 159–72. **56** The precise date of this foundation is unclear. E. Johnston, 'Powerful women or patriarchal weapons? Two medieval Irish saints', *Peritia*, 15 (2001), 302–10; Ó Riain, *Dictionary*, pp 228–9; T. Ó Carragáin, 'The archaeology of ecclesiastical estates in early medieval Ireland: a case study of the kingdom of Fir Maige', *Peritia*, 24–5 (2014), 266–312. **57** L. O'Connor, 'Faughart investigation 1966,' *CLAHJ* 17 (1966), 125–9; *MRHI*, p. 384; Ó Riain, *Dictionary*, pp 123; Boazman, 'The material

and the few archaeological investigations that have been undertaken is somewhat surprising.[58] No intrusive excavations have been undertaken at the Nuns' Church, Clonmacnoise, but there was a magnetometer survey, though results were somewhat disappointing.[59] Geophysical survey at Glendalough was more successful and has revealed evidence of industrial activity to the west and south-west of St Mary's Church.[60] Of those that have been excavated, as at Inishleena, Co. Cork, and Faughart, Co Louth, results were inconclusive, hampered by later use of the sites, and nothing specifically related to female religious was uncovered.[61]

Excavation at Ballyvourney, Co. Cork, undertaken in the early 1950s, was more fruitful, though the supposed site of the early female foundation was unsuitable for excavation due to its continued use for burial. Evidence of extensive metalworking and occupation activity was recovered from a hut site known as 'St Gobnait's house', now the first station in the modern penitential route at Ballyvourney.[62] These archaeological findings are interesting as some have suggested that Gobnait's name indicates an association with the metalworking deity Goibhne.[63]

The body of St Lupait (Lubaid),[64] sister of St Patrick, was reputedly discovered in 1633 at Temple-na-Ferta, Armagh. Lynn's much later excavations revealed early medieval occupation, graves, and later activity there. Important information on early medieval burial was recovered, though none was positively identified as a female religious.[65] More recent excavations at Aghavea, Co. Fermanagh – associated with the female St Lasair – revealed intensive occupation and use in both the early and later medieval periods, including extensive industrial activity, but nothing clearly associated with early female religious.[66]

Early medieval burial evidence is currently unclear in regard to the positive identification of female religious. Indeed, the nature of burial evidence from this period is such that it may be difficult to ever conclusively identify the remains of female religious in the archaeological record.[67] Placename evidence may indicate such segregated burial, as the suffix 'na mban' and its derivatives is the Irish for women, as seen at Tempullnamban and Relicnamban on Inishmurray, Co. Sligo, Relignaman, Co.

culture of self-promotion'. **58** O'Sullivan et al., *Early medieval Ireland*. C. Manning, 'Excavation at Kilteel church, Co. Kildare', *JCKAHS*, 16 (1982), 173–229; S. Greene, 'Killeen Cormac Colbinstown: an ecclesiastical site on the Kildare–Wicklow border', *Co. Kildare Online Electronic History Journal* (2011), http://www.kildare.ie/library/ehistory/2011/03/killeen_cormac_colbinstown _an.asp, accessed 23 April 2022. **59** For excavations elsewhere at Clonmacnoise, see H. King (ed.), *Clonmacnoise studies, volume 1* (Dublin, 1998); H. King (ed.), *Clonmacnoise studies, volume 2* (Dublin, 2003); H. Mytum, 'Surface and geophysical survey at Clonmacnoise: defining the extent of intensive monastic settlement' in King (ed.), *Clonmacnoise studies, volume 2*, pp 42, 45. **60** Seaver et al., 'A monastery among the glens'. **61** E.M. Fahy, 'Inishleena Abbey and other sites in the Lee Valley', *JCHAS*, 62 (1957), 65–76; O'Connor, 'Faughart investigation 1966'. **62** O'Kelly, 'St Gobnet's house'; Edwards, *Archaeology of early medieval Ireland*, p. 87. **63** Ó Riain, *Dictionary*, pp 276, 278–9. There is not universal agreement on this suggested association. **64** Ó Riain, *Dictionary*, p. 406. **65** Lynn, 'Excavations in 46–48 Scotch Street, Armagh', pp 80–3; Ó Carragáin, *Churches in early medieval Ireland*, p. 64. **66** Ó Baoill, 'Excavations at Aghavea', p. 162. **67** M.J. O'Kelly, 'Church Island near Valentia, Co. Kerry', *PRIA*, 59C (1958), 57–136 at pp 132–3; E. O'Brien, *Mapping death: burial in late Iron Age and early medieval Ireland* (Dublin, 2020).

Tyrone, and also on Inishglora, Co. Mayo.[68] Several of these sites were ecclesiastical and so it is possible that segregated burial was practised – though there is little contemporary historical evidence to show that it was.[69] These segregated burial places are frequently on the edge of ecclesiastical sites, perhaps embodying liminal qualities, and are thought to have had a variety of functions.[70]

While it is sometimes suggested that cemeteries or ecclesiastical sites containing female toponyms were once female religious communities there is not universal agreement on this interpretation.[71] As such, while these sites *may* represent satellite female religious communities, the evidence is far from conclusive.

ARTEFACTS

There is a small number of artefacts associated with early female saints or their ecclesiastical sites. Surprisingly, there are just two objects associated with St Brigit of Kildare, excluding her popular reed cross – a mantle or cloak, and a shoe – with several possible relics at Glastonbury, England, Cologne, Germany, and a skull fragment at Lisbon, Portugal.[72]

There are four other artefacts associated with early medieval female saints: St Lasair with a book shrine, the *Domnach Airgid*; St Damhnat (Dympna), with a crosier; and St Attracta with a (now lost) cross and cup.[73] A rare survival is a timber statue of St Gobnait once retained by the O'Herlihys, who were official keepers of her church and custodians of her cult (Fig. 1.4).[74]

Although the book shrine and the crosier date to the early medieval period, they were substantially modified in the later Middle Ages, while the remainder of the objects mentioned are likely later medieval in date, rather than being contemporary with their respective female saint. There are two early carved stones that may be interpreted as commemorating women. One from Clonmacnoise includes the suffix 'ingen' or daughter, that Swift has suggested may have been for an ecclesiastical wife and the other from Inishmurray that includes the phrase *Máel Brigte* or 'servant of Brigit' and a female name, which O'Sullivan and Ó Carragáin have suggested may hint at female religious burials there, despite 'Máel' usually denoting a male servant.[75]

---

68 A. Hamlin and C. Foley, 'A women's graveyard at Carrickmore, Co. Tyrone, and the separate burial of women', *UJA*, 46 (1983), 41–6.   69 S. Leigh Fry, *Burial in medieval Ireland, 900–1500* (Dublin, 1999), p. 180.   70 T. Ó Carragáin, 'From family cemeteries to community cemeteries in Viking Age Ireland?' in C. Corlett and M. Potterton (eds), *Death and burial in early medieval Ireland in the light of recent archaeological excavations* (Dublin, 2010), pp 217–26 at p. 221. 71 Harrington, *Women in a Celtic church*, p. 230. Dr Edel Bhreathnach pers. comm.   72 H.F. McClintock, 'The mantle of St Brigid at Bruges', *JRSAI*, 6, 1 (1936), 32–40; R. Ó Floinn, *Irish shrines and reliquaries of the Middle Ages* (Dublin, 1994), p. 44; L. Bitel, *Landscape with two saints* (Oxford, 2009), p. 199.   73 Ó Floinn, *Irish shrines and reliquaries*, p. 30, 45; M. MacDermott, 'The crosiers of St Dympna and St Mel and tenth-century Irish metal-work', *PRIA*, 58C (1957), 167–95; Hall, *Women*, p. 117.   74 Ó Riain, *Dictionary*, p. 368.   75 Macalister, *Memorial slabs of Clonmacnoise*, p. 10; R.A.S. Macalister, *Corpus inscriptionum insularum Celticarum*, vol. II (Dublin, 1949), p. 46; P. Lionard, 'Early Irish grave slabs', *PRIA*, 61C (1961), 95–169 at p. 113; C. Swift,

1.4 A timber statue of
St Gobnait, Ballyvourney,
Co. Cork. Image © Care of
the Church Committee.

The current outline of the archaeological evidence can only be tentative, as from a historical perspective it is arguable if dedicated female religious communities following a distinctive rule over several generations were even commonplace in the early medieval period in Ireland.[76] It also remains debatable as to what extent archaeology can actually reveal the everyday lives of female religious, as none of the excavations so far have indicated any gender bias in favour of females, although, perhaps we should not expect

'Sculptors and their customers: a study of Clonmacnoise grave slabs' in King (ed.), *Clonmacnoise studies*, vol. 2, p. 109. It may record a priest associated with a female community, though opinions differ on this interpretation. The inscription dates to the twelfth century or later. J. O'Sullivan and T. Ó Carragáin, *Inishmurray: monks and pilgrims in an Atlantic landscape, vol. 1: archaeological survey and excavations, 1997–2000* (Cork, 2008), pp 99, 152.   **76** E. Bhreathnach, 'The *Vita Apostolica* and the origin of the Augustinian canons and canonesses in medieval Ireland' in Browne and Ó Clabaigh, *Households*, pp 1–27 at pp 20–6.

the archaeological record to show such binary divisions as male and female religious in this period.[77]

CURRENT EVIDENTIAL ISSUES

The main evidential issue in this early period is the sheer number of sites recorded. It has been estimated that there are over 5,000 ecclesiastical settlements dating from the fifth to the twelfth century in Ireland, many of which are dedicated to a female saint.[78] There is a peculiar density of minor church sites in Ireland at this time, in comparison with elsewhere. Ó Carragáin suggests that this was due to the diffuse nature of power structures in Ireland, which permitted a higher proportion of the lay population to found their own churches.[79] This is problematical, as it cannot be definitively asserted that a female dedication alone is sufficient to indicate a female religious community at a specific site. Moreover, it cannot be presumed that these sites were continually occupied by religious females. The dedication may show that a royal woman donated her bride-price to the church, or that she was a female religious during her own lifetime.[80]

Site names incorporating Brigit or its derivatives may also indicate a female religious use, though this is probably a simplification of a more complex transmission of the cult of Brigit of Kildare – and several other Brigits over time – in a similar manner to Finnbarr of Cork.[81] Bhreathnach has demonstrated for parts of Leinster that ecclesiastical families aligned themselves with particular saintly cults, and the saint's cult could be geographically extensive.[82] Despite these reservations, there may indeed be an engendered aspect to the spread of the cult of a female saint, and sites dedicated to female saints – for example St Brigit – may have specifically housed female religious.

The second evidential issue in the study of early female religious sites is that a distinction must be drawn between those foundations established by a woman who lived a religious life, like Brigit of Kildare, Íte, Monenna, and Samthann; and those foundations that are dedicated to those saints but were clearly not founded by them. An example of the former is Clenor, Co. Cork, believed to have been established by the female saint Cránaid sometime in the sixth century and dedicated to her.[83] Historical and archaeological evidence from the early medieval kingdom in which Clenor was situated – Fir Maige – undertaken by MacCotter and Ó Carragáin suggests that it was the centre of a female religious ecclesiastical estate, which had a

77 The same is true of excavations abroad; see e.g. G. Thomas, 'Life before the minster: the social dynamics of monastic foundation at Anglo-Saxon Lyminge, Kent', *The Antiquaries Journal*, 93 (2013), 109–45.   78 https://monasticon.celt.dias.ie/, accessed 23 April 2022. See also Ó Riain, *Dictionary*.   79 T. Ó Carragáin, 'The architectural setting of the Mass'; Ó Carragáin, *Churches in early medieval Ireland*, p. 226.   80 See Bhreathnach, 'The *vita apostolica*'.   81 *MRHI*, p. 323; Harrington, *Women in a Celtic church*, map 2; P. Ó Riain, *The making of a saint: Finnbarr of Cork, 600–1200* (Dublin, 1997); Ó Riain, *Dictionary*, pp 124, 332–4.   82 Bhreathnach, 'The genealogies of Leinster'; Harrington, *Women in a Celtic church*, maps 1–4.   83 Callan, *Sacred sisters*; Johnston, 'Powerful women or patriarchal weapons?', pp 305–8; Ó Riain, *Dictionary*, pp 228–9.

demonstrably different settlement pattern to two contemporary male ecclesiastical estates in the same region.[84]

The third evidential problem is that while there is a broadly consistent morphology or 'look' of early ecclesiastical sites and churches in Ireland – one or more usually circular or sub-circular enclosing elements with one or more small rectangular churches – to date no particular features have been recognized in the field that distinguish female religious foundations from the rest. Current archaeological evidence suggests that size and layout was related to the site's status, and there is also some regional variation. For example, Kildare, arguably the most important female religious foundation, was a large ecclesiastical complex in its own right, comparable to other contemporary major sites such as Armagh, Glendalough or Kells. It had similar archaeological features to these complexes and currently cannot be differentiated from them on the basis of the community's predominant gender. Additionally, the reuse of many of these sites – some up to the present day as burial grounds – means that their earliest archaeological levels have been at best disturbed and at worst completely removed.

CONCLUSIONS

Notwithstanding the current lack of substantial archaeological evidence for early female communities in Ireland, what is clear from the sheer numbers of female religious in the sources is that not all lived in the identified seven major religious communities. Rather, they lived in a wide spectrum of locations that included satellites to large ecclesiastical complexes, regionally important churches and ecclesiastical sites, and at family churches. Some of these churches may have held religious women's relics.[85] Indeed, the definition of female religious in this period might be expanded to include additional roles such as priests' wives, hermits, and recluses. Even married couples followed a particular path of religious life by being continent on particular days.[86]

It would appear from the current evidence that early medieval female religious communities were rarely completely single-sexed or strictly enclosed. It is likely that many ecclesiastical centres and smaller churches had a vowess or a community of female religious attached in some form. The history and documentary evidence of early religious women shows them to be a surprisingly diverse group, which complements very well the current corpus of archaeological evidence outlined here.

---

84 Ó Carragáin, 'The archaeology of ecclesiastical estates in early medieval Ireland'.   **85** N. Wycherley, *The cult of relics in early medieval Ireland* (Turnhout, 2015).   **86** Etchingham, *Church organization in Ireland*, p. 66.

Locating female saints and their foundations in the early medieval Irish martyrologies

ELVA JOHNSTON

THE IRISH MARTYROLOGIES AND THEIR CONTEXTS

The commemoration of the saints, both female and male, connected Christian communities with their pasts, humanizing them through their presence. The inclusion of local saints brought them into the daily lives of believers. This was as true of Ireland as elsewhere in the Christian world. One of the most important sources for tracing these commemorations are texts known as martyrologies. At their simplest, martyrologies list the daily feasts of saints, often adding details such as Old Testament figures, relic translations, octaves, vigils and a range of liturgical feasts. More complexly they sometimes embed stories of the saints in prose and verse.[1] The Irish vernacular martyrological tradition grew directly from continental inspiration, especially the hugely influential Hieronymian martyrology, while simultaneously grounding it in the island's imagined sacred topographies. This localization can be traced from the ninth to the twelfth century in a series of directly linked texts, especially three martyrologies, those of Tallaght, Óengus and Gorman (Plate 4).[2] To what extent can we trace the role of women within the Irish church through them? Their significance within texts operating within a recognizable tradition, one whose very weight tends towards continuity, has yet to be deeply researched. The aim of this chapter is to make a preliminary investigation through comparing these connected documents. These illuminate aspects of the culture of Irish ecclesiastics at different points in the island's history. Do differences between them shape the approach to female saints or are genre conventions and expectations paramount? Are these sources that help locate not only women but the landscapes and foundations to which they contributed?

The extant Irish martyrological tradition was deeply influenced by the *Céli Dé*, literally 'clients of God', an ecclesiastical group within the Irish church that had strong interests in asceticism and liturgical practice. They drew their inspiration from Máel Ruain (d. 792), founder of Tallaght. The *Céli Dé* prized obedience and emphasized

---

1 J. Dubois, *Les martyrologes du moyen âge Latin* (Turnhout, 1978) and F. Lifshitz, *The name of the saint: the martyrology of Jerome and access to the sacred in Francia, 627–827* (Notre Dame, IN, 2006); see, also, J. Hennig, 'Ireland's contribution to the devotion to Old Testament saints', *Irish Ecclesiastical Record*, 104 (1965), 333–48.   2 R.I. Best and H.J. Lawler (eds), *The martyrology of Tallaght from the Book of Leinster and MS 5100–4 in the Royal Library, Brussels*, HBS, 68 (London, 1931, repr. Woodbridge, 2010) [henceforth *Mart. Tallaght*]; W. Stokes (ed. and trans.), *Félire Óengusso Céli Dé: The martyrology of Oengus the Culdee*, HBS, 29 (London, 1905, repr. Dublin, 1984) [henceforth *Fél. Óengusso*]; Stokes (ed. and trans.), *Félire Húi Gormáin: The martyrology of Gorman* (London,

practical asceticism.[3] There is evidence that the *Céli Dé* became affiliated with a number of the major Irish monasteries during the ninth century while also contributing to the prestige of their own foundations, including Tallaght and Finglas, both in county Dublin. In fact, the first of these texts, and the one upon which the martyrologies of Óengus and Gorman rely, is the Martyrology of Tallaght. Scholarly consensus places its production near the beginning of the ninth century.[4] Only a single imperfect medieval manuscript copy of the martyrology survives, although this can be supplemented with Mícheál Ó Cléirigh's early modern transcription of material, now missing owing to lost leaves.[5] The text combines a breviate version of the Hieronymian martyrology, which probably reached Tallaght via northern Britain, with extensive lists of Irish saints. Some of these may have been added at centres such as Iona, Bangor and Moville as suggested by Pádraig Ó Riain in his ground-breaking studies of the Irish martyrologies.[6] These lists provide around 2,000 personal names, although not every name commemorates a separate individual. Throughout, there are demonstrable examples of doublets as well as saints celebrated on multiple feastdays.[7] In addition, it is also worth noting that these individuals are 'saints' in a loose sense: it is probably better to think of the majority as locally venerated figures whose sanctity originated in communal acclaim rather than any formal process. The geographical spread of dedications in the Martyrology of Tallaght is remarkable. It seems that no site and no cult is too small or insignificant for inclusion: the entire island is represented. Does this include women and their foundations?

The Martyrology of Tallaght was the direct source for *Félire Óengusso*, the Martyrology of Óengus. This text was written by Óengus ua Oiblén, probably between 797 x 808.[8] Óengus was a bishop and appears to have held significant status within the community of Tallaght. The *Félire* itself is far more selective than its source,

1895) [henceforth *Fél. Húi Gormáin*].   **3** W. Follett, *Céli Dé in Ireland: monastic writing and identity in the early Middle Ages* (Woodbridge, 2006).   **4** D. Dumville, '*Félire Óengusso*: problems of dating a monument of Old Irish', *Éigse*, 33 (2001), 19–48 at 37–46, suggests that the base martyrological text may have been at Tallaght as early as 774 while P. Ó Riain, *Feastdays of the saints: a history of Irish martyrologies*, Subsidia Hagiographica, 6 (Brussels, 2006), pp 75–98, argues that it took its current form 828 x 33; see also, Follett, *Céli Dé in Ireland*, pp 128–32.   **5** Dublin, UCD-OFM MS A 3, pp 1–11, online at www.dias.isos.ie. The *lacunae* account for 30 January–11 March, 20 May–31 July, and 1 November–16 December. There is also a loss of part of 1 September, all of 2–3 September, and a partial loss of 4 September.   **6** Ó Riain, *Feastdays*, pp 68–9. There are significant clusters of saints from northern Britain commemorated in the martyrology, strongly suggesting the influence of that region on the evolution of the text.   **7** There are very many examples. Colmán moccu Béognae (d. 611), a historically attested individual, has a feastday on 22 January in *Mart. Tallaght*, p. 11 and as Colmán Ela on 26 September with his nativity on 3 October, *Mart. Tallaght*, pp 74, 77. Mo Máedóc mac Migna has three feastdays: 23 March, 18 May and 13 August in *Mart. Tallaght*, pp 26, 44, 63.   **8** The *Félire* does not include an authorship attribution but the tradition associating it with Óengus is strong: Follett, *Céli Dé in Ireland*, pp 119–21. R. Thurneysen, 'Die Abfassung des *Félire* von Oengus', *Zeitschrift für celtische Philologie*, 6 (1908), 6–8 proposed the 797 x 808 date; L. Breatnach, 'Poets and poetry' in K. McCone and K. Simms (eds), *Progress in medieval Irish studies* (Maynooth, 1996), pp 65–77 agrees; Dumville, '*Félire Óengusso*: Problems of dating', 19–48, suggests caution, but places the text before 870; Ó Riain, *Feastdays*, pp 75–98, argues for a date of 829 x 833.

incorporating significantly fewer saints. Furthermore, it is a verse martyrology with a prologue and epilogue that reflect its author's understanding of the Irish past within the sweep of Christian history. The *Félire* is an artistically sophisticated text that was admired and influential.[9] It eventually acquired an extensive apparatus of gloss and commentary. These form the so-called Commentary on Óengus whose compilation has been dated to the second half of the twelfth century.[10] However, this should not be considered as a single document. As Nike Stam has shown what we now call the Commentary is a complex series of intersecting texts, of widely varying dates, that defy simplification into a single definitive version.[11] These texts take the saints of the *Félire* and elaborate their cults with narrative detail, filling out stories only hinted at in the allusive phrases of Óengus.

The other key document that will be considered sits directly within the tradition established by the Martyrology of Tallaght and the *Félire*. This is the Martyrology of Gorman, a verse text that also drew heavily on international examples such as the Carolingian Martyrology of Usuard (d. *c*.875).[12] Its author was Máel Muire Ua Gormáin, abbot of Knock Abbey near Louth, Co. Louth, who died around 1181.[13] He was probably a member of an important ecclesiastical family that included Flann Ua Gormáin (d. 1174), a cosmopolitan official at Armagh who had been to England and the Continent, as well as Find Ua Gormáin (d. 1160) who was associated with the Cistercians.[14] Máel Muire was an Augustinian canon, a member of the order that was most popular among Irish ecclesiastical houses during the reform era.[15] The Martyrology of Gorman was completed after the deaths in 1174 of Gilla Meic Líac (Gelasius), archbishop of Armagh, and Gilla Mo Chaidbeo (Machabeus), abbot of Sts Peter and Paul, Armagh, since chronologically they are the latest saints recorded in the text. These seem to have been included, either by Máel Muire or a later writer, after the rest of the main text was written as a clearly alive Gelasius is mentioned in the dedicatory preface.[16] Máel Muire's world was on the cusp of profound political and social change as new Norman lordships upended old certainties and began to redraw the political landscape. Fascinatingly, Máel Muire makes no overt references to these

---

9 It survives in eight manuscripts. Ó Riain, *Feastdays*, pp 74–7, usefully lists them.   **10** The currently most accessible edition of a version of the Commentary texts is Stokes, *Félire Óengusso Céli Dé*.   **11** N. Stam, *Typology of code-switching in the commentary to the* Félire Óengusso (Utrecht, 2017); Stam, '"Hij Die Niet Leest Is Een Dweil": Nieuw Licht Op de Commentaartraditie van de *Félire Óengusso*', *Kelten* 81 (March 2020), 4–10 contains a detailed analysis of the variations between and within recensions.   **12** For the Martyrology of Usuard, see J. Dubois, *Martyrologes: d'Usuard au Martyrologe romain* (Abbeville, 1990), pp 43–149. Máel Muire also draws on the Martyrology of Ado. Various influences are discussed in Ó Riain, *Feastdays*, pp 166–7.   **13** Ó Riain, *Feastdays*, pp 149–54; Ó Riain, 'Ua Gormáin, Máel Muire', DIB, online at http:// dib.cambridge.org/viewReadPage.do?articleId=a8739.   **14** Ó Riain, 'Ua Gormáin, Máel Muire'.   **15** P.J. Dunning, 'The Arroasian Order in medieval Ireland', *IHS*, 4:16 (Sept. 1945), 297–315. The best introduction to the reform of the Irish church remains Flanagan, *Transformation*; see more recently, D. Ó Corráin, *The Irish church, its reform and the English invasion* (Dublin, 2017). For the canonical movement in medieval Ireland see the contributions to Browne and Ó Clabaigh (eds), *Households*.   **16** *Fél. Húi Gormáin*, pp 4–5 (preface), 62–3 (Gilla Mac Líac, March 27), 66–7 (Gilla Mo Chaidbeo, March 31). Both saints are added at the end of the relevant verses.

transformations. This is all the more striking in that Louth was an area of Norman interest and by the 1180s, within a decade of Máel Muire's martyrology, English settlers had arrived.[17] However, this apparent silence does not mean that the text is not politically informed. The preface pointedly elevates Irish-language sources and accords them a special importance. It identifies both the *Félire* and the Martyrology of Tallaght as inspirations, privileging the latter. Máel Muire remarks that he turned to Tallaght because while Óengus had made use of it he had included few of its saints.[18] Overall, Máel Muire in his Martyrology of Gorman adds over 100 Irish saints to the Tallaght corpus, roughly 6 per cent of the total, and excludes less than 5 per cent of the saints recorded in the Martyrology of Tallaght.[19] His addition of this material, while relatively small, is significant for what it tells about his own times. Furthermore, Máel Muire's retention of almost all the Irish saints in the Martyrology of Tallaght contributed to the image of Ireland as an island of saints, an idea that had gained traction over the course of the twelfth century.[20]

The extant text of the Martyrology of Gorman now exists in a single manuscript, a seventeenth-century transcription by the Irish Franciscan friar Mícheál Ó Cléirigh (d. *c.*1643) from a now lost original.[21] The only other witness is a Franciscan manuscript, dating to the late fifteenth century, which contains a copy of *Félire Óengusso* accompanied by a full version of the Commentary texts. It includes a list of the majority of Irish saints in the Martyrology of Gorman appended at the end of most entries.[22] In this context it is worth drawing attention to the extensive genealogical and toponymic notes that supplement the Martyrology of Gorman in the Ó Cléirigh manuscript, usually as interlineal glosses. It has been often assumed that these notes were originally written by Máel Muire. It is possible, perhaps even more likely, that they are the work of a later continuator.[23] Linguistically the glosses are Middle Irish and difficult to pin down definitively, although there are some potential contextual clues that point to the early thirteenth century. For example, the notes to 9 June gloss the famous saint, Columba, with a reference to the black monks (*manaig dubh*) at Derry.[24] The date of the establishment of the religious house of Augustinian Canons Regular at Derry, to which this may refer, is debatable, with suggestions ranging from the late 1160s to around 1230.[25] However, it was in the immediate years after Máel Muire's death that Derry was decisively incorporated into the reformed ecclesiastical structures that ultimately replaced older models of church authority.[26] A date no later

17 B. Smith, *Conquest and colonization in medieval Ireland: the English in Louth, 1170–1330* (Cambridge, 1999), esp. pp 10–52.   **18** *Fél. Húi Gormáin*, pp 4–5 (preface).   **19** It is impossible to give absolute percentages due to the number of repetitions and/or confusions of saints between the martyrologies.   **20** L. Gougaud, 'The Isle of Saints', *Studies*, 13 (1924), 363–80.   **21** Brussels, KBR MS 5100–5104, ff 124a–197b, online at www.dias.isos.ie.   **22** Dublin, UCD-OFM MS A7, online at www.dias.isos.ie. The following days lack these lists: 1–3, 5, 15, 22, 31 January; 8–10, 12, 14 February; 4, 19 March; 17–18 April; 17, 24, 31 May; 16 June; 18–19, 24 August; 12 September; 10 October; 28 November; 30–1 December.   **23** They existed by the time UCD-OFM MS A7 was produced as their content are partially included in the Gorman material preserved in that manuscript.   **24** *Fél. Húi Gormáin*, pp 112–13 (gloss 1).   **25** *MRHI*, p. 153, suggests around 1230 while B. Lacey, *Medieval and monastic Derry: sixth century to 1600* (Dublin, 2013), pp 66–76, argues for an earlier date.   **26** M. Herbert, *Iona, Kells and Derry: the history and*

than the first quarter of the thirteenth century seems a likely *terminus ante quem* for the glosses and the significance of this will be explored later in the chapter.

IDENTIFYING FEMALE SAINTS IN THE MARTYROLOGIES

So, where do female saints and their foundations fit into this picture? Most of those commemorated in the Irish martyrologies were men, reflecting the patriarchal nature of Irish society. Women represent 12 per cent of saints in the Martyrology of Tallaght, with over 200 separate examples. The Martyrology of Gorman matches this percentage, adding at least fifteen further female saints. The *Félire*, as previously mentioned, is highly selective, drawing directly on the Martyrology of Tallaght. It does not add saints. Figures cannot be completely precise as some of the entries commemorate multiple women, identified by kinship relations but not individually or with exact numbers.[27] Despite the disparity, the number of women commemorated is large enough to allow patterns to be identified and extrapolated. Moreover, the martyrologies mention relatively more female saints than other hagiographical sources. For example, the surviving Irish saints' Lives from the medieval period, both in Irish and in Latin, overwhelming concentrate on men with holy women reduced to anecdotal appearances, either incorporated into the Lives of male saints or in short ancillary texts.[28] The impressive textual tradition associated with St Brigit is an outlier that is more comparable with that of important male saints than of other women.[29]

However, identifying women within the martyrologies is not necessarily always straightforward, especially for those not known from other documents such as saints' Lives, chronicles and genealogies. Generally, the major factors that establish identification are names, titles and pronouns. Names and titles are particularly representative of cultural norms and expectations. Among these were expectations of gender. A large number of names matched grammatical with biological gender. For example, masculine and feminine diminutive suffixes, *án* and *-nat* respectively, are common in distinguishing male and female names.[30] Similarly, those with *Dar/Der* in initial position are female, originating in an archaic word for daughter, while names with *neth/nad*, ultimately derived from a term for champion, are male.[31] The use of certain nouns can also indicate biological sex, sometimes through association with a wider vocabulary that denoted ideas of masculinity and femininity. A good example

hagiography of the monastic familia *of Columba* (Oxford, 1988, repr. Dublin, 1996), pp 109–26. **27** See, for instance, *Fél. Húi Gormáin*, pp 148–9 (Fachtna's daughters, 3 August), 170–1 (Mechar's daughters, September 6).   **28** E. Johnston, 'Powerful women or patriarchal weapons? Two medieval Irish saints', *Peritia*, 15 (2001), 302–10, examines examples of both types.   **29** An excellent introduction to the saint and her extensive cult is T. Charles-Edwards, 'Brigit [St Brigit, Brigid] 439/52–524/26)', *ODNB*, online at doi.org/10.1093/ref:odnb/3427.   **30** Representative examples are *Mart. Tallaght*, pp 16 (Gobnait, 11 February), 50 (Damnat, 13 June); *Fél. Húi Gormáin*, pp 240–1 (Ségnat, 18 December).   **31** *Mart. Tallaght*, pp 14 (Dar Lugdach, 1 February), 54 (Dar Erca, 6 July); the prolific allomorph *derb-* is considered in M.A. O'Brien, 'Etymologies and notes', *Celtica*, 3 (1956), 168–84 at 178. *Mart. Tallaght*, p. 5 (Nad Fróich, 6 January); *Fél. Húi Gormáin*,

is *cú* (hound) and related words that are used to identify men. The hound had a deep symbolic resonance in Irish literature and it was frequently paired with a masculine warrior ethos. It is no coincidence that the greatest of all early Irish literary heroes was Cú Chulainn (hound of Culann).[32] In contrast, there are male names derived from *báeth* meaning foolish or stupid, such as Baíthéne, that are given to some ecclesiastics.[33]

This negative nomenclature is fascinating and may indicate personal choice upon the part of the holders or even function as apotropaic. For instance, an early list of the abbots of Iona claims that Baíthéne, Columba's immediate successor, was originally called Conin, making Baíthéne his name in religion.[34] On the other hand, the use of hypocorisms (a type of nickname), mainly but not exclusively for men, demonstrates an empathic bond between saint and follower that cuts against hierarchical differences.[35] Male clerics are also identified by the ubiquitous *máel* 'tonsured', although that name element also became popularized in secular contexts.[36] There is less of an obvious ecclesiastical emphasis in the names assigned to female saints in the martyrologies. However, some of them have social resonances, such as the use of -*flaith* (sovereignty, ale) in final position, strongly reflecting a basic political ideology in which women were seen as embodying but not possessing sovereignty.[37] But it is not always so clearcut. Ambisexual names feature making it more difficult to determine biological sexual identity. Colum and Comgall are striking examples, especially as famous holders of these names, Columb Cille/Columba (d. 597) of Iona and Comgall (d. 602) of Bangor, were among the most important Irish ecclesiastics of their era.[38] However, both names were also held by women and there are several examples in the Martyrology of Tallaght.[39] Fortunately, the frequent use of *ingen* (daughter), *mac* (son) and *ua* (grandson),

---

pp 88–9 (Neth Chóeme, 1 May).   **32** Hounds and hound-like heroes are ubiquitous in early Irish literature. See, for instance, K. McCone, '*Aided Cheltchair maic Uthechair*: hounds, heroes and hospitallers in early Irish myth and story', *Ériu*, 35 (1984), 1–30; M. Boyd, 'On not eating dog' in Matthew Boyd (ed.), *Ollam: studies in Gaelic and related traditions in honour of Tomás Ó Cathasaigh* (Madison, NJ, 2016), pp 35–46.   **33** For the semantic range of *báeth* see eDIL *s.v. báeth* online at dil.ie/5139. Examples of the name Baíthéne include *Mart. Tallaght*, pp 7 (12 January), 18 (19 February), 45 (22 May), 49 (9 June), 77 (6 October), 79 (12 October), 80 (15 October). **34** W. Stokes and J. Strachan (eds), *Thesaurus paleohibernicus: a collection of Old Irish glosses, scholia, prose and verse*, vol. 2 (Cambridge, 1903), p. 281. I owe this reference to my colleague Prof. Dáibhí Ó Cróinín.   **35** The use of hypocorisms is ubiquitous. P. Russell, 'Patterns of hypocorism in early Irish hagiography' in J. Carey, M. Herbert and P. Ó Riain (eds), *Studies in Irish hagiography: saints and scholars* (Dublin, 2001), pp 237–49, examines their origins and use.   **36** There are nearly 40 examples across the Martyrology of Tallaght-related texts and it remained productive through the entire period. See, for example, the commemoration of Malachias /Máel Máedóc Ua Morgair (d. 1148), now better known as Malachy, at *Fél. Húi Gormáin*, pp 210–11 (gloss 6 gives the Irish form).   **37** A good example is *Mart. Tallaght*, p. 5 (7 January), but the name form is relatively uncommon compared to its use in secular society. See eDIL *s.v. flaith*, online dil.ie/22281. The association between women, sovereignty and the giving of alcoholic drink is well-established in early Irish literature. Particularly striking cases are discussed by M. Ní Mhaonaigh, 'Tales of three Gormlaiths in medieval Irish literature', *Ériu*, 52 (2002), 1–24.   **38** Good introductions are: A. Breen, 'Comgall', *DIB*, online at http://dib.cambridge.org/viewReadPage.do?articleId=a1902; M. Herbert, 'Columba [St Columba, Colum Cille] (*c.*521–597)', *DNB*, online at doi.org/10.1093/ref:odnb/6001.   **39** *Mart. Tallaght*, pp 54 (Comgell inghen Diarmata, 7 July), 72 (Comgell *uirgo*,

and Latin equivalents, usually offers definitive identification. However, this is not always the case and some saints cannot be assigned as biologically male or female when the name alone is used and it would be a mistake to assume a male biological identity. The numbers are small but significant.

Titles can also help establish biological gender. For example, the martyrologies often describe a woman as a virgin or a nun. However, there is a marked contrast between the ubiquity of institutional titles such as bishop, abbot, deacon or priest given to men and their rarity for women, with a few exceptions such as noting if a woman was an abbess.[40] Strikingly, the primary identity of many female saints is expressed biologically, through their virginity or genealogically, by the name of their father. Men are also situated genealogically but this is usually in addition to their institutional roles. This echoes the realities of early medieval Irish ecclesiastical hierarchies where men were perceived as holding the most important roles. Moreover, even though church organization changed dramatically between the ninth and twelfth centuries, men remained dominant as powerbrokers. Thus, there was very little reason for Abbot Máel Muire to change the basic deployment of gendered identities that he found embedded in the Martyrology of Tallaght.

Perceived hierarchy is one underlying cause of gender imbalance in the martyrologies. A related factor is the way that hierarchy impacted on real people and their communities. In early medieval Irish society women frequently had more limited rights and greater challenges in establishing property ownership than men, although these rights were relative rather than absolute and rooted in socio-economic distinctions.[41] This basic difficulty in acquiring land and enlarging ecclesiastical estates may be reflected in the small size of many female foundations, particularly in the early medieval period.[42] It is likely that a large number of female religious communities may not have lasted past the lifetime of their founder, meaning that the chances of holy women surviving long enough in communal memory to be recorded were smaller.[43]

19 September) (Comgell, one of three sisters, 26 October), 3 (Columba *uirgo*, 31 December), 25 (Columb ingen Buti, 25 March). In comparison, Comgall is used for a man six times, *Mart. Tallaght*, pp 41 (10 May), 57 (24 July), 66 (26 August), 68 (4 September), 75 (29 September), 77 (7 October). Columb and its variants is common, with 25 examples of Colum(b) alone, not counting hypocoristic forms.   **40** This is inconsistently noted. For example, Tuilelaith, an early abbess of Kildare, is marked as such in *Mart. Tallaght*, p. 5 (6 January) but the more famous Dar Lugdach, Brigit's immediate successor, is not, nor for that matter is Brigit. A gloss in *Fél. Húi Gormáin*, pp 28–29 (gloss 1), identifies Dar Lugdach as a *banabb*, abbess, after Brigit.   **41** There is a large literature on women, and gender, in early Irish law. The basic legal principals are explored in F. Kelly, *A guide to early Irish law* (Dublin, 1988), pp 7–16, 68–79. More detailed studies include D. Ó Corráin, 'Women and the law in early Ireland' in M. O'Dowd and S. Wichert (eds), *Chattel, servant or citizen: women's status in church, state and society* (Belfast, 1995), pp 45–57; H. Oxenham, *Perceptions of femininity in early Irish society* (Woodbridge, 2016), considers the intersection of law and literary representation.   **42** The story of Cummen, recorded in the *Additamenta* of the Book of Armagh, offers a fascinating glimpse of a woman in the religious life circumventing these difficulties. See, L. Bieler (ed. and trans.), *The Patrician texts in the Book of Armagh* (Dublin, 1979), pp 174–5.   **43** K. Hughes, *Early Christian Ireland: introduction to the sources* (London, 1972), pp 234–35; L. Bitel, 'Women's donations to the churches in early Ireland', *JRSAI*, 114 (1984), 5–23. The most recent important study is Collins, *Female monasticism*, pp 28–40.

Some female foundations appear to be effectively churches established within the kindred, in effect family or proprietorial foundations, with sisters sharing the same site.[44] Perhaps such family churches gave a kin-group extra status, making it worthwhile to invest in a female foundation.

The combination of scale and ephemerality may be one reason why so many of the women mentioned in the martyrologies are not associated with any site, although this is also the case with a significant number of men. In addition, these factors conspire to make many named female sites difficult to locate.[45] However, those that can be identified broadly share the same toponymic elements as male sites. Thus, female foundations are often named after the founder or are located in a variety of landscape types with toponyms indicating areas suitable for pasture as well as uplands, wooded areas, lake environments and so on. Generally, there is no difference in the ecological types favoured by men and women. *Dísert* toponyms, derived from Latin *desertum* (desert), is one possible exception.[46] These placenames are testament to the ideals, if not the actualities, of ascetic retreat among Irish ecclesiastics. They suggest that the sites are located in wilderness areas or are emblematic of particular ascetic ideologies. However, several of the foundations named as *díserta* were major ecclesiastical centres whose locations little resembled the wilderness.[47] Intriguingly, every single *dísert* placename recorded in the martyrologies is connected with a churchman, perhaps reflecting the idea that ascetic 'desert' retreat was perceived to be more appropriate for men than women. However, this may be a bias of the source or a reflection of the greater visibility of male foundations. For example, the well-attested cult of Canir of Bantry, Co. Cork, associates this female saint with a *dísert* site, demonstrating that a gendered trend is not absolute when other genres are considered.[48] Moreover the idea of female hermits living apart from the world is described as early as the Life of Columbanus, written by the Italian monk Jonas in the first half of the seventh century.[49]

The same trends of toponymic comparability between male and female sites holds true of the built environment, which is indicated through a range of onomastic terms.

---

44 A few examples will suffice to demonstrate the wider pattern: *Mart. Tallaght*, pp 49 (daughters of Laisrén at Cell Cúle, 11 June), 53 (daughters of Cathbad at Aired, 2 July), 54 (three daughters of Ernéne at Enach Dirmaige, 6 July). In all cases the site cannot be securely identified. **45** *MRHI*, p. 307; See also the contribution to this volume by Collins. **46** There are 11 examples of *dísert* placenames recorded in the martyrologies, with a particular emphasis in the glosses to Gorman. A good example is Dísert Maíle Tuile, now Dysart, Co. Westmeath. The founder saint is commemorated on 30 July in *Mart. Tallaght*, p. 59, but the site is not recorded. The additional information is provided by *Fél. Húi Gormáin*, pp 146–7 (gloss 2). **47** For example, Dísert Díarmata (Castledermot, Kildare), *Mart. Tallaght*, p. 51 (21 June), was a major foundation. **48** See E. Johnston, 'A woman's voice? The cult of St Canir of Bantry in the early Middle Ages', *Journal of the Bantry Historical and Archaeological Society* 4 (2022), 124–36, which argues for a connection between Reendisert, near Bantry, Co. Cork, and the saint. **49** B. Krusch (ed.), *Ionae Vitae Sanctorum Columbani, Vedastis, Iohannis*, MGH (Hanover and Leipzig, 1905), I.3, 157; the passage is translated by A. O'Hara and I. Wood, *Jonas of Bobbio: Life of Columbanus, Life of John of Réomé and Life of Vedast* (Liverpool, 2017), 99–100; discussed by E. Johnston, 'Exiles from the edge? The Irish contexts of *peregrinatio*' in R. Flechner and S. Meeder (eds), *The Irish in early*

The most famous is *cell*, derived from Latin *cella*.[50] However, one significant exception is provided by *ernaide*, usually anglicized as Urney/Nurney. The onomastic element is derived from the verbal noun *airnigde* (act of praying) and it is applied to a number of female churches in the martyrologies.[51] The term is frequently translated as oratory into English, a reasonable reflection of the scale involved. For instance, Gobnait, a saint of the Múscraige in the south of the island, is placed in Ernaide in Múscraige Mittine in the Martyrology of Tallaght. But a toponymic gloss in the Martyrology of Gorman locates her in Móin Mór (Ballyvourney, Co. Cork).[52] These sites were geographically very close and may even be identical but the toponymic note provides valuable additional detail. It is arguable that the change in Gobnait's dedication from Ernaide to Móin Mór is reflective of her growing local importance, one which increased dramatically over time.[53] She became too popular to be only associated with a small oratory. Further contextual evidence is provided by the *Vita* of Samthann (d. 739), a widely admired abbess. Samthann, who will be discussed in more detail shortly, began her religious career at a place called Ernaide, before going to the larger Clonbroney, Co. Longford, and it is the latter church with which she was most associated.[54]

Taken as a whole, the placename evidence suggests that although men and women used similar geographical sites, the way their built environment was perceived varied. Large female ecclesiastical centres such as Kildare were the exception rather than the norm in the early medieval Irish church.[55] Furthermore, while there were a multitude of small male foundations this is counterbalanced by the many medium and large monasteries that were founded by and for men. These were dominant in church politics and the ecclesiastical economy throughout the early Middle Ages and still held that position when Máel Muire was writing in the twelfth century.

THE *CÉLI DÉ* AND FEMALE ASCETICISM

Female saints in the martyrologies can be analysed in other more fine-grained ways. Treated as a group it is possible to identify clusters of holy women within the martyrologies. There are at least three basic types: those based on geographical

medieval Europe: identity, culture and religion (Basingstoke, 2016) pp 38–52.   **50** There are over 130 examples across the Tallaght-related martyrologies, although several of these are multiple references to particular sites.   **51** eDIL *s.v. airnigde*, online at dil.ie/2324. Examples are *Mart. Tallaght*, pp 12 (Mo Chonna, 25 January), 16 (Gobnait, 11 February), 59 (Mica, 1 August); *Fél. Húi Gormáin*, pp 34–5 (Coccnat, 11 February, gloss 8), 148–9 (daughters of Fachtna, 3 August, gloss 5), 170–2 (Ness, 4 September, gloss 2). Of these Mo Chonna is an ambisexual name and Coccnat's association with an Ernaide may well be a displacement from Gobnait on the same day.   **52** *Mart. Tallaght*, p. 16; *Fél. Óengusso*, p. 60 (*Félire*); pp 72–3 (Commentary); *Fél. Húi Gormáin*, pp 34–5 (gloss 1). The Commentary names both Ernaide and Móin Mór.   **53** D. Ó hEaluighthe, 'St Gobnet of Ballyvourney', *JCHAS*, 72 (1952), 43–61.   **54** Vita Sancte Samthannae Virginis' in Charles Plummer (ed.), *Vitae Sanctorum Hiberniae Partim Hactenus Ineditae*, vol. 2 (Oxford, 1910), pp 253–61 at 254 (§3), where it is spelled 'Ayrnaidy'. The Life is translated by D. Africa, 'Life of the holy virgin Samthann' in T. Head (ed.), *Medieval hagiography: an anthology* (London, 2000), pp 97–110.   **55** See Collins, this volume.

networks between churches, diachronic clusters at a single site and those related to specific forms of ascetic practice. By far the most obvious are those centred around St Brigit and her church at Kildare. It boasts multiple saints as do major male foundations such as Armagh and Clonmacnoise, Co. Offaly. For example, apart from Brigit herself, three abbesses of Kildare are commemorated in the Martyrology of Tallaght, emphasizing Kildare and its cults; male ecclesiastics are also represented.[56] Yet, it must be remembered that Kildare is remarkable, benefitting from the gravitational pull of the figure of Brigit, the star around which many other saints orbit. Arguably, the sheer scale of Brigit's cult means that it is not the best starting point for exploring specific attitudes towards female sanctity on behalf of the compilers of the martyrologies. Evidence for intentionality must be sought elsewhere, beginning with the *Céli Dé.*

Their deep interest in practical asceticism extended to holy women and, arguably, to their commemoration within the Martyrology of Tallaght. A good example is the solidly attested cult of Samthann of Clonbroney, Co. Longford.[57] Her *Vita*, which is noteworthy for its emphasis on the lived religious life, presents her as a great ascetic.[58] Samthann's feastday is celebrated on 19 December, appearing in both the Martyrology of Tallaght and the more selective *Félire Óengusso.*[59] Óengus even devotes an entire quatrain to her, something that is usually reserved for important saints. Furthermore, she appears in the so-called 'Tallaght Memoir' as an authority on asceticism and as an expert on how to defeat the pervasive dangers of sexual desire.[60] This text likely dates to before 840 and was produced by the same community that was responsible for the near-contemporary Martyrology of Tallaght and *Félire.*[61] In the Tallaght Memoir, Máel Ruain is portrayed as valuing Samthann's advice. Her heroic austerity is emphasized in an anecdote where she pierces her face to the cheekbone with the pin of a brooch. Samthann is so pure that no blood flows from the wound, echoing a long-standing medical and theological tradition that associated excess of blood with impurity.[62] It is only after squeezing the wound that Samthann is able to wring a single drop of water

---

56 *Mart. Tallaght*, pp 3 (Comnat, 1 January), 5 (Tuilelaith, 6 January), 14 (Dar Lugdach, 1 February), which, however, only identifies Comnat by name and Tuilelaith by office (abbess). They are explicitly placed in Kildare in the glosses of *Fél. Húi Gormáin*, pp 6–7, 10–11. Among male ecclesiastics, the bishop Máel Doborchon (d. 709) on 19 February, Cogitosus, author of a seventh-century Life of Brigit, on April 18 and Brigit's supposed contemporary bishop Conláed on 3 May, all receive commemoration. See *Mart. Tallaght*, pp 18, 34, 39 and *Fél. Húi Gormáin*, pp 38–9 (gloss 6), 78–9, 88–9 (gloss 1).   **57** See Swift, this volume.   **58** 'Vita Sancte Samthannae', pp 253–61. For further context see Elva Johnston, 'Samthann', *DIB*, online at http://dib. cambridge.org/viewReadPage.do?articleId=a7908.   **59** *Mart. Tallaght*, p. 87; *Fél. Óengusso*, p. 252; *Fél. Húi Gormáin*, pp 242–3. The founder of Clonbroney, Funech, has a commemoration on December 11, which coincides with a missing leaf in the Martyrology of Tallaght, but appears in *Fél. Húi Gormáin*, pp 236–7 (gloss 2).   **60** E.J. Gwynn and W.J. Purton (eds and trans.), 'The monastery of Tallaght', *PRIA* 29C (1911–12), 115–79 at 149–51 (§ 61).   **61** Follett, *Céli Dé in Ireland*, pp 98–9, 101–14.   **62** For general context see P. Brown, *The body and society: men, women and sexual renunciation in early Christianity* (New York, 1988); J. Salisbury, *Church Fathers, independent virgins* (London, 1991), examines the tangled relationship between sexuality and female asceticism. Samthann is also a virginal bride of Christ. The general idea is explored by E.A. Clarke, 'The celibate bridegroom and his virginal brides: metaphor and the marriage of Jesus in early Christian

from it. The anecdote suggests that Máel Ruain should strive to surpass Samthann's level of ascetic purity and that until then he should avoid the companionship of women.[63] Samthann's treatment in the Memoir demonstrates her importance in communal memory.

Scíath of Ardskeagh, Co. Cork, had a similar although less prominent role for the *Céli Dé*. Scíath's feastday is noticed in the Martyrology of Tallaght on 1 January and she makes a brief appearance in the *Vita* of Ailbe of Emly (Co. Tipperary).[64] Furthermore, she is included in a *Céli Dé* litany, suggesting that she was highly respected.[65] Nonetheless, it is the arrival of her relics in Tallaght, celebrated on 6 September in the martyrology, that seems the most significant detail.[66] The *Céli Dé* emphasized the cult of relics, something they tied into their liturgical interests; relics also cemented the idea of the monastic space being particularly holy. However, relics are often referenced in general and collective terms in the Martyrology of Tallaght: Scíath is an instance of relics being tied to a particular individual, again implying that Scíath was more than just a name to the *Céli Dé*.[67] Why were her relics worth emphasizing?

Both Samthann and Scíath appear in a range of *Céli Dé* sources and it is likely that they were appreciated as holy women whose values of asceticism aligned with those of the Tallaght community. However, a close examination of the Martyrology of Tallaght suggests that there was also a complementary interest in a geographical cluster of female saints located near their main centres of Tallaght and Finglas. Some of these cults probably long pre-dated the *Céli Dé* but they certainly had a geographical relevance and included important centres such as Kilmainham, Co. Dublin.[68] There are even closer connections such as the commemoration of Crón of Tallaght on 25 February.[69] Perhaps the most intriguing entry of this type is that concerning Ethne and Sodelb, who are celebrated in the Martyrology of Tallaght and the *Félire* on 29 March.[70] The Commentary texts to the *Félire* and the toponymic glosses in the Martyrology of Gorman locate them in a small church beside the important Columban foundation at Swords, Co. Dublin.[71] The toponymic detail is late but plausible because the two saints

exegesis', *Church History*, 77:1 (March 2008), 1–25.   **63** Gwynn and Purton, 'Monastery of Tallaght', 149–51 (§61). I would like to thank my colleague Dr Exequiel Monge Allen for sharing his convincing translation and interpretation of this passage with me.   **64** *Mart. Tallaght*, p. 3 (she is in Fert Scéithe). The episode is in Plummer, *Vitae Sanctorum Hiberniae*, vol. 1, pp 58–9 and also in W.W. Heist (ed.), *Vitae Sanctorum Hiberniae ex Codice olim Salmanticensi, nunc Bruxellensi* (Brussels, 1965), p. 127.   **65** Follett, *Céli Dé in Ireland*, pp 135–6; P. Ó Riain, *Dictionary* (Dublin, 2011), p. 550.   **66** *Mart. Tallaght*, p. 68; Dumville, 'Félire Óengusso: problems of dating', 42–3, places this event before 825.   **67** *Mart. Tallaght*, pp 27 (Sillán's relics, 27 March), 62 (Máel Ruain brings relics to Tallaght, 10 August), 75 (Sedrac's relics, 29 September), 77 (relics of saints of Ireland, 5 October).   **68** *Mart. Tallaght*, pp 17 (Lasar of Clonmethan, 18 February), 84 (the sisters Dar Inill, Dar Bellin and Comgell in Kilmainham, 26 October); *Fél. Húi Gormáin*, pp 204–5 (gloss 5), adds an extra sister, Cóel, and places them in Killininny near Tallaght but this may be based on a misreading of Maignend from Cell Maignend (Kilmainham) as 'na n-ingen'. *Fél. Húi Gormáin*, pp 220–1 (17 November), notes Dúilech of Clochar in Fingal at a point where there is a lost leaf in the Martyrology of Tallaght.   **69** *Mart. Tallaght*, p. 19.   **70** *Mart. Tallaght*, p. 28; *Fél. Óengusso*, p. 84.   **71** *Fél. Óengusso*, pp 102–3 (Commentary); *Fél. Húi Gormáin*, pp 64–5 (gloss 3).

are the subject of a micro-narrative in the Martyrology of Tallaght. The short narratives in the martyrology are in Latin and, given their content, several can be confidently attributed to the Tallaght community, being strongly reflective of its interests.[72] They are usually extremely brief, often little more than a sentence, and explanatory in nature. In this case, Eithne and Sodelb are described as breast-feeding Jesus, reminiscent of the more famous story of St Íte (d. 570/77) of Killeedy, Co. Limerick. In the Old Irish poem 'Ísucán', she describes suckling the baby Jesus in the first person.[73] The underlying assumption is that these women have such a superabundance of sanctity and a devotion to purity that they embody virginal and maternal characteristics at one and the same time.[74] Unlike Samthann, little can be reconstructed of the biographies of these women. Nonetheless, taken as a cluster, they suggest that the *Céli Dé* valued female sanctity, placing particular emphasis on ascetic virtue.

It is arguable that this emphasis amounts to a strategic concern with types of female sanctity among the *Céli Dé*. Tellingly, the Tallaght Memoir shares some of the interests implicit in the martyrology, in particular around the nexus of female sexuality, asceticism and temptation. The world of the Tallaght Memoir is one inhabited by men and women. They frequently come into contact with each other and, as in the case of Samthann and Máel Ruain, use messengers to remain in communication. For all the emphasis on purity, this is not a male-only landscape. Laywomen and nuns feature regularly in the anecdotes. It is considered normal, if somewhat fraught, for male and female religious to converse regularly with each other and with laypeople.[75] There is no suggestion that strict segregation of the sexes is desirable apart from within their actual monasteries or as a personal ideal. However, its author believed that women were a third more prone to sexual temptation than men, echoing ubiquitous patristic tropes. He tells the story of Copar, sister of Mo Laisse (d. 564) of Devenish, Co. Fermanagh. In order to measure her tendency to sexual sin he sticks a pin into her palm, causing it to bleed. He then puts her on a strict abstinent diet. After three years, no blood flows from Copar's hand and she achieves the state of chastity. This anecdote is both reversed and recapitulated in the story of Samthann that immediately succeeds it.[76] Read together, as they should be, these narratives present Samthann as worthy of emulation because she has a greater weakness to overcome than a man. And, unlike Copar, she suggests the appropriate ascetic regime to a man, rather than it being imposed upon her. Moreover, the dedications to female saints in the Tallaght area show a familiarity with female religious communities in the martyrologies that accords well with the world of the Memoir. The emphasis on the holiness of women such as Samthann,

72 J. Hennig, 'Studies in the Latin texts of the *Martyrology of Tallaght*, of *Félire Óengusso* and of *Félire hÚi Gormáin*', *PRIA* 69:4C (1970), 45–112.   **73** The poem appears in *Fél. Óengusso*, p. 44 (Commentary) while there is a modern edition with commentary by E.G. Quin, 'The early Irish poem Isucán', *Cambridge Medieval Celtic Studies*, 1 (1981), 39–52. Her cult is the subject of E. Johnston, 'Íte: patron of her people'? *Peritia*, 14 (2000), 421–8.   **74** See Swift, this volume. **75** For example, Dublitter of Finglas reprimands another cleric for not helping an elderly woman: Gwynn and Purton, 'Monastery of Tallaght', p. 139 (§7).   **76** Gwynn and Purton, 'Monastery of Tallaght', p. 149 (§60).

Scíath, Crón, Ethne and Sodelb speaks to an ascetic sensibility that was both ideological in content and practical in its acknowledgment of a diverse religious landscape. It demonstrates that martyrologies are far more than long lists of names and can be usefully read alongside contemporary texts.

FEMALE SAINTS IN A CHANGING POLITICAL LANDSCAPE

Intentionality is more difficult to detect in the Martyrology of Gorman because Máel Muire was so intent on including as much from his sources as possible. Therefore, in order to examine whether gender played a meaningful role in his martyrology, it is worth looking at where he adds to the Tallaght corpus. As mentioned earlier he includes additional female saints that are not in the Martyrology of Tallaght. The first example is a cluster that has its ultimate origin in the Martyrology of Tallaght but which is greatly expanded in the Martyrology of Gorman. This is related to the notable female foundation at Cloonburren, Co. Roscommon, one which is well-attested in the medieval chronicles.[77] A number of early medieval inscribed stone fragments, including cross fragments, also survive from the site. Cloonburren lay along a pilgrim route that went through Clonmacnoise, and was situated almost directly across the Shannon from it.[78] In fact, Cloonburren was at one of the key crossings of the river, linking Clonmacnoise with the Slige Mór, the major routeway connecting the east and west coasts of the island. It is very likely that Cloonburren benefitted materially from this highly strategic location. The martyrologies commemorate Caírech (9 February), its founder and reputed sister of the early sixth-century Énda of Aran, and two other saints, Gubsech (20 June) and Mugain (15 December).[79] The two latter are primarily known through their attestation in the Martyrology of Gorman and accompanying toponymic glosses. Mugain also appears in the Commentary texts of the *Félire*. The political and religious relevance of the site has not yet been explored in detail,[80] but the martyrological evidence suggests avenues of enquiry. Cloonburren's appearance in the Martyrology of Tallaght coincides with a period of influence through the eighth century and into the ninth, when a bridge across the Shannon was first constructed near the site.[81] Yet, it cannot be said to receive any particular attention in Tallaght, for while Caírech is referred to and distinguished through her epithet 'dergain', the site

---

77 The Annals of Ulster, a core chronicle, include the deaths of Scanlaige *s.a.* 753, Sithmaith, an abbess *s.a.* 778 and Lerben, the female superior *s.a.* 794. The burning of Cloonburren is recorded *s.a.* 780.   **78** M. Herity, D. Kelly, and U. Mattenberger, 'List of early Christian cross slabs in seven north-western counties', *JRSAI*, 127 (1997), 80–124 at 115–16; L. Doran, 'Medieval communication routes through Longford and Roscommon and their associated settlements', *PRIA* 104:3C (2004), 57–80 at 63–8; Collins, *Female monasticism*, pp 34–5. I would also like to thank Gary Dempsey who provided me with further details about the Cloonburren Cross. **79** *Mart. Tallaght*, p. 15 (Caírech); *Fél. Húi Gormáin*, pp 32–3 (Caírech, gloss 3), 120–1 (Gubsech, gloss 4), 238–9 (Mugain, gloss 1); *Fél. Óengusso*, pp 260–1 (Commentary).   **80** Discussion usually occurs within the context of other female foundations as in C. Harrington, *Women in a Celtic church: Ireland, 450–1150* (Oxford, 2002), pp 85–6.   **81** Doran, 'Medieval communication routes'.

itself is not named. Centuries later the politics had changed and previously secure frontiers were contested within a transformed ecclesiastical landscape. Cloonburren became the location of a Norman motte, possibly built around 1200, but which had returned to Irish control by 1215, arguably within the timespan covered by the glosses to the Martyrology of Gorman.[82] The extra saints and onomastic detail gives Cloonburren a far greater significance in the Martyrology of Gorman than in its predecessors. The Irishness of Cloonburren is emphasized through remembering its female saints; it may well be meaningful that one of these, Gubsech, is mentioned for the first time in the Martyrology of Gorman. Moreover, Cloonburren's location on the borderlands of Connacht and its connection with the Ua Conchobair kings gave it a geopolitical resonance during an age in which the authority of that dynasty as kings of Ireland was in steep decline. The difficulty lies in ascertaining whether this emphasis is due to Máel Muire or a continuator. Either way, it demonstrates that the site of a female foundation could carry a political weight in late twelfth- and early thirteenth-century Ireland.

The Cloonburren saints are easier to analyse in terms of intent compared to the other additional female saints commemorated by Máel Muire, particularly as the majority of them are not accompanied by toponymic detail, provided either in the main texts or the glosses. In the case of Agna of Druim Dá Dart, Máel Muire simply expands on information already provided by the Martyrology of Tallaght.[83] In most instances, however, extra onomastic clues come from the glosses. These show a distinct bias towards Leinster and Connacht. In one case, it is arguably possible to detect Máel Muire's own interest. On 27 July Máel Muire mentions Luit who is placed in Fotharta Mara (Forth, Co. Wexford) by the glosses.[84] The name, Luit, is highly unusual and is given to only a single other individual in the martyrologies. This is Luit of Druim Airbrech, mentioned on 30 April by both Tallaght and Gorman.[85] Suspiciously, both saints named Luit are located among the Fothairt, perhaps suggesting two localizations of the cult of a single individual. Several groups of Fothairt were situated within the Uí Bairrche sphere of influence and the Ua Gormáin family were a branch of the Uí Bairrche. It is plausible that the double attestation of Luit echoes Máel Muire's knowledge of the Fothairt saints providing a rare glimpse into the role of personal affiliations in the choices made by a medieval Irish writer.

CONCLUSIONS, CHANGES AND CONTINUITIES

The Irish martyrologies provide a large database of place and personal names on a scale that makes them amenable to analysis. This chapter concentrated on female saints as the language of biological identity and affiliation is inherent in any listing of saints; it

---

82 B. J. Graham, 'Medieval settlement in Co. Roscommon', *PRIA*, 88C (1988), 9–38 at 25. **83** *Mart. Tallaght*, p. 45 (May 22), has the three nuns of Druim Dá Dart, which is probably Drumdart in Co. Leitrim. *Fél. Húi Gormáin*, pp 102–3, names one as Agna while gloss 6 interprets Cassin and Luigsech as completing the trio.   **84** *Fél. Húi Gormáin*, pp 144–5 (gloss 2).   **85** *Mart. Tallaght*, p. 38; *Fél. Húi Gormáin*, pp 86–7 (gloss 3).

is also central to many early Christian ideologies. By taking the Martyrology of Tallaght as the starting point and comparing it with the Martyrology of Gorman, which used it as a source, it was possible to begin identifying areas of continuity and change. It emerged that despite the lower representation of women in the corpus they were not insignificant. Women were as likely as men to use a variety of geographical locations for ecclesiastical sites but with exceptions such as Kildare and Cloonburren, their foundations tended, on the whole, to be smaller. More intriguingly, the Tallaght community prized female asceticism and this likely inspired the commemoration of a distinctive group of female saints in the vicinity of Tallaght and Finglas. It also informed their celebration of women such as Samthann. This interest of the community is currently under-explored but it seems central to their self-identity. In contrast, Máel Muire does not appear to share these motivations. It is probable that he added saints that he knew of personally and emphasized sites that had political associations. Several of these included women but it appears that their main attraction was what they contributed to the vast number of Irish saints, repurposed for a new era. Throughout, the names of the saints remained remarkably consistent, echoing across centuries of Irish history. However, the martyrologies while conserving information were not monolithic or unchanging. The ascetic sensibilities of the Tallaght community and the political resonances of Máel Muire's text, written on the cusp of a transformational time, are witnesses to its ongoing vitality.

Soul sisters: two Irish holy women in their late antique context

CATHERINE SWIFT

INTRODUCTION

The role of women in early Irish historical and literary studies is a study often entangled with modern concepts and values.[1] A primary aim of this chapter is to examine our early Irish material for two Irish holy women, Sts Brigit and Íte, and their roles in Irish society within the conceptual frameworks available to the contemporary writers of the time. These can be inferred from the writings of the Church Fathers that circulated in Ireland, including those of the late antique Greek-speaking church, as well as from Irish legal sources from both vernacular and canon law traditions.

Unfortunately, we do not have contemporary accounts of early medieval Irish female communities as they operated on a day-to-day basis. To fill this gap, we have to draw on the incidental details in hagiographical biographies projected back into a heroic age of saints in the fifth and sixth centuries. Saint Brigit of Kildare is the best documented of the female Irish saints and the medieval accounts of her upbringing by druids and association with Ireland's conversion period have greatly enhanced both scholarly and popular interest in her life.[2] Accounts of other Irish holy women also

---

[1] S. Sheehan, 'Loving Medb' in S. Sheehan, J. Findon and W. Follett (eds), *Gablánacht in Scélaigecht: Celtic studies in honour of Ann Dooley* (Dublin 2013), pp 171–86; M. Hepplethwaite, 'Woman of fire', *The Tablet*, 19 March 2022, pp 8–10. [2] Given the prevalence of the doctrine of a fifth- and sixth-century 'Age of Saints' that marked the first centuries of Christianity in Ireland, the death dates of early Irish saints in the annals are highly unreliable but for what it is worth, Brigit is said to have died in 524/526. The high level of interest in her makes it impossible to provide a full bibliography in a paper of this length. On the topics covered in this paper, see D.A. Bray, 'Secunda Brigida: St Íta of Killeedy and Brigidine tradition' in C.J. Byrne et al. (eds), *Proceedings of the Second North American Congress of Celtic Studies* (Halifax, 1989), pp 27–38. The main primary sources for Irish female religious life have been assembled by M. Ní Dhonnchada, 'Mary, Eve and the church *c*.600–1800' in A. Bourke et al. (eds), *The Field-Day anthology of Irish writing*, volume IV: *Irish women's writing and traditions* (Cork, 2002), pp 45–165. A recent discussion of this material (somewhat influenced by modern Catholic interests) can be found in M. Callan, *Sacred sisters: gender, sanctity and power in medieval Ireland* (Amsterdam, 2019) while an earlier overview of Irish women in religion was attempted by C. Harrington, *Women in a Celtic church: Ireland, 450–1150* (Oxford, 2002). For a discussion which contextualizes Brigit within wider early Christian practice, see L. Bitel, *Landscape with two saints: how Genovfa of Paris and Brigit of Kildare built Christianity in Barbarian Europe* (Oxford, 2009). On later female communities in Ireland see D. Hall, *Women*; Collins, *Female monasticism* and the contributions to this volume by Lennon, Lyons, McShane, Ó Clabaigh, Ó Riain-Raedel and Seale.

existed, most notably that of St Íte of Killeedy,[3] Co. Limerick (Plate 3), who was specifically identified in her hagiography as another St Brigit. Using sources such as these allows us to compare the Lives of Irish female religious with those described in late antique sources. The result of such comparisons suggests that the closest parallels between Brigit and Íte's communities are not with geographically closer groups from the western Mediterranean but rather with the early Cappadocian communities of central Turkey who followed the precepts of St Basil and St Macrina.[4]

BACKGROUND: BIBLICALLY-BASED COMMENTARY ON WIVES AND HUSBANDS IN IRISH SOURCES

Let us first look briefly at the picture painted of secular women in relation to husbands in the Irish sources as a backdrop to the consideration of holy women, discussed later. 'Arisball dicrist infer et isball dindfiur inben' – for a man is a limb of Christ and a woman is a limb of man.[5]

This phrase, written by an Irish commentator writing between AD 750 and 800,[6] was interpreting the apostle Paul's Letter to the Ephesians: 'Let women be subject to their husbands, as to the Lord: Because the husband is the head of the wife, as Christ is the head of the church.'[7] It forms part of an extensive commentary in both Irish and Latin that Jean-Michel Picard has described in the following terms: 'It is not a question of formal commentary by an expert but rather notes intended to explain the biblical text from a variety of perspectives and to awaken the curiosity of the reader by providing insights into the many complexities of the sacred text.'[8]

Picard has identified the work of many early Fathers in the marginal and interlinear explanations (known as glosses) in this Würzburg manuscript including Pelagius, Cassiodorus, Origen, Augustine, Jerome and Gregory the Great. Included in his list is the Byzantine writer, John Chrysostom[9] who also wrote a homily devoted to this section of the Letter to Ephesians. The homily's opening section reads 'even from the very beginning, from man sprang woman' and goes on to say 'neither on the one hand did He form her from without, that the man might not feel towards her as towards an alien.'[10]

---

3 The Annals of Ulster provide two death dates for St Íte in 570 and 577 and name her as Íte of *Cluain Credail*, later Killeedy, Co. Limerick.   **4** D. Farmer, *The Oxford dictionary of saints* (5th ed., 2011): 'Basil the Great' (*c.*AD 330–79), bishop of Caesarea; 'Macrina the Younger' (AD 327–79).   **5** W. Stokes and J. Strachan (eds), *Thesaurus Palaeohibernicus: a collection of Old Irish glosses, scholia, prose and verse*, 2 vols (Dublin, 1903), I, p. 640 (gloss 9).   **6** P. Ó Néill, 'The Old-Irish glosses of the *prima manus* in Würzburg m.p.thf.12 – text and context reconsidered' in M. Richter and J.-M. Picard (eds), *Ogma: essays in Celtic studies in honour of Próinséas Ní Chatháin* (Dublin, 2002), pp 230–42, at pp 230–3.   **7** Ephesians 5:22–3.   **8** J.M. Picard, 'L'Exégèse irlandaise des Épîtres de Saint Paul: les gloses latines et gaéliques de Würzburg', *Recherches augustiniennes et patristiques*, 33 (2003), 155–67, p. 163. The above is my translation of the original: 'Il ne s'agit pas d'un commentaire magistral formel, mais de notes destinées à éclairer le texte biblique sous des angles divers et à éveiller la curiosité du lecteur en lui faisant entrevoir la complexité plurielle du texte sacré.'   **9** Farmer, *Oxford dictionary of saints*: 'John Chrysostom', archbishop of Constantinople (*c.*AD 347–407).   **10** St John Chrysostom, *Commentary on the Epistle to the Galatians and homilies on*

These references to the Book of Genesis serve to highlight the physical specificity of the Irish phrase and suggest the Irish commentator may have known the original Byzantine text.

In summary, Chrysostom's homily argues that successful relationships between men and women are the closest of human partnerships. When they are in harmony, the Greek bishop writes, 'the children too are well brought up, and the domestics are in good order, and neighbours, and friends, and relations partake of the fragrance. But if it be otherwise, all is turned upside down, and thrown into confusion.'[11] The homily insists that just as Christ is saviour of humankind, the husband owes care to his wife, even to the point of laying down his life. Unlike a servant whom one might control by fear, a wife was to be loved and respected 'for she is the body and if the head despise the body, it will itself also perish'.[12]

While we can only speculate whether John Chrysostom's homily was known to our Irish commentator, this understanding of a woman's inherent status was certainly closer to that of eighth-century Irish churchmen than it is to the views of many of us today.[13] In the *Collectio Canonum Hibernensis*, for example, it is stated baldly: 'Paul: Let women be subject to their husbands, as to the Lord'.[14] In the same source, female religious communities were placed under the authority of their *pastor*, whether that be a bishop or a priest.[15] Any consideration of the early Irish 'Brides of Christ' must be grounded within this wider reality: almost all women in early Ireland, including holy women, lived their lives under the authority of menfolk on whom they had to rely to safeguard themselves from their own perceived weakness. As Elva Johnston has pointed out, St Íte's Life describes that saint as saying bluntly to her female companion: 'Handmaid of God, unless the bishop comes with you, your journey will not prosper as demons greatly beguile our sex'.[16]

OVERLAPPING ROLES OF MARRIED AND PROFESSED HOLY WOMEN IN EARLY IRELAND

Another reality is that women who were not professed religious, as well as their children, would have lived on many Irish church settlements. Modern Irish understands the word *caillech* as an old woman, a hag or, in some contexts, a witch, but originally the word was an adoption of the Latin word *pallium* 'cover' and meant one who was

---

the *Epistle to the Ephesians* trans. Anon. (Oxford, 1840), Homily XX, 312–35, p. 313. See also Genesis 2:21–23. **11** Ibid., pp 313–14. **12** Ibid., pp 316–17, 321. **13** For a modern writer whose conclusions are close to those of John Chrysostom and whose arguments are based, in part, on the Letter to Ephesians, see J. Piper, 'A vision of biblical complementarity: manhood and womanhood defined according to the Bible' in J. Piper and W. Gruden (eds), *Recovering biblical manhood and womanhood* (Wheaton, 1991), pp 25–55 and for a rather different interpretation, John Paul II, *The theology of marriage and celibacy* (Boston, 1986), pp 296–9. **14** R. Flechner, *The Hibernensis* (Washington, 2019), pp 372, 752, §45.23. **15** Flechner, *Hibernensis*, pp 355, 740 §44.12. **16** F. Kelly, *A guide to early Irish law* (Dublin, 1988), pp 68–9; E. Johnston, 'The "pagan" and "Christian" identities of the Irish female saint' in M. Atherton (ed.), *Celts and Christians: new approaches to the religious traditions of Britain and Ireland* (Cardiff, 2002), pp 60–78, at p. 77.

veiled. As Máirín Ní Dhonnchadha has shown, wives, widows and women vowed to the church were all veiled leading to a degree of semantic confusion about this term. She draws attention to the citation in *Berrad Airechta* referring to a married priest, his *caillech* and 'mac berar dó iar techt graidh' – a son who is borne to him after he entered the priesthood.[17] Similarly, a verse in the notes to *Félire Oengusso* refers to a priest visiting his *caillech* and the consequences for his celebration of communion and baptism.[18] In the *Book of Armagh* account of the first Leinster bishop, Dubthach maccu Lugair, he is described not only by the Pauline rubric as a man of one wife but also as the father of one child.[19]

In the Latin penitentials, there is mention of *clientellae* or former wives who had vowed themselves to God after their husbands had risen to the rank of deacon or above. All of these references are in accordance with Pope Leo I's fifth-century regulations that allowed churchmen in sub-clerical grades to be married but expected them to give up sexual relations once they had been ordained.[20] References to *caillecha* on church settlements are thus highly ambiguous and where a *caillech* ringing a bell is identified as one of the three *airgarta* or prohibitions of a church,[21] this is not necessarily a professed religious as Kuno Meyer assumed. In fact, it seems considerably more likely that such a person was a woman whose role belonged somewhere along the spectrum ranging between spouse and housekeeper. The *senior caillech craibdech* living near Brigit's father may have been 'an old pious nun', as Donncha Ó hAodha suggested, but she may also have been a Christian married woman from the neighbourhood as in the Latin account of the same incident.[22]

The use of *caillech* as a term for professed religious women is found in *Bethu Phátraic* or the Life of St Patrick, a Middle Irish text describing a wide variety of ecclesiastical establishments throughout Ireland.[23] One describes the situation at Clonbroney, Co. Longford: 'it is the administrator (*airchindech*) of Granard who always appoints the leader of the veiled women (*cenn caillech*) in Cluain Bronaig. Now when Patrick blessed the veil on the aforesaid virgins, their four feet went into the stone, and their marks remain in it still.'[24]

Airchindech is usually used of monastic stewards but in *Bethu Phátraic*, it is used of Pope Celestine, so the assumption is that this is a reference to the bishop of Granard. There are other instances in *Bethu Phátraic* where St Patrick blesses the veil on women's

17 Ní Dhonnchadha, 'Caillech', 71–96 at 78.   18 W. Stokes (ed.), *Félire Óengusso Céli Dé: The martyrology of Oengus the Culdee* (London, 1905), pp 228–9; *An electronic dictionary of the Irish language, based on the contributions to a Dictionary of the Irish language* (Dublin, 1913–76) (www.dil.ie 2019) s.v. *comman* (accessed 29 November 2021).   19 1 Tim. 3:2; Ludwig Bieler, *The Patrician texts in the Book of Armagh*, Scriptores Latini Hiberniae 10 (Dublin, 1979), pp 176–7.   20 Ni Dhonnchadha, 'Caillech', 85–7; C. Swift, 'Early Irish priests in their own locality' in F. Edwards and P. Russell (eds), *Tome: studies in medieval Celtic history and law in honour of Thomas Charles-Edwards* (Woodbridge, 2011), pp 29–40, at pp 33–5.   21 K. Meyer, *The Triads of Ireland*, Royal Irish Academy Todd Lecture Series 13 (Dublin, 1906), p. 8 §66.   22 D. Ó hAodha, *Bethu Brigte* (Dublin, 1978), p. 3 §11; S. Connolly, 'Vita Primae Sanctae Brigitae: background and historical value', *JRSAI* 119 (1989), 5–49, p. 16 §15.   23 Patrick was a fifth-century Roman Briton remembered as apostle of Ireland whose key site is Armagh; Ó Riain, *Dictionary*, pp 526–31. 24 K. Mulchrone, *Bethu Phátraic: the Tripartite Life of Patrick* (Dublin, 1939), p. 55.

heads, consecrating them to religious lives, including two instances where the woman is identified as *mainches*, translating Latin *monacha* or nun.[25] These women are normally identified as the daughters of important families whose male progenitor was also blessed by Patrick. Young married women apparently had coloured and embroidered coverings, while the white veil of consecration could be given to young girls of marriageable age, which in early Ireland could be as young as twelve.[26] Either before or after having received the veil, a number of the consecrated girls were taught to read by either men or women.[27] An episode in *Bethu Brigte* refers to an ongoing relationship between the women being blessed and their bishop when the *cét-idbairt* or first gifts received by the female community were passed on to the bishop who had consecrated them.[28]

The lifestyles open to religious women depicted in *Bethu Phátraic* were varied. In two instances, a single woman, identified as the sister of multiple male siblings, lives with them on an ecclesiastical settlement, probably filling the housekeeping role discussed above.[29] In another type of arrangement, a woman is described as living alone as a hermit. She was dependent on food being delivered to her by Patrick's young disciple, Benén.[30] A third reference is to a bishop living with his *siur* (sister) 'in aentegdais oc ernaigthi frisin Coimdid' (in a single household, praying to the Lord).[31] Despite the fact that nothing untoward had happened, Patrick stated: 'Let men and women be apart, so that we may not be found to give opportunity to the weak, and so that the Lord's name be not blasphemed by us, a situation we avoid.'[32]

The two were sent to live apart with the hill of Brí Leith between them. This accords with the fact that Granard, Co. Longford, is some ten kilometres from Clonbroney while the female site of Cell Forgland in north Co. Mayo was also geographically separated both from the earlier episcopal site of Domnach Mór and the later episcopal centre at Killala.[33] At Clonmacnoise, Co. Offaly, the Nuns' Church (and presumably the ancillary settlement) is located roughly half a kilometre outside the main enclosure, while St Mary's Church at Glendalough, Co. Wicklow, is in a similar location.[34] Given the dispersed nature of Irish settlement in general, it seems probable that a symbolically significant distance separated most female religious establishments from those of their male counterparts.

Also found in *Bethu Phátraic* are the *caillecha* who made *anairt altora* or altar cloths. These included a woman named Lupait who was one of Patrick's *druinecha* or embroideresses but whether she was also the Lupait identified as Patrick's sister, whom

25 Mulchrone, *Bethu Phátraic*, pp 60, 65, 107, 112. **26** Ní Dhonnchadha, 'Mary, Eve', p. 114; S. Connolly and J.-M. Picard, 'Cogitosus' Life of St Brigit: content and value', *JRSAI*, 117 (1987), 5–27, pp 16 §12, 17 §14; Flechner, *Hibernensis*, p. 793 §54.8. **27** Mulchrone, *Bethu Phátraic*, pp 107, 109. **28** Ó hAodha, *Bethu Brigte*, p. 7 §22. **29** Mulchrone, *Bethu Phátraic*, pp 65, 67. **30** Ibid., p. 139. **31** eDIL s.v. *siur* (accessed 6 December 2021); R. Reynolds, 'Virgines subintroductae in Celtic Christianity', *Harvard Theological Review*, 61:4 (1968), 547–66 at 554–5. For reasons which are unclear, Reynolds has interpreted this woman as the bishop's aunt. **32** Mulchrone, *Bethu Phátraic*, 55, 82–3. **33** C. Swift, 'The social and ecclesiastical background to the treatment of the Connachta in Tírechán's seventh-century Collectanea' (D.Phil., Oxford, 1994), pp 331–3. **34** See the contribution by Collins to this volume.

Patrick condemned for becoming pregnant (and whether the latter was a professed religious), is not made clear in our sources.[35] Both professed religious and married women produced embroidered cloth for church furnishings in the Ireland of the twelfth century and later.[36] *Druinecha* worked in the household of Joseph, bishop of Armagh, who died in 936, as well as in that of Fedlimid mac Crimthaind, king of Munster but also at least a quasi-professional churchman.[37] Cogitosus tells how Brigit replaced exotic vestments of foreign manufacture, while in the *Vita Prima* Brigit was instructed to make Patrick a shroud. Sewing and embroidery were skills seen as particularly important for aristocratic females, but all women were expected to make cloth.[38] Later commentary on the legal text *Bretha Crólige* identifies the *ben lamtoruid* or 'woman of profitable handcraft' as a *druinech* and as somebody exceptional when it came to awarding maintenance to victims of violence, suggesting that embroidery could be seen as a professional craft. To what extent qualified *druinecha* may have formed an important cohort among early Irish female communities or what their status in such communities might have been is unknown, but *Vita Prima* tells how Brigit acquired a gifted weaver from a laywoman as a servant.[39]

SAINT BRIGIT

Among Irish female saints, St Brigit is not only the most famous but by far the best attested with four different medieval Lives: Cogitosus' Life, the *Vita Prima*, *Bethu Brigte* and the metrical Life (Fig. 3.1). The precise dating of these has been subject to considerable debate but commentators are agreed that all belong to the period before the mid-ninth century. In addition there are two Latin Lives of later date, the biographical accounts in the *lectiones* of various high medieval offices of St Brigit, and a Middle Irish homily.[40] There are also four early Irish poems addressed to Brigit: *Slán seiss a Brigit co mbúaid* in the Book of Leinster; *Brigit bé bithmaith* and *Ní car Brigit búadach bith* as well as the Latin hymn *Phoebi diem* in the eleventh-century *Liber Hymnorum*, a

35 Mulchrone, *Bethu Phátraic*, pp 147, 140, 155.   36 J. Ní Ghrádaigh, 'Mere embroiderers? Women and art in early medieval Ireland' in Therese Martin (ed.), *Reassessing the roles of women as 'makers' of medieval art and architecture* (Leiden/Boston, 2012), pp 93–128, p. 124.   37 A. Mac Shamhráin, 'Fedelmid', *Dictionary of Irish biography*, https://www.dib.ie/biography/fedelmid-feidlimid-a3034 (consulted 14 March 2022).   38 Connolly and Picard, 'Cogitosus's Life', p. 23 §28; Connolly, 'Vita Prima', p. 30 §58; L. Bitel, *Land of women: tales of sex and gender from early Ireland* (Ithaca and London, 1996), pp 126–31.   39 D. Binchy, 'Bretha Crólige', *Ériu*, 12 (1938), 1–77, 24–7 §31; Connolly, 'Vita Prima', p. 36 §74.   40 Some of the more recent are: K. McCone, 'Brigit in the seventh century: a saint with three lives?', *Peritia*, 1 (1982) 107–45; R. Sharpe, 'Vita S. Brigitae: the oldest texts', *Peritia*, 1 (1982), 81–106; D. Howlett, 'Vita I Sanctae Brigitae', *Peritia*, 12 (1998), 1–23; D. McCarthy, 'The chronology of St Brigit of Kildare,' *Peritia*, 14 (2000), 255–81; L. Maney, 'The date and provenance of Vita Prima Sanctae Brigitae', *Proceedings of the Harvard Celtic Colloquium*, 23 (2003), 200–18; R. Sharpe, *Medieval Irish saints' Lives* (Oxford, 1991), pp 139–208; A. Buckley, 'Music and musicians in medieval Irish society', *Early Music*, 28:2 (2000), 165–90, p. 187; W. Stokes, *Three Middle Irish homilies on the Lives of St Patrick, St Brigit and St Columba* (Calcutta, 1877), pp 51–87.

3.1 An image of St Brigit in stained glass in the Church of St Michael and St John, Cloughjordan, Co. Tipperary. Image © Catherine Swift.

praise poem, *Brigit búadach* and a Middle Irish prayer attributed to Brigit herself, *Ropadh maith lem*.[41]

Clare Stancliffe has drawn attention to the extent to which the miracles in the hagiography of Brigit differ from those of both continental and Irish male saints in their large number of 'folk-lore miracles' and the relative scarcity of 'vertical miracles' when the saint calls directly on the help of God. Stancliffe suggests that one reason for the extraordinary number of Brigit's 'miracles of plenty' is because the attributes of a pagan goddess Brigit were transferred to her Christian namesake. She also toys, briefly but intriguingly, with the idea that Patrick and Brigit were complementary saints 'with the male Patrick standing for the forceful vindication of Christianity and its rights, whereas the female Brigit represents its caring aspect'.[42]

Common themes in the early hagiography of Brigit include an emphasis on her Christian faith (which is what enabled her to perform miracles) as well as a pronounced

41 Ní Dhonnchadha, 'Mary, Eve', pp 62–3; 71–5; J.H. Bernard and R. Atkinson, *The Irish Liber Hymnorum*, HBS 13, 2 vols (London, 1898), I, pp 107–28, p. 161. 42 Clare Stancliffe, 'The miracle stories in seventh-century Irish saints' Lives' in J. Fontaine and J.N. Hillgarth (eds), *The seventh century: change and continuity* (London, 1992), pp 87–115 at pp 89–94.

interest in charity and hospitality, including miracles of fecundity in relation to the multiplication and preservation of food.[43] There is a concern with chastity, but one which is marked by forgiveness for those who might have failed to adhere to it, and there is a relatively strong theme of obedience of women religious to their bishop, including the offering of hospitality and other resources to the clergy in exchange for Masses and access to the sacraments.[44] There are also episodes showing reciprocal episcopal care of female religious: for example, Bishop Mel provides support for Brigit when she is physically suffering; Bishop Ibar provides her with grain; and Bishop Brón came to visit her with gifts.[45] (Such stories provide part of the context for the famous story in *Bethu Brigte* that St Brigit was accidentally ordained bishop,[46] the 'accident' having come about because of the holy woman's close involvement with bishops and episcopal activities.) All the early *vitae* also lay considerable emphasis on Brigit's travels across large parts of Ireland and her generous involvement in wider lay society.

The early Irish poetry dedicated to St Brigit have not been subjected to the same degree of scrutiny as the Latin Lives. *Slan seiss a Brigit co mbúaid*, thought to be by the Kildare bishop Orthanach who died in AD 840, deals primarily with the glories of the secular fort at *Ailenn* or Knockaulin, a hill neighbouring Kildare.[47] *Brigit bé bithmaith* is credited in *Liber Hymnorum* to the seventh-century Bishop Ultán of Ardbraccan, but has been dated to the ninth century. Brigit is addressed as a *caillech* in the prose introduction, while the poem itself is essentially a *lorica* or breastplate prayer, seeking the saint's protection.[48] *Ní car Brigit*, or Broccán's hymn, is a much longer work summarizing some key miracles in the saint's life.[49] *Brigit búadach* is an early praise poem while *Ropadh maith lem* is an intriguing depiction of an ale-feast for the people of heaven with guests being served mercy and charity from great vats or *dabaig*. Such vats, usually containing ale, were prominently placed in the centre of banqueting halls according to the *Tech Midchúarta* seating plan in the Book of Leinster (folio 29a).[50]

A MODEL OF FEMALE CHARISM: SAINTS ÍTE AND BRIGIT COMPARED

The surviving Lives of St Íte are rather later than the early Brigit material (Fig. 3.2). The *Magnum Legendarium Austriacum*, dated by Diarmuid Ó Riain to 1170 x 1185, contains a Life of Íte recently edited by Claudia Gundacker.[51] Another occurs in the Dublin collection dated to between 1185 and 1226 and edited by Plummer.[52] The two Lives are sufficiently close that most commentators have suggested that they both derive

43 K. Ritari, 'The image of Brigit as a saint: reading the Latin Lives', *Peritia*, 21 (2010), 191–207. 44 Ó hAodha, *Bethu Brigte*, pp 9 §28, 13 §38, 14 §40; Connolly, 'Vita Prima', pp 22 §38, 23 §39, 24 §40, 26 §49, 29 §55, 31 §61, 42 §92.   45 Connolly, 'Vita Prima', pp 20, §29, 27 §52, 39 §85. 46 Ó hAodha, *Bethu Brigte*, p. 24 §19.   47 K. Meyer, *Hail Brigit: an Old-Irish poem on the Hill of Allen* (Dublin, 1912).   48 Stokes and Strachan, *Thesaurus*, II, pp 323–6.   49 Ibid., pp 327–49. 50 Ní Dhonnchadha, 'Mary, Eve', pp 72–4.   51 C. Gundacker, 'Die Viten Irischen Heiliger im *Magnum Legendarium Austriacum*' (M.Phil., Vienna, 2008), pp 119–174; D. Ó Riain, 'The *Magnum Legendarium Austriacum*: a new investigation of one of medieval Europe's richest hagiographic collections', *Analecta Bollandiana*, 133 (2015), pp 87–165.   52 C. Plummer, *Vitae Sanctorum*

3.2 An image of St Íte in stained glass in the Church of St Michael and St John, Cloughjordan, Co. Tipperary. Image © Catherine Swift.

from a twelfth-century original, although Dorothy Africa has recently suggested that there may be an earlier Life of late eighth- or early ninth-century date lying behind these.[53] References to Íte in the hagiography of Brendan, Mochutu and Mochoemóg have been dated by Richard Sharpe to the thirteenth century.[54]

Hiberniae, 2 vols (Oxford, 1910), II, pp 116–30; Sharpe, *Saints Lives*, p. 394.   **53** Ó Riain, *Dictionary*, p. 376; D. Africa, 'The chronology of the Life of St Íte and the architecture of theft', *Eolas: The Journal of the American Society for Irish Medieval Studies*, 12 (2019), 2–25, at 8–12; see also Bray, 'Secunda Brigida', pp 27–8.   **54** Sharpe, *Saints Lives*, pp 394–6.

Íte was identified by her hagiographers as 'sancta Yta secunda Brigida meritis et moribus' – a second Brigit through merits and customs – and the two saints are described as discussing Christ together in Brigit's *Vita Prima*.[55] Given the chronological differences in our sources, it is perfectly plausible that specific rules governing Íte's community may well have evolved from those evidenced in the earlier documentation for Brigit, but the phrase suggests they were both seen as sharing a common sense of charism. In her study, Johnston highlighted the description of Íte as *matrona ipsius gentis* and the proposition that a leader of a female religious community wielded authority in the wider community.[56] In Hiberno-Latin texts, Latin *patronus* is, however, glossed by the Irish term *sruith-athair* or ancestral father together with a female equivalent, *sruith-máthair*, where *sruith*, means aged and venerable but also revered mother. The description as *matrona* may, therefore, be a way of stressing Íte's status and authority as ancestral, rather than as one representing the normal social status attached to heads of female communities.[57]

Johnston further suggested that the use of the word *matrona* represented an Irish knowledge of late antique Christianity when religious women were seen as absorbing the status accorded to the secular Roman *matrona* because of their role in household management. In this regard, it is worth stressing that Íte was not described as *matrona* in isolation, but rather in partnership with Senan of Scattery Island, Co. Clare, who was both bishop and abbot (Fig. 1.1).[58] A tenth-century bishopric centred on Scattery extended to both sides of the Shannon estuary and was included in the arrangements for the synod of Kells in 1151, with its last known bishop, Aodh Ó Beacháin, dying in 1188.[59] The description of Íte and Senan is thus very similar to that of the seventh-century description of Brigit and Conlaed in Cogitosus' Latin Life: 'primate of all the bishops and the most blessed chief abbess … [who] … governed their primatial church by means of a mutually happy alliance,' at Kildare.[60] In the case of Íte, the description is explicitly extended beyond her church to include lordship over a local population but given the increased use of territorial descriptions for Irish bishoprics in the eleventh and twelfth centuries,[61] this change is not surprising.

Íte's Lives explicitly state that as *matrona* of the Uí Chonaill, she was in a position to ensure military victory for them through her prayers. In exactly the same way, the *Vita Prima* and the Fragmentary Annals identify Brigit as ensuring the success of her Leinster troops.[62] This notion of females having military oversight is very much to the

55 Bray, 'Secunda Brigida', p. 27; Connolly, 'Vita Prima', p. 47 §121.   56 E. Johnston, 'Íte: patron of her people?', *Peritia*, 14 (2000), 421–8, at 425–7.   57 eDIL s.v. *sruith*; *Annals of Ulster* s.a. 570, 577.   58 Plummer, *Vitae* (1910), p. 118 §8; Gundacker, *Irisher Heiliger* (2008), p. 121 §5 where Íte is simply told 'civitatem habebis et genti Hu Conil una cum sancto Senano donante Deo dominaberis' – see however, pp 135 §28, 136 §29, 137§31 where she is explicitly called *matrona*. Senan is normally identified as a sixth-century figure though no dates for him survive: Ó Riain, *Dictionary*, pp 557–60.   59 L. Breatnach, 'An edition of *Amra Senáin*' in D. Ó Corráin, L. Breatnach and K. McCone (eds), *Sages, saints and storytellers: Celtic studies in honour of Professor James Carney* (Maynooth, 1989), pp 7–31; *Annals of Inisfallen*, s.a. 958, 974 *Annals of Ulster* s.a. 995; H.J. Lawlor, 'A fresh authority for the synod of Kells', *PRIA*, 36C (1921–4), 16–22, at 18.   60 Connolly and Picard, 'Cogitosus' Life', p. 12, §4.   61 C. Etchingham, *Church organization in Ireland, AD 650 to 1000* (Maynooth, 1999), pp 177–93.   62 Plummer, *Vitae* (1910), p. 128 §33;

fore in *Slán seiss a Brigit* with its opening description of Brigit as 'banflaith buidnib slúaig fil for clannaib Cathair Máir' – a female lord with army troops over the families of Cathair Mór.[63] The poem's author further identified her as overlord of the *tír* (land) with a reputation surpassing a king, and the poem finishes with a reference to her *bithflaith lasin ríg* – her eternal lordship with the king. Similar royal and lordly imagery is found in *Ní car Brigit buadach* where Brigit is called *máthair mo ruirech* 'mother of my over-king' as well as best-born of the *nime flatha* or lords of heaven. In the final stanza, she is described as having *fóesam*: the ability to offer the lordly protection that could offer commoners legal redress from attack.[64] In *Brigit bé bithmaith*, there is reference to her ability to remove *cís*, the word used for taxes levied by kings, although in Brigit's case it is *císu col* or taxes of sin.

This royal imagery is in stark contrast to the hagiographical depiction of Brigit where her mother's status as a slave and Brigit's involvement in domestic and even servile tasks is stressed. Because Brigit is often called 'another Mary', even in the potentially sixth-century origin-legend of the Fotharta,[65] the assumption has often been made that such descriptions reflect Mary's status as Queen of Heaven. Such a characterization is rather later than our texts, however, and the Virgin Mother does not normally command military forces. Another, perhaps more plausible, biblical analogy might be Deborah, prophetess, judge, *mater in Israhel* and leader of the Israelite army along with Barak son of Abinoam.[66] Both Brigit and Íte are thus depicted as saintly overseers of their peoples with similar gifts of prophecy, lordship and military power. It remains an open question whether such authority and respect in secular society was enjoyed by contemporary female religious leaders but a vernacular legal phrase 'ben sues sruta cocta for cula' – a woman who turns back the streams of war – is identified in later commentary with the abbess of Kildare.[67]

MOTHERING, FOSTERING AND CARING

This emphasis on female military protection also stands in stark contrast to the famous poem associated with Íte known as *Ísucán* or 'Baba Jesus'[68] in which Íte is depicted crooning to the Christ-child at her breast.[69] While Ernest Gordon Quin's edition concentrates on the legal and contractual vocabulary in this poem, the humming onomatopoeia, and the frequent use of the diminutive *-án*, gives it what David Greene termed its 'ingenuousness'. It has been suggested by Thomas Owen Clancy that it was

Gundacker, *Irisher Heiliger* (2008), pp 135–6, §28; Connolly, 'Vita Prima', p. 41 §88, §89; J. Newlon Radner, *Fragmentary annals of Ireland* (Dublin, 1978), pp 70–1. **63** Plummer, *Vitae* (1910), p. 128 §33; Gundacker, *Irisher Heiliger* (2008), pp 135–6, §28 (1978), pp 70–1. **64** Stokes and Strachan, *Thesaurus*, II, p. 349; C. Swift, 'Tírechán's motives in compiling the *Collectanea*: an alternative interpretation', *Ériu*, 45 (1994), 53–84, at 75–6. **65** Ó hAodha, *Bethu Brigte*, p. 42. **66** Vulgate, Judges 4 & 5, especially verse 7. **67** Binchy, *Bretha Crólige*, pp 26–7, §32. **68** Baba is my colloquial translation of the dimunitive '-án' which Gerald Murphy translated as 'little Jesus', Whitley Stokes as 'Jesukin' and David Greene as 'Jesuseen'. **69** G. Murphy, *Early Irish lyrics: eighth to twelfth centuries* (rept. Dublin, 1998), pp 26–7; Stokes, *Félire*, p. 103; D. Greene and F. O'Connor (eds), *A golden treasury of Irish poetry, AD 600–1200* (2nd ed., Dingle, 1990), pp 102–3.

'designed for the consumption and performance by monastic women'.[70] Brigit, too, is called the mother of Christ in *Brigit bé bithmaith* while in *Ní car Brigit buadach bith*, the saint is said to sleep fitfully for the sake of her son, and she is termed *oenmáthair Maicc Ríg Máir* 'the unique mother of the son of the Great King'.[71]

This shared emphasis on the Christchild, on motherhood and on rearing can also be linked to the statement in Paul's First Letter to the Thessalonians where he describes the Christian mission in terms of a nurse cherishing her children.[72] The Irish glossator adds two comments to this: first, an interlinear statement to the effect that the apostles were instructed as a nurse might sing of great deeds to young children, and second, a rather longer quotation in the margin: 'Ceist in innonn less *parbulus* et *nutrix* náde æm isinnon arisbésadb nammuimme dogníc deidbléan di ocmunud ádalti horbi accobur lænebud dó innoidenacht nachgeín síc fuimus uobis ol pol.' (Question, does he deem *paruulus* and *nutrix* the same? Verily it is the same: for it is the custom of the foster-mother [*muimme*] to make a weakling [*deidblén*] of herself instructing her fosterling [*dalta*], since she hath a desire that he should not be in infancy for any long time: *sic fuimus uobis* [so we were to you] saith Paul.)

The relationship between a *dalta* and his *muime* or between fosterling and foster-mother was one of the eight personal attachments recognized in vernacular Irish law.[73] The emphasis on loving support here reminds one of Stancliffe's emphasis on Brigit's caring aspect, while the reference to the frailty or poverty (for *deidblén* covers both) of a foster-mother is illustrated perfectly by the late anecdote of Íte being gnawed by a giant beetle whom she was fostering in the *Liber Hymnorum*'s prose preface to *Ísucán*.[74] Jenny Bledsoe has used the story of Íte's beetle to argue that 'the female monastic community [operated] as a safe haven for socially outcast women and children, a site for earthly – and spiritual – nurturing.'[75] This is a development of Lisa Bitel's position that merely refers to the fosterage of children by female religious.[76] In her article, Bledsoe discusses the wider fosterage context indicated by the story of the stag beetle, the poem *Ísucán* and Íte's fostering of saints, such as St Brendán and St Mochaemóg.[77] Her argument that female communities sheltered outcasts in particular – rather than women and children in general – is dependent on a story of St Íte's rescue of a fallen

70 E.G. Quin, 'The Early Irish poem Ísucán', *Cambridge Medieval Celtic Studies*, 1 (1981), 39–52; T.O. Clancy, 'Women poets in early medieval Ireland: stating the case' in C. Meek and K. Simms (eds), *The fragility of her sex: medieval Irish women in their European context* (Dublin, 1996), pp 43–72 at p. 62; M. Callan, 'Líadáin's lament, Darerca's Life and Íte's *Ísucán*: evidence for nuns' literacies in early medieval Ireland' in V. Blanton, V. O'Mara and P. Stoop (eds), *Nuns' literacies in Europe: the Kansas City dialogue* (Turnhout, 2015), pp 209–27, at p. 219.   71 Stokes and Strachan, *Thesaurus*, II, p. 342; D. Peters Auslander, 'Gendering the *Vita Prima*: an examination of Brigit's role as "Mary of the Gael"', *Proceedings of the Harvard Celtic Colloquium*, 20–1 (2000/1), pp 187–202.   72 1 Thessalonians 2:7.   73 C.M. Eska (ed.), *Cáin Lánamna: an Old Irish tract on marriage and divorce law* (Leiden, 2010), pp 84–5, §2.   74 Stokes, *Félire*, pp 42–5.   75 J.C. Bledsoe, 'St Íte of Killeedy and spiritual motherhood in the Irish hagiographical tradition', *Proceedings of the Harvard Celtic Colloquium*, 32 (2012), 1–29, at p. 2.   76 Bitel, *Land of women*, p. 185.   77 St Brendan is linked to dioceses of Ardfert (Co. Kerry) and Clonfert (Co. Galway) and his death dates are listed as 576 and 583 while St Mochaemóg is attached to the church of Leigh, Twomileborris, Co. Tipperary, with a death date of AD 656; Ó Riain, *Dictionary*, pp 115–17, 459–61.

woman. There are similar stories in the Lives of other female saints including St Brigit, but also St Samthann and St Monenna, and most specifically in the birth tale of St Cumaine Fota.[78] The earliest version of this was published by Gearóid Mac Eoin:

> Cumaine Fota, son of Fiachna of the Eoganacht of Caisel, Fiachna begot him on his own daughter in drunkenness, for the girl used to sleep with her mother. And her father put her on her word as to who the boy's father was, and the woman confessed that he was his. He ordered the boy to be cast to the beasts and said that he and his daughter would never look on each other. The child was taken from her in a little vessel in which there used to be milk and was left on the arm of a cross at the door of a church, with purple cloth about him and sixty ounces of silver under his side. The prior found him on the following day and said that he was his own son. The monastery to which he was brought, it is thither she [his mother] went to take the veil, and she remained there in religion in the company of the abbesses.[79]

Brigit was reared by a Christian *muime* when she returned home to her father as a young girl and is herself referred to as *mumme Goidel* 'foster-mother of the Irish'.[80] Bledsoe's more concrete suggestion about children in need can be supported by some legal sources although, as Bronagh Ní Chonaill has pointed out, *altram seirce* or fosterage undertaken through love was of minimal interest to vernacular lawyers as it did not involve fees or liability for crimes.[81] Legal commentary indicates that the foster-mother was particularly engaged in the feeding and clothing for the fosterling whereas the foster-father, in contrast, was the *fethathair* 'knowledge-father' who was given responsibility for teaching (*forcetal*).[82] The same commentary makes it clear that, on occasion, the foster-mother could be solely responsible for the rearing of a child. This situation is replicated in the collection of maxims known as the *Sechtae*: seven occasions when rearing by women alone could occur. Examples include cases when the father was a slave, a stranger, or an otherwise prohibited person, including penitent men in holy orders. Similarly, if the child was born to a *báitsech*, 'a woman who slept with multiple men', the woman was also given sole responsibility for rearing.[83]

Commentary on *Córus Bésgnai* reinforces this by implication in that it forbids lawfully married parents to provide the offspring of a *ben taide* (a synonym for *báitsech*)

---

78 St Samthann of Clonbroney, Co.Longford, with an obit AD 739; St Monenna of Killevy, Co. Armagh, obit AD 517; St Cumaine Fota of Clonfert, Co. Galway and south Munster, obit 662; Ó Riain, *Dictionary*, pp 545–6, 495–7, 243–5. **79** G. Mac Eoin, 'The Life of Cumaine Fota' *Béaloideas*, 39/41 (1971–3), 192–205, at 201. The last sentence in the original is more specific that the mother joined a community of veiled women: 'An ceall dia rucad-sum is ed do-cuaidh-side do gabail chaille cu mbai a caillecht innti hi cumbaid na mbanoircindeach.' As noted by Mac Eoin, the identification of the site in question as *Cell Íte* or Íte's church comes from a variant reading in the *Liber Hymnorum*. **80** Ó hAodha, *Bethu Brigte*, p. 2 §8; Connolly, 'Vita Prima', p. 16 §12; Ní Dhonnchadha, 'Mary, Eve', p. 72. **81** B. Ní Chonaill, 'Child-centred law in medieval Ireland' in R. Davis and T. Dunne (eds), *The empty throne: childhood and the crisis of modernity* (Cambridge, 2008), pp 1–31, at p. 11; D.A. Binchy, *Corpus Iuris Hiberniae*, 5 vols (Dublin, 1979), I, 83:23–5; V 1764:29–34. **82** Eska, *Cáin Lánamna*, pp 94–97. **83** Binchy, *Corpus*, I

as their own first-fruit child to the church.[84] The laws recognized a *mac builg* – son of a satchel – whose mother had no other resources and who might be abandoned 'at the arm of the cross'. In exchange, the mother would become the church's possession with one commentary stating 'gním doire ar Dia geibes a tigh espoic conid cumal air' – it was a deed of servitude to God, her removal into the bishop's house so that she becomes his servant.[85] What the word *tech* or house means in this context is not clear – it may have meant the episcopal residence, but it may also denote the wider group of settlements, including female religious establishments, over which the bishop had direct authority. Yet another vernacular legal commentary refers to the church feeding orphan children who are without kin, without land and without wealth, but without specifying the nature of the churches providing such support.[86]

In the Latin canons, identification of churches with abandoned children is made more explicit:

> A Hibernian synod: Let those who abandon young children in a church of God without the abbot's knowledge do penance for three and a half years if there are bishops buried or present in it … If, however, it has no bishop but instead is a small church, let them do penance for a year and a half … Concerning those to whom belong children that have been abandoned in a church. A child who has been brought to a church is its slave unless he is redeemed through payment … If the church received money from his parents in whatever amount, after the fashion of fosterers, it shall take the place of the parents.[87]

Foundling children could thus be brought to both the higher status settlements in which bishops resided but also, on occasion, to lesser churches. It seems reasonable to infer that these last included female religious establishments, especially given that these were often described in terms that stressed their small size and relative poverty. In Íte's case, for example, her *vitae* state that the original foundation controlled only four ploughlands though this was later expanded.[88] Brigit's Kildare seems exceptional in this regard although it is worth noting that despite the prestige of her abbess, we have no evidence for the actual size or landed endowment of the early female community there. There is, however, reference to Brigit's cook, to a guest-house, and to a *proindtech* or a dining hut, though this last was located at Cell Lasre.[89]

Brigit's *vitae* do not show the same concern for children visible in St Íte's hagiography although they do include similar tales of empathetic support and forgiveness of women struggling with celibacy.[90] If, however, we view her depiction

21:27–22:22; V 1894:27–32; II 547: 21–3.   **84** L. Breatnach (ed.), *Córus Bésgnai: an old Irish law tract on the church and society*, Early Irish Law Series 7 (Dublin, 2017), p. 163 §43.   **85** R. Thurneysen, *Irisches Recht: Díre. Ein altirischer Rechtstext* (Berlin, 1931), p. 7.   **86** Eska, *Cáin Lánamna*, pp 102–3.   **87** Flechner, *Hibernensis*, p. 794.   **88** Plummer, *Vitae*, p. 119, §9; Gundacker, *Irischer Heiliger*, p. 122 §6.   **89** Ó hAodha, *Bethu Brigte*, pp 16 §44, 18 §7; Connolly, 'Vita Prima', pp 38 §82, 45–6 §109. The location of Cell Lasre is unfortunately now unknown. **90** Plummer, *Vitae*, p. 121 §16–17; Gundacker, *Irischer Heiliger*, pp 124–5 §11§12, 136, §29; Connolly and Picard, 'Cogitosus' Life', p. 16 §9; Connolly, 'Vita Prima', pp 44 §97, 45 §103.

through the wider prism of concern and care for the vulnerable, Brigit clearly shares a similar vocation to that of Íte – what Dorothy Bray has characterized as 'her compassion for the poor, oppressed and imprisoned'.[91] Famously, this extended to hungry dogs and pet foxes, as well as to slaves and lepers. One of the most evocative descriptions is the story in the *Vita Prima*, which tells of Brigit's concern that an elderly woman should be kept warm and dry indoors while she lay dying, while at the same time, the laundresses of Kildare were miraculously saved from having to wash the clothes of the deceased outdoors in winter weather.[92] As with many stories of female religious, the focus is on material assistance and the provision of physical comforts to those lacking them.

FEMALE FREEDOM TO TRAVEL

For the most part, as Stancliffe and others have noted, Íte and Brigit also shared a common ability to travel freely and to cross the boundaries of secular kingdoms. Whether Íte travelled originally from the Waterford lands south of the Suir as most have assumed, or from the rather nearer group of Déis Bec (the barony of Smallcounty, Co. Limerick), the fact remains that as a young girl she is described as having moved outside her Déis kin-group to set up her foundation in west Limerick.[93] Nor is this ability to move freely limited to Íte and Brigit; in *Bethu Phátraic*, for example, reference is made to a group of ten daughters of the kings of Lombardy and Britain who travelled to visit Patrick at Armagh.[94] Saint Monnena, accompanied by a group of young women, together with a widow and her child, is said to have travelled across Ireland from Faughart, Co. Louth, on the east coast to the Aran Islands in the west.[95]

Even a female hermit living alone might move across country to seek fire and provisions at the local episcopal settlement of Mo-chulla of Tulla, Co. Clare, although she did require a miracle to rescue her from brigands.[96] Christina Harrington has suggested that this freedom of movement by religious women came under increasing scrutiny in the eleventh and twelfth centuries. Certainly it is easy to interpret the mysterious trip taken by St Íte to receive the Eucharist at Clonmacnoise, Co. Offaly, when her absence went entirely unnoticed by her fellows, as an oblique reference to a growing belief that Irish religious females should, in fact, live enclosed.[97]

91 D.A. Bray, 'The *Vita Prima* of St Brigit: a preliminary analysis of its composition' in Joseph Eska (ed.), *Narrative in Celtic tradition: essays in honor of Edgar M. Slotkin, Celtic Studies Association of North America Yearbook 8–9* (New York, 2011), pp 1–15, p. 3.   **92** Connolly, 'Vita Prima', p. 42 §93.   **93** Plummer, *Vitae*, p. 118 §8; Gundacker, *Irischer Heiliger*, p. 121 §5.   **94** Mulchrone, *Bethu Phátraic*, p. 139.   **95** 'The Life of St Monenna by Conchubranus Part I', ed. Ulster Society for Medieval Latin Studies, *Seanchas Ard Mhacha*, 9:2 (1979), 250–73, pp 258–9.   **96** 'Vita S. Mochullei episcopi', *Analecta Bollandiana*, 17 (1898), 135–54, pp 145–8 §11–12.   **97** Harrington, *Celtic church*, pp 226–46; Plummer, *Vitae*, pp 122–3 §20; Gundacker, *Irischer Heiliger*, p. 127 §15.

MODELS OF FEMALE CHARISM IN LATE ANTIQUE EUROPE

In contrast to Ireland, Mediterranean cultures strongly encouraged early female religious to observe enclosure. The most famous early rule is that by Bishop Caesarius of Arles (in the south of modern France) called *Regula ad virgines*. It was compiled by 534 for his sister, Abbess Caesaria, who lived in a walled establishment beside the church, close to where her brother resided. Caesarius had been a monk at Lérins (472–501) before becoming bishop of Arles where he founded a monastery dedicated to St John. In his testament, Caesarius makes the bishop's jurisdiction over his sister's community explicit:

> And I entreat you my noble daughters by the holy and inseparable Trinity and by the Second Coming of our Lord Jesus Christ to direct your requests respectfully, as if through the Lord, to the bishop who by the will of God worthily succeeds my unworthy self. Esteem him with a pure heart and do not sadden him by your disobedience … I ask you again and again, holy bishop, through divine grace that above all you treat the monastery of holy virgins as having been entrusted to your very great care and that you very kindly allow the community of these women to be provided for. And if anyone wishes to give you bad advice, dutifully answer that arrangements that were made or granted with the advice of a bishop … cannot be in any way reversed. And especially because the holy Popes of Rome have also confirmed this by their authority.[98]

As against this, however, Pope Hormisdas wrote Caesarius a letter confirming that the bishop's authority over the women's monastery was to be limited 'so that the virgins consecrated to God might be free of all disturbance and annoyance' and that none of their endowment was to be alienated by episcopal decree. According to Caesarius' *Regula*, sisters who had made their vows should not leave the women's monastery till death. No man was allowed within their enclosure save for the bishop, priests and lectors or the steward who looked after the monastery's assets. No secular woman was allowed visit and no meals should be prepared for outsiders.[99] The account of Caesarius' Life describes the lifestyle of the enclosed women: 'in the midst of psalms and fasts, vigils and readings, the virgins of Christ beautifully copy out the holy books'.[100]

In a variant approach, in fourth-century Milan, St Ambrose wrote *De Virginibus* for his sister Marcellina, after she had been consecrated with a veil by Pope Liberius in a public ceremony. Ambrose was writing for women who were resident in their parental homes. Although he commends Marcellina for her particular devotion to long-term fasting and exhorts her and others to be chaste, to avoid visits, to remain quiet during celebration of the mysteries, to avoid dancing and to read certain prayers in their rooms at night,[101] he does not provide a rule for female religious as such.

---

98 W.E. Klingshirn, *Caesarius of Arles: Life, testament, letters* (Liverpool, 1994), pp 73–4 §7–§8.   **99** A. de Vogüé and J. Courreau, *Césaire d'Arles: Oeuvres Monastiques Tome I: Oeuvres pour les moniales*, Sources Chrétiennes 345 (Paris, 1988), pp 170–273.   **100** Ibid., pp 27–8, 39, 120–2.   **101** *Ambrose:*

These are very different models of female religious life from the arrangements described in texts on Brigit and Íte although, as noted above in relation to the situation in Granard, there was at least memories of Irish siblings who acted as bishop and female head of community. An earlier example than Granard occurs with reference to a shared establishment of Aghagower, Co. Mayo, in a seventh-century description.[102] It must be remembered, of course, that there could well have been other types of female religious community in Ireland apart from those represented in the Lives of Brigit and Íte. It is not clear either whether Ambrose's advice about virgin lifestyles was known in early Ireland. We do know that Íte fasted as a form of devotion and Brigit is described as praying in cross-vigil at night. Ambrose also provides an anecdote about a woman opposing her parents in her choice of religious life, reminding one of Brigit and Íte's similar determination.[103] We also know that Ambrose's companion piece, *De Viduis* 'On Widows' inspired certain canons in the Irish *Collectio* making it seem more probable that his *De Virginibus* may have been known in Irish circles.[104]

Another continental example of a fourth-century model of siblings sharing church leadership comes from Cappadocia (central Anatolia, modern Turkey) in the monastic household of Macrina and Peter, siblings of Bishop Basil of Caesarea and Gregory, bishop of Nyssa.

Gregory wrote an account of Macrina's death which took place in AD 379. In this he states that Macrina supervised the women's house, which was inhabited by virgins and widows, while her younger brother Peter, who had been ordained a priest, was in charge of the men. After her fiancé died, Macrina had refused to get married and instead acted as Peter's nurse: 'she became everything for the little boy: father, teacher, tutor, mother, counsellor in all that was good.' At the same time, she also prepared food for her mother and helped her run her estates, advised her brother Basil and studied Christian writings. When the women's house was founded, all differences of rank were removed with slave-girls, servants and family members becoming sisters and they all shared the same food and the same type of bed. In times of famine, beggars were never turned away, and one story noted that when the corn supply was distributed according to people's necessities, it never grew less (a particular characteristic of Brigit's charity also). Another miracle attributed to Macrina was the curing of a child's eye, and in more general terms she was also credited with the casting out of devils, prophecies of the future and rescuing children orphaned through famine.[105]

Bishop Basil's own sense of monasticism shows the clear imprints of his older sister's regime. The most recent editor of the *Regula Basilii*, the translation of his thinking into Latin by Rufinus of Aquileia (*c*.354–411), has written:

Select works and letters, trans H. de Romestin and H.T.F. Duckworth, Nicene and Post-Nicene Fathers, Series II volume x (2nd printing, Massachusetts, 1995), pp 361–87, pp 382–4. **102** Bieler, *Patrician texts*, pp 150–3 §37. **103** Ibid., pp 372–3; Plummer, *Vitae*, pp 116 §1, 117 §5, 118 §6, 119 §10, 117 §4; Gundacker, *Irischer Heiliger*, pp 120 §4; 122 §7; Ó hAodha, *Bethu Brigte*, pp 1 §4, 4–5 §14–15. **104** Flechner *Hibernensis* pp 352–3 §44:6, §44:7. **105** J.M. Petersen (trans.), *Handmaids of the Lord* (Kalamazoo, MI, 1996), 51–86, esp. pp 53–5, 57, 59, 61, 68, 74, 80–2.

Macrina and her direction of the community at Annisa in the late 350s and early 360s was a determinative influence in the early maturing of Basil's conception of the Christian ascetic community. Basil was never Macrina's spiritual father. Rather, in more than one sense, she was his spiritual mother … the family household reached its final transformation into a dedicated ascetic community, comprising a house of virgins, a house for dedicated men or monks, a house for children and a house for guests, with a common 'house of prayer'.[106]

The principles under which this mixed community lived are clearly articulated in the opening sections of the *Regula*:

Question 1: … is there any order and sequence in the commandments of God? The Lord himself imposed an order among the commandments, saying the first and the great commandment is to love God with the whole heart and the whole mind, the second however … is to love your neighbour as your very self. … For behold, the Lord too did not deem the mere teaching of the word sufficient but wished to deliver to us an example of humility in very deed when he, having girded himself with a linen cloth, washed the feet of his disciples [John 13:5]. Whose feet then will you wash? For whom will you perform the duties of care?[107]

Washing feet, in fact, is a particular feature of Brigit's *Vita Prima* but is also attested in Íte's Lives.[108] The *Collectio* cites Basil's teaching in the *Regula Basilii* on a number of occasions and it is clear that the Cappadocian Fathers were known to Irish canonists even if, as Roy Flechner has suggested, some of the quotations ascribed to them were actually by Irish writers.[109] Perhaps more surprisingly, because rather less well disseminated in the West than the *Regula*, there are also extensive quotations in Irish canon law from the fourth-century Council of Gangra in Cappadocia: these covered their prescriptions with regard to fasting on Sundays, donations (including feasts) to the poor, the abandonment of children, ceasing to support parents, relationship with slaves, tonsuring of women and the lawful forms of meat.[110]

CONCLUSION

Any analysis of female religious organization should consider both those who found such a life inspiring, and also, the manner in which such communities may have impacted on wider society. It is clear that the early Irish church drew widely from an eclectic range of Christian writings and it seems almost certain that there must have

---

106 A.M. Silvas, *The Rule of St Basil in Latin and English* (Collegeville, MN, 2013), 6–7. **107** Ibid., p. 54 §4, 81 §34 §35.   **108** Connolly, 'Vita Prima', pp 17 §17, 20 §31, 22 §36, 23 §38, 39 §85; Plummer, *Vitae*, p. 123 §20; Gundacker, *Irischer Heiliger*, p. 128 §15.   **109** Flechner, *Hibernensis*, pp 851, fn.171, 983.   **110** Ibid., pp 986–7, 526, 781, 787, 825.

been considerable variety in the regimes adopted by individual religious communities, particularly if one factors in chronological change through time.

The particular approach to female religious life witnessed in the writings related to Brigit and Íte was one rooted in the common experience of those secular Irish women who were accustomed to sharing the authority of running households with their *cétmuinter* or spouse. For handmaids of Christ, the equivalent male in early Ireland was apparently their bishop whose status in society was equivalent to that of the local king.[111] As such, they were integral to the pastoral activities within their local territories, providing material support and sustenance, rearing the young, supporting the abandoned, looking after the sick and caring for the old. Their hagiographers could thus describe their founders as *matrona* and *banflaith*, helping their bishop to support and safeguard the women of their own communities, the tenantry over whom they exercised authority, and the local population at large. In a different context, Caroline Walker Bynum has written of twelfth-century Cistercian spirituality: 'To speak of God, of apostles and bishops, abbots and novice masters, and of oneself, as *mater et pater* perfectly expressed an ideal of discipline plus affectivity'.[112] It is the contention of this chapter that the Irish female communities who followed Brigit and Íte provided a good deal of church 'affectivity' in the territories of their respective bishops.

The traditions of the Roman Mediterranean, with their emphasis on enclosed women living under the rule of family relatives, shared with their Irish counterparts episcopal oversight, public veiling ceremonies, fasting and night prayers. On the whole, however, the lifestyle of Brigit's and Íte's followers do not strongly mirror those of northern Italy and southern France. Instead, the strongest parallels for the form of religious female life, documented in the surviving texts on Brigit and Íte, apparently lie with the more egalitarian and more socially engaged Cappadocian communities of St Macrina, with their tradition of men and women working together and their strong focus on charity, love of their neighbours, and humble service to others. As Íte explained to her *dalta* (student), Bishop Brendan of Clonfert: 'Faith with a true heart, religious simplicity, generosity with charity; these three are enough for God.'[113]

111 C. Etchingham, 'Bishops in the early Irish church: a reassessment', *Studia Hibernica*, 28 (1994), 35–62, pp 39–43.   **112** C. Walker Bynum, 'Jesus as mother and abbot as mother: some themes in twelfth-century Cistercian writing', *Harvard Theological Review*, 70:3–4 (1977), 257–84, at 280. **113** Plummer, *Vitae*, pp 123–4 §22; Gundacker, *Irischer Heiliger*, p. 129 §17.

The other *Peregrinatio*: pilgrim nuns in medieval Regensburg and their Irish connections

DAGMAR Ó RIAIN-RAEDEL

INTRODUCTION

When writing in the Irish Benedictine monastery dedicated to St James (Jakob) and St Gertrud, the so-called *Schottenkloster* at Regensburg, the thirteenth-century author of the *Libellus de fundacione ecclesie Consecrati Petri* included his new home among the four most important imperial cities in Europe, the others being Rome, Trier and Cologne. The last two had previously hosted Irish colonies of monks and may well have been visited by the author on his journey from Ireland to Bavaria.[1] *Frater* Marcus, who had written his *Visio Tnugdali* in the same place a century earlier, also placed Regensburg at the centre of a world that stretched from Ireland to Jerusalem. He set the vision, said to have taken place in Cork in 1149, within the same year as the second year of the crusade to Jerusalem of the German king Konrad, the fourth year of the pontificate of Pope Eugene III and the year of the deaths of St Malachy of Armagh at Clairvaux and of Nehemias, bishop of Cloyne.[2]

On hearing an account of the vision from Tnugdal, Marcus is said to have rushed to Regensburg, where he converted the tale from Irish into Latin and presented it there for copying to a yet-to-be identified Abbess 'G'. The often-asked question as to why an abbess in far-away Bavaria should have been interested in the fortunes experienced by Irish kings and bishops in heaven and hell, as depicted in the *Visio*, receives at least a partial answer through the presence of a number of Irish religious women in Regensburg, most likely in the twelfth and thirteenth centuries. The presence of such

---

1 P. Breatnach, *Die Regensburger Schottenlegende-Libellus de fundacione ecclesiae consecrati Petri. Untersuchung und Textausgabe* (Munich, 1977), pp 127–39, 158. For connections with Cologne, see D. Ó Riain-Raedel, 'New light on the beginnings of Christ Church Cathedral, Dublin' in S. Duffy (ed.), *Medieval Dublin XIII* (Dublin, 2019), pp 63–80 and D. Ó Riain-Raedel and P. Ó Riain, 'Weitreichende Verbindungen: Köln und Irland im 11. Jahrhundert' in H. Horst (ed.), *Mittelalterliche Handschriften der Kölner Dombibliothek. Achtes Symposium der Diözesan- und Dombibliothek Köln zu den Dom-Manuskripten (30 November und 1 Dezember 2018)*, Libelli Rhenani, 24 (Cologne, 2019), pp 113–52. **2** For the *Visio Tnugdali*, see B. Pfeil, *Die 'Vision des Tnugdalus' Albers von Windberg'. Literatur- und Frömmigkeitsgeschichte im ausgehenden 12. Jahrhundert* (Frankfurt am Main – Berlin, 1999); E. Gardiner, 'The vision of Tnugdal' in R.M. Pollard (ed.), *Imagining the medieval afterlife* (Cambridge, 2020), pp 247–63; St J. Seymour, 'Studies in the Vision of Tundal', *PRIA*, 37 C (1926), 87–106; H. Spilling, *Die Visio Tnugdali: Eigenart und Stellung in der mittelalterlichen Visionsliteratur bis zum Ende des 12 Jahrhunderts* (Munich, 1975); J.M. Picard and

women in Regensburg can plausibly be explained by reference to the Irish Benedictine community there from the second half of the eleventh century onwards, during what has been termed the fourth (and last) 'wave' of Irish monastic expansion abroad.[3]

This essay will first briefly examine the evidence for Irish female pilgrims on the Continent and then look at twelfth- and thirteenth-century Regensburg, its *Schottenkloster* and the three female monasteries of Obermünster, Mittelmünster and, especially, Niedermünster.[4] Lastly, it will attempt to place the *peregrinae* in the context of contemporary ecclesiastical establishments at home in Ireland.

FEMALE PILGRIMS TO THE CONTINENT

In the year 747, St Boniface wrote to Archbishop Cuthbert of Canterbury, reporting on the outcome of the Council of Soissons, which he had attended. As a postscript, he remarked that he felt impelled to ask Cuthbert to 'provide a certain shield against vice' by forbidding 'matrons and veiled women to make these frequent journeys back and forth to Rome' as, allegedly, 'a great number of them perish and few keep their virtue'.[5] By then, a number of nuns had joined the 'apostle of Germany' in his endeavours to bring Christianity to Germanic lands and they, by all accounts, contributed greatly to his efforts and were his steadfast supporters. But Boniface was apparently more exercised about the affairs of female pilgrims to Rome, finishing with the remark that there were 'few towns in Lombardy or Frankland or Gaul where there is not a courtesan or a harlot of English stock. It is a scandal and a disgrace to the whole church'.[6] These women, one assumes, would have been inspired by the same pilgrimage spirit as their male counterparts and, rather than celebrate the inclusion of women in the community of Christ, Boniface here instead seems to fear that they might become an embarrassment to its (male) constituents.

Irish female pilgrims

Nothing of this kind is noted of any Irish female pilgrims but, then, hardly any are recorded. As far as is known, no group of émigrés who left for the Continent, from the times of Columbanus and Fursa up to the time of Marianus Scotus (Muiredach mac Robartaig, d. *c*.1082) in Regensburg, included women. The Life of St Odilia of Hohenburg in Alsace reports that female pilgrims from *Scotia* (as well as those from *Britannia*) visited the saint's foundation, but no other information is provided.[7] It is

Y. de Pontfarcy, *The vision of Tnugdal* (Dublin, 1989).　**3** The various 'waves' of medieval Irish emigration are listed in L. Weisgerber, 'Eine Irenwelle an Maas, Mosel und Rhein in ottonischer Zeit?' in *Aus Geschichte und Landeskunde. Forschungen und Darstellungen. Franz Steinbach zum 65. Geburtstag gewidmet von seinen Freunden und Schülern* (Bonn, 1960), pp 727–50.　**4** The topic was previously discussed in D. Ó Riain-Raedel, 'Irish Benedictine monasteries on the Continent' in M. Browne and Ó Clabaigh (eds), *The Irish Benedictines: a history* (Dublin, 2005), pp 25–63.　**5** E. Emerton (trans.), *The letters of St Boniface* (New York, 1940), p. 140.　**6** Ibid.　**7** W. Levison (ed.), *Vita Odiliae abbatissae Hohenburgensis*, MGH Scriptores Rerum Merovingicarum IV (Hannover and Leipzig, 1913), pp 24–50 at pp 25, 45. Until the twelfth century, when it was replaced by *Hibernia*,

nonetheless feasible that Irish pilgrims stayed there on their way to Rome in a hospice for pilgrims founded at the foot of the Hohenburg mountain. It, too, was called Niedermünster and is often confused with the like-named nunnery/female monastery in Regensburg. In fact, as will be seen later, *Vita Ste Odiliae* was used by the author of the eleventh-century Life of St Erhard, patron saint of the Regensburg convent.

A study of Irish female attitudes towards *peregrinatio* is outside the scope of this essay, but it may be useful to look at the two women who informed the life of Columbanus before his emigration and who, according to Elva Johnston, 'play typecast roles: they are either opponents of the saint or the bearers of holy inspirations'.[8] The role played by his mother is contradictory, as, on the one hand, his future greatness was prophesized to her but, at the point of his departure, she is depicted as attempting to stop him. Equally complex is the role of the female hermit in this text, but her description of *peregrinatio* as the lesser one being within Ireland and the superior one abroad, may well reflect Columbanus's own views. However, the female temptresses who allegedly had tormented the saint may rather represent the views of the biographer Jonas.[9] The experience of the saint's female adviser, though, may explain the paucity of female pilgrims. Having lived for twelve years as a hermit in Ireland, she regretfully comments that, 'if the weakness of my sex had not prevented me, I would have crossed the sea and chosen a better place among strangers as my home', in what would have amounted to a *potior peregrinatio*.[10] Sadly, what would have been of interest in the present context, namely the reason why she could not travel abroad, and thereby achieve perfection, is not elucidated. One may wonder whether travel of women was discouraged by their families because, *pace* Boniface, it may have been they who needed protection from the unwanted advances of the opposite sex. Whatever the reason, there is no doubt that, where Irish female pilgrims are on record, they travelled with their husbands or in family groups.[11]

Only one such 'family' pilgrimage to Rome is recorded in the Irish annals, namely that of Laidchenn, son of Máelán Ua Leocháin, lord of Gailenga, and his wife, the daughter of Gott Ua Máelshechlainn, who are said in the Annals of the Four Masters for the year 1051 to have died 'in the east', on their way back from Rome. Judging by the names provided by Bernadette Cunningham, which span the years from 1320 to 1580, and which include some fifty men but only three women, female pilgrimage to

Scotia was the term generally used for Ireland or the wider Gaelic world. **8** E. Johnston, 'Movers and shakers? How women shaped the career of Columbanus' in A. O'Hara (ed.), *Columbanus and the peoples of post-Roman Europe* (Oxford, 2018), pp 69–89 at p. 74. **9** Ibid., p. 75. **10** '… et nisi fragilis sexus obstasset, mare transacto, potioris peregrinationis locum pertissem': B. Krusch (ed.), *Ionae Vitae Sanctorum Columbani, Vedestis, Iohannis*, MGH Scriptores Rerum Germanicarum in usum scholarum 37 (Hannover and Leipzig, 1905), pp 144–294 at p. 156. **11** King Sitriuc of Dublin's pilgrimage to Rome in 1028, in the company of a large retinue, may also have included his wife Sláine, the daughter of Brian Boru. For Sitriuc's pilgrimage in Cologne, see Ó Riain-Raedel, 'New light'. For the pilgrimages undertaken by Sitriuc's son in 1032 and Brian's son Donnchad in 1064, see D. Ó Riain-Raedel, 'St Koloman: ein irischer Pilger?' in M. Niederkorn-Bruck (ed.), *Ein Heiliger unterwegs in Europa. Tausend Jahre Koloman-Verehrung in Melk (1014–2014)* (Vienna/ Cologne/ Weimar, 2014), pp 219–38 at pp 223–4.

Santiago de Compostella was also infrequent.[12] These were likely to have been aristocratic women who travelled with 'a suitable entourage of male protectors as well as maids'.[13] Whether the Irish women documented in Regensburg had also been on pilgrimage, to Rome or to other holy places, is not known, but they probably had left Ireland on a lifelong *peregrinatio*, in the same way as their male compatriots had done for centuries.

While Regensburg would not have formed part of the customary itinerary to Rome, its location on the river Danube had always favoured travellers, as is shown by its role as a starting point of the second crusade to the Holy Land, which left from there in 1147 (Fig. 4.1).[14] Following the construction of the so-called *Steinerne Brücke* over the river in the years 1135–46, accompanied by the building of nearby hospices and hospitals, Regensburg catered for crusaders, merchants and pilgrims, and became the agreed gathering place for the settling of disputes between such neighbouring regions as Bohemia, Hungary and Poland.[15] Although not chosen as the seat of an archbishop, an honour which went to Salzburg, it was the political and economic centre of Bavaria, benefitting from intersecting trade routes leading north to the Baltic and south over the Alps to Italy, as well as eastwards along the Danube towards Hungary and Byzantium. Furthermore, after the absorption of Bavaria into the Carolingian empire, it became the most favoured residence (*Pfalz*) for German kings and emperors, whose itinerant lifestyles relied on the availability of suitable accommodation in numerous centres within the realm. Although such royal and imperial visits bestowed great prestige on Regensburg, they also proved a heavy financial burden for the local religious and civic institutions.

During the time under consideration here, Regensburg was at the height of its importance and, apart from being a *Roma secunda*, it was also, according to an eleventh-century writer, a 'second Athens', a place where learning and philosophy flourished.[16]

---

12 As the annals generally focus on aristocratic travellers many other pilgrims went unnoticed: B. Cunningham, *Medieval Irish pilgrims to Santiago de Compostela* (Dublin, 2018), pp 165–7; see also Hall, *Women*, pp 29–30.   **13** Cunningham, *Medieval Irish pilgrims*, p. 20; Hall, *Women*, pp 29–30. **14** This crusade is referenced by the author of the *Visio Tnugdali*, who composed his work shortly afterwards in the *Schottenkloster* in Regensburg: Picard and de Pontfarcy, *The vision of Tnugdal*, p. 110.   **15** P. Schmid, 'Die Bischöfe und die Hauptstadt: Residenzen der bayerischen Bischöfe in Regensburg', in Peter Morsbach (ed.), *Ratisbona sacra. Das Bistum Regensburg im Mittelalter* (Ausstellung anläßlich des 1250 jährigen Jubiläums der kanonischen Errichtung des Bistums Regensburg durch Bonifatius 739–1989) (Munich/Zurich, 1989), pp 93–5. See also H. Flachenecker, *Schottenklöster*, pp 77–81 and H. Flachenecker, 'Irische Stützpunkte in Regensburg – Weih Sankt Peter und Sankt Jakob im Mittelalter' in Stephan Acht and Paul Mai (eds), *Scoti Peregrini in Sankt Jakob. 800 Jahre irisch-schottische Kultur in Regensburg* (Bischöfliches Zentralarchiv und Bischöfliche Zentralbibliothek Regensburg Kataloge und Schriften 21), (Regensburg, 2005), pp 13–24.   **16** G. Schwaiger, 'Bischof Wolfgang von Regensburg (ca. 924–994). Geschichte, Legende, Verehrung' in G. Schwaiger and P. Mai (eds), *Wallfahrten im Bistum Regensburg. Zur Tausendjahrfeier des Todes des hl. Bischofs Wolfgang* (Regensburg, 1994), pp 7–36 at p. 22.

4.1 Former Obermünster nunnery, Regensburg, view from the north; copper engraving in Paul Mai and Stephan Acht (eds), *Obermünster Regensburg: from the beginnings to the present day; exhibition in the Episcopal Central Library Regensburg, July 18 to October 2, 2008.* Catalogs and publications/ Episcopal Central Archive and Episcopal Central Library Regensburg; vol. 24, back cover. Image © Dr Raymond Dittrich and Dr Wolfgang Neiser.

By the end of the twelfth century it accommodated within the town walls and suburbs a cathedral and eleven monasteries, four hospitals and thirty-three chapels, one of which was the Irish monastery dedicated to St James (Jakob) and St Gertrud.[17]

Within such an overabundance of religious institutions, it is not surprising that there existed a modicum of rivalry between them, forcing their scriptoria to produce writings that laid emphasis on particular rights not enjoyed by other houses. During the eleventh and twelfth centuries, St Emmeram, the most venerable of the monasteries, exerted much effort, not only in falsifying charters but also in claiming the relics of St Dionysius, which were allegedly stolen by emperor Arnulf in 899 from St Denis in Paris, the burial place of the Pippinid ancestors of Charlemagne. Otloh of St Emmeram spent much of his writing career attempting to claim for Regensburg and particularly for his monastery a role in East Francia comparable to that held by St Denis in West Francia. Efforts were also made in St Emmeram to prove that Ludwig the German's wife, Hemma, was buried (as her husband was) in its church, a privilege contested by the convent of Obermünster, which claimed for itself the burial place of their foundress. This may have been an attempt to construct a Carolingian past for the

---

17 A. Dirmeier, 'Regensburg – ein "Idealtypus der Urbanität". Klöster, Stifte und Spitäler einer mittelalterlichen Stadt' in H. Flachenecker and R. Kiessling (eds), *Urbanisierung und Urbanität. Der Beitrag der kirchlichen Institutionen zur Stadtentwicklung in Bayern* (*Zeitschrift für Bayerische Landesgeschichte* Beiheft 36) (Munich, 2008), pp 101–26 at p. 112. For its foundation and history,

monastery, thus matching Niedermünster's claims to antiquity. By the eleventh century, Niedermünster had begun to promote St Erhard who was buried in the church *c.*700.[18] A claim to putative Carolingian connections was also made in the *Schottenkloster* in the thirteenth century with the composition of the *Libellus de fundacione ecclesiae consecrati Petri*, the so-called '*Schottenlegende*', much of it based on twelfth-century sources.[19] Furthermore, by choosing St Gertrud as second patron for their church, the Irish monks not only referenced her as seventh-century advocate of both Irish *peregrini*, and, as will be argued below, *peregrinae*, but also as a member of the Pippinid family, ancestors of the Carolingians.[20] We can be thankful to these and other ecclesiastical rivalries within Regensburg for initiating a spate of scribal activity which, in the case of the *Schottenkloster* texts, also include valuable witnesses to twelfth-century Irish history. The *Schottenkloster* was only one contributor to the significant amount of Latin and Middle High German literature composed or copied in eleventh- and twelfth-century Regensburg, earning it the distinction of '*Literaturstadt*' and the cradle of German literature.[21]

The Irish monastery of St James and St Gertrud (Schottenkloster) *in Regensburg*

The Irish *peregrini* in Regensburg first made their mark as scribes when, *c.*1070, the inaugural group, led by Marianus Scotus (Muiredach mac Robartaig) of an Ulster ecclesiastical family, but then based in Kells, Co. Meath, arrived in the city.[22] According to his late twelfth-century Life, the *Vita Mariani*, and also according to the *Libellus*, Marianus and his companions were on a pilgrimage to Rome but, on arrival in Regensburg, they were persuaded, thanks to divine intervention, to remain as scribes in two female monasteries, the Niedermünster and the Obermünster (Figs 4.1 and 4.2).[23] Subsequently, in 1075, the abbess of Obermünster provided the Irish pilgrims

---

see Flachenecker, *Schottenklöster*.　**18** C. Märtl, 'Die Damenstifte Obermünster, Niedermünster, St Paul' in P. Schmid (ed.), *Geschichte der Stadt Regensburg*, vol. 2 (2000), pp 745–63 at p. 747; G. Leidinger, 'Bruchstücke einer verlorenen Chronik eines unbekannten Regensburger Verfasser des 12. Jahrhunderts', *Sitzungsberichte der Bayerischen Akademie der Wissenschaften Philosophisch-historische Abteilung*, Jahrgang 33 Heft I (Munich, 1933), 3–72 at 16–55.　**19** Breatnach, *Die Regensburger Schottenlegende*.　**20** J.F. Kenney, *The sources for the early history of Ireland* (ecclesiastical): *an introduction and guide* (New York, 1929, repr. Dublin, 1979), pp 504–5; Flachenecker, *Schottenklöster*, pp 84, 86.　**21** E. Feistner, 'Das spätmittelalterliche Regensburg als Literaturstadt: Werke, Sammlungen, Fragmente' in P. Schmid (ed.), *Regensburg im Spätmittelalter. Bestandsaufnahme und Impulse* (Regensburg, 2007), pp 125–36. On the *Kaiserchronik*, see D. Ó Riain-Raedel, 'German influence on Munster church and kings in the twelfth century' in A. Smyth (ed.), *Seanchas: studies in early and medieval Irish archaeology, history and literature in honour of Francis J. Byrne* (Dublin, 2000), pp 323–30 at pp 326–7.　**22** The Regensburg *Schottenkloster* and its daughter-houses have been extensively covered in Flachenecker, *Schottenklöster* and L. Hammermayer, 'Die irischen Benediktiner-„Schottenklöster" in Deutschland und ihr institutioneller Zusammenschluss vom 12.-16. Jahrhundert', *Studien und Mitteilungen zur Geschichte des Benediktinerordens*, 87 (1976), 249–339.　**23** S. Weber, *Iren auf dem Kontinent. Das Leben des Marianus Scottus von Regensburg und die Anfänge der irischen "Schottenklöster"* (Heidelberg, 2010); Breatnach, *Die Regensburger Schottenlegende*. The manuscripts of Marianus and his group have recently been re-examined by H. Hoffmann, 'Irische Schreiber in Deutschland im 11. Jahrhundert', *Deutsches*

4.2 Portrait of Maria Anna Freiin von Böttigheim, canoness of Obermünster, Regensburg, watercolor on parchment, eighteenth century, in Paul Mai and Stephan Acht (eds), *Obermünster Regensburg: from the beginnings to the present day; exhibition in the Episcopal Central Library Regensburg, 18 July to October 2, 2008*. Catalogs and publications/ Episcopal Central Archive and Episcopal Central Library Regensburg; vol. 24, p. 21. Image © Dr Raymond Dittrich and Dr Wolfgang Neiser.

with a small church, *Weihsanktpeter*, subsequently a priory of the *Schottenkloster*.[24] As this remained the property of Obermünster, it later became an object of dispute.[25] Partially in order to counteract Obermünster claims, the author of the *Libellus* went to great trouble to prove its foundation for the Irish by Charlemagne himself, while St Peter was brought in person to consecrate it.[26] A charter dated to 1089 referred to 'certain Irishmen, who had exiled themselves from their homeland for the torment of the body and the salvation of the soul, and who, after spending a long time visiting places of prayer, had come finally to Regensburg'.[27] Towards the beginning of the twelfth century, an unprecedented influx of new recruits from Ireland led to the construction of a new monastery, dedicated to St James and St Gertrud, which, following its completion in 1111, was consecrated in 1120 (Fig. 4.2).[28]

Archiv für Erforschung des Mittelalters, 59 (2003), 97–120.   **24** Named in the Vita Mariani as *mater peregrinorum* – the mother of pilgrims: Weber, *Iren auf dem Kontinent*, pp 112, 122. **25** Flachenecker, *Schottenklöster*, pp 59–69, 126–36; D. Ó Riain, 'The *Schottenklöster* and the legacy of the Irish *sancti peregrini*' in W. Keller and D. Schlüter (eds), *'A fantastic and abstruse Latinity': Hiberno-continental cultural and literary interactions in the Middle Ages* (Münster, 2017), pp 141–64 at p. 146.   **26** Breatnach, *Die Regensburger Schottenlegende*, pp 203–7.   **27** *Quidam Scottigenae pro cruciando corpore salvandaque anima patria sua exulerant ac diu orationum*. D. Ó Riain, '*Monachi peregrini*. The mobile monks of the Irish Benedictine houses in medieval Germany and Austria' in O. Delouis, M. Mossakovska-Gaubert and A. Peters-Custot (eds), *Les mobilités monastiques en Orient et en Occident de l'Antiquité tardive au Moyen Âge (ive–xve siècle)* (Rome, 2019), pp 337–52 at p. 340.   **28** For the following, see Flachenecker, *Schottenklöster*, pp 83–98.

The new monastery became the mother house of a series of foundations throughout Southern Germany, with some of the more important located in Würzburg, Erfurt, Nürnberg and further east, in Vienna and Kyiv. To provide recruits for these monasteries, at least two priories were founded in Ireland, St Mary's in Rosscarbery, Co. Cork, and St Mary's at Cashel, Co. Tipperary. The spread of the foundations on the Continent commenced in the 1130s during the abbacy of Christianus Mac Carthaig and continued under his successor Gregorius. During the latter's incumbency a collection of Irish saints' Lives was assembled that subsequently found its way into the voluminous *Magnum Legendarium Austriacum*, 'medieval Europe's richest hagiographical collection'.[29] Included among these Lives are some that were first recorded in Ireland up to two centuries later.[30]

In the present context, there is one *Schottenkloster* document that deserves particular attention, namely a necrology (Book of the Dead), which began to be compiled around the middle of the twelfth century and is extant in a seventeenth-century copy made at St James in Würzburg and now preserved in the Vatican library.[31] The text lists the names of up to one thousand individuals, mainly abbots and monks of the *Schottenklöster*, as well as monks of befriended houses in and around Regensburg and benefactors of the monastery in both Regensburg and Ireland. For all those named, the monks undertook to pray annually on the anniversaries of their deaths. The mainly twelfth-century entries, which include Munster bishops and kings, incidentally provide an invaluable insight into Irish, and particularly Munster, politics of the period. To this document we also owe evidence of the presence of Irish women in Regensburg, although these, regrettably, have left little more than their names.

Recorded Irish women in twelfth-century Regensburg

Three female religious are commemorated in the *Schottenkloster* necrology, two of whom are identified by the epithet *scotigena*. These are *Beatrix monacha scotigena* (7 July), who is also commemorated in the Niedermünster necrology as *Beatrix soror nostra*, and *Gertrudis monacha scotigena* (19 August).[32] A third, '*Brechta Schottin*', presumably named Bertha, appears under the year 1126 in an eighteenth-century text relating to the same nunnery/female monastery and, although the text has to be used with caution, there appears to be no need to query her existence.[33] Bertha is too common a name for her

29 D. Ó Riain, 'The *Magnum Legendarium Austriacum*: a new investigation of one of medieval Europe's richest hagiographical collections', *Analecta Bollandiana*, 133 (2015), 87–165. **30** D. Ó Riain-Raedel, 'Cashel and Germany: the documentary evidence' in D. Bracken and D. Ó Riain-Raedel (eds), *Ireland and Europe in the twelfth century: reform and renewal* (Dublin, 2006), pp 176–217, at pp 196, 211. **31** Vat. lat. 10 100; D. Ó Riain-Raedel, 'Das Nekrolog der irischen Schottenklöster. Edition der Handschrift Vat. lat. 10 100 mit einer Untersuchung der hagiographischen und liturgischen Handschriften der Schottenklöster', *Beiträge zur Geschichte des Bistums Regensburg*, 26 (1992), 1–119. For references to Irish kings and bishops see D. Ó Riain–Raedel, 'Irish kings and bishops in the memoria of the German Schottenklöster' in P. Ní Chatháin and M. Richter (eds), *Irland und Europa: die Kirche im Frühmittelalter* (Stuttgart, 1984), pp 390–404. **32** F.L. Baumann (ed.), *Necrologium monasterii inferioris Ratisbonensis*, MGH Necrologia Germaniae 3 (Berlin, 1905), pp 273–89, at pp 280, 319. **33** J.C. Paricius, *Allerneueste und bewährte Historische Nachricht Von Allen in denen Ring-Mauren der Stadt Regensburg gelegenen*

to be identified in the Niedermünster necrology, although it is tempting to equate her with the *Berhta monacha de Inferiore monasterio* in the martyrology/necrology of St Emmeram on the same day and in the same hand as *Beatrix monacha scotigena* (4 July) in the corresponding Niedermünster text. Beatrix re-appears in the same document on 7 July, the day on which she is mentioned in the *Schottenkloster* necrology. The name Beatrix is rare enough to support the assumption that the same person is intended in both entries.[34] Although nothing else is known of them, it is fair to assume that these women came from the same areas as their male counterparts, in whose company they also probably travelled.

For the author of the *Vita Mariani* the concept of *peregrinatio* was paramount, and his interest mainly lay in elucidating 'why our predecessors and we also, the poor of Christ, following from a western land naked the naked Christ for the salvation of our souls, leaving behind our homeland and our dear relatives out of love and desire for a heavenly life'.[35] Indeed, the *Libellus* hones in on this and earlier comments by continental writers to the effect 'that Irishmen and the concept of the *peregrinatio pro Christo* were inextricably linked' by asserting that the early Irish *peregrini* 'introduced the custom from that day forward for all Irishmen to visit sacred places and peregrinate'.[36]

There is nothing to show that the pioneering Irish *peregrinae* would have felt differently. Significantly, as *Damenstifte* in Regensburg and elsewhere were reserved for ladies of aristocratic background, we may conclude that these Irish women were associated with the Munster nobility as portrayed in the *Visio Tnugdali*, namely the families of the kings of Desmond, the Meic Carthaig, and the kings of Thomond, the Uí Briain, and their courts.[37] A background of this kind may be confirmed by the appearance in the *Schottenkloster* necrology (8 April) of a fourth name, *Sophia comitissa* 'countess', whose name also appears in the Niedermünster necrology and who, therefore, is likely to have belonged to the latter nunnery/female monastery.[38]

In view of their probably adopted names, these four Irishwomen appear to have immersed themselves completely in their German milieu, so much so that other Irish women may be hidden among the many German names recorded in the necrologies. One Irish name was occasionally retained, namely Brigida, which is represented by Brigida of Niedermünster (18 January and 19 August),[39] Brigida monacha of

Reichs-Stifftern, Haupt-Kirchen und Clöstern Catholischer Religion (Regensburg, 1753), p. 197. **34** E.D. Freise et al. (eds), *Das Martyrolog-Necrolog von St Emmeram zu Regensburg*, MGH Libri memoriales et necrologia, Nova series 3 MGH Libri Mem. N.S., 3 (Hannover, 1986), pp 195, 196, 232; Baumann, *Necrologium monasterii inferioris Ratisbonensis*, p. 280.   **35** *Quapropter antecessores nostri nos quoque Christi pauperes pro remedio animarum de finibus occidentis nudum Christum nudi sequentes, patriam carosque propinquos amore ac desiderio uitę cęlestis derelinquentes ... commendabo.* Weber, *Iren auf dem Kontinent*, pp 92–4; Ó Riain, 'The Schottenklöster and the legacy of the Irish *sancti peregrini*', p. 154.   **36** *Et duxerunt in consuetudinem omnes Scoti ab illo die invisere loca sancta Christi et peregrinari*: Breatnach, *Die Regensburger Schottenlegende*, p. 183; D. Ó Riain, 'The Schottenklöster and the legacy of the Irish *sancti peregrini*', p. 154.   **37** Ó Riain-Raedel, 'Das Nekrolog', 29–30, 69, 71.   **38** Baumann, *Necrologium monasterii inferioris Ratisbonensis*, p. 277; Ó Riain-Raedel, 'Das Nekrolog', 63.   **39** Baumann, *Necrologium monasterii inferioris Ratisbonensis*, pp 274, 282.

4.3 Niedermünster Abbey, Regensburg, art collections of the diocese of Regensburg, picture archive. Image © Dr Raymond Dittrich and Dr Wolfgang Neiser.

Obermünster (23 August),[40] and Brigida monacha (without provenance) (21 July).[41] The Brigida abbatissa commemorated on 20 August in the late eleventh-century *Notae necrologiae* of the Niedermünster chapter book may refer to the first abbess of Mittelmünster, a daughter of duke Heinrich der Zänker, 'the Wrangler' (951–5), to whom we will return below.[42] As a rule, Irish women were connected specifically to the Regensburg Niedermünster, but it cannot be ruled out that further Irish women lived in other nunneries (Fig. 4.3).

Women's monasteries at Regensburg with Irish connections

The three female religious institutions under discussion here are named relative to their location within the walled city of Regensburg, Obermünster ('upper monastery') dedicated to St Mary and Niedermünster ('lower monastery') dedicated to St Mary and St Erhard, both of which foundations can be traced back to the eighth century. The third, Mittelmünster ('middle monastery'), dedicated to St Paul, was founded by Bishop Wolfgang (972–94).[43] Part of Wolfgang's reform agenda included the transformation of the two older female religious houses from Augustinian into Benedictine nunneries.[44] He was supported by duke Heinrich 'der Zänker' (the Wrangler, so named for his disputes with his cousin, emperor Otto II), whose mother, Judith, had chosen Niedermünster as the dynastic burial place. Whether this and the Obermünster had at some stage followed the Rule of St Benedict is uncertain but, by the tenth century, they were thought to be in urgent need of reform, especially since some of the women had begun to leave the nunnery and return to secular (and implicitly immoral) life, an accusation regularly aimed at canonesses.[45] As Katrinette Bodarwé has shown, comments of this kind must be viewed in the light of attempts made by the bishop, together with other (male) clergy and lay rulers, to exert control over female religious communities. Duke Heinrich's concern for the spiritual life of the canonesses was matched by his attempts to confine these women to a cloistered milieu, which would have curtailed any move on their part towards more independence.[46] It appears that the reformers did not shy away from expelling those unwilling to live under the Benedictine rule and replace them with more compliant candidates. Furthermore, by way of follow-up, Wolfgang and Heinrich established a new Benedictine nunnery, the

---

40 Ibid., p. 343: Brigida monacha ex nostris; also in Niedermünster: ibid., p. 322: Brigida monacha de Superiori monasterio.   **41** Ibid., p. 320; Freise, *Das Martyrolog – Necrolog von St Emmeram zu Regensburg*, pp 197, 233.   **42** For the Niedermünster manuscripts, see A. Risse, *Niedermünster in Regensburg. Eine Frauenkommunität in Mittelalter und Neuzeit* (Beiträge zur Geschichte des Bistums Regensburg Beiband 24), (Regensburg, 2014), pp 147–50.   **43** For the architectural history of St Jakob and the other foundations see L.-M. Dallmeier, H. Giess and K. Schnieringer, *Stadt Regensburg Ensembles – Baudenkmäler Archäologische Denkmäler* (Regensburg, 1997), pp 314–24 (St Jakob), pp 424–34 (Obermünster), pp 232, 406–17, 702 (Niedermünster), p. 324 (Mittelmünster), pp 197–222 (St Emmeram).   **44** For the following, see Märtl, 'Die Damenstifte'.   **45** The cases cited typically referred to those females who had left the convent school. K. Bodarwé, Katrinette, 'Immer Ärger mit den Stiftsdamen: Reform in Regensburg' in E. Schlothuber, H. Flachenecker and I. Gardill (eds), *Nonnen, Kanonissen und Mystikerinnen. Religiöse Frauengemeinschaften in Süddeutschland* (*Studien zur Germania Sacra* Band 3, Göttingen, 2008), pp 79–102 at p. 99.   **46** Ibid., pp 101–2.

Mittelmünster, dedicated to St Paul.[47] In male monasteries of the period, a 'distinguishing emphasis [developed] between the contemplative and the active life, between ascetic withdrawal from the world by monks and the more vocational provision of pastoral care and preaching within lay society by canons'.[48] Similarly, canonesses tended to become involved in urban activities including public functions and supervision of schools, activities which were thought to be less suited to regulated nunneries. For the noble dynasties, which provided their daughters, sisters and widows, the female monasteries played an important role and their relative flexibility meant that they were adjustable if and when familial relationships changed.[49] At the same time, however, it was precisely this relative autonomy that was a source of concern for lay and clerical men of authority. By the twelfth century, while the religious observances within the three Regensburg nunneries are less than clear, all three can be seen to have their own Irish connections.

Obermünster

The Obermünster is first referred to in ninth-century charters as *monasterium superioris puellarum*.[50] According to his Life, Marianus and his companions were hospitably received here by Abbess Hemma, styled *mater peregrinorum*.[51] In reality, however, the abbess at the time was Willa (d. before 1089), Hemma being the nunnery's ninth-century foundress, who is remembered as such on 15 February in the *Schottenkloster* necrology.[52] It may be that the author of the *Vita* wished to push back the time-line of the local Irish presence, and possible friction at the time of writing between the abbot of the *Schottenkloster* and the abbess of Obermünster concerning her right to Weihsanktpeter must also be borne in mind. If there was friction, it did not apply to devotion to the blessed Mercherdach (*dilectus frater Murchertacus*), who, according to the *Vita*, was an *inclusus* at the Obermünster. He was said to have had arrived long before Marianus, and it was on his advice that the group abandoned their Roman pilgrimage plans and instead remained in Regensburg. More likely, however, he was one of Marianus' companions who stayed on as an *inclusus* at Obermünster after the others settled in Weihsanktpeter. His alleged advisory role is omitted in the *Libellus* which instead gives this role to an angel.[53]

However, his legend lived on and later, though uncorroborated, some sources claimed that the *inclusus* was visited by Pope Leo IX on the occasion of the canonization of Sts Wolfgang and Erhard, which may represent an attempt on the part of

47 J. Gruber, 'Geschichte des Stiftes Obermünster in Regensburg' in P. Mai (ed.), *Obermünster Regensburg. Von den Anfängen bis heute* (Ausstellung in der Bischöflichen Zentralbibliothek Regensburg St Petersweg 11–13, 18. Juli bis 8. Oktober 2008) (Regensburg, 2008), pp 10–11 at p. 10. When the Benedictine observance in the three houses lapsed is not known, but this could have already occurred in the late eleventh century: Risse, *Niedermünster in Regensburg*, pp 60–1. **48** Flanagan, *Transformation*, p. 137. **49** I. Crusius, 'Sanctimoniales quae se canonicas vocant', p. 37. **50** Gruber, 'Geschichte des Stiftes Obermünsters in Regensburg', pp 10–11. **51** This is apparently not a scribal error, as the same name appears again later in the narrative: Weber, *Iren auf dem Kontinent*, pp 112–13, 122–3. **52** Ó Riain-Raedel, 'Das Nekrolog', 59. **53** Breatnach, *Die Regensburger Schottenlegende*, pp 201, 205.

Obermünster to obtain a standing similar to that of the Niedermünster.[54] It is certainly noteworthy that Mercherdach, alias Murchertachus *inclusus*, is the only Irish entry in the Obermünster necrology, on the same date as in the *Schottenkloster* necrology (3 August).[55] His chapel in the Obermünster church, which is said to have been built over his cell, is the only part to have been rebuilt after near-destruction in 1945. A thirteenth-century tomb stone in the chapel, which names him as S. MERCHERTACH, portrays him as a pilgrim and the reliquary containing his corporeal relics is now placed under the altar.[56]

The Benedictine nunnery dedicated to St Paul (Mittelmünster)[57]

Bishop Wolfgang's efforts to persuade the canonesses of Obermünster and Niedermünster to adopt the Rule of St Benedict are chronicled in his Life, which was written by Otloh, a monk of St Emmeram (*c*.1010–70).[58] As reported by Otloh, the deplorable lifestyle of the canonesses, which deteriorated to the point of being detrimental to their spiritual life, was revealed to the bishop during one of his nightly prayers at the tomb of St Erhard in Niedermünster. Acting on the vision, Wolfgang undertook to establish a new nunnery under the Rule of St Benedict, the Mittelmünster (Fig. 4.4). It was founded as an episcopal *Eigenkloster* (proprietary monastery), a move that may explain its dedication to St Paul in apparent reference to the cathedral's patron St Peter, and its consecration took place on the feast of Sts Peter and Paul in 983. Although the rules may have been relaxed over time, by the fourteenth century the occupants were still called *moniales* (nuns) and wore black habits. Recurrent scarcity of novices led to its dissolution and, in 1588, it became a Jesuit *collegium*, followed by a diocesan seminary in 1781 and ultimate destruction in the wars of 1809.

No visible remains of the nunnery survive and there is little knowledge of its original appearance.[59] It owed its foundation to the close connection between Wolfgang and Duke Heinrich the Wrangler whose four children were educated by the bishop.[60] The first abbess was Brigida, daughter of the duke, and as Wolfgang probably had baptized Brigida, he may have been responsible for suggesting the Irish saint's name, which he would have known from his earlier career in places associated with Irish *peregrini*, such as Reichenau, Würzburg, St Maximin in Trier and the Hofkapelle of Archbishop Brun of Cologne.[61] Little is known of Brigida's successors or whether her family had any further involvement in the nunnery.[62]

54 Weber, *Iren auf dem Kontinent*, p. 351. **55** Baumann, *Necrologium monasterii superioris Ratisbonensis*, p. 342; Ó Riain-Raedel, 'Das Nekrolog', 70. **56** Weber, *Iren auf dem Kontinent*, pp 120–1, 347–57; Flachenecker, *Schottenklöster*, pp 72–4. **57** Märtl, 'Die Damenstifte', p. 746. **58** G. Waitz (ed.), *Othloni Vita sancti Wolfkangi episcopi*, MGH SS 4 (Hannover, 1841), pp 521–42 at pp 533–4. **59** Morsbach, *Das Mittelmünster in Regensburg – Nur ein Straßenschild ist geblieben*, Haus der Bayerischen Geschicht, Klöster in Bayern: https://www.hdbg.eu/kloster/index.php/pdf?id=KS0337, accessed 7 March 2022. **60** These were the future duke of Bavaria, Heinrich IV (who later became king and, from 1014, Emperor Heinrich II), Bruno, bishop of Augsburg, Gisela, wife of King Stephen of Hungary and Brigida, the future abbess, the latter variously located at the Nieder- or Mittelmünster in 983: Schwaiger, 'Bischof Wolfgang von Regensburg (ca. 924–994)', p. 23. **61** Waitz (ed.), *Othloni Vita Sancti Wolfkangi episcopi*, pp 521–42 at p. 534. **62** P. Mai (ed.), *100 Jahre Stift St Paul (Mittelmünster) in Regensburg Jubiläumsausstellung* (Regensburg,

4.4 Niedermünster Abbey, Regensburg, tombs of St Erhard and St Albert.
Image © High Contrast, CC BY 3.0, via Wikimedia Commons.

The Visio Tnugdali: *written at Mittelmünster?*

The references at the beginning of this essay drew attention to literary works written in the *Schottenkloster* about the middle of the twelfth century. Among these was an account of a vision allegedly seen by Tnugdal in Cork, which was speedily brought to Regensburg by its author Marcus and there sent for copying to Abbess 'G'.[63] The only

1983), p. 9; J. Geier, 'Das Traditionsbuch des Klosters St Paul in Regensburg', *Verhandlungen des Historischen Vereins für Oberpfalz und Regensburg*, 111 (1971), 169–71.   **63** The reading of 'G' has

Abbess 'G' securely identifiable in Regensburg at this time is Gisela of Mittelmünster who was in charge from *c.*1040 to 1060, and the putative presence of Irish nuns there may have prompted her interest in the otherworld fortunes of Munster kings. Marcus did not stint in his praise for 'G', who was 'devoted to God and abbess by God's gift'. Moreover, she was held in high esteem in the local *Schottenkloster*, which remembered her in its necrology on 24 February.[64] Overall, however, the identification of Marcus's 'G' with Abbess Gisela of Mittelmünster cannot be established with certainty, especially since we do not know the name of the contemporary abbess of Niedermünster, where, as will be seen, an interest in Irish affairs would have been more likely.[65]

Niedermünster

The *Libellus* places Marianus and his group exclusively in the Niedermünster and their presence there in 1074 is confirmed by glosses in the above-mentioned psalter, written by Marianus.[66] Here was also home for the four Irish women known by name, although these may not have arrived until the following century. Niedermünster is the most thoroughly researched of all Regensburg nunneries, not least because its medieval fabric, including a Romanesque basilica, survives relatively intact. As excavations have shown, it was built on strata going back to prehistoric settlements, followed by the Roman *Castra Regina* and, from the late seventh century onwards, a succession of church buildings which took account of the tomb of St Erhard on its north wall.[67] Documentary evidence for the church becomes available from the tenth century onwards when it was chosen as their mausoleum by the Luidolf junior line of the Ottonian imperial family. Perhaps originally founded as a Benedictine nunnery, and still described as such in a charter of 1002, the house seems to have evolved into a community of canonesses, a so-called '*Damenstift*', although, as in other houses, efforts to introduce the Benedictine rule continued.[68] Situated close to the ducal *Pfalz*, its benefactors included Judith, wife of the Bavarian Duke Heinrich I, younger brother of Emperor Otto I, whose burial there was followed by Judith's assumption of the role of abbess until her death in 987.[69] The relics brought back from Judith's pilgrimage to Jerusalem added greatly to the status of the community and her *memoria* as foundress

been accepted generally but, as the archetype of the text is lost, this is uncertain. A number of manuscripts substitute full names, such as Gisela, Gertrud and Conegonde / Kunigunde: Spilling, *Die Visio Tnugdali*, p. 17.   **64** Picard and de Pontfarcy, *The vision of Tnugdal*, p. 109. Alber of Windberg, whose Middle-High German translation of the vision was produced towards the end of the twelfth century, places Abbess Gisela in St Paul. See B. Pfeil, *Die 'Vision des Tnugdalus' Albers von Windberg'*, pp 88–9; Ó Riain-Raedel, 'Das Nekrolog', 30; Geier, 'Das Traditionsbuch des Klosters St Paul in Regensburg'; Spilling, *Die Visio Tnugdali*, pp 18–19.   **65** For the list of known abbesses, see Risse, *Niedermünster in Regensburg*, pp 53, 260–1. Abbess Richiza I died at some time after 1129 and Kunigunde II is first attested in 1175.   **66** Breatnach, *Die Regensburger Schottenlegende*, p. 202.   **67** For a comprehensive bibliography on Niedermünster see Risse, *Niedermünster in Regensburg*, pp 1–8, 9–40.   **68** A. Cohen, 'Abbess Uta of Regensburg: Patterns of patronage around 1000', *Aurora: The Journal of the History of Art*, 4 (2003), 39–49 at 37; Risse, *Niedermünster in Regensburg*, pp 20, 152–5. For Niedermünster copies of the Rule of St Benedict and a *Rituale monialium ex pontificali Romano-Germanico*, see, ibid., p. 81.   **69** Märtl, 'Die

was kept not only here but also at the *Schottenkloster* where the anniversary of her obit was added to the house's martyrology on 27 June.[70]

This Regensburg family connection became irrelevant when the childless emperor was succeeded by the first Salian king and emperor, Konrad II (d. 1039). His support was more directed at the Obermünster, to judge by his presentation to it of his sceptre. At this point, Niedermünster activity began to focus on possession of the relics of St Erhard, as is shown by the attention paid to his Mass in the Uta Evangeliary (Bayerische Staatsbibliothek Clm 13601), suggesting that devotion to the saint was already well established before his *translatio* in 1052, an event that led to the commissioning of the saint's Life (Fig. 4.4).[71]

The cult of St Erhard at Niedermünster

Erhard's cult reached its peak in 1052 when, in the presence of Emperor Heinrich III, Pope Leo IX elevated the saint 'to the honour of the altars', a day after he had also canonized St Wolfgang.[72] In unison with the *translatio*, a Life was commissioned by a Fulda monk, Paul Iudeus, which seems to be based on limited sources, such as the Lives of the above-named Odilia of Hohenburg and that of Hildulf of Trier. Writing of the saint's background, the author provided a contradictory, and yet to be resolved, narrative by asserting that the saint was '*Narbonensis gentilitate, Nervus civilitate, genere Scoticus*'.[73] A century later, this enabled the *Schottenkloster* scriptorium to make selective use of Paul's biography by transforming Erhard into an archbishop of Armagh.[74] Furthermore, Erhard was provided with a friend and fellow pilgrim, allegedly a Londoner named St Albart/Albert, archbishop of Cashel, Co. Tipperary, who was

Damenstifte', p. 747. **70** The name is difficult to decipher but the date can be verified from other sources. See P. Ó Riain, *The martyrology of the Regensburg Schottenkloster* (London, 2019), p. 182. **71** Cohen, 'Abbess Uta of Regensburg', 47. **72** Schwaiger, 'Bischof Wolfgang von Regensburg (ca. 924–994)', 28–30. **73** W. Levison (ed.), *Vita Erhardi episcopi Bavarici auctore Paulo*, MGH SS rer Merov VI (Hannover & Leipzig, 1913), pp 1–21; Risse, *Niedermünster in Regensburg*, pp 152–4, for the Life of St Erhard and the subsequent use of it by the *Schottenkloster* scriptorium, see D. Ó Riain, 'The *Schottenklöster* and the legacy of the Irish *sancti peregrini*', pp 142–53. One of the earliest mentions of Erhard is in the list of diocesan founders in the Salzburg *Verbrüderungsbuch* compiled under its Irish bishop Virgilius (d. 784). Although this also includes one of the earliest references to Kilian of Würzburg, it is uncertain if Virgilius considered Erhard a compatriot. See D. Ó Riain-Raedel, 'St Kilian and the Irish network in early Carolingian Europe' in W.R. Keller and D. Schlüter (eds), '*A fantastic and abstruse Latinity?' Hiberno-Continental cultural and literary interactions in the Middle Ages*, Studien und Texte zur Keltologie 12 (Münster, 2017), pp 31–53 and D. Ó Riain-Raedel, 'Wide-reaching connections': the list of abbots from Iona in the *Liber confraternitatum ecclesiae S. Petri* in Salzburg' in E. Mullins and D. Scully (eds), *Listen, O Isles, unto me: studies in medieval word and image in honour of Jennifer O'Reilly* (Cork, 2011), pp 60–72. **74** […] *beatus Herhardus, in Hybernia natus et conversatus, sanctitate magnificus, dignitate episcopus in civitate que dicitur Artmacha*, '[…] the blessed Erhard, born and raised in Ireland, magnificent in sanctity, holding the dignity of a bishop in a city called Armagh': D. Ó Riain, 'The Schottenklöster and the legacy of the Irish *sancti peregrini*', p. 143; S. Weber, 'Die Konstruktion eines fabulösen ›irischen‹ Heiligenlebens? Der heilige Albert, Regensburg und die Iren' in D. Walz and J. Kaffanke OSB (eds), *Irische Mönche in Süddeutschland. Literarisches und*

destined to find his last resting place next to the tomb of St Erhard in the Niedermünster.[75]

This narrative, which was first aired in the *Schottenkloster*'s *Vita Sti Albarti*, may have been written in the context of the discovery of a further tomb in the vicinity of that of Erhard in the aftermath of a fire in 1152.[76] The narrative was revisited in the thirteenth-century *Libellus* whose author added a third saint to the group, Hildulf by name.[77] While all these texts relate later versions of the narrative, one may wonder whether Marianus and his companions had already made use of Erhard's Irish connection, however tenuous, in order to receive preferred treatment in the Niedermünster. In this way, the *Schottenkloster* scriptorium possibly also made clever use of a 'single ambiguous expression' in the Life of Niedermünster's patron saint Erhard in order to forge a close bond between the two houses, perhaps in support of the Irish women living there. The *Vita Albarti* would then join the *Visio Tnugdali* in including the Irish women in the author's target audience and it may be no coincidence that both texts were written around the middle of the twelfth century. The kings mentioned in the *Visio* were singled out for their support of the monastic institutions in both Munster and Regensburg, while the *Vita* extolled the merits of *peregrinatio*, depicting Albart and Erhard leaving Ireland on the advice of an unnamed bishop of Lismore (Co. Waterford).[78] The female Irish aristocrats had indeed 'left behind everything they possessed', only to live out their lives near the tombs of the two saints in Regensburg.

As the remains of their library show, the nuns/canonesses of Niedermünster enjoyed (and provided) a first-class education, as is also shown by their literary interests and correspondence.[79] They are known to have entertained an extensive correspondence (often described as 'Love letters') with their (male) teachers in an unspecified monastery but among their correspondents were also recipients like Hildegard of Bingen (d. 1179).[80] One may wonder whether this visionary nun, who wrote a Life of St Disibod, alleging him to be of Irish descent, might have relied on information received from Regensburg.[81] While this is mere speculation, the scribal activity of the twelfth-century women at Niedermünster is well documented and, just as Marcus had sent his *Visio Tnugdali* to Abbess 'G' to have it copied and corrected, the Benedictine monk,

kulturelles Wirken der Iren im Mittalalter (Heidelberg, 2009), pp 229–304.   **75** Apart from the head reliquaries of the two saints, now preserved in a Gothic shrine, other secondary relics of Erhard included a stole and an ivory staff ('Erhardistab'), both of twelfth-/thirteenth-century date: Risse, *Niedermünster in Regensburg*, p. 127.   **76** The tomb may have been discovered in 1146 when abbess Richiza commissioned Lombardic masons to build a new Romanesque church: Risse, *Niedermünster in Regensburg*, p. 42; D. Ó Riain, 'The *Schottenklöster* and the legacy of the Irish *sancti peregrini*', pp 144–5.   **77** Ó Riain, 'The *Schottenklöster* and the legacy of the Irish *sancti peregrini*', pp 152–3.   **78** *Qui non reliquerit omnia qui possidet, non potest meus est discipulus*: Ó Riain-Raedel, 'Cashel and Germany: the documentary evidence', p. 183.   **79** Dirmeier, 'Regensburg – ein "Idealtypus der Urbanität", p. 124.   **80** Risse, *Niedermünster in Regensburg*, pp 186–7.   **81** The Life of Disibod, written in 1172, is edited in *Acta Sanctorum* July II, pp 581–97; cf. J. Kenney, *Sources*, pp 513–14. In this Life, St Disibod, born of aristocratic parents, left his native *Hibernia* in the seventh century with Gillilaldus, Clemens and Sallust, and travelled for ten years through Gaul, before he settled at the river Nahe in what is now Disibodenberg, where Hildegard had spent her early years.

Master Idung, sent his *Dialogus duorum monachorum*, which was completed in 1153, to Abbess 'K' of Niedermünster (probably Kunigunde) with the express wish that it be given to her nuns/canonesses, not only to copy the text carefully but also to correct and improve his Latin, surely a strange request from a *rector scholarum* of the cathedral school.[82] If this and the evidence provided by the *Visio* are reliable, these scriptoria must have been renowned for their learning and scribal prowess, exemplified also, perhaps, by their Irish inmates, in continuation of a scribal tradition established by their male compatriots a century or so earlier.

By the twelfth century, then, an Irish link could be claimed for all three Regensburg female monasteries, a situation arguably influenced by the *Schottenkloster*, in a combined effort 'to exploit and build upon the positive legacy associated with the Irish monastic and missionary tradition on the Continent in the early medieval period'.[83] The nuns are likely to have agreed with the motto provided by the author of the *Vita Mariani*: 'I will commend to you why our predecessors and we also, the poor of Christ, following from a western land naked the naked Christ for the salvation of our souls, leaving behind our homeland and our dear relatives out of love and desire for a heavenly life.'[84] Sadly, their names apart, they did not leave any obvious traces in Regensburg and, as the following will demonstrate, not many more in Ireland.

THE IRISH-REGENSBURG CONNECTIONS: POSSIBLE ORIGINS

The Irish nuns in Regensburg most likely came from the same region as their male compatriots and one may assume that they had already received an adequate education in Ireland before they set out on their travels.[85] As discussed above, there are quite a few references to scribal activity in Niedermünster during the twelfth century but whether Irish women were involved is not known.[86] As seen above, however, Marcus sent the *Visio Tnugdali* to Abbess 'G' 'for copying under your vigilance'.[87] If this can be taken literally, the text would have been in Irish script and somebody in the Mittelmünster scriptorium would have been needed to convert this into Carolingian letters. However tempting this suggestion may be, it is much more likely that Marcus had been resident in the *Schottenkloster* for quite some time, and would by then have adjusted to the local script.

No firm conclusions can be drawn as regards the literacy of Irish female religious in the twelfth century. In the *Visio*, Marcus credited St Malachy with the founding of

82 Risse, *Niedermünster in Regensburg*, p. 187.   **83** D. Ó Riain, 'The *Schottenklöster* in the world: identity, independence and integration' in E. Hovden, C. Lutter and W. Pohl (eds), *Meanings of community across medieval Eurasia: comparative approaches* (Leiden, 2016), pp 388–416 at p. 397. **84** Weber, *Iren auf dem Kontinent*, pp 92–4.   **85** Alternatively, they may have been sent to Regensburg as girls for their education, as was often the case with their German aristocratic counterparts. See Risse, *Niedermünster in Regensburg*, p. 57.   **86** On the education at Niedermünster, see Risse, *Niedermünster in Regensburg*, pp 186–7.   **87** Picard and de Pontfarcy, *The vision of Tnugdal*, p. 109.

fifty-four congregations of monks, canons and nuns 'to whom he provided all the necessities of life and kept nothing at all for himself'.[88] If he founded any female communities in Munster before his death in 1148, their records do not survive; nor is it known whether the *Schottenklöster* daughter houses at Rosscarbery, Co. Cork, and, possibly, Cashel, Co. Tipperary, also functioned as recruiting houses for female Benedictines.[89] As has been shown by Marie Therese Flanagan, Malachy's foundations for the most part housed Cistercian monks and Augustinian canons, with little evidence for nuns.[90] Indeed, as Flanagan states, 'recovering information about the role of women religious in the medieval period is notoriously difficult, but especially so in relation to the twelfth-century church, given the overall paucity of evidence'.[91]

The Irish women at Regensburg are likely to have shared a Munster provenance with their male counterparts, whose writings repeatedly attest to an interest in the province's affairs, the *Visio Tnugdali* being just one of these texts. If the nuns were skilled in manuscript writing, where would they have acquired this skill? Also, which women were allowed to undertake the *peregrinatio* in the first place, and in what way would they have been sponsored by their assumedly aristocratic families. In spite of Marcus's praise for Tnugdal's patron, Cormac mac Carthaig, there is no evidence to show that he founded a female religious house comparable to his foundation of Gill Abbey in Cork, nor is anything known of the twelve churches he is said to have founded in Lismore, Co. Waterford.[92] There are the remnants of a church at Mahoonagh, Co. Limerick, where he was killed in his 'house' in 1138. This appears to have Romanesque features, but no indications as to its founder, occupants or rule are extant.[93] Overall, when Irish nunneries first appear in late twelfth-century documents, they are said to have followed the Augustinian rule.[94]

Clare Abbey, Co. Clare, and its patrons

The charter allegedly given to Clare Abbey by Domnall Ua Briain in 1159 has been shown to be a fifteenth-century forgery issued by Thaddeus Mac Craith, bishop of Killaloe.[95] While the text may be an attempt to reclaim properties alienated from Clare

---

88 Ibid., p. 155.   **89** D. Ó Riain-Raedel, 'Cashel and Germany: the documentary evidence', pp 179–80, 182–3, 215; D. Ó Riain, 'New light on the history of St Mary's priory, Rosscarbery', *JCHAS*, 113 (2008), 56–68.   **90** Flanagan, *Transformation*, pp 123–35 (Cistercian monasticism), pp 136–54 (Customs of Arrouaise), pp 154–61 (others). For a comprehensive survey of male and female Augustinian observance, see Collins, 'The archaeology of Augustinian nuns in later medieval Ireland', pp 87–92 and her contribution to this volume. For the beginnings, see also *MRHI*, pp 307–9.   **91** Flanagan, *Transformation*, p. 73.   **92** On Gill Abbey, see *MRHI*, pp 167–8; E. Bolster, *A history of the diocese of Cork from the earliest times to the Reformation*, pp 74–8, 95–101, 135–40, 199, 296–7; Hall, *Women*, pp 87–9. The nunnery founded by the Mac Carthaig family in Ballymacadane appears to be of fifteenth-century date: *MRHI*, p. 513; Hall, *Women*, pp 89–100. For the reference to Lismore, see S. Ó hInnse (ed.), *Miscellaneous Irish annals (AD 1114–1437)* (Dublin, 1947), s.a. 1138.   **93** T.J. Westropp, 'A survey of the ancient churches in the county of Limerick', *PRIA*, 25 (1905), 325–480, at 414–15.   **94** E. Bhreathnach, 'The *Vita Apostolica* and the origin of Augustinian canons and canonesses' in Browne and Ó Clabaigh, *Households*, pp 1–27.   **95** For an edition and analysis see Flanagan, *Charters*, pp 325–31. For earlier attempts to decipher

4.5 Clare Abbey, Co. Clare. Image © Frank Coyne.

Abbey over the years, at least part of it is likely to retain earlier material, and its description of Domnall as 'king of Limerick' reflects twelfth-century rather than fifteenth-century reality. Domnall did not succeed to the kingship of Thomond until 1168 and a foundation date of 1159 for the abbey is not reconcilable with his reign, which may be the reason why it was corrected by later commentators to 1189, a date since generally used. Domnall was reputed to have been a great church founder but the source document could have contained an oblique reference to an (unofficial) foundation date of 1159, possibly by Domnall's father Toirdelbach (d. 1167), a suggestion that lends weight to the argument that Abbot Gregorius of the Regensburg *Schottenkloster* may have been associated with the abbey before his consecration after 1150. While an official act of foundation is likely to have taken place during Domnall's reign, the abbey is not securely documented until 1216.[96] The abbey's architecture,

the text, which was then believed to be genuine, see A. Gwynn and D. Gleeson, *A history of the diocese of Killaloe*, pp 201–5. The monastery was said to be situated in 'the place that is Kimony', possibly a reference to an existing foundation (Kilmoney?). See L. McInerney, *Clerical and learned lineages of medieval Co. Clare: a survey of the fifteenth-century papal registers* (Dublin, 2014), pp 115–17; idem, 'A 1555 papal *bulla* for Clare Abbey', *JRSAI*, 141 (2011), 128–48; T.J. Westropp, 'The Augustinian houses of the County Clare: Clare, Killone and Inchicronan', *JRSAI*, 30 (1900), 118–35; *MRHI*, p. 162; G. Hull and S. Joubert, 'Medieval monastic occupation and post-medieval military activity at Clare Abbey, Co. Clare', *The Other Clare: Journal of the Shannon Archaeological and Historical Society*, 32 (2008), 21–6. **96** Flanagan, *Charters*, pp 165–6; McInerney,

which has yet to be studied in detail, shows few signs of a twelfth-century date but recent excavations outside the western wall by Graham Hull have recovered activity stretching from the eleventh century to the early thirteenth century, which would give credence to an earlier foundation (Fig. 4.5).[97]

The Mac Craith cleric responsible for the forged charter was bishop of Killaloe and his interest in Clare Abbey was well founded since, from at least the fifteenth century onwards, the family of Clann Chraith acted as hereditary coarbs of Clare Abbey. Indeed, the family had a history of producing 'career-minded clerics, many of whom were appointed to higher positions'.[98] A family member is recorded in a papal bull of 1555 in connection with Clare Abbey as '*Mac Crath nisi Brican…al[ias] Kylbrigan ex*', in reference to the ancient site of Kilbreckan, near Clare Abbey, which owes its name to St Brecán, whose cult was promoted by the Uí Briain in the twelfth century.[99] As Luke McInerney has argued, the residence of the abbots of Clare Abbey may have been located at Kilbreckan, where, as was often the custom among the Augustinians, the abbot's house was located away from the monastery, here on a site where the abbot's kin-group had proprietorial interests.[100] In the present context, this may be important as St Brecán was awarded special praise in the Life of St Flannán of Killaloe where he is described as the outstanding teacher who fostered and educated many of the future saints of Ireland.[101]

If there was a link between Clare Abbey and Abbot Gregorius in Regensburg, it may have found expression in the high praise given to St Brecán as educator of saints, thereby identifying as a centre of learning the monastery in which he himself was tutored. Gregorius may have brought back to Regensburg dossiers of Clare saints (arguably copied in the abbey), as he is known to have visited Ireland on a number of occasions, once before Muirchertach Ua Briain died in 1151 and again in 1163/6, when he witnessed a miracle in Lismore.[102] Although evidence is scarce, the abbey may thus

'A 1555 papal *bulla* for Clare Abbey', 133, 136. The list of witnesses provides no help for dating to 1159, or 1189, but the presence of 'B', bishop of Limerick, may point to an involvement of Briccius / Brictius, who may have joined one of the *Schottenklöster* after retirement. See Ó Riain-Raedel, 'Irish kings and bishops in the *memoria* of the German *Schottenklöster*', 396.   **97** Graham Hull, 'N18 Ennis bypass and N85 western relief road, Clare Abbey, Co. Clare' (2008). For St Brecán, see Ó Riain, *Dictionary*, pp 112–13.   **98** For interaction between members of old-established monasteries and the new religious orders, see McInerney: *Clerical and learned lineages*, pp 59–86.   **99** St Brecán gave name to Kilbreckan in the parish of Doora, Co. Clare, where a church and holy well still survive, although his main association is with Tempall Brecáin on Inis Mór. The present-day nearby church of Doora was probably Brecán's church and may be the same as the chapel called 'Carntemple' in Dooragh parish, consisting of 'very ancient and massive foundations of an oratory in townland of Noughaval', see Gwynn and Gleeson, *A history of the diocese of Killaloe*, pp 33, 323, 328. The connections with Clare saints mentioned in the Life of Flannán continues in the nearby church site of Killoe, which is arguably dedicated to St Lua, eponym of Killaloe. See Westropp, 'Augustinian houses of Co. Clare', 126.   **100** McInerney, 'A 1555 papal *bulla* for Clare Abbey'.   **101** D. Ó Corráin, 'Foreign connections and domestic politics: Killaloe and the Uí Bhriain in twelfth-century hagiography' in D. Whitelock, R. McKitterick and D. Dumville (eds), *Ireland in early medieval Europe* (Cambridge, 1982), pp 213–31, at pp 217–18.   **102** The event which occasioned the miracle took place in 1163, but when Gregorius subsequently visited Lismore is uncertain, perhaps on the occasion of a synod held

have existed before Domnall Ua Briain's alleged foundation and, if there is any truth in Abbot Gregorius' previous connection with Clare Abbey, he might well have persuaded Muirchertach Ua Briain to give the abbey financial support, thus bringing about fresh building activity.[103]

Many members of the Uí Briain family can be linked directly to ecclesiastical foundations in Ireland and Germany and their frequent commemoration in the Regensburg necrology confirms the support received from them. Some eight kings are remembered, including Brian Boru (d. 1014), his son Donnchad (d. 1064), Muirchertach (d. 1119), Conchobar (d. 1142), Muirchertach (d. 1151), Domnall (d. 1194), Donnchad (d. 1242) and Conchobar na Siudane (d. 1268).[104] If there is one who is singled out in the *Schottenkloster* documents, it is Conchobar '*Slapar Salach*' (d. 1142), as named in the *Libellus*, and described in the necrology as *frater noster* and in the *Libellus* as *fundator noster*. In a supplication to the papal curia in 1420, abbot Donatus of the *Schottenkloster* asked for confirmation of the stipulation attributed to Conchobar, here called 'former king of Ireland', that only Irish monks should be admitted as monks or abbots.[105]

It was Conchobar who received the first fundraising expedition to Ireland, led by Gregorius's predecessor Christianus Mac Carthaig, and he is encountered in the *Visio Tnugdali*, together with his inveterate enemy, Donnchad Mac Carthaig, brother of the more famous Cormac. We are told that he merited his place in the *campus letitie* because, when sick for a long time, he vowed to become a monk (perhaps following the example of his uncle Muirchertach), apparently at Killaloe, where he died in 1142.[106] No foundation can be directly linked to him but, since Conchobar who (together with his brother Toirdelbach) was responsible for the bestowal of the Munster kingship on Cormac Mac Carthaig, his rule coincided with a peaceful seven-year phase in Munster politics. If the internal politics at the Regensburg *Schottenkloster* mirrored those at home, it may also have been a period of fruitful collaboration. One would expect Conchobar to have attempted to emulate the building activities of his ally Cormac Mac Carthaig, who commenced his eponymous chapel in Cashel in 1127 and had it consecrated in 1134, before he met his death in 1138 (at the instigation of Conchobar's brother Toirdelbach). However, it was Domnall Mór Ua Briain, son of Toirdelbach, who emerged in the literature as the main founder of monasteries, and this may have prompted Thaddeus Mac Craith to claim him as the founder of Clare Abbey.[107] According to a seventeenth-century source, his son, Donnchad Cairbrech, followed his father's example by founding and endowing no fewer than eighty monasteries.[108]

---

there in 1166 which all bishops of Munster attended. See Ó Riain-Raedel, 'Cashel and Germany: the documentary evidence', p. 211.   **103** Breatnach, *Die Regensburger Schottenlegende*, pp 20, 263.   **104** Listed in Ó Riain-Raedel, 'Irish kings and bishops in the *memoria* of the German *Schottenklöster*'.   **105** Breatnach, *Die Regensburger Schottenlegende*, p. 238; McInerney, *Clerical and learned lineages*, p. 83.   **106** Ó Riain-Raedel, 'Irish kings and bishops in the *memoria* of the German *Schottenklöster*', p. 399; Picard and de Pontfarcy, *The vision of Tnugdal*, p. 143.   **107** The charters are in favour of Holy Cross Abbey, Brictius, bishop of Limerick, Kilcooly Abbey and, possibly spuriously, Clare Abbey. In contrast to the last, the other charters provide strong indications of papal and German imperial charter usage: Flanagan, *Charters*, pp 127–74.   **108** McInerney, quoting Antonius Bruodinus: *Clerical and learned lineages*, p. 81. He reputedly

Dál Cais sponsorship of church building has been extensively covered by Donnchadh Ó Corráin but foundation dates are at times difficult to assess.[109] As is shown by Marie Therese Flanagan, many of the Irish kings who supported native monasteries (as seen in the case of the notices inserted into the Book of Kells between 1033 and 1161) were just as eager to sponsor the houses of the newly arrived foreign orders.[110] In how far benefactions to native monasteries continued after this still needs to be ascertained. During the twelfth-century reform, many of the older communities were absorbed into the diocesan system and, in the case of Killaloe, which became a diocesan centre in 1111 under the patronage of St Flannán, coarbs were still recorded in the twelfth century. Surprisingly, however, no Augustinian chapter seems to have been introduced at the cathedral in Killaloe and no monastery of the order was built in the vicinity, as happened, for example, at Cork.[111] Many of the lesser houses may have been absorbed into the newly introduced orders and Augustinian religious houses may not only have taken over some of the personnel of the older churches but also continued to promote the cults of local saints.[112] Transmission of power may, therefore, have been gradual and, as far as is known, uncontested.

Thirteenth-century Uí Briain connections with Regensburg

The *Schottenkloster* necrology provides further evidence of the connections between Regensburg and Thomond by commemorating Donnchad Cairbrech Ua Briain (d. 1242) as *piae memoriae Donatus Karbrah Rex Rauminensis* (7 March).[113] In addition, *Sabba comitissa soror nostra*, commemorated on 6 April, can be identified as Donnchad's wife Sadb, whose death in 1241 is reported by the Annals of Innisfallen.[114] Her father,

founded the Dominican priory at Limerick and the Franciscan friary in Ennis. See Gwynn and Gleeson, *Killaloe*, pp 268–71. **109** D. Ó Corráin, 'Dál Cais-church and dynasty', *Ériu*, 24 (1973), 52–63; see also T. Ó Carragáin, 'Patterns of patronage: churches, round towers and the Dál Cais kings of Munster (*c.*950–1050)' in R. Stalley (ed.), *Medieval art and architecture in Limerick and south-west Ireland. British Archaeological Association Conference Transactions Series*, 34 (Leeds, 2011), pp 23–41. **110** Flanagan, *Transformation*, pp 164–6. On the problem of Cistercian foundation dates, see C. Swift, 'Lands that time forgot: the early Cistercian settlement of Monasternenagh, Co. Limerick', *Proceedings of the Harvard Celtic Colloquium*, 38 (2018), 259–304. **111** Gwynn and Gleeson, *Killaloe*, pp 5–15; Coarbs of St Flannán are recorded up until the eleventh century: *MRHI*, pp 86–7. 'Rodericus Luensis abbas', commemorated in the necrology on 1 April, would seem to refer to *Ruaidhri, comharba Flannáin* of the Clann Eodach (i.e., the Uí Maoldúin?), a branch of the Dál Cais, who, using a generation count in a genealogy, lived in the latter part of the twelfth century. See Ó Riain-Raedel, 'Das Nekrolog', pp 27, 63, 110. **112** As Flanagan has demonstrated, Monasterboice seems to have lapsed as a monastic community, 'certainly, its decline into obscurity coincides with the establishment of Mellifont [in 1142], with which it would have to compete for lay patronage and funds'. Indeed, the personnel at Mellifont might have been recruited from the older monastery and the new foundation proceeded to foster the cult of St Buite, the eponymous saint of Monasterboice, and commissioned his Life. Flanagan, *Transformation*, pp 162–3. **113** Ó Riain-Raedel, 'Irish kings and bishops in the *memoria* of the German *Schottenklöster*', 398. Donnchad's day of death is known from the inscription on his (now lost) epitaph in the Dominican priory of Limerick, which records his death on 8 March 1241; it is given as 7 March in the necrology. See Begley, *Limerick*, p. 349. **114** Ó Riain-Raedel, 'Das Nekrolog', p. 63; S. Mac Airt (ed.), *The Annals of Inisfallen: MSS Rawlinson B503* (Dublin 1951),

Donnchad Ua Cennétig, is likewise mentioned as *Duncanus Kennedie nobilis Scotus* on 6 May.[115] Donnchad Cairbrech and Sadb had six known children, of which the eldest, Conchobar na Siudane (d. 1268), succeeded to the kingship of Thomond; he is remembered in the Regensburg necrology as king of Ireland: *Cornelius Obrin Rex Hiberniae* (22 May) and his day of death is corroborated by the Annals of Innisfallen.[116] The same title was accorded to Donnchad's father, Domnall Mór, who is commemorated on 3 May as *Donallus rex Hyberniae*.[117] All of these names are underlined in the seventeenth-century copy by the scribe who may have been following the example of his *Vorlage*.

This cluster of related Ua Briain family members also figures in three charters given in favour of the monastery of Cîteaux. The first two were given in 1224 x 1226, one by Donnchad and his wife Sabina, another by nobles of Thomond. The third, in which Conchobar pledged to deliver the funds promised by his father Donnchad, was issued in 1251 x 1254.[118] Sabina was here used as the Latin version of the name Sadb, whose father, Donncúan Ua Cennétig, lord of Airmumu (Ormond), also makes an appearance, together with his wife Gormlaith, in the charter given by the nobles of Thomond and the leaders of well-known Dál Cais families. The congruence of this group with those remembered in the necrology is telling and one may assume that other members of the Dál Cais nobility are hidden among some unidentifiable Irish *comites* and *laici* in the necrology who may have issued comparable letters or charters pledging funds for the Regensburg *Schottenkloster*.

Killone, Co. Clare

The Clare Abbey charter names the nunnery of Killone as one of its possessions and there is no reason to doubt this statement (Plate 5).[119] The nunnery receives its first mention in 1242 but an association with the nearby male religious house may have existed previously. By the later Middle Ages, at the latest, a close connection between Killaloe, the ceremonial seat of the Uí Briain, and Killone is attested, and this suggests that the nunnery was an *Eigenkloster* of the family which provided all three recorded abbesses.[120] The first of these was Sláine whose death as 'abbess of Cell Eóin, the most pious, the most charitable, and the most generous woman in all Munster' is recorded in 1259 (AI). She was a daughter of Donnchad Cairbrech and Sadb and a sister of Conchobar na Siudane, who is known from both the Regensburg necrology and the

s.a. 1241: 'Sadb, daughter of Ó Cennétig [and] wife of Donnchad Cairprech, died'. **115** Ó Riain-Raedel, 'Das Nekrolog', p. 65. On the Uí Chinnéide, see Gwynn and Gleeson, *Killaloe*, pp 149–50. **116** Ó Riain-Raedel, 'Irish kings and bishops in the *memoria* of the German Schottenklöster', p. 401; Flanagan, *Charters*, p. 371. Conchobar Ó Briain, i.e., king of Tuadmumu and head of the Gaedil of Ireland, and his son Ioán and other nobles, were slain on the Tuesday [i.e., 22 May] before Pentecost by Diarmait, son of Muirchertach Ó Briain: *Annals of Inisfallen*, s.a. 1269. **117** Ó Riain-Raedel, 'Irish kings and bishops in the *memoria* of the German Schottenklöster', p. 400. **118** Flanagan, *Charters*, pp 357–72. **119** On history and architecture, see T.J. Westropp, 'The Augustinian houses of the Co. Clare'; *MRHI*, pp 321–2; Gwynn and Gleeson, *Killaloe*, pp 206–8. Killone and its daughter houses are discussed in Hall, *Women*, pp 74–6 and by Collins in her contribution to this volume. **120** The Meic Consaidín were descended from Considine, bishop of Killaloe (d. 1194), brother of Domnall Ua Briain: McInerney, *Clerical and learned lineages*, p. 56. For the abbesses of Killone, see Gwynn and Gleeson, *Killaloe*, pp 207–8.

Cîteaux charters. Whether there were previous abbesses is not known but Sláine's appearance ties in neatly with the removal of the royal residence of the Uí Briain from Limerick city to Clonroad, now near Ennis, Co. Clare, by Donnchad Cairbrech *c*.1210.[121] The new residence was situated at an important crossing point of the river Fergus, close by Clare Abbey and less than five kilometres from Killone.[122]

While Clare Abbey may have been established on or near an already existing religious foundation dedicated to St Brecán, there is no evidence of an earlier church at Killone, which may well have developed as a companion house of Clare Abbey for women religious. The canonesses would have depended on Clare Abbey for the provision of priests for sacramental needs. St Peter's priory in Limerick, which is also said to have been founded by Domnall, may have been used as the nunnery's 'town house' in the diocesan and administrative centre of Limerick.[123]

The writing and transmission of history and hagiography

Notwithstanding the dubious nature of the charter, and the uncertainty surrounding the date of its foundation, Clare Abbey emerged as the dominant Augustinian priory in Dál Cais, where it possibly supplied an 'official' scriptorium for the Uí Briain. The possession of the coarbship by the Meic Craith clerical family, which is documented from the fifteenth century onwards, led Luke McInerney to suspect that Séan mac Ruaidrí, son of the Ruaidrí Mac Craith whom the annals style *ollamh Leithe Mogha le dán* (ollamh of the southern half of Ireland in poetry) on his death in 1343, may have compiled the mid-fourteenth century *Caithréim Thoirdhealbhaigh* at Clare Abbey.[124] The Meic Craith were known as chronicler-poets of the Uí Briain from at least the eleventh century onwards and may also have been responsible for the previous records on which the text is based, which, in that case, would have been kept at Clare Abbey.[125] McInerney points out that, although the text shows the influence of a bardic school, the sources used, which included annals, point to an ecclesiastical milieu. Importantly in the present context, these sources also seem to have included a necrology. The keeping of necrologies was extremely rare in medieval Ireland but the obits of Munster kings and bishops in the *Schottenkloster* necrology must have been drawn from one or more similar Irish documents. It is hardly conceivable that a messenger would have

---

121 After abandoning their traditional residence at Kincora (Killaloe) at some time before it was burnt in 1119, the Uí Briain settled in Limerick and, after 1210, in Clonroad. See B. Ó Dálaigh, 'History of an O'Brien stronghold: Clonroad, *c*.1210–1646', *Journal of the North Munster Archaeological Society*, 29 (1987), 16–31. Limerick had been a stronghold of the Uí Briain since the late tenth century, see Flanagan, *Transformation*, pp 147–9.   **122** Ó Dálaigh, 'History of an O'Brien stronghold: Clonroad, *c*.1210–1646', 21.   **123** Gwynn suggests that some later Augustinian nunneries may have followed the Rule of St Benedict in the initial stages of their establishment: *MRHI*, p. 322; St Peter's Cell was probably identical with Monaster ne Callow Duffe or Black Abbey in Limerick, Begley, *Limerick*, p. 377. Monasternicalliagh (Ballynagallagh) near Lough Gur in Co. Limerick, although perhaps a Norman foundation, may have been later added to the Killone group: *MRHI*, p. 313; Hall, *Women*, p. 89.   **124** L. McInerney, 'Was *Caithréim Thoirdhealbhaigh* written at Clare Abbey in the mid-fourteenth century?', *The Other Clare: Journal of the Shannon Archaeological and Historical Society*, 45 (2021), 26–32.   **125** Séan Mac Craith is styled as 'the hereditary historian of the Dalcassian kings' in Gwynn and Gleeson,

PLATES

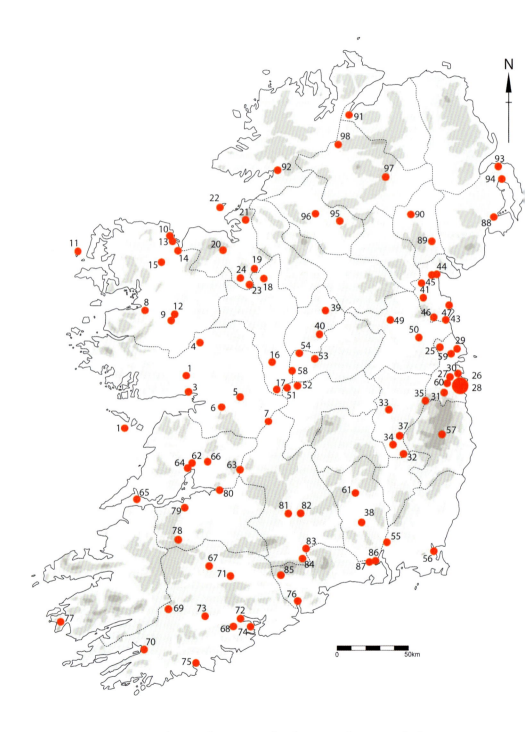

1. Map showing places associated with women religious in Ireland, mentioned in the text. Drawn by Frank Coyne.

Map no.	Place name mentioned in text	County	Map no.	Place name mentioned in text	County
1	Annaghdown	Galway	51	Clonmacnoise	Offaly
2	Aran Islands	Galway	52	Lemanaghan	Offaly
3	Galway	Galway	53	Ballymore Loughsewdy (Plary)	Westmeath
4	Kilcreevanty	Galway	54	Bethlehem Lough Ree	Westmeath
5	Kilreekil	Galway	55	New Ross	Wexford
6	Loughrea	Galway	56	Wexford	Wexford
7	Portumna	Galway	57	Glendalough	Wicklow
8	Aghagower	Mayo	58	Athlone	Westmeath
9	Annagh	Mayo	59	Grace Dieu	Dublin
10	Cell Forgland	Mayo	60	St Mary Del Hogges	Dublin
11	Inishglora	Mayo	61	Kilkenny	Kilkenny
12	Mayo	Mayo	62	Clare Abbey	Clare
13	Moyne	Mayo	63	Killaloe	Clare
14	Rosserk	Mayo	64	Killone	Clare
15	Templenagalliagdoo	Mayo	65	Scattery Island	Clare
16	Cam	Roscommon	66	Tulla	Clare
17	Cloonburren	Roscommon	67	Ardskeagh	Cork
18	Trinity Island, Lough Key	Roscommon	68	Ballymacdane	Cork
19	Carricknahorna	Sligo	69	Ballyvourney	Cork
20	Court	Sligo	70	Bantry	Cork
21	Drumcliffe, Ballynagalliagh	Sligo	71	Clenor	Cork
22	Inishmurray	Sligo	72	Cork	Cork
23	Killaraght	Sligo	73	Inishleena	Cork
24	Moygara Castle	Sligo	74	Legan/Monkstown	Cork
25	Ballymacdun	Dublin	75	Rosscarbery	Cork
26	Dublin (Christchurch)	Dublin	76	Youghal	Cork
27	Finglas	Dublin	77	Killabuonia (Kilbuaine)	Kerry
28	Kilmainham	Dublin	78	Killeedy	Limerick
29	Lusk	Dublin	79	St Catherine's Shanagolden	Limerick
30	Swords	Dublin	80	St Peter's Cell	Limerick
31	Tallaght	Dublin	81	Athassel	Tipperary
32	Graney	Kildare	82	Cashel	Tipperary
33	Kildare	Kildare	83	Inishloughaught	Tipperary
34	Kilkea	Kildare	84	Molough	Tipperary
35	Kilteel	Kildare	85	Lismore	Waterford
36	Oughterard	Kildare	86	Waterford	Waterford
37	Timolin	Kildare	87	Kilculliheen	Waterford
38	Jerpoint	Kilkenny	88	Downpatrick	Antrim
39	Clonbroney	Longford	89	Killevy	Armagh
40	Kilglass	Longford	90	Temple Na Ferta/St Brigit's	Armagh
41	Ardee	Louth	91	Derry	Derry
42	Donoughmore	Louth	92	Donegal	Donegal
43	Drogheda	Louth	93	Bangor	Down
44	Dundalk	Louth	94	Movilla	Down
45	Knock Abbey	Louth	95	Aghavea	Fermanagh
46	Mellifont	Louth	96	Devinish	Fermanagh
47	Termonfeckin	Louth	97	Donoughmore	Tyrone
48	Clonard	Meath	98	Religmaman (Carrickmore)	Tyrone
49	Kells	Meath	99	Urney (Ernaide)	Tyrone
50	Lismullin	Meath			

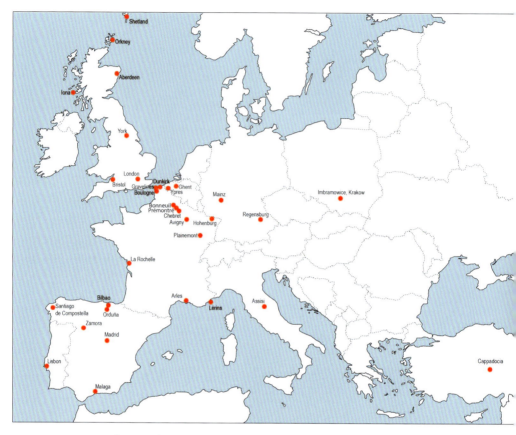

2. Map showing places associated with women religious abroad, mentioned in the text.
Drawn by Frank Coyne.

3. Killeedy, Co. Limerick. Image © Frank Coyne.

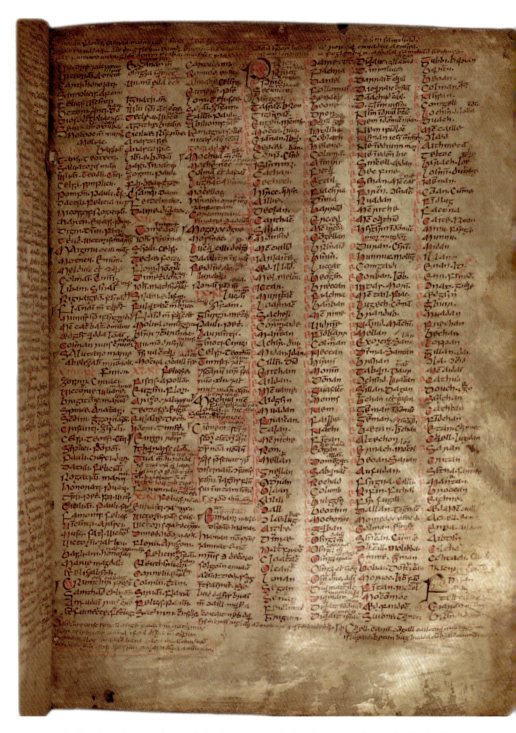

4. The feastday of St Samthann of Clonbroney recorded in the Martyrology of Tallaght (first column, third name from the bottom). UCD Franciscan MS A3, p. 11. Image © UCD-OFM Partnership.

5. Killone, Co. Clare. Image © Frank Coyne.

6. The west doorway of the nunnery church of St Catherine's, Co. Limerick. Image © Tracy Collins.

7. Effigy of a vowess in St Canice's Cathedral, Kilkenny, thought by some to represent
Elicia Butler, abbess of Kilculliheen. Image © Frank Coyne.

8. *Madonna della Misericordia*, Sano di Pietro (1405–81), painting *c.*1440. Image © Wikipedia Commons http://www.aiwaz.net/gallery/sano-di-pietro/gc343.

hanc cum grege t' ardua
in districti die iudicii. dño
incontaminata represen
tan ualeas. ipse te adiu
uare dignetur. Qui cum
deo pře in unitate sps sci
ds uiuit et regnat p o. s.
s. Tunc tradat ei baculu
dicens. Accipe baculum
pastoralis officii. quem p
feras caterue tibi 2 misse
ad exemplum uistre seueri
tatis. et pie correpcionis.
Domine T Orm̄s
deus omps. qui so
rorem moysi mariā pre
euntē cum ceteris uirgini
bus inter cquiuocas unda
cum timpanis et choris
letam ad litus maris ue
nire fecisti: te simplices de
precamur p fideli famu
la tua. Z. que hodie in
cathedra materna super
uniuersas subditas tibi
abbatissa constituitur. ut
ita canonica norma cue
atur amictas famulas
tuas. quatinus ad etiã
gliam te auxiliante cũ

omnibz illis introeat leta
tibi q̃ exultans ai agnis
canens cantica noua. se
quatur agnum quoaiq̃
ierit. ihm xpm dñm nr̃m.
Amen Oremus.
Famulam tuam q̃s
domine tua semper gra
a tue Dicat. et sacu
pabilem ad uitam pdu
cat eternam. P dũ. nr̃m.
Postea pagatur missa
suo ordine. ablatissa sta
te a remotis cum baculo
suo uk in finem misse. Et
dicta. recepta benedictione
epi. abscedat. In missal
latione abbatisse. fiat ut
sup sicut in installatione
abbatis.

Consecracio uirginis
que in diebz solen

ac et enducat : ordies sit
et alias instruat . amicos
et inimicos p̄ tui nois
amore amet et diligat :
humilitatem et utilitate
teneat eque et exerceat .
castimoniam et pudiciā
am corde et corpore āplec
tatur et teneat . pacienciā
et longanimitatem arri
piat atq̄ custodiat . ieiu
nium et abstinenciam stu
deat simul et amet . genu
ui et oronem desideret ar
mugilet : precata sua in
cessanter cum lacrimis z
suspirijs accuset . et te d̄
um omnipotentē corde z
opere circumferat atq̄ de
seruiat . Suscipe te dn̄e
q̄sumus pr̄ omp̄s hāc
famulam tuam quam
de huius seli naufragns
z piaculis erui . et ad mo
nasticam vocare digna
tus es gr̄am : concede p̄pi
cius . ut arctam et angul
tam quam p̄fessa est vi
am igitur teneat . dili
gat atq̄ sectetur : q̄sumus

ad eternā quam in te p̄
seuerantib: p̄mitte dig
natus es gloriam p̄ue
nire mereatur . P̄ dn̄m.
Post hec d̄ euāgelium.
Et p̄fessa remaneat uir̄
altare p̄strata in oracōe
us; ad finem misse . Et osc
ulata manu ep̄i : et ab
eo benedicta recedat ī pace
Incipit benedicio uel
las uidue ul’ uiduar:
Ante euāgelium uel
ad missam ueniat illa ī
uestre consueta : portās se
cum alias uestes fuscas
cum linctramine capitis.
et genuflectens ponat ant
ep̄m ul’ sacerdote sedente . Q
alloquatur eam de p̄posito
castitatis . et sponsione
frā b̄dicat pallium cū

11. Lady Margaret Beaufort by Meynnart Wewyck, *c.*1510, St John's College, Cambridge.
Reproduced by permission of the Master and Fellows of St John's College, Cambridge.

honor tu gaudium. tu in
merore solacium. tu in dubii
bignitate consilium. tu
in iniuria defensio. in tri
bulacione paciencia. in
pauptate habundancia. i
ieiunio cibus: atque in infir
mitate sis ei medicus et
mediana. Per te que
diligere sup omnia appe
tit. quod est professa cus
todiat. ut et hostem anti
quum te auxiliante de
uincat. et uigorum squa
lores expungit. Centenus
sexagesimu fructus domo
decorari omnium que uir
tutum lampadibus exorna
ri: et inter electarum tua
rum uiduarum consorcia
te donante mereatur co
locari. Submisse: P dñ
nmuum nrm. In unitate
eiusdem. sequitur. Oremus
Famulam tuam do
mine tue custodi
a muniat pietatis. ut
uiduitatis sce positum
qd te inspirante suscepit
te protegente semp illesu

custodiat. P dñ.
euangelium offerat si uo
luit. Et sic remaneat ari
ul' iuxta altare pstructa
ut ad communionem. Et tñ
accedat ad epim et comu
nicetur. Et sic finita mis
sa: pstructa gremiu: recipi
at benedictionem episcopi
et recedat.

Oredo ad reclurendum
Ordusuum. Si feria
sit: pauium iaceat in occi
dentali pte ecclie. ut mos
e feminis histare. Si ma'
aulis et laicus ad ostium
chori iaceat. Si dicius ul'
sacerdos: pstratus in me
dio chi nudis pedibus: in
oratione iaceat. Tunc duo
clerici stantes ante gradus
decantent totam letaniam

12. Enclosure of an anchoress, Cambridge Corpus Christ College MS 79, f. 96.
Image © Parker Library, Corpus Christi College, Cambridge.

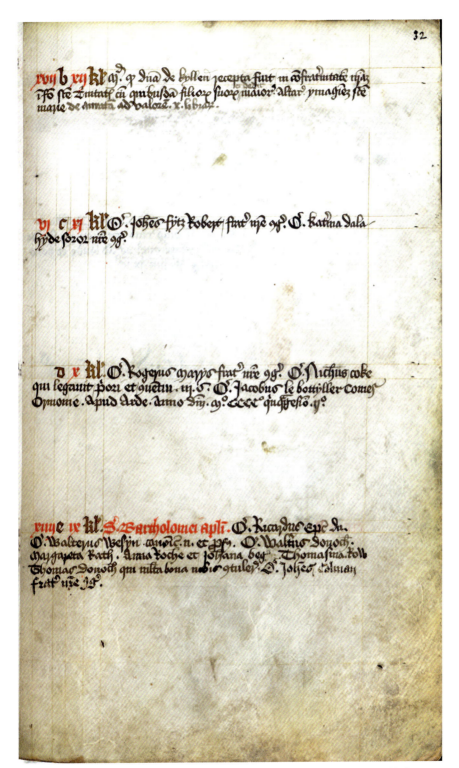

xvij b xij kł aj. q̄ dña de kyllen recepta fuit in cõfraternitate n̄ra ifõ fr̄e ɔmtatı̄ cū quibusda filior̄ suor̄ maior̄ altar̄ ymagier̄ sr̄e marie de anunta ad valore. x. libraŕ.

vj c xj kł. Ơ. Joħes fῑtʒ Robert frͤt ñͤ qg̈. Ơ. katina dala hyde soror ñͤ qg̈.

d x kł. Ơ. Rogeꝰ maypo frͤ ñͤ qg̈. Ơ. Nichꝰ coke qui legauit pon et quetu. iij. s̄. Ơ. Jacobꝰ le botyller comes Ơmome. apud arde. añ o d̄ͥi. aj o ɔɔɔc gͣtrefs. yo

xiiije ix kł. S. Bartholomei apłi. Ơ. Ricardꝰ eps du. Ơ. Walteꝰ Welyn mͣior̄. n̄. et ps̄. Ơ. Waltιɿ donoͨ. mͣgareta kath. amia Roche et Johana bey. Thomasſma toll Thomas donoͨ qui milta bona nɷⁱꝰ gͭules̄ Ơ. Johes̄ calmany frͤt ñͤ yͦ.

14. Portrait of Abbess Mary Butler. Image courtesy of the Benedictine Monastery Archive, Kylemore Abbey, Co. Galway.

been dispatched to Germany soon after each king's death with a view to having him included on the correct day in the Regensburg necrology. It is, therefore, more likely that a comparable record was kept in one of the Munster churches and, in view of the Mac Craith connection, Clare Abbey emerges as one of the main contenders.

Just such a combination of secular lore with a religious text, together with an interest in promoting the fame of lay benefactors, may also lie behind the Lives of such Clare saints as Mochuille and Flannán. The idiosyncrasies of the author of these texts, who also composed the Life of Marianus and was, therefore, resident in Regensburg, have been described by Donnchadh Ó Corráin.[126] The strong Uí Briain bias evident in these two works is not matched by the other two *Magnum Legendarium Austriacum* Lives of saints from the general vicinity of the Shannon area, those of Íte and Senán, the patron saints of the Uí Chonaill Gabra, a branch of the Uí Fhidgente, located on the southern shore of the Shannon estuary, an area now roughly equivalent to the extent of the diocese of Limerick.[127]

Further connections? Killeedy and Shanagolden, Co. Limerick

In the present context examination of a text connected with a female saint such as Íte could be promising, together with an examination of the site most closely linked to the saint, that is Cluain Credail, now Killeedy, in the barony of Glenquin, Co. Limerick (Plate 3).[128] Possible Romanesque fragments at the church testify to a twelfth-century revival but whether it was here that Íte's hagiographical dossier was compiled is uncertain. Furthermore, it may not be without relevance that it and the other local church named for the saint, Kilmeedy (Cell m'Íde), were located in the vicinity of Mahoonagh, near Newcastle West, Co. Limerick, where Cormac Mac Carthaig, eponym of Cormac's chapel at Cashel, was murdered in 1138, 'in his own house'.[129]

Íte's cult may have been cultivated at nearby Shanagolden, where a house of Augustinian canonesses, St Catherine de O'Conyl, was founded, perhaps already in the twelfth century.[130] The architectural history of this nunnery has been comprehensively researched by Tracy Collins who credits John FitzThomas Fitzgerald of Shanid (d. 1261) with its foundation (Plate 6).[131] While the architecture points to a thirteenth-century Norman foundation, a previous secular structure (possibly a chamber-tower or hall house) seems to have been re-used at the west range and, since the nunnery was built on episcopal land, the previous structure may have been associated with the nearby

---

Killaloe, p. 269. **126** Ó Corráin, 'Foreign connections and domestic politics'. **127** On Iniscathaig/ Scattery Island, see Gwynn and Gleeson, *Killaloe*, pp 15–23. Begley, *Limerick*, pp 1–26. **128** T.J. Westropp, 'A survey of the ancient churches in the county of Limerick', 404–5. *MRHI*, p. 392. According to Begley, 'the church was situated in the tuath of Cleanglass, 'the ancient home of the O'Cuilens, lords of the Hy Connail', Begley, *Limerick*, pp 44–50, 111–12, 44–56; *MRHI*, p. 392; Ó Riain, *Dictionary*, p. 375. **129** His murder took place either on 5 July or 23 August: Ó Riain-Raedel, 'Irish kings and bishops in the *memoria* of the German *Schottenklöster*', pp 401–2. Maigh Tamhnach, later Mahoonagh / Castlemahon, later became a Norman manor: Begley, *Limerick*, pp 167–70. **130** Westropp, 'A survey of the ancient churches in the county of Limerick', p. 396. **131** *MRHI*, pp 323–4; Collins, 'The archaeology of Augustinian nuns in later medieval Ireland', pp 93–100; eadem, 'Unveiling female monasticism in later medieval Ireland: survey and excavation at St Catherine's, Shanagolden, Co. Limerick',

manor of the bishops of Limerick.[132] A medieval church also existed to the west of the present village of Shanagolden, and a holy well dedicated to St Senán indicates a possible earlier cult.[133] Importantly, the nunnery is not far from Shanid, later the *caput* of a branch of the Fitzgeralds.[134]

The earlier importance of the site is shown by the successful battle fought here in 834 by the Uí Chonaill Gabra against the Vikings, and also by the local name Shanid (*senaid*), from Latin *senatus*, with the meaning of synod, later a place of assembly.[135] The area around Shanagolden may, therefore, have had special meaning for the Uí Chonaill Gabra, which gave added importance to the nunnery and which possibly led to promotion there of the cult of the saint of Killeedy.

CONCLUSIONS AND POSSIBILITIES

Most of the Lives in the *Magnum Legendarium Austriacum*, including those of Íte and Senán, still await editors and the relationship between the putative 'intermediate circulating collection' at Regensburg and the later Irish collections has yet to be established.[136] If a Regensburg redactor had an input into the shape taken by these two Lives, as can be demonstrated in those of Mochuille and Flannán, we may possibly find in them some hints of the relationship fostered between the Irish women and men in Regensburg. In fact, the Life of Íte describes the two Uí Chonaill Gabra saints as *patronus* and *matrona* respectively, the latter being an unusual expression when '*patrona*' might have been expected. For Elva Johnston this was no more than the usual portrayal of a female saint as 'a nurturer and / or mother, proper depictions for a woman, however holy, that served to reinforce the sexual stereotyping prevalent in early medieval Irish culture'.[137]

Íte's Regensburg Life, however, has several distinctive features that differ from the versions contained in the later Irish collections, and may thus tell us more about its target audience.[138] Of particular interest is the extensive use of biblical parallels, mainly in reference to apostles, including extracts from the pseudo-Isidorian *Liber der Ortu et Obitu Patrum*, which chronicles the various fates endured by the apostles. This text is also cited in the *Libellus*, which shows that a copy of it was to hand in the *Schottenkloster*

PRIA, 119C (2019), 103–71. **132** Collins, 'Unveiling female monasticism', 142. **133** St Catherine's de O'Conyl of Shanagolden (Seanghuala) is first mentioned in documents of the late thirteenth century: Begley, *Limerick*, pp 63, 111, 374–7. See also J. Wardell, 'The history and antiquities of St Catherine's, Old Abbey, County Limerick' (with a description of the conventual buildings by T.J. Westropp), *JRSAI*, 14 (1904), 41–64 at 52–3, 64. **134** Westropp, 'A survey of the ancient churches in the county of Limerick', 398. **135** MacCotter, *Medieval Ireland: territorial, political and economic divisions* (Dublin, 2008), p. 187. **136** D.C. Africa, 'The chronology of the Life of St Íte and the architecture of theft', *Eolas: the Journal of the American Society of Irish Medieval Studies*, 12 (2019), 2–25, at 4. For an edition of the Life, see von Vaupel Klein, *The Lives and times of St Íte of Killeedy*. **137** The use of *matrona* is unusual. See E. Johnston, 'Íte: patron of her people?', *Peritia*, 14 (2000), 421–8 at 425. It recalls the description of Abbess Hemma of Obermünster as *mater peregrinorum*: Weber, *Iren auf dem Kontinent*, pp 112, 122; for the Life, see Africa, 'The chronology of the Life of St Íte'. **138** A comparison of the various manuscript witnesses is provided by Africa, 'The chronology of the Life of St Íte'.

scriptorium.[139] Of special interest are the many references to St Paul, patron of the Mittelmünster nunnery in Regensburg. According to Lisette von Vaupel Klein, this material, which is absent from the Irish collections, was directed at a more cosmopolitan and sophisticated audience.[140] Moreover, it reflects a tendency of *Schottenkloster* redactors to parade their knowledge and impress by emphasizing the holy lives of their saintly predecessors, marked by both striking miracles and ascetic and austere lifestyles. In this way, the Lives were consciously instrumentalized as a means of boosting the status of the twelfth-century Regensburg Irish, women and men. Against this, the 'belligerent and knightly' attitude displayed by Íte in her continental Life, which is accentuated by her description as *ductrix* and *bellatrix*, though out of place in a nunnery, may point to the aristocratic background of many of the Irish in Regensburg.

At the time the Lives were written, Regensburg was, of course, at the centre of crusader spirit, but, as Dorothy Africa has noted, many episodes in Íte's Life also depict the companiable rapport enjoyed between female and male religious, as is brought out by the regular and uncontroversial reciprocal visits depicted in the texts.[141] A clue as to when the Lives were compiled is provided by an episode in the Life of Íte that refers to an event said to have taken place *in nostris temporibus* and draws a comparison between one of the saint's miracles and a similar one related to the Bavarian saint Herluca (d. 1127).[142] A twelfth-century redaction of the text would conform with the dating criteria provided by the Lives of Flannán (and Mochuille), where mention of a recent miracle at Lismore, Co. Waterford is datable to 1163.

Arguably, the revival of the cult of Íte who, after Brigit, was the most important Irish female saint, would have been of interest in both female and male monasteries in Regensburg. Also, in view of the shared Uí Chonaill Gabra patronage of the two saints, Senán's biography might be regarded as a companion text to that of Íte, so that one may well suppose that the same scriptorium was responsible for both texts.[143] Perhaps they were planned with a view to portraying the two saints as Munster equivalents of

---

139 Breatnach, *Die Regensburger Schottenlegende*, pp 151–6.   **140** L. von Vaupel Klein, *The Lives and times of St Íte of Killeedy*, xl–xli; D. Ó Corráin, 'Foreign connections and domestic politics'. The multiple references to the Trinity and biblical figures, notably St Paul, are particularly noteworthy and would repay further investigation.   **141** Dr D. Africa, pers. comm. See also: Africa, 'The chronology of the Life of St Íte', 6. For the various attempts to date the 'original' and the 'common' Life underlying the later recensions, see ibid., and Johnston, 'Íte: patron of her people?'. In the absence of a single text witness before the Life's appearance in the late-twelfth-century *Magnum Legendarium Austriacum*, it is difficult to draw definitive conclusions. **142** L. von Vaupel Klein, *The Lives and times of St Íte of Killeedy*, 6. The reference in this context to 'our beloved priest Gebhard', presumably Gebhard of Bernried (d. 1156), may be of importance. Together with his companion and mentor Paul (author of a Life of Herluca) he founded the Augustinian abbey of St Mang on the outskirts of Regensburg. See C. Märtl, 'Regensburg in den geistigen Auseinandersetzungen des Investiturstreits', *Deutsches Archiv für Erforschung des Mittelalters*, 42 (1986), 145–91 at 179–80. For the connections of Paul and Gebhard with the *Schottenkloster* and their use of Irish manuscript material, see P. Ó Riain, *Feastdays of the saints*, p. 244.   **143** On Íde and Senán, see Ó Riain, *Dictionary*, pp 375–8; 557–60. Ó Riain proposes Abbeyfeale as a possible place of origin of the Life of Íde, but also points to apparent Augustinian influences on the Life, suggestive of links with Rathkeale or Shanagolden: ibid.,

the two patrons of Ireland, Patrick and Brigit, in yet another twelfth-century attempt to stress the early Christianization of Munster.[144]

The political implications of the inclusion of these Lives in the Regensburg collection have yet to be teased out. If based ultimately on base texts produced in Ireland in Munster, the scriptorium, or scriptoria, must be sought there, most likely in an Augustinian religious house eager to provide itself with an 'ancient history'. It is tempting to assume that their composition coincided with the elevation of Inis Cathaig to a diocesan centre in 1152, in which case Clare Abbey, with its connections to Killone, and probable possession of some islands in the Shannon estuary, such as Canon Island, might have played a role.[145] It may be no coincidence that Áed Ua Becháin (*Edanus episcopus Cathagensis*), who died in 1188, is commemorated in the Regensburg necrology on 8 March.[146]

Further examination of the Lives in the *Magnum Legendarium Austriacum* may reveal more information relating to the backgrounds of the Irish women in Regensburg. The time frame indicated by the events portrayed in some of the Lives lies in the 1160/70s. However, if the *Visio Tnugdali* was addressed to an Irish female audience, this must have been already in place *c*.1150, or even earlier, if credence is given to the above mentioned 1126 citation of Brechta Schottin.[147] Furthermore, the known group of Uí Briain sponsors of the *Schottenkloster* about the middle of the thirteenth century would suggest that some Irish female religious may still have been there a century later. The abbots returning from the three fundraising expeditions chronicled in the *Libellus*, which date to the times of Conchobar Ua Briain (d. 1142), Donnchad Mac Carthaig (d. 1142/3) and Muichertach Ua Briain (d. 1168), most likely also brought with them new recruits, arguably including some women.[148]

The Irish women in Regensburg may have left nothing but their names but, as I hope to have shown here, some information may yet be extracted from the literary and hagiographical works of the local Irish community there. Their texts seem also to have carried appeal for a wider Regensburg audience which was apparently eager to learn about the lives led by imaginary or real predecessors of the *Scoti* who lived in their midst. As far as the Irish in Regensburg were concerned, they certainly never tired of reminding their German audience of the *insula sanctorum* they had left behind when embarking on their *peregrinatio*.

pp 376–7; 559.   **144** D. Ó Riain-Raedel, 'The question of the "Pre-Patrician" saints of Munster' in M.A. Monk and J. Sheehan (eds), *Early medieval Munster: archaeology, history and society* (Cork, 1998), pp 17–22; eadem, 'The other paradise: perceptions of Ireland in the Middle Ages' in R. Simek and A. Ivanova (eds), *Between the Islands – and the Continent: papers on Hiberno-Scandinavian-Continental contacts in the early Middle Ages* (Vienna, 2013), pp 167–92.   **145** The dependency of Inis Cathaigh on Clare Abbey, as allegedly claimed in the monastery's charter, is disputed. Gwynn and Gleeson, *Killaloe*, p. 203; *MRHI*, pp 96–7; Flanagan, *Charters*, p. 326; L. McInerney, 'The clerical lineages of Inis Cathaigh', 57–8.   **146** Ó Riain-Raedel, 'Irish kings and bishops in the *memoria* of the German *Schottenklöster*', p. 392.   **147** J.C. Paricius, *Allerneueste und bewährte Historische Nachricht*, p. 197.   **148** Breatnach, *Die Regensburger Schottenlegende*, pp 244, 256, 260. I wish to thank Dr Raymond Dittrich (Bischöfliche Zentralbibliotek Regensburg) and Dr Wolfgang Neiser (Abteilung Kunst- und Denkmalpflege, Kunstsammlungen des Bistums Regensburg) for permission to publish figures 4.1, 4.2 and 4.3.

Putting women in order: a comparison of the medieval women religious of Ballymore-Loughsewdy and Prémontré

YVONNE SEALE

INTRODUCTION

The question of what an *ordo* ('order') was in the Middle Ages, and what constituted membership of one, may seem both obscure and trifling to a general modern audience.[1] Yet the concept of *ordo* was one that historically has mattered a great deal – to many medieval people, and to generations of later historians, including those antiquarian and nineteenth-century scholars whose ideas still shape so much of how we think of medieval Christianity. The term's very prominence in the Middle Ages is what has given rise to so much study of it, especially since *ordo* could be used in such a multiplicity of ways. Giles Constable provides us with a useful working definition of an order as something which a person entered into, something 'marked by a way of life and an internal discipline as well as exterior distinctions and obligations', but equally reminds us of the many questions which we must ask about the realities underpinning the use of the term, and of the disagreements that scholars have had as to how women 'fit' into such medieval schemas.[2]

Understanding the use of the term *ordo*, then and now, requires us to think about concepts of belonging and exclusion, of hierarchy and authority. This is especially the case when studying the history of women religious in the Middle Ages. In trying to better understand what belonging to an 'order' meant for such women, whether there were gendered differences in understandings of membership in a given monastic order, and who got to define the shape and contours of a monastic identity, historians may often find themselves frustrated by the limitations of the source base and by some of the assumptions that permeate the existing historiography.

This chapter will explore some of these issues through a comparative study of women's monastic communities in Ireland and France from approximately the twelfth through to the sixteenth centuries. First, this chapter will undertake an examination of the history and historiography of one house of women religious in the Irish Midlands, that of Loughsewdy in Westmeath. Since its foundation in the early

---

1 For an overview of the development of reformed monastic orders in the high Middle Ages, see G. Melville, 'The institutionalization of religious orders (twelfth and thirteenth centuries)' in Beach and Cochelin, *CHMMLW*, pp 783–802. 2 G. Constable, *Three studies in medieval religious and social thought: the interpretation of Mary and Martha, the ideal of the imitation of Christ, the orders of society* (Cambridge, 1995), pp 255, 259–61.

thirteenth century, this community has been claimed by – or it might be more accurate to say, assigned to – various religious orders, primarily the Cistercian Order. This essay will then more generally survey some communities of women religious in France – primarily in the northern region of Picardy – the affiliations of which with the Premonstratensian Order have often been downplayed in ways that obscure women's presence and roles within that order during the Middle Ages. For both these French and Irish women religious, we shall explore under which circumstances the categorization of their communities into a particular order may help us to better understand their history, and under which it may actually better inform us about the concerns of their male contemporaries or later chroniclers.

None of these communities may have been of high historical importance in its own right – none of them was particularly wealthy or large, nor was home to any influential mystics or theologians, nor served as a major pilgrimage destination.[3] Yet their very ordinariness makes them more compelling as representative of the kinds of female religious communities often overlooked in the historiography and yet most commonly encountered in the medieval landscape – and they were common indeed. Bruce Venarde has argued that by the twelfth century, virtually no one in England or France was 'more than a day's journey from a female monastic community, and most were closer', and the picture in Ireland may not have been much different.[4] Each of these communities would have been profoundly shaped both by the local communities and landscapes of which they were such vibrant parts, and the broader institutional networks or orders of which they may have been members.[5]

THE WOMEN OF BALLYMORE-LOUGHSEWDY

Today, Ballymore is a small town located just to the south of Lough Sewdy and about twenty kilometres west of Mullingar, Co. Westmeath, but in the thirteenth century, it was a borough lying near the western border of the holdings of the de Lacy lordship. Then one of the most powerful families in Ireland, the de Lacys' influence ensured that Ballymore was a prosperous local trade hub, and from 1204 the site of an eight-day fair.[6]

---

3 We have little insight into the devotional lives of these women. As shown below, there is little surviving contemporary documentation associated with Loughsewdy, and nothing either devotional or written by its members. The medieval Premonstratensian Order produced only one notable female mystic, Christina of Hane (*c.*1269–92), who lived in a Premonstratensian community in the Rhineland and who left no writings. For her *vita*, see R. Kirakosian, *The Life of Christina of Hane* (New Haven, CT, 2020). **4** B.L. Venarde, *Women's monasticism and medieval society: nunneries in France and England, 890–1215* (Ithaca, NY, 1997), p. 16. **5** For a broader discussion of this topic, see J. Röhrkasten, 'Regionalism and locality as factors in the study of religious orders' in G. Melville and A. Müller (eds), *Mittelalterliche Orden Und Klöster Im Vergleich. Methodische Ansätze Und Perspektiven*, Vita Regularis. Abhandlungen, 34 (Berlin, 2007), pp 243–68. **6** T. Duffus Hardy (ed.), *Rotuli chartarum in turri Londinensi asservati* (London, 1837), i, pp 136–7. For an overview of the history of the de Lacy family, see C. Veach, *Lordship in four realms: the Lacy family, 1166–1241*, Manchester Medieval Studies, 12 (Manchester, 2014).

This fair would have taken place on a site somewhere between the de Lacys' castle to the north, and to the south a monastery for women, Loughsewdy.[7]

This community of women religious was most likely founded as a Cistercian community by the de Lacys in around 1205.[8] No foundation charter or other contemporary documentation attests to a patronage link between the house and the de Lacys, but it seems highly probable given the proximity of castle and monastery. According to local tradition, Loughsewdy stood not far from the medieval town, on a flat stretch of land that is now sandwiched between two modern housing estates.[9] If so, this means that Loughsewdy was in the kind of secluded but not isolated location that, as Tracy Collins has pointed out, was fairly typical of late medieval Irish houses of women religious; many were located near or sometimes within walled towns or other built environments.[10]

The de Lacys' foundation of such a community would also fit with the general pattern identified by Dianne Hall of the first generation of Anglo-Norman tenants-in-chief in Ireland favouring the establishment of communities of women religious.[11] Doing so permitted them to display their piety, wealth, and dominance in a new land – and in a way perhaps that also offered some plausible deniability about that being an assertion of power in the first place. An instructive parallel here might be the tenures of the roughly contemporary Countesses Jeanne (*c.*1199–1244) and Marguerite (1202–80) of Flanders. These sisters worked hard to assert the independence of their county in the face of the increasingly powerful French kingdom to their south. Erin Jordan has argued that the countesses' establishment of new monastic houses, particularly houses of women, in the hotly contested border region was a display of power that was difficult to contest because it was a display of piety – and indeed, what powerful monarch would want to seem threatened by a mere house of nuns?[12] The de Lacys were the founders or patrons of a number of other monastic institutions in Ireland, including the Augustinian abbey of St Thomas in Dublin, the Benedictine community at Fore in Westmeath, and the Cistercian houses of Bective in Meath, and Beaubec in Louth.[13]

---

7 To avoid confusion, I will refer to the town as Ballymore and the monastic community as Loughsewdy, although both names (together with Lox, Lough Sunderlin and Plary/Clary) were used interchangeably and in a variety of spellings in the medieval and early modern sources. 8 Some sources state a foundation date of 1218, but I have argued elsewhere that this is incorrect. Y. Seale, '*De Monasterio Desolato*: patronage and politics in a frontier Irish convent', *JMMS*, 4 (2015), 23–4. 9 There is some disagreement as to the exact location of the community. See T. Collins, *Female monasticism in medieval Ireland: an archaeology* (Cork, 2021), pp 138, 488, fn. 137. 10 T. Collins, 'Timolin: a case study of a nunnery estate in later medieval Ireland', *Anuario de Estudios Medievales*, 44/1 (2014), 55; T. Collins, 'Isolated in the wilderness? An archaeological exploration of nunneries in the medieval landscape of Ireland' in J. Lyttleton and M. Stout (eds), *Church and settlement in Ireland* (Dublin, 2018), pp 142–56. 11 Hall, *Women*, p. 81. 12 See E. Jordan, *Women, power and religious patronage in the Middle Ages*, The New Middle Ages (New York, 2006), particularly chapter 3. 13 For discussion of the de Lacy patronage practices, see R. Masterson, *Medieval Fore, Co. Westmeath*, Maynooth Studies in Local History, 112 (Dublin, 2014), pp 9–29; J. Hillaby, 'Colonization, crisis-management and debt: Walter de Lacy and the Lordship of Meath, 1189–1241', *Ríocht Na Midhe: Records of Meath Archaeological and Historical Society*, 8:4 (1993), 34. For closer studies of these monastic communities, see A. Gwynn, 'The early history of St Thomas's Abbey, Dublin', *JRSAI*, 84:1 (1954), 1–35; Masterson, *Medieval Fore*; G. Stout

In addition, across their lordship the de Lacys frequently reused earlier ecclesiastical or secular status sites, established parish churches, or granted tithes to religious houses in order to facilitate the colonization process.[14] The reorganization of the diocese of Meath was also key in the consolidation of the de Lacys' power.[15] In addition, female Cistercian communities often functioned as 'high prestige necropolises' and as focal points of support for aristocratic families, particularly those like the de Lacys who found themselves working to exert power in a border region.[16]

When taken together, these probabilities – of location, founder and patronage relationship – provide us a very rough outline sketch of Loughsewdy as a fairly typical foundation for women religious in Ireland during this time period. It is also typical in having extremely little by way of surviving contemporary documentation. We can assume that the women of Loughsewdy observed a daily round of *ora* and *labora* as did most Cistercian communities, although we do not know the precise schedule they may have followed.[17] There are no extant papers from the house itself, and so our most detailed knowledge of Loughsewdy's history comes from references in the papal registers that we can track across the fourteenth and fifteenth centuries. These generally document legal disputes initiated by third parties concerning the nuns' rights as holders of lands, tithes and benefices, and give us glimpses of their prioresses as diligent defenders of their community's rights.[18]

To these fragmentary accounts we can add what we know of the history of Ballymore and its hinterland more generally. Their location on the western border of the de Lacys' lordship was a potentially vulnerable one in times of conflict – which happened with increasing frequency over the course of the Middle Ages. The town was burned multiple times in the 1310s, in 1363, and again in 1394.[19] In the 1420s, an *inquisition post mortem* valued 'the manor of Loxheuedy' as 'worth nothing because it lies waste'.[20] Even allowing for some exaggeration in this description, in the late Middle Ages even the most able prioress would surely have found it a challenge to maintain the viability of her community in the face of such difficult conditions. These, coupled with the fragmentation and eventual disappearance of the independent lordship of

and M. Stout, *The Bective Abbey project, Co. Meath: excavations, 2009–12* (Dublin, 2016); G. Stout, 'De Bello Beco: A French foundation in the Boyne Valley', *CLAHJ*, 29:2 (2018), 194–204.   **14** M. Murphy, 'Rural settlement in Meath 1170–1660: the documentary evidence' in M. Deevy and D. Murphy (eds), *Places along the way: first findings on the M3*, NRA scheme monographs, 5 (Bray, 2009), pp 157–8.   **15** J.A. Watt, *The church in medieval Ireland* (Dublin, 1972), pp 92–4. For a broader discussion of the connections between monasticism and colonialism in an Irish context, see C. Ó Clabaigh, 'Monasticism, colonization, and ethnic tension in late medieval Ireland' in Beach and Cochelin, *CHMMLW*, pp 901–99 at pp 908–12.   **16** E. Jamroziak, *Survival and success on medieval borders: Cistercian houses in medieval Scotland and Pomerania from the twelfth to the late fourteenth century*, Medieval Texts and Cultures of Northern Europe, 24 (Turnhout, 2011), p. 57.   **17** For a general discussion of daily life in a Cistercian cloister, see J. Burton and J. Kerr, *The Cistercians in the Middle Ages* (Woodbridge, 2011), pp 103–24.   **18** For a more detailed discussion of these disputes, see Seale, 'De Monasterio', pp 28–30. For a map of Loughsewdy's holdings, see Collins, *Female monasticism*, 380.   **19** *MRHI*, p. 160.   **20** P. Crooks (ed.), 'Close Roll 1 Henry VI', *CIRCLE: A calendar of Irish chancery letters, c.1244–1509* (2021), https://chancery.tcd.ie/document/Close/1-henry-vi/25 [accessed 17 December 2021].

Meath by the middle of the fifteenth century, may well have been contributing factors to the demise of Loughsewdy as a religious community. By 1479 at the latest, there were no more nuns at Loughsewdy. In March of that year, the Knight Hospitaller, Cornelius Ykayssy, described it as 'an abandoned monastery of nuns.'[21] Ykayssy's letter provides a quiet coda to some two centuries of the history of Loughsewdy, one which in what has been outlined so far seems unexceptional amongst the other female religious communities affiliated with a monastic order which were founded in Ireland in the twelfth and thirteenth centuries.[22]

Yet the letter also points us toward one of the quirks of Loughsewdy's appearance in the historiography, for Yksayssy refers to the nuns as having been 'of the order of Saint Augustine'.[23] This is despite the fact that most modern scholars, as we shall see below, refer to Loughsewdy as a Cistercian community. This confusion over the house's affiliation is of long standing. In the mid-seventeenth century, the antiquarian Sir James Ware compiled his *De Hibernia et antiquitatibus eius*, a catalogue of medieval Irish monasteries. In it, Ware stated that Loughsewdy was described as Cistercian in 'an Antient book of the Statutes of [*that*] Order', but that he believed Loughsewdy had been 'of the Order of Gilbertins [*sic*] or de Sempringham, wherein the Canons were of the Premonstratensian Order and the nuns Cistercians, but living in separate houses.'[24] Two hundred years later, Samuel Lewis' *Topographical dictionary*, a work still regularly referred to by historians of Ireland, stated that Loughsewdy was home to Premonstratensian men and Benedictine women who lived in separate parts of the same building.[25] The reference work of first resort for present-day undergraduates, Wikipedia, shows how much influence these texts have had on popular ideas of Loughsewdy's history. At the time of writing this essay, Wikipedia asserts that 'Plary Abbey' (a name sometimes used for Ballymore, particularly in the later Middle Ages) was home to canons who were both Gilbertine and Premonstratensian, and to nuns who were Benedictine.[26]

None of this makes much sense. The Gilbertine Order was founded within a decade of the Premonstratensian Order in the early twelfth century; like the Premonstratensians, many of its early houses were double communities, home to both men and women. However, with the exception of a short-lived house in Scotland, the Gilbertines never established a community outside England, and only one of its double

21 M.A. Costello, A. Coleman and W.H. Grattan Flood (eds), *De Annatis Hiberniæ: A calendar of the first fruits' fees levied on papal appointments to benefices in Ireland*, AD 1400 to 1535 (Dundalk, 1909), p. 71. **22** For discussion of the foundation of female religious houses, their archaeology, and their role in church reform in Ireland during the earlier part of this period, see T.E. Collins, 'Transforming women religious? Church reform and the archaeology of female monasticism in Ireland' in E. Breathnach, K. Smith and M. Krasnodebska-D'Aughton (eds), *Monastic Europe: medieval communities, landscapes and settlement*, Medieval Monastic Studies, 4 (Turnhout, 2019), pp 277–301. **23** Costello, Coleman and Flood, *De Annatis Hiberniæ*, 71. **24** J. Ware, *De Hibernia et antiquitatibus ejus, disquisitiones*, (2nd ed., London, 1658), p. 197. **25** S. Lewis, *A topographical dictionary of Ireland: comprising the several counties; cities; boroughs; corporate, market and post towns; parishes and villages with historical and statistical descriptions*, 2 vols (London, 1837), i, p. 153. **26** 'Ballymore, Co. Westmeath', *Wikipedia*, 2021, https://en.wikipedia.org/w/index.php?title=Ballymore,_Co._Westmeath&oldid=1050468073 [accessed 17 December 2021].

houses was founded after the mid-twelfth century.[27] The order's canons were not simultaneously Gilbertine and Premonstratensian, although both groups structured their lives around the Rule of Augustine.[28] The regulations governing Gilbertine women were strongly influenced by Cistercian statutes, but equally, Gilbertine women were Gilbertine, not Cistercian. Moreover, while there were a number of Premonstratensian houses established in Ireland, mostly in Connacht, none of them are known to have had female members.[29] The idea of a house being affiliated to more than one monastic order at the same time (as opposed to switching from one affiliation to another) seems implausible.

The exact origin of the confused understanding of the affiliation of Loughsewdy that was held by Ware, Lewis, and later scholars is unknown, although we can speculate that it arose from the fact that Ballymore was also home to a small priory of Augustinian canons during the Middle Ages.[30] While members of a separate community, both physically and institutionally, the Augustinians may have fulfilled the role of 'nuns' priests', saying Mass for the women's community.[31] For our purposes here, what is sufficient to note is that the confusion over Loughsewdy's affiliation is one of great antiquity. This is undoubtedly in part due to the paucity of surviving records about the house, but it may also reflect the much-contested historiography as to which medieval religious orders did or did not accept female members at which particular phase of their history, and what form that membership took. The question of whether there were Cistercian nuns in the twelfth century, for instance, has caused the spilling of much ink.[32]

The balance of probability is that the women of Loughsewdy were Cistercian, or at least thought of themselves as following its *ordo*, its way of life, even if they were not formal members of the order in an institutional sense. 'Cistercian' is the affiliation most often cited for the nuns in modern scholarship. For example, Geraldine Carville has argued that the community was Cistercian, and indeed that membership in an order which emphasized strict enclosure for women was the reason behind Loughsewdy's

27 B. Golding, *Gilbert of Sempringham and the Gilbertine Order, c.1130–c.1300* (Oxford, 1995), p. 219. 28 While some scholars have seen a strong Premonstratensian influence on the early Gilbertine statutes, Katharine Sykes has argued that this is tenuous and there is more evidence for a Cistercian connection. K. Sykes, *Inventing Sempringham: Gilbert of Sempringham and the origins of the role of the master*, Vita Regularis. Abhandlungen, 46 (Münster, 2011), pp 172–4. 29 Collins, *Female monasticism*, p. 86. For the most recent studies of the Premonstratensians in medieval Ireland, see M. Clyne, 'The founders and patrons of the Premonstratensian houses in Ireland' in J. Burton and K. Stöber (eds), *The regular canons in the medieval British Isles*, Medieval Church Studies, 19 (Turnhout, 2011), pp 145–72; M. Clyne, 'Premonstratensian settlement in the Czech lands and Ireland, 1142–1250', *JMMS* 7 (2018), 127–52; M. Clyne, 'The monasteries of the Canons of Prémontré, *c.*1180–*c*1607' in Browne and Ó Clabaigh, *Households*, pp 62–86. 30 Seale, '*De Monasterio*', p. 28.   31 Much work remains to be done on the relationship between nuns and priests during the Middle Ages, but see F.J. Griffiths, *Nuns' priests' tales: men and salvation in medieval women's monastic life*, The Middle Ages Series (Philadelphia, 2018).   32 For two contrasting views on the topic, see S. Thompson, 'The problem of the Cistercian nuns in the twelfth and early thirteenth centuries' in D. Baker (ed.) *Medieval women* (Oxford, 1978), pp 227–52; C.H. Berman, 'Were there twelfth-century Cistercian nuns?', *Church History*, 68:4 (1999),

ultimate failure.[33] Nuns who were unable to at least occasionally venture out to oversee their community's holdings would not be able to serve as effective stewards of its economic resources. It is true to say that the Cistercian Order was far from being the most popular choice for women religious in Ireland, and that those women who did wish to profess as Cistercians faced some hierarchical hostility there. Stephen of Lexington, abbot of the English Cistercian house of Stanley, was sent to Ireland as visitor on behalf of the order in 1228, roughly a generation after the probable foundation of Loughsewdy. He opposed women joining the order in Ireland, and in a set of regulations for Irish Cistercian houses likely composed in August of that year, Stephen decreed that no woman 'ever in future be received as a nun [*by the Cistercians*] on account of the greatest disorders and scandals arising throughout Ireland from such practices.'[34] Exactly what these 'disorders and scandals' might have been is not clear, if indeed they happened at all. Many Cistercian men in the Middle Ages were ambivalent or anxious about the presence of women within their order, fearing both sexual pollution and an additional demand on economic resources. Bernard of Clairvaux, possibly the most famous of all Cistercians, wrote that it was easier to raise the dead than to refrain from sex when alone with a woman.[35] While such misogynistic ideas were not characteristic of the thinking of all medieval Cistercian men, or indeed all men in reformed monastic orders, they may well have formed the basis for a hierarchical opposition to women joining the order in any great numbers in Ireland.[36]

Yet despite this, and while the overwhelming majority of religious communities founded for women in Ireland in the twelfth and thirteenth centuries were Arroasian Augustinian, there are several other known examples of Irish Cistercian female communities from the Middle Ages. Priories of Cistercian nuns were founded in Derry and Downpatrick in the early thirteenth century, while there may have been short-lived communities of women associated with the male Cistercian houses of Jerpoint, Kilkenny; Inislounaght, Tipperary; and Mellifont, Louth, in the twelfth century.[37] References to Loughsewdy as Cistercian predate modern scholarship. An early seventeenth-century manuscript made for Bishop James Ussher (1581–1656) and now at Trinity College Dublin may hold a copy of part of that 'ancient book of statutes' to

824–64. **33** G. Carville, 'Cistercian nuns in Medieval Ireland: Plary Abbey, Ballymore, Co. Westmeath' in J.A. Nichols and L.T. Shank (eds), *Hidden springs: Cistercian monastic women*, 3 vols (Kalamazoo, MI, 1995), iii, Part 1, pp 62–84; reprinted with minor amendments in G. Carville, *The impact of the Cistercians on the landscape of Ireland, 1142–1541* (Ashford, Wicklow, 2002), pp 233–56. **34** On his return to Stanley Abbey in 1229, Stephen likely drew up another document in which this point was reiterated. Stephen of Lexington, *Letters from Ireland: 1228–1229*, trans. by B.W. O'Dwyer (Kalamazoo, MI, 1982), pp 163, 211. Stephen does not mention Loughsewdy in his letters, and it is unlikely that he visited it. He largely focused on visiting houses in Munster; the only monasteries north of Dublin that he visited in person were Bective and Mellifont. Stephen of Lexington, *Letters*, pp 11–12. **35** J.-P. Migne (ed.), *Patrologiae cursus completus. Series Latina*, 221 vols (Paris, 1879), vol. 183, col. 1091. **36** For a more detailed discussion of women's roles within the monastic reforms of the twelfth and thirteenth centuries, see F.J. Griffiths, 'Women and reform in the central Middle Ages' in J.M. Bennett and R. Mazo Karras (eds), *The Oxford handbook of women and gender in medieval Europe* (Oxford, 2013), pp 447–63. **37** Hall, *Women*, pp 207–9.

which Ware referred in his *De Hibernia*. The manuscript contains a list of Cistercian communities in medieval Ireland, including one *Ballimornan in Loghsuedy*.[38] This is a post-medieval copy, however, and there is no firm contemporary documentary evidence that Loughsewdy was ever formally a Cistercian community. The surviving pieces of evidence from medieval sources are contradictory. There are two references in the papal registers to the house as Cistercian. The first is a petition from 1360 concerning a benefice belonging to 'the Cistercian prioress of Lochsewdy'; the second, from 1417, refers to 'Margaret, prioress, and the convent of the Cistercian priory of St Mary, Lochseudy.'[39] However, a 1395 entry in the papal registers refers to a benefice belonging to 'the Augustinian prioress and convent of Lochsed', while as we have seen above, in 1479, Cornelius Ykayssy referred to the then-abandoned community as 'of the order of Saint Augustine.'[40] Given the chronological overlap here, this does not seem to be a simple case of Loughsewdy moving from one affiliation (Cistercian) to another (Augustinian) over time.

So what are we to make of all of this: of Loughsewdy as a community that has been variously represented as Cistercian, Augustinian, Premonstratensian, Benedictine, or Gilbertine, or as having a multiplicity of simultaneous identities. Is this merely a case of occasional errors by medieval scribes, amplified by their disproportionate representation in a scanty source base and therefore confusing to antiquarian scholars? Is it a reflection of a historiographical tendency to distinguish between 'official' Cistercian communities and those which were (with an implicit 'merely') 'imitating' or 'emulating' Cistercian practices?[41] Or is it a hint at a more complex situation than we can now recover, of a community whose identity was fluid or situational? These are issues to which we shall return, but first let us move south to consider the role of women in the Premonstratensian Order in medieval France.

THE SISTERS OF PRÉMONTRÉ

The Premonstratensian Order was one of a number of reformed monastic orders to emerge in western Europe in the twelfth century, and during the Middle Ages was one of the most successful.[42] At the order's height, the Premonstratensians were second only to the Cistercians in the sheer number of their communities, which spanned Europe from Ireland in the west to Jerusalem in the east, and from Norway south to Spain.[43]

---

38 J.T. Gilbert (ed.), *Chartularies of St Mary's Abbey, Dublin: with the register of its house at Dunbrody, and Annals of Ireland*, 2 vols (London, 1884), ii, p. 218.   **39** W.H. Bliss (ed.), *Calendar of entries in the papal registers relating to Great Britain and Ireland*, 17 vols (London, 1896), vol. 1, p. 359; J.A. Twemlow, *Calendar of entries in the papal registers relating to Great Britain and Ireland*, 17 vols (London, 1906), vol. 7, p. 83.   **40** W.H. Bliss and J.A. Twemlow (eds), *Calendar of Papal Registers relating to Great Britain and Ireland*, 17 vols (London, 1902), vol. 4, p. 513; Costello, Coleman and Flood, *De Annatis Hiberniæ*, p. 71.   **41** Burton and Kerr, *The Cistercians in the Middle Ages*, pp 53–4.   **42** A comprehensive English history of the Premonstratensian Order remains to be written, but see B. Ardura, *Prémontrés histoire et spiritualité*, CERCOR Travaux et recherches, 7 (Saint-Etienne, 1995); U.G. Leinsle, *Die Prämonstratenser* (Stuttgart, 2020); D.-M. Dauzet, *L'ordre de Prémontré: Neuf cents ans d'histoire* (Paris, 2021).   **43** C.J. Bond, 'The Premonstratensian Order: a preliminary

5.1 The abbey at Prémontré as it appeared in the eighteenth century. Tavernier de Jonquières, 'Abbaye de Prémontré', *c.*1780s. Source: gallica.bnf.fr/Bibliothèque nationale de France. Image © https://gallica.bnf.fr/ark:/12148/btv1b7741202h.

The order's founding figurehead, Norbert of Xanten (*c.*1080–1134), was a charismatic wandering preacher. A number of his followers would become the first generation of the Premonstratensian Order. This new order – which took its name from the mother house at Prémontré in Picardy – placed an emphasis on a renewed apostolic life, one devoted to preaching and pastoral service (Fig. 5.1). There were many women among the early Premonstratensians. The monk-chronicler Herman of Tournai (d. *c.*1147) wrote with admiration of the 'more than ten thousand women' (*plusquam decem millia feminarum*) whom Norbert had inspired to enter the religious life within just a few years of Prémontré's foundation in 1120.[44] Herman was undoubtedly exaggerating the numbers, but not the general level of enthusiasm among women in northern France and the Rhineland for this new order.

Yet where the women of Loughsewdy are notable by the number of monastic orders to which later scholars have assigned them, those of the Premonstratensian Order have been more defined by the extent to which the boundaries of their order's identity have been drawn in order to exclude them. In part this reflects the medieval sources. The two *vitae* which were written about Norbert during the Middle Ages tell us that the first group of fourteen Premonstratensian men had settled at Prémontré by Easter 1120 and professed their vows there on Christmas Day, 1121.[45] What these *vitae* omit,

survey of its growth and distribution in medieval Europe' in M. Carver (ed.), *In search of cult: archaeological investigations in honour of Philip Rahtz* (Woodbridge, 1993), pp 153–85. **44** J.-P. Migne (ed.), *Patrologiae cursus completus. Series Latina*, 221 vols (Paris, 1880), vol. 156, cols pp 996–7. **45** T.J. Antry and C. Neel (eds), *Norbert and early Norbertine spirituality*, Classics of Western

however, is the likely presence of women in this fledgling community, although this is known to us from other sources. For instance, Ricwera, lady of Clastres, is reputed to have been the first vowed Premonstratensian woman, and she served as something of a role model for later Premonstratensian sisters (Fig. 5.2).[46]

A local noblewoman who entered the religious life at Prémontré in the 1120s, Ricwera helped to run the community's *xenodochium*: part inn for travellers and pilgrims, part hospital for the sick. The order's earliest surviving statutes, which date to around 1135, give us a glimpse of the kind of daily routine followed by Ricwera and her fellow sisters: a mixture of devotional life, care of the community's sick and counsel of local lay women, and manual labour such as cooking, cheese making and wool production.[47] This way of life would have been emulated by women in dozens of other Premonstratensian communities across what is now France, whether living in houses just for women or those physically separate from but institutionally united with houses of men.

It is beyond the scope of this chapter to provide a full recounting of the history of these French Premonstratensian sisters. What I will focus on instead is how that history has been characterized by some modern historians, with a focus on those who have written works on medieval religious history aimed at a more general audience. For example, R.W. Southern, in his *Western society and the church in the Middle Ages* (1970), discussed Premonstratensian women religious in a section of his book titled 'Fringe Orders and Anti-Orders', and framed their history within the order as one of decline and repression from the very end of the twelfth century. He supported this with a rather vituperative quotation from Konrad, abbot of the Premonstratensian community of Marchtal in what is today south-western Germany: one in which Konrad rejects any new female entrants into the religious life because 'the wickedness of women is greater than all the other wickedness of the world' and 'the poison of asps and dragons is more curable and less dangerous to men than the familiarity of women.'[48] Konrad was no great champion of women religious, that much is clear. Yet what is not clear from Southern's chapter is that Konrad was writing in the latter half of the thirteenth century, not near the end of the twelfth, and that rather than supporting a blanket ban on women entering the order, he was instead arguing more narrowly against women entering his own community of Marchtal. Southern's framing is confused, but also representative of a broader set of misconceptions about some late twelfth-century papal decrees that has led some to assume that there were essentially no female Premonstratensians, at least in France, after the early 1200s.[49] This narrative about

Spirituality (New York, 2007), p. 146.   **46** No medieval biography of Ricwera has survived, but for a brief seventeenth-century account of her life, see J. Le Paige, *Bibliotheca Praemonstratensis ordinis*, 2 vols (Paris, 1633), i, p. 438. For more on Premonstratensian women generally, see B. Krings, 'Die Prämonstratenser und ihr weiblicher Zweig' in I. Crusius and H. Flachenecker (eds), *Studien zum Prämonstratenserorden* (Göttingen, 2003), pp 73–106.   **47** For an edition of and commentary on these statutes, see R. van Waefelghem, 'Les premiers statuts de l'Ordre de Prémontré. Le Clm. 17. 174 (XIIe siècle)', *Analectes de l'Ordre de Prémontré*, 9 (1913), 1–74. **48** R.W. Southern, *Western society and the church in the Middle Ages* (London, 1970), p. 314.   **49** For more extensive discussion of this issue, see Y. Seale, '"Ten thousand women": gender, affinity

Klosterfrau Prämonstratensér Ordens.
Religieuse de l'Ordre de Premontré.

5.2 A sister of the Premonstratensian Order. C.F. Schwan, 'Klosterfrau Prämonstratenser Ordens. Religieuse de l'Ordre de Premontré', *c*.1787. Source: gallica.bnf.fr/Bibliothèque. Image © https://gallica.bnf.fr/ark:/12148/btv1b100503015.

Premonstratensian women continues to be an influential one, with Kevin Madigan in his *Medieval Christianity* (2015) writing about the 'plight of the female Norbertines' and asserting that the Premonstratensians 'decided in 1198 on a policy of complete detachment: no more women would be admitted to the order. Once approved by Pope Innocent III ... this decision destined the female branch of the Norbertines to a slow disappearance.'[50]

It may well have been the case that the average Premonstratensian brother in the Middle Ages was not overly enthusiastic about women's membership in the order – such attitudes are extremely difficult for us to recover now. Yet the documentary and archaeological record clearly demonstrates that women continued to be an active, if minority, part of the Premonstratensian Order in France until the early modern period. For example, Bonneuil in the Somme was one of the most important dependent communities of Prémontré, and the abbey's economic hub in the diocese of Noyon.[51] We know that women religious lived at this house until well after 1198. Not only does a 1240 charter concerning the way of life at Bonneuil stipulate the number of women who could be sisters there (a maximum of 20), it also appointed a *magistra* to be their head.[52] Prémontré's obituaries document sisters at Bonneuil into the fifteenth century, such as the prioresses Johanne de Baluim and Marie.[53] If we look further west, in the heart of the coastal city of La Rochelle stand the remains of Sainte-Marguerite-des-Soeurs-Blanches, a monastery once inhabited by a community of Premonstratensian sisters.[54] This house does not appear in the documentary record until the fourteenth century, but then persisted until after the Reformation, when La Rochelle became a Huguenot stronghold and the number of Catholics in the city dwindled. The last sister of Sainte-Marguerite, one Marie Pichier, ceded the property to the city's Catholics to use as a place of worship in 1579. One last example to mention here is Aubeterre, a mid-twelfth-century foundation nestled in Auvergne in the heart of France.[55] Its surviving chapel, with its vivid late twelfth- or early thirteenth-century murals, provides some of the best testimony we have of female Premonstratensian spirituality in medieval France.[56] However, we know that Aubeterre as a community outlasted the Middle Ages, as its last known prioress, one Diane d'Apchon, was installed in 1603.[57]

---

and the development of the Premonstratensian Order in Medieval France' (PhD, University of Iowa, 2016), especially 33–41.   **50** K. Madigan, *Medieval Christianity: a new history* (New Haven, CT, 2015), p. 164.   **51** N. Backmund, *Monasticon Praemonstratense, id est historia circariarum atque canoniarum candidi et canonici ordinis Praemonstratensis*, 3 vols (Straubing, 1952), ii, p. 484.   **52** Beauvais, Archives départementales de l'Oise, H 6009. This charter is also copied into the thirteenth-century cartulary of Prémontré. Soissons, Bibliothèque Municipale, MS 7, f. 112v.   **53** R. Van Waefelghem (ed.), *L'Obituaire de l'abbaye de Prémontré (XIIe s., ms. 9 de Soissons)* (Louvain, 1913), pp 38, 168.   **54** N. Backmund, 'Sainte Marguerite de La Rochelle, un couvent de moniales prémontrées', *Bulletin de la Société des Antiquaires de l'Ouest et des musées de Poitiers*, 2 (1956), 441–5.   **55** Aubeterre was closely linked with the nearby male Premonstratensian community of Neuffontaines (or Neuffonts). Both were founded by Gilbert and Pétronille, lord and lady of Escolles. N. Backmund, *Monasticon Praemonstratense, id est historia circariarum atque canoniarum candidi et canonici ordinis Praemonstratensis*, 3 vols (Straubing, 1956), iii, pp 142–3, 151–3.   **56** P. Tiersonnier, 'La chapelle de l'ancien prieuré d'Aubeterre', *Bulletin de la Société d'émulation et des beaux-arts du Bourbonnais*, 10 (1902), 80–2.   **57** G. Malvielle, 'Le prieuré d'Aubeterre, ses

It is true that many of the communities known to have been established for Premonstratensian women in France in the twelfth century trail off in the documentary record in the thirteenth or fourteenth centuries, and that most of the order's double houses in France split in two along gender-segregated lines during the twelfth century. The women's communities of Plainemont, Meuse; Avigny, Haute-Marne; and Chebret, Aisne, for instance, seem neatly representative of the narrative of 'slow disappearance': the documentary record leaves no definitive evidence as to when these communities were dissolved, and there are no extant archaeological remains or local traditions associated with them, to the best of my knowledge.[58] They may have lasted only two or three generations and never been home to more than a handful of sisters at any one time.

But the histories of these communities cannot simply be paired with the existence of anti-female statutes and allowed to stand for the history of all Premonstratensian women in the Middle Ages. The narrative of 'slow disappearance' only fits with the history of Premonstratensian sisters in France over the very long term indeed, and not at all in other parts of Europe. Shelley Wolbrink's research on the Premonstratensians of northwestern Germany has demonstrated that female communities flourished there long after the posited 1198 watershed, while Elsanne Gilomen-Schenkel has documented spiritual cooperation between male and female Premonstratensians in Switzerland into the later Middle Ages.[59] In Poland, the female Premonstratensian community at Imbramowice near Krakow has had an unbroken existence since the early thirteenth century.[60] It is clear that the resilience and vibrancy of any given community of Premonstratensian sisters is not one that can be predicted based on reference to prescriptive texts alone. Local circumstances were very important. Equally it is clear that we must revise our narratives about these communities in order to better illuminate women's actions and persistence.

A COMPARATIVE LENS

We must be conscious that a religious identity, an understanding of one's self as a member of a given monastic order, was not something created out of whole cloth by a (male) hierarchy and imposed on a passive group of women. As Anne Lester has pointed out in her work on Cistercian female communities in Champagne, the order's

prieures et prieurs', *Bulletin de la Société d'émulation du Bourbonnais: lettres, sciences et arts*, (1951), 111–17 at 113–14.   **58** Backmund, *Monasticon*, ii, pp 447, 495; iii, 92–3.   **59** S.A. Wolbrink, 'Women in the Premonstratensian Order of northwestern Germany, 1120–1250', *The Catholic Historical Review*, 89:3 (2003), 387–408; S.A. Wolbrink, 'Necessary priests and brothers: male–female cooperation in the Premonstratensian women's monasteries of Füssenich and Meer, 1140–1260' in F.J. Griffiths and J. Hotchin (eds), *Partners in spirit: women, men, and religious life in Germany, 1100–1500*, Medieval Women: Texts and Contexts, 24 (Turnhout, 2014), pp 171–212; E. Gilomen-Schenkel, 'Double monasteries in the south-western Empire (1100–1230) and their women's communities in Swiss regions' in Griffiths and Hotchin (eds) *Partners in spirit*, pp 47–74 at pp 56–8. **60** J. Gil-Mastalerczyk, 'Premonstratensian convent complex in the Polish lands: Imbramowice in the past and today', *IOP Conference Series: Materials, Science and Engineering*, 603:5 (2019), 52089.

statutes can be read not as simply exclusionary but rather as showing it responding to women's actions and defining what it meant to be a Cistercian nun in a way that took into account what these women were already independently doing.[61] Equally, Lucy Barnhouse has demonstrated through her work on the hospital sisters of late medieval Mainz that the identity of women religious could be more anchored in their work – in this case, tending to the sick – than in their affiliation with a given order.[62] The Mainz sisters' invocation of a Cistercian identity during negotiations with external authorities might have been more rooted in a practical understanding of legitimacy and political leverage than in a sense of their own 'Cistercianness.' Alison More, in her study of extra-regular and non-monastic pious laywomen in the late Middle Ages, equally argued that such women were often less concerned with how to cultivate particular institutionalized religious identities than in how they could make a difference within their society.[63] It might be useful for us as historians to think about whether the same might have held true for the sisters of Prémontré or of Loughsewdy: what did they centre themselves around? What did it mean for a woman to purposefully cross the threshold of these communities, intent on one day making her final vows there? And how can we unpick those motivations from the concerns of her male contemporaries or of later historians?

This is not to say that the concept of a monastic *ordo* as currently understood is meaningless, or that communities that professed the same identity, whether formally or informally, had nothing in common. Even if an order's internal coherence and *uniformitas* was sometimes more an ideal than a reality, it was still a shared ideal. Yet it remains a complicated issue with which to engage. Much of the recent historiography on medieval female religious has tended to focus more on the reciprocity and variety of relationships that these women had with others rather than on issues of *ordo* categorization, narratives of decline, or on women as a 'problem'.[64] Some recent scholarship on women's monastic history in the Middle Ages may provide us with some useful methodological exemplars here, such as Constance Berman's work on the Cistercian women of France, or Catherine Mooney's untangling of the Chiara Offreduccio of history from the St Clare of hagiography.[65] Both Berman and Mooney urge historians to consider documents of practice rather than simply prescriptive texts in order to get a better sense of the lives of medieval women religious, and in turn to read those prescriptive texts with more attention to what they tell us about power and gender.

61 A.E. Lester, *Creating Cistercian nuns: the women's religious movement and its reform in thirteenth-century Champagne* (Ithaca, NY, 2011).   **62** L. Barnhouse, 'Disordered women? The hospital sisters of Mainz and their late medieval identities', *Medieval Feminist Forum: A Journal of Gender and Sexuality*, 55:2 (2020), 60–97.   **63** A. More, *Fictive orders and feminine religious identities, 1200–1600* (Oxford, 2018), p. 15.   **64** For a discussion of this trend with a particular focus on the issue of double monasteries, see A.I. Beach and A. Juganaru, 'The double monastery as a historiographical problem (fourth to twelfth century)' in Beach and Cochelin, *CHMMLW*, pp 561–78, at pp 565–6.   **65** C.H. Berman, *The White Nuns: Cistercian abbeys for women in medieval France*, The Middle Ages Series (Philadelphia, 2018); C.M. Mooney, *Clare of Assisi and the thirteenth-century church: religious women, rules and resistance*, The Middle Ages Series (Philadelphia, 2016).

CONCLUSION

Unless some well-hidden cache of documents comes to light, we will likely never learn much more about the history of Loughsewdy or any of these female Premonstratensian houses than what has been sketched out above – and even then such documents may have been written by male administrators and would not necessarily give us much more insight into how the women of these communities understood their vocation or their membership in a particular monastic order. It is frustrating to be able to point to issues with the existing narratives told about these communities, but not to necessarily have new ones to offer in their place. However, by studying carefully what evidence we do have about these communities and their histories, and revisiting the conclusions that past historians have drawn about them, we can come to a better understanding of how to study the history of women religious in the Middle Ages.

Moreover, even if comprehensive proof one day comes to light of Loughsewdy's Cistercian affiliation, or a more defined chronology for some of the houses of French Premonstratensian sisters emerges, we should resist the temptation to then impose a more homogenous notion of identity – of 'Cistercianness' or 'Premonstratensianness' – on these communities. Each one of the communities I have discussed here was distinct, and so too perhaps may have been their understanding of their monastic identity and vocation.

It has not been my goal here to argue that there were necessarily any stronger parallels between the lives of the women of Loughsewdy and of their rough contemporaries in France than between them and any other particular community of women religious. However, a comparison of what we know of the histories of these communities, and of how scholars have framed those histories, underlines the individuality of these houses. As much as the desire to put things – communities, people – in 'order' is a tempting one, it must always be tempered by an awareness of the specific local contexts in which they flourished.

Keeping it in the family: familial connections of abbesses and prioresses of convents in medieval Ireland

MARY ANN LYONS

INTRODUCTION

In recent years, our understanding of female religious houses in medieval Ireland has deepened in several important respects thanks in large part to the pioneering scholarship of Christina Harrington, Dianne Hall, Gillian Kenny and, more recently, Tracy Collins and Bronagh Ann McShane among others.[1] Working within constraints imposed by highly fragmented sources, these scholars have assiduously pieced together tissues of evidence to shed fresh light on the foundation, operation, staffing, resources and significance of the country's nunneries in contexts shaped by major shifts in the country's geopolitical landscape and waves of ecclesiastical re-organization. We now have a clearer sense of the relative size of convents and their communities in Ireland. According to Collins, approximately 65 nunneries are known to have existed in the later medieval period in Ireland (as compared to almost 153 in England, 15 in Scotland and 3 in Wales): the great majority of these were founded in the late twelfth and early thirteenth centuries and not all were in use at the same time.[2] Furthermore, Hall contends that in comparison with nunneries in England, the number of nuns in Irish convents was smaller, with many never having more than a dozen nuns at any one time, usually less.[3] Certain claims, such as that nunneries were typically poorer than men's monasteries and that they played a supplementary role to male houses in the early stages of Anglo-Norman colonization, have also been disproved, with Collins showing that

---

1 C. Harrington, *Women in a Celtic church: Ireland, 450–1150* (Oxford, 2002); D. Hall, 'Towards a prosopography of nuns in medieval Ireland', *AH*, 54 (1999), 3–15; eadem, *Women and the church in medieval Ireland, c.1149–1540* (Dublin, 2003); G. Kenny, *Anglo-Irish and Gaelic women in Ireland, c.1170–1540* (Dublin, 2007); T. Collins, 'Timolin: a case study of a nunnery estate in later medieval Ireland', *Anuario de Estudios Medievales*, 44:1 (Jan.–June 2014), 51–80; T. Collins, *Female monasticism in medieval Ireland: an archaeology* (Cork, 2021); B.A. McShane, *Irish women in religious orders, 1530–1700: suppression, migration and reintegration* (Woodbridge, 2022); B.A. McShane, 'Negotiating religious change and conflict: female religious communities in early modern Ireland, c.1530–c.1641', *British Catholic History*, 33:3 (2017), 357–82; B.A. McShane, 'The pre-profession record of Sister Catherine Browne ('in religion' Sister Catherine of St Francis), Poor Clare convent, Bethlehem, County Westmeath, 1632', *AH*, 70 (2017), 284–93; B.A. McShane, 'The roles and representations of women in religious change and conflict in Leinster and south-east Munster, c.1560–c.1641' (PhD, Maynooth University, 2015); Browne and Ó Clabaigh (eds), *Households*. 2 Collins, 'Timolin', p. 54; Collins, *Female monasticism*, pp 77–90. 3 Hall, *Women*,

in the case of Co. Kildare at least, convents were relatively wealthy compared to monasteries for men. Through their systematic trawl of archival and printed sources, the aforementioned scholars have unearthed most if not all of the extremely limited body of evidence for medieval religious women in Ireland that has survived. In so far as that evidence permits, this essay examines the lives of abbesses and prioresses of convents in Ireland, focusing on how their familial connections shaped the fortunes of these women and of the communities in their charge.

There were four main waves of foundation of nunneries in medieval Ireland, the first occurring during the early medieval era.[4] In the second wave, as a result of native twelfth-century reform, nunneries were founded by Gaelic kings and formed part of an extensive re-organization of Irish monasticism.[5] The third wave, which occurred when the first generations of Anglo-Normans 'altered the course of native reform, hastened changes to diocesan and parochial structures and redistributed conquered lands'[6], saw more individual Augustinian, Benedictine and Cistercian houses, most of which were established by the second stratum in the hierarchy of Anglo-Norman settlers. Although fewer in number than the foundations for male religious, these nunneries played a significant role in the colonization of Ireland. The fourth and much smaller wave of foundations occurred during the fifteenth-century reform movement that proved especially popular in Gaelic Ireland and mainly involved the mendicant orders.[7] The focus in this essay is mainly on convents founded during the second, third and fourth phases.

WOMEN AS PATRONS AND FOUNDERS OF CONVENTS

There is no evidence to suggest that women were more likely to sponsor nunneries than male religious houses in medieval Ireland. In general, women tended to channel their expendable resources towards religious communities that were favoured by their husbands' family or were close by geographically instead of patronizing a more distant nunnery. Women frequently made donations of money, furnishings, altar plate and other items to religious communities in their own right; however, grants of land in both Gaelic and Anglo-Norman regions required the consent of their male relatives. In that context, it is unsurprising that only a handful of women were instrumental in founding nunneries and in each case, the material support of male relatives was vital in the realization of their plans.[8]

Around 1242, a widow, Alicia de la Corner (*fl.* 1240), and her brother, Richard de la Corner (d. 1252), of the de Anglo family of Meath, barons of Navan, jointly founded the priory of the Holy Trinity for Augustinian nuns at Lismullin in that county, and Alicia became it first prioress (Fig. 6.1). Richard, who was bishop of Meath, facilitated the venture by orchestrating the enfeoffment of the site to Alicia who then used it to

p. 181.   **4** See Collins this volume.   **5** Hall, *Women*, p. 63; C. Ó Clabaigh, 'The church, 1050–1460' in B. Smith (ed.), *The Cambridge history of Ireland*, volume 1: *600–1550* (Cambridge, 2018), pp 364–75.   **6** Hall, *Women*, p. 63.   **7** Ibid.   **8** Ibid., pp 42–3, 58, p. 60.

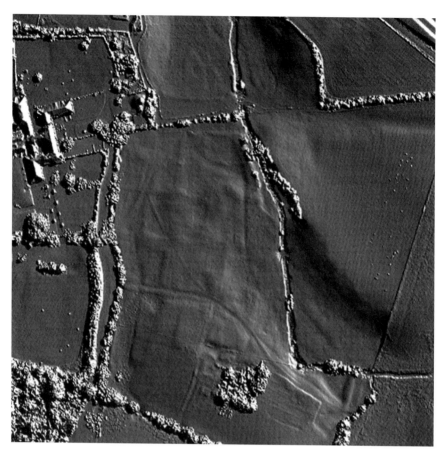

6.1 LIDAR image of the site of Lismullin, Co. Meath. Image courtesy of Dr S. Davis, School of Archaeology, UCD, and T. Collins.

found the convent. Subsequently, Richard generously augmented the priory's possessions through grants of the manors of Dunsink and Ballygodman, and the temporalities of Ardmulchan church. The foundation of Lismullin convent was part of Richard's drive to introduce ecclesiastical reform by exerting tighter episcopal control over the spiritualities of Meath that had been granted to other religious houses. The priory's location, together with its extensive estates, made it one of the most successful convents in Anglo-Norman Ireland.[9]

In the late 1290s, when Agnes de Hareford, a recluse in Cork around whom a group of pious women had gathered, initiated proceedings to formalize that community by having a convent built, she is thought to have relied upon a male relative for financial support. The official notices of Agnes's proposed foundation marked the culmination

9 *MRHI*, p. 322; Hall, *Women*, pp 86–7; idem, 'The nuns of the medieval convent of Lismullin, Co. Meath, and their secular connections', *Ríocht na Midhe*, 10 (1999), 58–70; A. Mac Shamhráin, 'Corner, Alicia (Avicia) de la' in J. McGuire and J. Quinn (eds), *Dictionary of Irish biography* (9 vols, Cambridge, 2004), sub nomine; idem, 'Corner, Richard de la', *DIB*, sub nomine.

of negotiations with local landowners for grants of land and income to finance the new house. The original petition stated that the nunnery was not yet securely established and did not have the funds to purchase lands. Following two inquiries into the granting of lands for the convent in preparation for a license from the Crown, the plans were approved. By 1301, Agnes and her community were living in the house of St John the Baptist on St John's Street on the outskirts of Cork. Her name features prominently in all of the records, attesting to her role in initiating and overseeing the arrangements but there is evidence to suggest that Agnes drew upon family connections for financial backing. Although the endowments came primarily from the Barry family of Cork, another donor, John FitzGilbert, also known as de Hereford, thought to have been a relative of Agnes, granted a half carucate of land and the advowson of two churches to support the foundation.[10]

In convents where the first abbess or prioress was a member of the founder's family, it is likely that those houses were established specifically to support that relative who may have been the driving force behind the foundation.[11] This appears to have been the case when Robert Fitz Richard De Valle, son of Richard, Lord of Norragh, founded St Mary's priory as an Augustinian house of Arroasian observance at Timolin in south Kildare in the 1190s: he had his granddaughter, Lecelina, appointed first prioress. The same was true of later foundations by wealthy families who allowed female relatives, inspired by the Observant reform movement of the mid-fifteenth century, to live in formal convent communities. This is best exemplified by the small nunnery at Ballymacadane in Co. Cork, founded[12] by Cormac Láidir Mac Carthaigh, lord of Muskerry, for his relative, Honor, and by the prominent Galway merchant, Walter Lynch's grant to his daughter in 1511 of a house near the Church of St Nicholas, afterwards known as 'the house of the poor nuns of St Francis'.[13] Some founders made specific provision for female relatives who may wish to enter the convent. When Walter de Burgo MacWilliam Oughter granted land to Cong Abbey in order to establish a convent at Annagh in Mayo in the early fifteenth century, he did so on condition that any female descendant who wished to become a nun should be admitted to that house to which he had a special attachment.[14]

CONVENTS UNDER MANAGEMENT OF FEMALE MEMBERS OF FOUNDING FAMILIES

Appointing a close relative as first abbess or prioress was also a priority for prominent Gaelic families who founded convents at Clonard in Meath, Killone in Clare (Plate 5), and Kilcreevanty in Galway during the twelfth and early thirteenth centuries, guaranteeing the founder control over the house, its lands and income, at least in its

10 *MRHI*, pp 315–16; Hall, *Women*, pp 60, 87–8. See also the contribution by Ó Clabaigh below. 11 Hall, *Women*, p. 60. 12 *MRHI*, p. 325; Hall, *Women*, pp 60, 82; Collins, 'Timolin', p. 63. Foundation dates differ with some sources giving 1450 and others 1472: see *MRHI*, p. 313; Hall, *Women*, p. 89 n.162. 13 *MRHI*, p. 317; C. Ó Clabaigh, *The friars in Ireland, 1224–1540* (Dublin, 2012), p. 98. 14 *MRHI*, p. 312; Collins, *Female monasticism*, p. 209.

early years and often for generations. St Mary's priory, Clonard, founded in 1144, had as its first abbess a relative of its founder, Murchad Ua Máelshechlainn, king of Mide (either a granddaughter or niece) and down to 1318, at least three family members were abbesses of that convent.[15] Similarly, the convent of St John's at Killone in Co. Clare, founded by Donnchad Cairpreach Ua Briain in the early thirteenth century, was under the direction of several O'Brien women; among the earliest was Donnchad's daughter, Abbess Slaine, who died in the convent in 1259. Between then and the closure of the house *c.*1540, six Uí Bhriain women were recorded as abbesses or nuns in that community.[16] The degree of control that families continued to exercise over their foundations through the appointment of relatives as abbesses and nuns is best illustrated in the case of Kilcreevanty Abbey in Galway, founded *c.*1200 by Cathal Crobderg Ua Conchobhair, king of Connacht (d. 1224), initially under the Benedictine rule, and later Arroasian and Cistercian: all nuns in that house whose names have been recorded were members of the Ua Conchobhair family.[17] Both were part of a grand plan of female and male monastic foundations during the period *c.*1148–*c.*1247 intended to serve the needs of the kingdoms of Connacht and Thomond.[18]

FAMILY AS A FACTOR IN WOMEN'S CHOICE OF CONVENT

Women who entered religious life in Ireland, as elsewhere, did so for a variety of reasons and at different stages in life. In addition to personal religious conviction, the lure of living a formal cloistered life, free of the trials of married domestic life and childbirth; the chance to become prioress or abbess and to exercise control over convent estates with a degree of independence otherwise denied them; the opportunity to live one's later years among a community of nuns, even the lack of alternative options – these all drew women to nunneries. Family invariably shaped their decision. Some entered with the support of relatives; others did so in response to family pressure, others still to escape or defy it. In the late twelfth century, when many women enthusiastically embraced the opportunity to join newly established convents, several were criticized for doing so without their families' approval. A reference in the Annals of Clonmacnoise to the Synod of Clonfert (1179), which states 'no portion Canons should be sought of women their husbands still living' is understood to mean that a woman whose husband was still living should not be admitted as a canoness.[19]

Choices about where to enter and which order were also strongly dictated by family.[20] Usually a woman entering religious life joined a local convent or another further afield where her relatives were or had been members of the community. It was common to find several family members in a convent community or within a network of affiliated nunneries and monasteries at one time. In 1353 two de Mandevilles – Anne

15 Hall, *Women*, p. 211; A. Mac Shamhráin, 'Ní Máelshechlainn, Agnetha ('An Cailleach Mór': 'the great nun')' in *DIB*, sub nomine.   16 See Ó Riain-Raedel, this volume.   17 Hall, *Women*, p. 75; A. Mac Shamhráin, 'Ua Conchobair, Cathal Mór Crobderg', *DIB*, sub nomine.   18 Hall, *Women*, pp 100–2. For an overview of patronage of nunneries see Collins, *Female monasticism*, pp 90–7.   19 Hall, *Women*, p. 68.   20 For religious orders and affiliation see Collins, *Female*

(prioress) and Margaret (nun) – were resident in the Cistercian convent of the Blessed Mary, Downpatrick.[21] In 1468, three members of the Hackett family were resident in the Arroasian priory of St Mary, Grace Dieu, Dublin – Elena, then prioress and Joan and Katherine, both nuns. The fact that Katherine later served as prioress suggests that she followed a relative's lead in entering Grace Dieu. In 1535 two members of the Wale family, Elizabeth and Agidia, were prioresses of Graney convent in south Kildare. This pattern is also evident in Gaelic Ireland. During the fifteenth and sixteenth centuries, three known abbesses of Killevy in Armagh were members of the Ó hAnluain family who exercised control over that area.[22] The less common practice of restricting admittance to members of the founding family occurred in extreme form at the O'Brien abbey at Killone in Clare and the O'Connor abbey at Kilcreevanty in Galway where all identified nuns and abbesses were members of those families. Notwithstanding the highly fragmented nature of surviving source material, the recurrence of local family names among abbesses, prioress and nuns in both Anglo-Norman and Gaelic areas across generations strongly suggests ongoing commitment to maintaining familial attachment to convent communities.

PERMEABLE WALLS: MAINTAINING CONNECTIONS WITH THE OUTSIDE WORLD

Claustration appears to have been practiced differently in various religious communities across Ireland, with no explicit reference to cloistering for nuns in Gaelic areas in the late medieval period.[23] As employers, landlords, legal agents, holders of rectories and collectors of tithes, abbesses and prioresses were obliged to engage either personally or through intermediaries in negotiations and disputes with various parties outside the convent walls, notably government officials, ecclesiastical authorities, and lay patrons, including (for good or ill) family. More so than family, they depended heavily on relationships that they forged with ecclesiastical authorities and local lay people when pursuing legal suits to defend their lands and entitlements to spiritual and temporal incomes.[24]

There is evidence that superiors and at least some nuns managed to maintain connections with their families. There is evidence, for example, that some abbesses and prioresses attended family weddings at which they were witnesses and that in certain instances, they were called upon in court cases to respond to questions about the legitimacy of those marriages. Indeed, Dianne Hall suggests that some women of high status may have been invited to attend weddings, either before or after they joined the convent, mindful of the weight that their evidence might carry in any future case contesting the legitimacy of those marriages. Certain nuns had such an intimate knowledge of consanguinity within their own families and others that they

monasticism, pp 81–6. **21** Hall, *Women*, p. 212; *MRHI*, p. 316. **22** Hall, *Women*, pp 213, 214, 179. **23** Collins, *Female monasticism*, pp 184–223. **24** Hall, *Women*, pp 132, 143–51. For a detailed discussion of the management of convent estates see ibid., pp 133–58. For an archaeological analysis of estates, see, Collins, *Female monasticism*, pp 374–416.

were capable of providing detailed, reliable evidence before ecclesiastical courts. Around 1455, for example, the abbess of St Brigid's, Benmon ingen OMellan, was summoned to give evidence before the archbishop of Armagh in a case where Felim McDomphnayll and Isabella ingen Neill were seeking dispensation to marry, despite being within prohibited degrees of affinity. The abbess' evidence proved that the couple were related within prohibited degrees, indicating that she was either a member of the Uí Néill family or had an exceptional knowledge of several generations of that clan. As in England, some nuns in Dublin convents joined confraternities which allowed them to maintain relationships with a wider circle of religious and laity, possibly including family members. Among these were Lady Matilda and Lady Alicia Bron, abbess and a nun of St Mary Del Hogges respectively, and Lady Katerine Hacket (*fl.* 1468), prioress of Grace Dieu, who were affiliated to the city's most prestigious confraternity – that of Christ Church Cathedral.[25] The fact that convent superiors such as Renalda Ní Bhriain, daughter of Tadhg an Chomhaid Ó Briain of Thomond and abbess of Killone (d. 1510) and Elicia Butler, abbess of Kilculliheen, were laid to rest in ancestral burial places strongly suggests that their primary and enduring affinity was with their family.[26]

ABBESSES AND PRIORESSES WITH PASTS

In both anglicized and Gaelic Ireland, there were abbesses and prioresses as well as nuns who had unions with one or more men and had children, not always in that order, prior to joining the convent. Elicia Butler, abbess of Kilculliheen convent in Kilkenny (Plate 7), was the daughter of Sir James Butler, seneschal of the earls of Ormond, and sister to Piers Roe Butler (*c.*1467–1539), eighth earl of Ormond and first earl of Ossory, described by David Beresford as 'perhaps the best exemplar of the use of naked ambition and political skill to achieve personal goals in late medieval Ireland'.[27] By 1478 and still only aged in her late teens or early twenties, Elicia had had unions with two men and given birth to at least two children when she entered Kilculliheen. There is no evidence that thereafter she maintained connections with her children or their fathers, or that she had a claim on any property or income arising from those unions. While the irregular nature of Elicia's unions did not prevent her from becoming a nun, they were cited by her opponents as significant impediments to her election as abbess. It was thanks to the strong support she received from her own family, the Butlers, who had the resources and ecclesiastical contacts to obtain the necessary papal dispensations, that Elicia was appointed abbess in 1478 in a calculated step to assert or re-assert Ormond control of the convent.[28]

25 Hall, *Women*, pp 163, 171–2, 213, 215. See Lennon's contribution below.   **26** NLI MS D 1978; B. Ó Dalaigh, 'Mistress, mother and abbess: Renalda Ní Bhriain (*c.*1447–1510)', *NMAJ*, 32 (1990), 50–63; Hall, *Women*, p. 38. For an archaeological overview of burial at nunneries see Collins, *Female monasticism*, pp 351–9.   **27** D. Beresford, 'Butler, Piers ('Piers Ruadh')', *DIB*, sub nomine. Note: Kilculliheen now lies in modern Co. Waterford.   **28** Kenny, *Anglo-Irish and Gaelic women*,

In contrast with Elicia Butler, Renalda Ní Bhriain was in her mid-fifties when she entered the convent at Killone and was appointed abbess at the behest of her brother, Toirdhealbhach Donn, *c.*1500. From her mid-teens, Renalda had resided in the Butler territories around Tipperary. She had two unions, the first with Sir John Ormond which was not canonically recognized and from which she had an illegitimate son, and the second, a marriage with Richard Butler, baron of Knockgraffon in Tipperary from which she had a second son. By 1475 she was widowed and it is likely that she continued to reside at Knockgraffon until she returned to her native Thomond in the wake of her brother's attack on Ormond territory in Autumn 1498. Her past was no impediment to her immediate appointment as abbess. Renalda's will, drawn up in 1510, reveals legacy issues relating to her Butler family connections. In 1509, Piers Roe Butler was consolidating his position as the most powerful Butler of Ormond. In February, he had Renalda's son, Thomas, surrender the manor of Knockgraffon to him in return for other properties in Kilkenny. Around that time, almost certainly at Piers Roe's prompting, Renalda drew up her will to dispose of her remaining interest in Ormond territory, namely a rent charge of 20 marks yearly from the manor of Killenaule in Tipperary which she had inherited through her husband Richard. She redeemed Killenaule from the friars of Kilkenny to whom it was mortgaged and pledged this holding to Piers Roe for 100 marks. The fact that she appointed him chief executor of her estate, despite his having been responsible for the death of her eldest son, is evidence of his dominance in Ormond. According to Brian Ó Dalaigh, 'the purpose of the will … was not just to dispose of Renalda's assets or to settle her debts, but rather to ensure that on her death Killenaule passed into the possession of Piers Ruadh' and enhanced his power.[29] After her debts were settled, the residue of her estate (sixty marks) was allocated for prayers for her own soul and for those of John, earl of Ormond (father of her first son, Sir James, who received no mention) and her husband, Richard Butler. To her legitimate son, Thomas or his children, she left ten marks. Finally, Renalda's request that she be interred in the friary at Ennis, the traditional burial place of the kings of Thomond, rather than in the graveyard of her convent, signalled her enduring affinity with her family.[30]

The case of the last abbess of Killone, Ónora Ní Bhriain, who had children and later married Sir Ruaidrí Ó Seachnasaigh either before or soon after the convent closed *c.*1540, provides a glimpse of the legacy issues that arose within such unconventional families. When the couple's grandchildren were at loggerheads in 1616, the fact that Ónora was a nun when her elder children were born was cited in an effort to discredit them and their offspring.[31]

pp 181–2; Hall, *Women*, pp 192–200. **29** Ó Dalaigh, 'Mistress', 54–5, 58, 60–1. **30** Will of Renalda Ní Bhrian, 1510 (NLI MS D 1978); Ó Dalaigh, 'Mistress'; Kenny, *Anglo-Irish and Gaelic women*, pp 168–9, 171; Hall, *Women*, p. 38; D. Duffy, *Aristocratic women in Ireland, 1450–1660: the Ormond family, power and politics* (Woodbridge, 2021), pp 40, 45–6. **31** Hall, *Women*, pp 179–80.

THE ROLE OF FAMILY IN EQUIPPING AND POSITIONING RELATIVES
FOR OFFICE

In addition to operating within a matrix of gendered expectations and constraints on
all aspects of women's conduct, there is evidence that convent superiors in both Anglo-
Norman and Gaelic society broadly complied with their family's expectations,
customary practices and the exercise of, at times, heavy-handed patriarchal control.
Family background was vital in determining a woman's progression prospects in
religious life in several important respects, starting with her legitimacy of birth. In the
fifteenth and early sixteenth centuries, religious communities in both Anglo-Irish and
Gaelic Irish areas appear to have adopted quite a relaxed stance on whether men or
women seeking to enter religious life were born in wedlock, except when it came to
preferment for ecclesiastical office. During that time, a small number of Gaelic and
Anglo-Norman nuns seeking preferment were granted papal dispensations on account
of being the daughters of clerics and unmarried women. These included Gormelina
Ní Chonchobair, a nun at Kilcreevanty Abbey (1446/7), the daughter of parents who
were not canonically married; Margaret Tuyt, a nun at St Mary's Abbey, Clonard in
Meath (1409) and Elizabeth Tanner at Grace Dieu priory in Dublin (1412), both
daughters of priests and unmarried women, and Joanna Barrett, a nun at Lismullin
priory in 1511 and the daughter of a lay woman and a canon. Although their names do
not re-appear in records, Hall believes it is safe to assume that some, if not all, of them
did succeed to office within their communities.[32]

Family also positioned women for preferment to office in religious life through
education and financial payments in the form of dowries or other donations. All
abbesses and prioresses of convents in Anglo-Irish areas were drawn from wealthy local
gentry families: women of this rank were expected to bring a dowry and to be able to
manage estates independently and were educated accordingly.[33] In Gaelic areas,
superiors of large convents came from the local ruling families. 'Their brothers became
chiefs, warriors and bishops, while their sisters made strategic marriage alliances,
facilitating the complex and delicate weave of negotiation and context between
different familial groups.'[34] One must assume that these women too had the requisite
financial backing of their families and were sufficiently educated to manage estates.

The guardians of convent estates, these women operated as 'feudal landholders,
engaged in maintaining, extending and defending their lands'. By virtue of their
familial connections, social standing, stewardship of these properties and control over
parish churches, many convent superiors exercised significant dominance over their
local communities. In certain instances, their style of management of estates mirrored
local and family practices. Molough priory in Tipperary was located on the border of
Butler and Poer (Power) holdings where a mixture of Gaelic and English customs
prevailed. Its last prioress, Joan Power, likely of local origin, was found to have been
extracting Gaelic in-kind payment of coign and livery from tenants, in line with local
practice. The extent of these superiors' control over parish life may be seen in the case

32 Ibid., pp 180–1.   33 Collins, *Female monasticism*, pp 59–75.   34 Hall, *Women*, pp 133–4.

of the Arroasian convent at Termonfeckin in Louth. In the fifteenth and early sixteenth centuries, its prioresses were very actively involved in the practical management of the parishes where they held land, partially subsidizing the priests and collecting tithes. In 1521 the prioress, Elina, even directed parishioners from Kylclogher, Co. Louth, not to go to their parish church but to go instead to nearby Calliaghstown church.[35]

THE SIGNIFICANCE OF THE POST OF ABBESS/PRIORESS

The wave of ecclesiastical reforms introduced during the decades preceding the Anglo-Norman settlement was shaped significantly by the political agendas of Gaelic kings engaged in power struggles within a context of shifting alliances and instability. Through their influential role in the foundation of convents and monasteries, the introduction of new religious orders into existing houses and the re-allocation of lands that formerly belonged to abandoned houses, rulers such as Diarmait Mac Murchadha, king of Leinster (d. 1171), had a major stake in foundations within their orbit of influence.[36] As part of their strategy for extending or consolidating their holdings and power in new territories, kings often brought religious houses in those areas under their control by affiliating them with their own foundations and networks. Appointing a close family member as superior of houses or motherhouses of a network was, therefore, important in confirming a dynasty's political claims to territory.[37] During the first half of the twelfth century, politically St Brigit's Abbey in Kildare town (established as a double monastery for nuns and monks in the fifth century) was one of the country's most important convents.[38] By then, the abbess and coarb of Brigid was in charge of both communities and took precedence over bishops at public assemblies.[39] Unsurprisingly, incumbents of this powerful office were members of Leinster's top tier ruling dynasties. Abbess Gormlaith (d. 1112) was daughter to Murchad (d. 1070), king of Dublin and likely half-sister to Domnall (d. 1075), also king of Dublin and to Donnchad (d. 1115), recognized as overking of Leinster from 1098.[40] While their role as stewards of this substantial property and income befitted their social standing and significantly extended their family's orbit of influence, it also occasionally placed abbesses at the centre of violent conflicts between rival dynasties. In 1127 Cearball Mac Fáeláin, king of the Kildare kingdom of Uí Fáeláin and prominent supporter of Toirrdelbach Ua Conchobair (d. 1156), high-king of Ireland, died while defending his daughter's rights as abbess of Kildare against Donnchad Ua Conchobair Failge who had a relative appointed to the office. Four years later, when Cearball's son-in-law, Diarmait Mac Murchada, king of Leinster, avenged Cearball's death by burning the abbey and killing 140 (or 170) people, he targeted the Ua Conchobair Failge abbess whom he abducted, raped and replaced with a member of his own family.[41]

---

35 Ibid., pp 15–18, 125, 171.   **36** M. Ní Mhaonaigh, 'Mac Murchada, Diarmait (MacMurrough, Dermot)', *DIB*, sub nomine. For an overview of nunnery patronage see Collins, *Female monasticism*, pp 90–7.   **37** Hall, *Women*, pp 69–70.   **38** See the contributions to this volume by Collins, Johnston and Swift.   **39** *MRHI*, pp 307, 319–20.   **40** E. O'Byrne, 'Mac Fáeláin, Fáelán', *DIB*, sub nomine; A. Mac Shamhráin, 'Ua Máelshechlainn, Murchad', *DIB*, sub nomine.   **41** Harrington,

The office of abbess of the head house in Ireland of the Arroasian canonesses, St Mary's Abbey in Clonard, founded by Murchad Ua Máelshechlainn, king of Mide (d. 1153), was another coveted position, reserved for female members of the most powerful ruling dynasties in Leinster which was used by that family for political advancement. At the time when Murchad Ua Máelshechlainn, king of Mide, founded the abbey in Clonard *c.*1144, he was consolidating his position within the diocese of Clonmacnoise. His inclusion of St Mary's Clonmacnoise and several smaller dependent convents in affiliation with his foundation, together with his appointment of a relative, Agnes, as first abbess of Clonard must be understood in that context.[42] At the time of her death in 1196, Agnetha 'An Caillech Mór' or 'the great nun', whom Ailbhe Mac Shamhráin identifies as Murchad's niece, was abbess. Given her family's prominence in the ecclesiastical sphere (her uncle, Conchobar Ua Máelshechlainn (*fl.* 1153) was abbot of Clonard when she is thought to have entered the convent and her relative, Derbfhorgaill, re-built Clonmacnoise nunnery in 1167), Agnetha's role at Clonard not only befitted her social standing; it was also strategic, empowering her to bolster her family's drive to gain ascendancy. This was especially true since following Murchad Ua Máelshechlainn's death in 1153, the family struggled to maintain 'a fitful kingship over an unstable province till the Anglo-Norman conquest reduced … [them] to the level of local rulers in the southern regions of the present Co. Westmeath.'[43] For her part, Agnetha ably protected the interests of both her order and her family. She preserved the very substantial property portfolio of St Mary's Abbey, Clonard, ensuring that it had thirteen dependent nunneries by the end of her term. In 1195 she overcame a serious challenge to her convent's holdings, ultimately securing papal protection for their possessions, including the houses of canonesses at Lusk and Termonfeckin, and that at Clonmacnoise.[44] After 1220, when the Ua Máelshechlainn dynasty was in decline, several of the nunneries affiliated to Clonard were claimed by the Uí Chonchobair for Connacht.[45]

CONVENTS AS AGENTS IN ANGLO-NORMAN COLONIZATION

It was during the late twelfth and thirteenth centuries, when the transfer of substantial tracts of land from the kings of Gaelic Ireland to Anglo-Norman settlers gave new lay landowners the resources to shape ecclesiastical change through sponsorship of religious foundations, that the upsurge in convent foundations in Ireland mirrored that which occurred in England and France.[46] The notion that the foundation of male religious houses was key to the success of the Anglo-Norman's initial colonization drive and that the founding of nunneries later consolidated those new settlements has recently been challenged by Tracy Collins. Her discovery that convents were, in fact, part of the

Women in a Celtic church, p. 212; Hall, *Women*, p. 65; O'Byrne, 'Mac Fáeláin, Fáelán'; Ní Mhaonaigh, 'Mac Murchada, Diarmait (MacMurrough, Dermot)'.   **42** J. Brady, 'The nunnery of Clonard', *Ríocht na Midhe*, 2:2 (1960), 4–7; *MRHI*, p. 314; Hall, *Women*, pp 70–2.   **43** Mac Shamhráin, 'Ua Máelshechlainn, Murchad'.   **44** Ailbhe Mac Shamhráin, 'Ní Máelshechlainn, Agnetha (An Cailleach Mór: 'the great nun')', *DIB*, sub nomine.   **45** Hall, *Women*, p. 78.   **46** Ibid., pp 69–70, 95.

initial phase of settlement, with nunneries being the first religious houses established in several localities,[47] prompts fresh reflection on the influence exercised by abbesses and prioresses in both cultural colonization and ecclesiastical reorganization in the Anglo-Norman settlement. Their dual role is best exemplified in the case of two convents that two of the larger Anglo-Norman landowners chose to establish as their main contribution to the new monastic foundations.

St Mary's convent in Timolin, south Kildare, was founded *c*.1191 by Robert Fitz Richard De Valle (Wale), son of Richard, lord of Norragh, after Robert received a grant of the area from Hugh de Lacy as part of his sub-infeudation of Leinster. St Mary's convent in Graney was founded *c*.1200 by Walter de Riddlesford who accompanied Strongbow to Ireland and was granted extensive lands around Bray in Wicklow and Kilkea in south Kildare. Eustace de Rupe, feudal tenant of de Riddlesford, was also an important patron of Graney.[48] Both houses conformed to the typical early Anglo-Norman foundation, being Augustinian and built close to their founder's castles. As was the custom, family members of the founding patrons were appointed prioress: Robert's Fitz Richard De Wall's granddaughter, Lacelina, was first abbess of Timolin and Eustace de Rupe's descendants, Matilda and Christina de Rupe, were prioresses of Graney (+1267–84 and 1317 respectively).[49] During this incubation phase, the founders and patrons adopted a hands-on approach in ensuring that the convents, situated on their estates, were protected and also integrated into the fabric of the nascent colonial settlements through endowments of lands and rectories and, in the case of Graney, through appropriation of a local church to the nuns. In the early thirteenth century, to mark the admission of Isabelle, a relative of Robert FitzRichard, to Timolin priory, Robert de Staunton, who is thought to have been Isabelle's brother or father, made a donation of land adjacent to the convent's holdings. With strong family support, the first superiors of Timolin and Graney contributed significantly to the consolidation of their Anglo-Norman ancestral presence, through purchase and exchange of land holdings, though, in line with superiors in general in Ireland, they did not embark on large-scale expansion of their substantial properties and incomes.[50]

However, from the late thirteenth century down to the 1530s, prioresses of houses originally located within close proximity of their founders' castles in anglicized areas, including Timolin and Graney, were struggling to maintain a foothold in their localities. When subjected to several attacks, they apparently received no protection from local families. Timolin was targeted by Gaelic raiders on several occasions between the late 1290s and 1310: first, in 1297 when one of its granges was robbed of livestock and cloth valued in excess of 20 marks, second in 1298–9, when corn was stolen twice, and third, in 1310 when three men scaled the walls of the priory close and robbed corn, malt and wheat.[51] By the early 1400s, south Kildare was a frontier. So vulnerable was the priory of Graney that in 1409 its prioress, Margery, had to request Henry IV's permission to converse with, shelter and give or sell provisions or clothing to Irish enemies and English rebels by whom the convent was surrounded on all sides.[52]

47 Collins, 'Timolin', p. 53; Collins, *Female monasticism*, p. 89.   **48** Hall, *Women*, pp 82, 178.
49 Collins, 'Timolin', p. 63.   **50** Hall, *Women*, pp 83, 135, 137.   **51** Hall, *Women*, p. 155.   **52** *MRHI*,

Furthermore, in 1422 Graney was caught up in the Talbot–Ormond conflict. Claiming that John Talbot (d. 1453) targeted the convent on account of it being under his patronage, the earl of Ormond accused his opponent of taking an enormous amount of provisions (worth over £40) for his men and houses from the convent.[53]

In the decades prior to their dissolution in 1539 and 1540 respectively, when both Timolin and Graney were in territory controlled by the Mac Murrough Kavanaghs and the lands of Timolin were largely overrun by the O'More, both had close ties with local landed families, several of their prioresses being local women, namely Ellen Wolfe at Timolin (1495–1518) and two members of the Wale family, Elizabeth and Agidia, in 1535. However, these connections counted for nothing at a time when it was proposed that 'young lords, knights and gentlemen out of England' were needed to suppress unrest in that area; neither family received a share of the spoils after the dissolution of either convent.[54]

FAMILY NETWORKS

Although fragmented sources make it difficult to identify abbesses and prioresses definitively and impossible to trace nuns whose first names alone were recorded, those few surnames that have survived strongly suggest their privileged family background and likely connections to local wealthy gentry family networks. The nuns at Lismullin, Co. Meath, came mainly from old landed gentry stock – Cusacks, Barnwalls and Eustaces – and two of their prioresses were Cusacks, Elianora in the early 1300s and Mary at the time of dissolution. A prioress of Termonfeckin, Co. Louth, Alsona Plunkett (d. 1535), was almost certainly a member of a very prominent Meath family. It is also likely that Jenet White, prioress of Termonfeckin in Co. Louth from c.1467 to c.1480, was local and may have been related to Alice White, a widow who in the early 1400s had land in Callystown in Co. Louth where the Termonfeckin convent also had lands and the rectory. At Kilculliheen priory in Co. Kilkenny,[55] several abbesses and nuns were members of eminent local families, among them, Desiderata le Poer (abbess c.1277), Elinia/Elicia Butler, abbess or abbesses from c.1478 until after 1540, and a nun, Anastasia Cantwell, at the dissolution.

Dianne Hall has adumbrated family connections between convent superiors and nuns and senior-ranking officer holders in government, the judiciary and the church. Notable among these are Katherine Mothing, abbess at Kilculliheen, who may have been related to Nicholas Mothing (d. 1568), chancellor of St Canice's Cathedral, Kilkenny, and Margaret de Broun, abbess of Hogges in 1316, may have been related to William Broun, escheator of Ireland in the mid-1300s. When opportunities for preferment, for advancement of family interests or protection of individual relatives presented themselves, several superiors capitalized on family connections to their

p. 318.   **53** D. Beresford, 'Talbot, John', *DIB*, sub nomine; Hall, *Women*, p. 156.   **54** *MRHI*, pp 318, 325; Hall, *Women*, pp 214, 219; M. Lyons, *Church and society in Co. Kildare, c.1470–1547* (Dublin, 2000), pp 59, 114–18, 120, 138, 140, 144, 147, 157, 158, 173, 177.   **55** Now located in

advantage. Through his involvement in the proceedings that led to the deposition of Elicia Butler, abbess of Kilculliheen in 1531, Nicholas Mothing, chancellor of St Canice's, almost certainly facilitated the preferment of Katherine Mothing, then a nun in that convent and a complainant against Elicia, as last abbess.[56] In Gaelic areas, ruling families made similar preferential arrangements for relatives. When Renalda Ní Bhriain, daughter of O'Brien of Thomond and long-time widow of Richard Butler, baron of Knockgraffon, was forced to return to the security of her native Thomond in the aftermath of her brother Toirdhealbhach Donn's attack on Ormond territory in Tipperary in Autumn 1498, her appointment as abbess of the Augustinian convent at Killone was almost certainly attributable to his influence.[57]

The importance of these high-level family connections were especially evident at the time of the dissolutions in both English and Gaelic areas in various forms of paternalistic protection and appropriation of confiscated monastic properties and revenues. At the time of the dissolution of Ireland's monasteries, in Gaelic areas in the West, convents were 'easy targets for Gaelic rulers looking for monasteries they could dissolve to appease the Crown officials and demonstrate their loyalty without great sacrifice.'[58] This was true in the case of Killone nunnery whose patron, Ó Briain, organized its closure and took possession of its lands in 1542; the property remained in the hands of the earls of Thomond in the early seventeenth century.[59] However, not all Gaelic patrons of convents managed to retain ownership post-dissolution. The O'Connor Kilcreevanty convent and its extensive holdings, surrendered by Abbess Dervorgilla Ní Chonchobair in 1543, passed out of the hands of its patrons and was granted, along with several other monasteries, to Richard Burke, earl of Clanricard, in 1562 as part of a suite of rewards granted by Elizabeth I to reward his loyal service in Connacht. Elizabeth had recently confirmed his earldom, appointed him a member of the Irish Privy Council (July 1559), granted him the customs revenues of the city of Galway and appointed him captain of Connacht for 1562–3.[60] This was more in keeping with the practice in anglicized areas where, in general, the most valuable and strategically positioned dissolved convent properties, such as St Mary de Hogges, Grace Dieu, Graney and Timolin, were granted to government officials or prominent landed gentry families who were not immediate relatives of the last abbess or prioress.

There were, however, some notable exceptions. Kilculliheen Abbey, whose patrons were the Butlers, earls of Ormond, was one of several dissolved monastic properties granted to Sir Edmund Butler in 1566.[61] The post-dissolution fate of Lismullin nunnery in Co. Meath illustrates how one family safeguarded their interest in the second wealthiest convent in the Pale (it was valued at £109, after Grace Dieu at £112). Arising from the priory's suppression in 1539, the last prioress Mary Cusack and her brother, Sir Thomas (*c.*1505–71), each made exceptional gains. Given that Thomas was one of the commissioners charged with surveying monastic properties in the Pale region for dissolution and his sister was prioress, it is no surprise that Mary was the only convent

modern Co. Waterford. **56** Hall, *Women*, p. 177 n.110, pp 178, 191–5. **57** Ó Dalaigh, 'Mistress', p. 58. **58** Hall, *Women*, p. 203. **59** Ó Dalaigh, 'Mistress', p. 60; Hall, *Women*, p. 202. **60** *MRHI*, p. 319; Terry Clavin, 'Burke (de Burgh), Richard', *DIB*, sub nomine. **61** *MRHI*,

superior to receive a pension that exceeded £10; in fact, she received £16. It is equally unsurprising that Thomas received a grant of Lismullin and all of its properties in 1547. He took possession of 'the best clothe and vestments and other furniture, including a chalice, from the chapel of Lessmlen' and subsequently bequeathed these to his local church in Trivet, his burial place.[62] Thomas used his political influence to acquire several lucrative former monastic estates in Meath, including the Dominican properties at Trim and Londerstown, the Augustinian priory at Skreen and Clonard Abbey. All were purchased or leased at rates far below their true value and he was permitted to accumulate substantial arrears on the lease payments due to the Crown. He also illegally took possession of Crown lands, acquired church lands in Meath for a fraction of their value, and was accused of taking bribes while Master of the Rolls. His corruption cost him his post as lord chancellor in 1555 and he was imprisoned in London. He was only released in late 1557 when he undertook to pay £1,500 to the Crown, a move that left him financially crippled for the rest of his life. From 1547 Thomas Cusack made Lismullin his residence and Mary seems to have spent the rest of her life resident on her brother's estate. Although she was young when the convent closed, she does not appear to have married. The fact that Mary loaned Thomas £100 which he only repaid before his death in 1571 suggests that she lived comfortably and independently on her pension which she continued to receive at least until 1574.[63]

PURPOSES SERVED BY CONVENTS FOR THE FAMILIES OF ABBESSES/PRIORESSES

Having a family member in the office of abbess or prioress of a convent served their interests and those of their families in a number of ways. They facilitated admission of female relatives who, for reasons both spiritual and mundane, sought refuge in the convent. Through their prayer and intercession, the provision of education and care for children, welfare in the form of alms and hospitality, and places of worship for parish congregations, they fulfilled their founder/patron's charitable and spiritual obligations. Killone Abbey is a case in point. Its church functioned as the parish church.[64] The nuns fed and clothed those in need. At the convent of St Peter's Cell, a dependency of Killone, the nuns were said to have educated the daughters of Limerick's leading merchant families while the orchards and gardens adjoining St Peter's were rented out to poor widows of that city.[65] Importantly, convents afforded ambitious and accomplished women from aristocratic and gentry families opportunities to live independently of their family, to hold the prestigious office of convent superior, and to exercise control over both convent and lay communities, all of which enhanced their families' prestige, reputation and influence. A glance at the assets of three convents at

p. 319.   **62** Hall, *Women*, pp 120, 128, 204.   **63** H. Gallwey, 'The Cusack family of county Meath and Dublin', *Irish Genealogist*, 5 (1974–9), 591–8; Hall, 'Lismullin', p. 66; T. Clavin, 'Thomas Cusack', *DIB*, sub nomine; B. Scott, *Religion and Reformation in the Tudor diocese of Meath* (Dublin, 2006), pp 94, 105–6, 126–7, 153–4.   **64** Several nunnery churches were at some time shared as parish churches, see Collins, *Female monasticism*, pp 250–8.   **65** Ó Dalaigh, 'Mistress',

the time of their dissolution provides an insight into their scale and appeal for an aspiring abbess or prioress. Grace Dieu priory had a house, church, and other buildings that were in good repair for the use of the farmer and parishioners. The church had been parochial from time immemorial. The site and demesne comprised 203 acres, with a water-mill, a horse-mill and a dove cote. The priory's possessions included another 632 acres with many messuages, cottages, unmeasured plots and an interest in six rectories. At a total gross value of £112, this was the wealthiest convent in Ireland. Second to it was Lismullin which had a church, a cloister, a dormitory and other buildings. The demesne lands comprised 225 acres with a mill and a messuage. The convent's possessions included approximately 2,412 acres, two manors, several farms, messuages and cottages, two more water-mills, and an interest in three churches. The total gross value was £109. Kilculliheen Abbey church served as the parish church. The convent also had a belfry, a hall, a dormitory, a chapter house, an infirmary with its own kitchen, a large kitchen which had an internal water supply, a bake house, furnace and granaries, approximately 800 acres, as well as many messuages, cottages and gardens, two mills, six salmon-weirs, and twelve appropriated churches. Its total gross value was £50.[66]

THE CORROSIVE EFFECTS OF THE PERMEABLE CLOISTER

Frequent reports of non-observance of celibacy from the mid-fourteenth century indicate that many parts of the church in Ireland were effectively laicized in respect of marriage and family inheritance of church office and property.[67] The lax condition in which nuns in Gaelic convents were cloistered suggests that they viewed celibacy in the same way as the abbots of monasteries in those areas who openly supported wives and families and whose sons succeeded them in church office. Killone Abbey is a tragic example of 'the convergence of Gaelic Irish attitudes to clerical celibacy' and 'the realities of strong family involvement in conventual affairs'.[68] The house was always under the patronage of the founder's family, the Uí Bhriain, and all abbesses and nuns identified there were from the most senior ranks of the family, generally the daughters of the kings of Thomond. Based on three dispensations for clerics in the late 1400s, Dianne Hall claims that at least one and possibly two of the abbesses bore children from incestuous unions. Cornelius and Tatheus Ó Briain, both clerics in Killaloe diocese, were granted dispensations, in 1482 and 1485 respectively, from defects of their births which were the result of fornication between their sister, the abbess of Killone, and her father. In 1501 Donald Ó Briain received a dispensation as the son of an abbess of Killone and a bishop who were related in the second degree of consanguinity and the double second of affinity. This open acknowledgment of their parentage combined with their preferment to ecclesiastical office would suggest that the office of abbess of Killone was secularized to a significant degree by the late 1400s.[69]

pp 59–60; Hall, *Women*, pp 174–6.   **66** *MRHI*, pp 317, 322, 319; Hall, *Women*, pp 112, 128.
67 Hall, *Women*, p. 165.   **68** Ibid., p. 166.   **69** C. Ó Clabaigh, *The Franciscans in Ireland,*

Albeit less shocking, there is evidence of advanced secularization in convents in anglicized areas by that time, too. The circumstances surrounding the deposition of Elicia Butler, abbess of Kilculliheen, in 1532 reveal how the intrusion of a member of a powerful family as abbess had a seriously corrosive impact of that convent community, which was left deeply divided. From the outset, Elicia had to overcome objections to her owing to claims that her profession was irregular as she received the veil not from her abbess nor from the local bishop of Ossory but from another bishop. However, she was granted dispensations for all impediments and soon after she obtained papal permission to be appointed to any office in the convent, she apparently imposed herself as abbess, backed by her Butler relatives. By the early 1530s, tensions between Elicia and her community finally erupted and ended in her dismissal from office in 1532 after a catalogue of damning evidence against her was presented at the court of Milo, bishop of Ossory, who also reported the charges to the archbishop of Dublin and later, the civil authorities.[70] Elicia was accused of having squandered the 'diverse goods, rights, rents, incomes and finances of the convent, through an arrangement made without consulting the other nuns, for her own profane and wicked uses.' Because it was said that she 'wretchedly and impiously actually stole from her fellow sisters', the nuns who testified against her claimed they were compelled to leave the cloister and convent in search of food and clothing at the houses of powerful lords and other friends, contrary to the rules of their order. Having 'notoriously and incestuously' fornicated with a member of a monastic house, she allegedly gave birth to a child. She was accused of having 'laid violent hands even to the shedding of blood on … [three] professed nuns of the convent', of mutilating a young man 'for which heinous behaviour she can only be forgiven by the pope', and of celebrating divine office in 'an irregular fashion'.[71] What exercised the nuns most was the breach of enclosure caused by this 'loud, scandalous and public rumour' about the goings on at Kilculliheen. Although the charges again Elicia were too damning for her brother, Piers Roe Butler, to prevent her dismissal as abbess or her excommunication, she appears to have had his support at the end of her life and was accepted back into the Butler family, as evidenced by her burial in St Canice's Cathedral (Plate 7).[72]

CONCLUSION

While stone walls surrounding convents represented the sharp, supposedly inviolate boundary between lay and religious spaces in late medieval Ireland, breaches in the walls, bridges and pathways served as vital points of contact between the nuns and neighbouring lay communities. Thus, members of these 'permeable cloisters' forged close ties with local gentry or burgess families from whom they recruited new entrants

1400–1534: from reform to Reformation (Dublin, 2002), pp 155–6; Hall, *Women*, pp 166–8.   **70** *Irish monastic and episcopal deeds, 1200–1600*, ed. N.B. White (Dublin, 1936), pp 179–80; Hall, *Women*, pp 190–200.   **71** J. Mulholland, 'The trial of Alice Butler, abbess of Kilculiheen, 1532', *Decies*, 25 (Jan. 1984), p. 45.   **72** *Irish monastic and episcopal deeds*, p. 179; Collins, *Female monasticism*, pp 354–5.

and continued to attract donations of land, rents, advowsons of churches and other form of support for centuries.[73] Although several abbesses and prioresses enjoyed the protection and support of their families, maintaining ties with influential relatives also impacted negatively on superiors, their communities and convent resources when external tensions and political machinations permeated the cloister walls. It is worth remembering that behind the events and personalities captured in the surviving records and featured in this essay, the majority of abbesses and prioresses appear to have gotten on with ensuring that their convents remained places for women to live their communal life under religious vows, in peace, for centuries.

---

73 Hall, *Women*, pp 121–2, 178–9.

Marginal figures? Quasi-religious women in medieval Ireland

COLMÁN Ó CLABAIGH OSB

INTRODUCTION

The detail of the kneeling nuns depicted on the cover of this volume is taken from a painting dating to *c.*1440 by the Sienese painter, Sano di Pietro (1405–81) (Plate 8). It is of a type known as the *Madonna della Misericordia* or Mother of Mercy, that depicts suppliants sheltered under the Virgin Mary's mantle. From the late thirteenth century it was deployed, particularly in Italian mendicant circles, to express devotion to the Virgin as patron and protector of various groups.[1] At first glance, the casual observer might think, 'Franciscan nuns' or 'Poor Clares', but, as the contributions by Collins, Johnston and Ó Riain-Raedel have demonstrated above, when it comes to female religious in medieval Ireland few things are as they appear and Sano di Pietro's image serves well as a metaphor for these ambiguities.

Closer examination of the image shows that not all the 'nuns' depicted are identical: some have black veils; some white; some are wearing grey mantles. Two are not even female: the diminutive figures in the foreground, though each wearing the Franciscan cord and the grey robe of a penitent, are adolescent males sporting the clerical tonsure. Clearly, all these characters have something 'Franciscan' in common. Less clear however is how they differ and what form their individual vocational commitments took. Some may indeed have been professed nuns, bound by formal vows of poverty, chastity and obedience and living in a cloister. Others may represent vowesses: widows or single women who professed chastity while maintaining control over their financial affairs and living and operating 'in the world'. Still others may depict Franciscan secular tertiaries, women who observed the austere, ascetic lifestyle of the Franciscan Third Order but within the context of marriage and family life. It is also possible that some passed from one state of religious commitment to another in the course of their lifecycle as their personal circumstances changed. The two boys may well have been the sons of one or other of the women depicted, being raised in devout households influenced by Franciscan spirituality and perhaps primed for careers as friars. Whatever their status, all were identifiable as having made a religious commitment that both differentiated them from, and made them identifiable to their secular contemporaries.

If the iconography of such 'quasi-religious' individuals is confusing, then the terminology is even more so. For instance, Mario Sensi, in his study of female solitaries

---

1 K.T. Brown, *Mary of Mercy in medieval and renaissance Italian art: devotional image and civic emblem* (Routledge, 2017). I owe this reference to Dr Rachel Moss.

in medieval Italy, identified six different phrases describing the phenomenon of the devout woman living chastely under mendicant auspices and engaging in activities ranging from charitable service of the poor to life as enclosed anchoresses.[2] In Ireland, Máirín Ní Donnchadha has identified eight distinct meanings for the phrase *caillech*, each with distinct religious connotations. The phrase ultimately derives from the Latin word *pallium* – veil – and is one of the earliest loan words from Latin into the Irish language. Ostensibly meaning 'a veiled woman', it could also designate a consecrated virgin or nun, a betrothed woman or a spouse, a veiled penitent, widow or vowess, or an old woman, and by extension, a supernatural female figure, a hag or a witch.[3] These varying manifestations of female asceticism and religious life are as confusing to modern scholars as they were to their medieval clerical counterparts who likewise struggled to impose order on this creative chaos. As Elizabeth Makowski has demonstrated, canon lawyers in particular, charged with formulating definitions and imposing order on these 'pernicious women', had a task akin to herding mice at crossroads.[4]

This contribution examines the various expressions of quasi-religious life undertaken by medieval Irish women from the twelfth to the sixteenth centuries. While these were never as numerous or as influential as the Beguines on the Continent, they included individuals who lived as vowesses, anchoresses or female recluses, Franciscan and Dominican tertiaries as well as religious sisters who staffed medieval Irish hospitals. It builds on the pioneering work of Máirín Ní Donnchadha, Dianne Hall and Gillian Kenny as well as on the recent scholarship of Tracy Collins and Bronagh Ann McShane.

VOWESSES, VIRGINS AND WIDOWS

Consecrated virgins and widows or vowesses represent the earliest form of religious life in Christianity, being mentioned in the New Testament writings of St Paul and in the Acts of the Apostles.[5] These women made a public commitment to a life of continence, piety, penance and charity that distinguished them within the Christian community. They were identifiable by their sober dress and distinctive head covering or veil and often occupied a prominent place in church during the liturgy.[6] By the high Middle Ages commitment to vowed life by both virgins and widows occurred during a liturgical ceremony performed by a bishop or his delegate. Consequently, the rite was included in the pontifical, a service book that contained the texts and rubrics for ceremonies usually reserved to a bishop or prelate. Cambridge, Corpus Christi College

2 M. Sensi, 'Anchorites in the Italian tradition' in L. Herbert McAvoy (ed.), *Anchoritic traditions of medieval Europe* (Woodbridge, 2010), pp 62–90 at p. 67. **3** Ní Dhonnchadha, 'Caillech' 71–96. See also the contributions to this volume by Johnston and Swift for further discussion of the term. **4** E. Makowski, *A pernicious type of woman: quasi-religious women and canon lawyers in the later Middle Ages* (Washington DC, 2005). **5** See, for instance, Acts 6:16; 9:36–42; 21:8–9; 1 Timothy 5:3–16. **6** E. Magnani, 'Female house ascetics from the fourth to the twelfth century' in Beach and Cochelin, *CHMMLW*, pp 213–31.

MS 79, an English pontifical dating to the first decades of the fifteenth century, is of particular interest as, in addition to the texts of the ceremonies, it also contains detailed illustrations depicting the various rites (Plates 8, 9, 12). Only one such pontifical survives from medieval Ireland, Trinity College Dublin MS 99, a late fourteenth-century volume that originated in either Italy or Avignon but which was used in the diocese of Meath in the fifteenth and sixteenth centuries.[7] Although the text is deficient and faded in parts, it contains the rite for dedicating a widow to a life of chastity along with a reference to the ceremony for consecrating a virgin.[8]

Given its antiquity, the consecration of a virgin was a lengthy ceremony usually celebrated during Mass on one of the solemnities of the liturgical year like the Epiphany, the Ascension, Pentecost, the Easter octave or on a feastday of the Virgin Mary or one of the apostles (Plate 9). Failing this, it could take place on any Sunday outside of Advent and Lent.[9] On the evening before the ceremony, the candidate was examined by the bishop or his delegate to ascertain her suitability. In addition to verifying her physical integrity and good reputation, each virgin had to be at least twenty-five years of age, and cognizant of the commitment she was undertaking.[10] During Mass the candidate, bearing a candle, was positioned in the nave of the church in sight of the bishop seated before the altar. Once the bishop was assured of her worthiness, she was led into the choir where, kneeling before him, she vowed to observe perpetual virginity, afterwards prostrating herself before the altar while the choir sang the litany of the saints. During this the bishop blessed the candidate while beseeching God to strengthen her in her calling.[11] He then blessed the veil, ring and crown as symbols of her consecration. In imposing the veil, he prayed that she would present it 'without stain to the tribunal of the eternal judge'. He then placed a ring on her right hand, as a sign of her status as a spouse of Christ. After a series of collects and prayers invoking God's blessing, the bishop proclaimed an anathema or curse on anyone who compromised her chastity or interfered with her property.[12] That such sanctions were occasionally necessary is evident from the 1401 petition of the Galway vowess, Margaret Ballagh, who sought royal protection in pursuing the chaste lifestyle she had vowed in her youth from the 'evilly minded people' who were harassing her.[13]

Although a less elaborate ceremony, the blessing of a widow also took place during Mass, generally before the gospel was proclaimed. In this case the woman, wearing her normal attire and accompanied by two male relatives, approached the bishop or, more frequently, his delegate who was seated in front of the altar. Over her left arm she carried the dark cloak and veil that were the symbols of her vocation (Plate 10). She then knelt before the celebrant and professed a vow of chastity. Depending on her level of literacy this took the form of either a verbal commitment or a written document, which she signed or marked with a cross. Surviving English examples indicate the

7 M.L. Colker, *Trinity College Library Dublin: Descriptive catalogue of the mediaeval and renaissance Latin manuscripts*, 2 vols (Aldershot, 1991), vol. 1, pp 198–201.   **8** TCD MS 99, fos 137v–41v.   **9** This description in based on M. Andrieu (ed.), *Le Pontifical Romain au Moyen-Age*, III: *Le Pontifical de Guillaume Durand* (Vatican City, 1940), pp 411–25.   **10** Ibid., p. 411.   **11** Ibid. p. 414.   **12** Ibid., pp 416–18, 423; TCD MS 99, ff 137v–141v.   **13** Hall, *Women*, p. 186.

SOVVENT ME SOVVIENT

7.1 Lady Margaret Beaufort in the habit of a vowess.
Image © National Portrait Gallery, London.

profession was normally made in the vernacular. The widow's mantle and veil were placed on the altar and blessed with holy water following which she was invested by an assisting cleric. A ring was also blessed and placed on her finger as a sign of her spousal union with Christ. The celebrant then continued with Mass, which included prayers for divine assistance in fulfilling the commitment and in resisting temptation and frailty. The newly consecrated widow received communion as part of the ceremony.[14]

The voluminous cloak worn by consecrated widows in England led to the phrase 'to take the ring and the mantle' becoming a synonym for the vocation. In addition to a dark or russet tunic, the widow wore a dark veil while her face was framed by a wimple and a pleated linen garment known as a *barbe* that covered the neck, chin and upper chest.[15] (Fig. 7.1; Plate 11) Similar attire was worn by anchoresses, tertiaries and nuns, which makes it very difficult to identify status from iconography alone. Despite this, two sepulchral effigies in St Canice's Cathedral, Kilkenny, are thought to represent vowesses. The first occurs on a fourteenth-century incised grave slab set in the floor near the west end of the cathedral. The figure wears a gown closely fitted at the neck with full sleeves extending to her mid forearms and with the sleeves of a kirtle visible underneath. The pleats in her outer garment may represent the folds of a cloak. She also wears a veil and a wimple and her hands are uplifted in a gesture of prayer.[16]

The second effigy (Plate 7) is positioned on a substantial chest tomb in the south aisle of the building. Although often described as the tomb of Elicia Butler, the somewhat colourful abbess of Kilculliheen, Co. Waterford, who courted notoriety between 1531 and 1540, John Hunt suggests that it depicts a consecrated widow or a vowess.[17] This figure is clad in a long gown over which she wears a voluminous mantle, the ends of which are held in her hands. Her waist is encircled with a buckled belt and over her throat and around her face she wears a wimple and *barbe*. This is surmounted by a veil that covers her head and shoulders and whose heavy folds overlie the pleated edge of the *barbe* and the forehead.

The religious life of a vowess or consecrated widow was generally conducted in a domestic setting although some found accommodation in the precincts of male and female monasteries. Dianne Hall suggests that the description of part of a section of Moygara Castle, Co. Sligo, as *Teach na calliagh* or 'the house of the nun' may indicate the presence of a vowess there at some stage in its history.[18] The relative independence of this way of life enabled the vowess to administer her affairs, control her finances and supervise her family. In their analyses of the surviving English material, Cullum, Burgess and Erler show that some late vowed widows were formidable characters in

---

14 Andrieu, *Pontifical Romain au Moyen-Age*, III, pp 426–7. See also M.C. Erler, 'English vowed women at the end of the Middle Ages', *Medieval Studies*, 57 (1995), 155–203. **15** M.M. Sauer, 'The meaning of russet: a note on vowesses and clothing', *Early Middle English*, 2:2 (2020), 91–7. **16** J. Hunt, *Irish medieval figure sculpture, 1200–1600*, vol. I (Dublin, 1974), p. 184. **17** Ibid., vol. I, p. 191. See M.M. Phelan, 'An unidentified tomb in St Canice's Cathedral, Kilkenny', *Old Kilkenny Review* 48 (1996), 40–4. For a nuanced treatment of Abbess Butler's career see Hall, *Women*, pp 191–200 and Lyons' contribution above. Alternatively, the effigy may represent an anchoress as an anchorite's cell was located on the north side of the cathedral. **18** Hall, *Women*, p. 187.

the mercantile communities of medieval Bristol, London and York.[19] Likewise, the elevated social status of the calling afforded strongminded, aristocratic women like Elizabeth de Burgh, Lady of Clare (d. 1360), Mary of St Pol, Countess of Pembroke (d. 1377) and Lady Margaret Beaufort (d. 1509), mother of Henry VII and matriarch of the Tudor dynasty, an opportunity to remain active in public life following the deaths of their husbands.[20] The various portraits of Lady Margaret in the habit of a vowess depict a singularly forceful individual (Fig. 7.1, Plate 11). The image from St John's College, Cambridge produced by Meynnart Wewyck, *c*. 1510 shows her kneeling at her devotions, the russet robe, *barbe*, wimple and veil of the vowess contrasting sharply with her sumptuous surroundings and the canopy of estate over her head.

This may have been the lifestyle adopted by various widows noted in the Irish sources for their piety and support of the church and the poor. These included Lady Isabella Palmer of Kilkenny who died on Palm Sunday, 1347, 'having lived about seventy years religiously and honourably in her widowhood and in virginity.'[21] A notable supporter of the Franciscans in Kilkenny, she was credited with building the choir screen in their church. The belief that she had preserved her virginity throughout her marriage provides a unique Irish example of the phenomenon of the 'chaste marriage' whereby spouses remained sexually abstinent for devotional reasons.[22] Likewise, in Galway, Margaret Ballagh Lynch, the widow of Thomas Martyn, a burgess of the city, was noted for her generosity to the Dominicans of Athenry. This benevolence earned her the soubriquet *hospita fratrum* – the hostess of the friars.[23] Devout women in Gaelic areas also embraced this way of life: in September 1456 Sawe ingen Oconnolan received the permission of Archbishop John Mey of Armagh to live chastely at the hospice at Donoughmore, Co. Louth, caring for the poor and the sick.[24]

ANCHORESSES AND RECLUSES

The evidence for female anchorites/anchoresses or recluses in late medieval Ireland is more abundant than for vowesses and widows. These were individuals who, under episcopal licence, adopted an extreme form of asceticism, opting for a lifetime of prayer and penance while enclosed in a small cell or anchorhold attached to the wall of a church or chapel. This vocation was open to both men and women and was widespread

19 C. Burgess, *The right ordering of souls: the parish of All Saints, Bristol on the eve of the Reformation* (Woodbridge, 2018), pp 119–62; M.C. Erler, 'Three fifteenth-century vowesses' in C.M. Barron and A.F. Sutton, *Medieval London widows, 1300–1500* (London and Rio Grande, 1994), pp 165–81; P.H. Cullum, 'Vowesses and female lay piety in the province of York, 1300–1500', *Northern History*, 32 (1996), 21–41. **20** M.K. Wood and M.G. Underwood, *The king's mother: Lady Margaret Beaufort, countess of Richmond and Derby* (Cambridge, 1992), pp 153, 160, 187–8. **21** B. Williams (ed.), *The annals of Ireland by Friar John Clyn* (Dublin, 2007), pp 241–2. **22** D. Elliott, *Spiritual marriage: sexual abstinence in medieval marriage* (Princeton, 1993). **23** A. Coleman (ed.), 'Regestum Monasterii Fratrum Praedicatorum de Athenry', *AH*, 1 (1912), 201–21 at 210–11. **24** Hall, *Women*, p. 189; W.H.G. Quigley and E.F.D. Roberts (eds), *Registrum Iohannis Mey*: the register of John Mey, archbishop of Armagh (Belfast, 1972), pp 336–7, no. 324. The license also contained an admonition to the O'Neill chieftain and his brothers not to molest or injure Sawe

across Britain and the Continent throughout the high and late Middle Ages.[25] Most practitioners seem to have been women however, with male solitaries generally opting for the less constrained life of a hermit.[26]

The surviving anchoritic material from Ireland consists of episcopal legislation governing the lifestyle, liturgical material relating to the rite of enclosure, anchoritic rules of life, evidence for support by benefactors and references to anchorites in contemporary literature. A number of anchorholds have been identified in archaeological surveys and two have recently been excavated.[27] Of particular importance is a dossier of anchoritic material recently discovered in Maynooth MS Renehan B 201. This is a seventeenth-century compendium of Irish hagiography and other religious material compiled by Dr Thomas Arthur, a Limerick physician, from earlier sources, including documents from the archives of the medieval archbishops of Armagh.[28] The anchoritic material closely parallels twelfth- and thirteenth-century English sources and is similar to texts found in TCD MS 97, a late thirteenth-/early fourteenth-century compendium of monastic legislation from the Victorine abbey of St Thomas in Dublin. It is possible that the Arthur compendium reflects the experience of late medieval recluses professed by the archbishops of Armagh. Although addressed to male recluses, both the Arthur compendium and the St Thomas' Abbey material could have been adapted for anchoresses.

As with virgins and vowesses, the bishop's involvement began with a thorough examination of the candidate to ensure that she possessed the psychological and spiritual maturity and the requisite finances to pursue her calling. No Irish examples of these preliminary investigations survive, but an illustrative account of one Irish anchoress' experience occurs in the register of Bishop Edmund Lacy of Exeter. In 1447, Christine Holby, an Augustinian canoness of Kildare, sought enclosure as an anchoress in the churchyard of St Leonard's Church in Exeter having fled from Ireland after her convent was attacked. Bishop Lacy commissioned Walter Collys, the precentor of the cathedral, to examine her to determine

> ... that Satan had not transformed himself into an angel of light to seduce her.
> Ensure that she has sure and certain sustenance to sustain her, and who will
> bestow it and sustain it until the end of her life, and of how much and of what
> things this manner of dowry ought to consist, so that we and our successors in
> this place shall never be burdened by this conclusion.[29]

or her goods.   **25** Important recent studies include P. L'Hermite-Leclercq, 'Reclusion in the Middle Ages' in Beach and Cochelin, *CHMMLW*, pp 747–65; A. Mulder-Bakker, *Lives of the anchoresses: the rise of the urban recluse in medieval Europe* (Philadelphia, 2005); T. Licence, *Hermits and recluses in English society, 950–1250* (Cambridge, 2011) and especially L. Herbert McAvoy (ed.), *Anchoritic traditions of medieval Europe* (Woodbridge, 2010).   **26** K. Jasper and J. Howe, 'Hermitism in the eleventh and twelfth centuries' in Beach and Cochelin, *CHMMLW*, pp 684–96 at pp 693–4.   **27** This section summarizes C. Ó Clabaigh, 'Anchorites in late medieval Ireland' in McAvoy (ed.), *Anchoritic traditions*, pp 153–77.   **28** St Patrick's College, Maynooth, Russell Library MS RB 201, ff 233–40. The text was identified by Dr Donna Thornton and an edition and translation by Senan Furlong OSB and Colmán Ó Clabaigh OSB is forthcoming.   **29** G.R. Dunstan (ed.),

Holby obviously satisfied these conditions as a subsequent entry in the register indicates that she had been enclosed in her cell.

Although the rite of enclosure for an anchorite is not included in the Meath pontifical discussed above (Trinity College Dublin MS 99), its principal elements can be reconstructed from English sources and from the abbreviated version of the rite contained in the Arthur compendium.[30] The ceremony combined elements of the funeral liturgy with that of religious profession. During Mass the candidate, holding a candle, made profession of the religious vows to the bishop or his delegate, promising to remain in the anchorhold, steadfastly devoted to prayer and penance. This was accompanied by the litany of the saints and after communion the prayers for the dying were recited and the anchorite was sprinkled with clay. Following this the bishop entered the adjacent anchorhold and blessed it. The anchorite then took possession of the cell and the bishop or his delegate sealed the door (Plate 12).

Whereas the Arthur compendium makes no reference to Mass, it describes the procession to the anchorhold, the blessing of the cell and its occupant and gives the *incipits* of the various collects and prayers recited during the ceremony:

> At the *introit* let there be a procession with the anchorite.
>
> At the entrance of an anchorite a procession is made by the bishop or abbot or prior and after they come to the anchorhold let him be led by the major prelates before the altar and let them say the seven penitential psalms. After the psalms let the prelate say the prayers *Salvum fac servum tuum. Deus meus sperantem in te. Mitte ei Domine auxilium de sancto, et de Syon tuere eum. Esto ei Domine turris fortitudinis, a facie inimici. Nihil proficiat inimicus in eo. Et filius iniquitatis non apponat nocere ei. Domine exaudi est et clamoretur*, etc.
>
> Let us pray: Bless O Lord this bridal chamber and this your servant J. living in it and may he remain in your love with fasting, prayers and vigils and may he day by day build up the clergy and people of God by leading a pure and religious life until the end of his life. Amen.

The text also gives the formula of profession used by the candidates:

> I, J., make profession to Almighty God and to the Blessed Mary, ever virgin and to all the saints whose feast is celebrated today in the church of God and of the rule constituted by the saints and fathers in the year of the Lord, 1401.[31]

In an age where prayer was regarded as a valuable commodity, anchoresses enjoyed a high social status and frequently featured as recipients of alms and beneficiaries of wills.

Register of Edmund Lacy, bishop of Exeter, 1420–1455 (Canterbury and York Society 60–3, 1963–71), vol. ii, pp 394–5; A.K. Warren, *Anchorites and their patrons in medieval England* (Berkeley, 1985), pp 74, 269. **30** E.A. Jones, 'Ceremonies of enclosure: rite, rhetoric and reality' in L. Herbert McAvoy (ed.), *Rhetoric of the anchorhold: space, place and body within the discourses of enclosure* (Cardiff, 2008), pp 34–49. **31** St Patrick's College, Maynooth, Russell Library MS RB 201, ff 239–40.

The making of testaments and wills became more common in Europe from the twelfth century and Irish examples survive from the thirteenth century onwards. The earliest record of a bequest to an Irish recluse occurs in 1275 when Katherine, wife of John le Grant, left a legacy to the anchoress of St Paul's chapel in Dublin, and to her servant Petronilla.[32] In 1326 Robert de Moenes, a wealthy citizen of Dublin, left bequests to a female recluse at St Paul's chapel and to two male anchorites at other churches in the city.[33] A single reference to a recluse in Drogheda occurs in 1335 when Richard Tanner bequeathed forty pence to the anchoress enclosed beside the Church of St Laurence.[34]

In England the Crown and aristocratic benefactors constituted the mainstay of many recluses' support networks.[35] This could include endowment of a specific anchorhold, a regular payment of alms, either in cash or in kind, or a one-off benefaction in response to specific needs. Occasionally the rent from properties was assigned to support a recluse. Similar arrangements were made in Ireland. Between 1270 and 1281 the Irish Exchequer Rolls record the annual grant of a robe and a daily stipend of one-and-a-half pence by King Henry III to the anchoress of the Church of St Mary del Dam in Dublin.[36] This church was adjacent to Dublin Castle, the seat of royal government in Ireland, and to the Irish Exchequer, which proximity may account for the patronage. Though rents provided a degree of financial security for the recluse, such involvements in temporal affairs also brought their own hazards. For example, in 1300 the anchoress Roesia de Naungles was forced to sue Adam of Trim in court for non-payment of a debt.[37]

As an act of charity religious houses occasionally undertook the support of recluses. In 1436, the Annals of Connacht record the death of the anchoress Gormalaigh at Holy Trinity Abbey, a house of Premonstratensian canons situated on Trinity Island in Loch Key, Co. Roscommon.[38] The Augustinian canonesses of Grace Dieu near Dublin supported the anchoress Felicia in their chapel at Ballymadun, Co. Dublin, at an unspecified date in either the fourteenth or fifteenth century.[39] Another community of Augustinian canonesses, at Graney, Co. Kildare, maintained an anchorhold at their church at Kilkea.[40] Tracy Collins suggests that a structure called 'the black hag's cell' at St Catherine's Abbey, Co. Limerick, indicates the presence of an anchoress there in the fifteenth century.[41] While these arrangements provided a degree of security for the recluse, they did not always end well as Maria, the anchoress of Aghade, discovered when the canonesses of St Mary de Hogges in Dublin began court proceedings to evict her.[42]

---

32 M.J. McEnery and R. Refaussé, *Christ Church deeds* (Dublin, 2001), no. 106, p. 54.   33 Trinity College, Dublin MS 1207/85–26. Cited by Hall, *Women*, pp 186–7.   34 C. McNeill and J. Otway-Ruthven (eds), *Dowdall deeds* (Dublin, 1960), pp 53–4.   35 Warren, *Anchorites and their patrons*, pp 127–221.   36 P. Connolly (ed.), *Irish Exchequer payments*, vol. 1: 1270–1326 (Dublin, 1998), pp 2, 6, 12, 17, 22, 25, 29, 37, 46, 50, 54, 60, 61, 66.   37 J. Mills (ed.), *Calendar of the Justiciary Rolls: Ireland, 1295–1303* (Dublin, 1905), p. 313; Hall, *Women*, p. 186.   38 A. Martin Freeman (ed.), *Annála Connacht: the annals of Connacht (AD 1224–1544)* (Dublin, 1944), pp 478–9. Gormalaigh was the daughter of David Ó Duibgennain and wife of Brian Mac Aedacáin who became a recluse at the end of her life.   39 M. Archdall, *Monasticon Hibernicum* (Dublin, 1786), pp 131, 216–17. Dianne Hall gives an alternative date of 1308 in *Women and the church*, p. 187, n. 182.   40 See below, pp 130–1.   41 Collins, *Female monasticism*, pp 265–70, 272, 426.   42 Hall, *Women*,

As the above mentioned case of Christine Holby demonstrates, it was possible for a nun to become a recluse but the opposite was also true. This generally occurred when disciples gathered around an anchoress, necessitating the formation of a coenobitic community.[43] This may be why Agnes of Hereford, formerly a recluse in Cork, sought permission in 1297 to establish a house for herself and other nuns at Clonboly in the city. Despite some misgivings about the financial implications of the foundation, the local gentry supported her petition as there was 'no other house of nuns where knights and other free men may have their daughters brought up and maintained.'[44] Here the educational requirements of a social elite outweighed an individual's desire for solitude. This incident also provides a unique example of an anchoress fulfilling a social and educational role in medieval Ireland. Though often frowned on by legislators, the anchoress as educator was an important and widespread phenomenon in England and on the Continent.[45]

The particular needs of the anchorite's vocation required specific legislation and from the ninth century, rules and spiritual treatises catering for the solitary life began to appear in Europe and England.[46] The earliest evidence for this material in Ireland is found in the abovementioned Trinity College Dublin MS 97, a compendium of monastic texts from St Thomas' Abbey, Dublin. These include unique copies of a work known as the 'Dublin anchorites rule' and a set of admonitions on the anchoritic life.[47] The Dublin rule consists of a prologue and twenty-four chapters and is an interesting mixture of the spiritual and the mundane. It combined material from the Rule of St Benedict, the *Regula solitariorum* of Grimlaic, St Aelred's *De institutis inclusarum* and the *Ancrene rule* and was compiled sometime between 1220 and 1312, probably in the first half of the thirteenth century. It also has close verbal and thematic similarities with the rule contained in British Library MS Vitellus E. IX, ff 39–53 and with the recently discovered 'Rule of Godwin of Salisbury' found in the Arthur compendium.

Although much of the Dublin rule is concerned with the practicalities of the reclusive life, the prologue contains a poetic meditation on the Christian vocation to praise and worship God:

> What is more natural for all creatures of God than that they should love their God and Father above all? He acts in accordance with nature who loves God above all, He who is called wisdom, the highest good. Where is wealth, where is beauty, where is light, where is fortitude, where is health, where is plenitude, where is joy, where is glory, where is the fullness of goodness, where is rest, where is any good unless with God?[48]

p. 187.　**43** J. Herbert, 'The transformation of hermitages into Augustinian priories in twelfth-century England' in W.J. Shiels, *Monks, hermits and the ascetic tradition*, Studies in Church History 22 (Padstow, 1985), pp 131–46.　**44** J. Mills (ed.), *Calendar of the Justiciary Rolls: Ireland, 1295–1303* (Dublin, 1905), p. 313; Hall, *Women*, p. 155.　**45** A. Mulder-Bakker, 'The reclusorium as an informal centre of learning' in J.W. Drijvers and A.A. MacDonald (eds), *Centres of learning: learning and location in pre-modern Europe and the Near East* (Leiden, 1995), pp 246–54.　**46** Warren, *Anchorites and their patrons*, pp 92–124; 294–8.　**47** Colker, *Descriptive catalogue*, vol. 1, pp 183–95; TCD MS 97 ff 187–91. The anchoritic material has been published by L. Oliger (ed.), 'Regulae tres reclusorum et eremitarum Angliae saec. XIII–XIV', *Antonianum*, 3 (1928), 151–90.　**48** Ibid.,

The first chapter urges the recluse to adopt Job as model, bearing patiently with poverty and infirmity if this is his lot. The second urged attention to the 'daily bread' of divine doctrine before dealing at length with what must have been an occasional temptation: the abuse of alcohol. Considerable attention is devoted to the maintenance of silence and the avoiding of gossip, scandal and detraction. The anchorite's voice was not to be heard raised in laughter or coming from the window of the anchorhold. Anchorites were not to have too many servants, nor to be avaricious nor to use the cell for inappropriate secular activities like storing valuables for others. Other sections were dedicated to the spiritual and liturgical aspects of the life. The anchorite was to receive communion each Sunday, having prepared appropriately by confessing his sins. The hours of the Divine Office were to be celebrated at the appropriate times and from the feast of All Saints (1 November) until Easter the recluse was to rise at midnight to recite Vigils. The Office of the Virgin Mary was also recited and the *Dirige* or Matins from the Office of the Dead was said after the midday meal during the summer, unless it was a feastday. Each day the recluse was instructed to recite the seven penitential psalms and the litany of the saints, to pray for their servants and benefactors. If they were illiterate, they substituted multiple recitations of the *Pater noster* for the psalmody. The final chapter was devoted to the seasons and manner of fasting and, if possible, the anchorite was urged to abstain from all inebriating drink, though this was not obligatory. The habit was to be black, white or grey in colour and the recluse was not to wear linen underclothing unless seriously ill.

The anchorite's rule contained in the Arthur compendium – Maynooth MS RB 201 – consists of a prologue and twenty-eight chapters and runs to approximately 370 lines of text. A colophon attributes its compilation to Canon Godwin of Salisbury who may be identical with the early twelfth-century writer whose *Meditationes* are preserved in Oxford Bodleian MS Digby 96.[49] Its content is remarkably similar to the Dublin rule and both texts draw on similar sources.

The solitary life also gave rise to a distinctive body of literature designed for a broad audience some of which circulated in late medieval Ireland. A particularly vivid example is preserved in the *Liber Exemplorum*, a collection of anecdotes for preachers, compiled by an English member of the Irish Franciscan province *c*.1275. One story, concerning the necessity of making a full confession, relates how an anchoress overhead the conversation of a gathering of demons in the graveyard outside her cell. One boasted that he was about to secure the damnation of the soul of a dying woman who, though well regarded for her piety, had omitted out of shame to confess a sin she had committed in her youth. Hearing this, the anchoress summoned the priest and relayed the information. He then approached the dying woman and interrogated her. Although now unable to speak, she began to weep when the priest identified the sin. This sign of repentance was sufficient to secure her salvation and when the demons next gathered, they heard that their colleague had been thwarted in his efforts. Again, all this was overheard by the anchoress.[50]

p. 171 (my translation).   **49** R. Sharpe, *A handlist of the Latin writers of Great Britain and Ireland before 1540* (Turnhout, 1997), p. 151.   **50** A.G. Little (ed.), *Liber exemplorum ad usum praedicantium saeculo*

7.2 Anchorite's cell at Athassel priory, Co. Tipperary. Image © Colmán Ó Clabaigh.

The exemplum illustrates a number of perceptions of the anchoritic life. First, it demonstrates that thirteenth-century Irish congregations were familiar with anchoresses. Second, the recluse's ability to eavesdrop on demons and her dwelling in the churchyard highlights her role as a liminal figure, conducting a spiritual warfare on behalf of the community in the twilight zone between the visible and invisible worlds. Finally, her ability to summon and instruct the priest on how to proceed indicates recognition of her authority in spiritual matters.

The anchoritic lifestyle gave rise to a distinctive architecture: the reclusiorium or anchorhold, a structure that allowed them to pursue their radically separate vocation while remaining at the heart of a community. While Tomás Ó Carragáin has convincingly proposed that the roof vaults in the twelfth-century stone churches at Cashel, Killaloe and Kells may have been occupied by recluses, the classic reclusorium normally abutted the north wall of a church or chapel and had an internal window or hagioscope through which the occupant could watch Mass and the Divine Office being celebrated within the church itself.[51] Another small window, set in an exterior wall, allowed the recluse to conduct business with servants and benefactors and to offer counsel and conversation to visitors. The earliest surviving example of this type of structure is the thirteenth-century example at the Augustinian priory of St Edmund, Athassel, Co. Tipperary. Here the cell is nestled in the angle between the north transept of the church and the north wall of the nave (Fig. 7.2). With internal measurements of 3 x 1.75 metres, it has a low internal window with a line of sight on a side altar in the

xiii compositus a quondam fratre minore Anglico de provincia Hiberniae (Aberdeen, 1918), p. 57. See also D. Jones, *Friars' tales: thirteenth-century exempla from the British Isles* (Manchester, 2011), pp 84–5.
51 T. Ó Carragáin, *Churches in early medieval Ireland: architecture, ritual and social memory* (New Haven and London, 2010), pp 255–91.

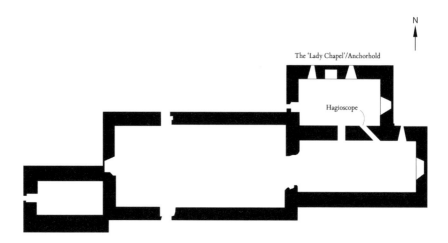

7.3 Anchorhold at Kilkea church, Co. Kildare. Redrawn by Frank Coyne. Reproduced by permission of the Committee of the County Kildare Archaeology and Historical Society.

north-east corner of the nave. Through this, the kneeling occupant could view Mass being celebrated and could hear the Divine Office being chanted by the Augustinian canons in the choir behind the roodscreen.

Tracy Collins has identified a small, freestanding structure at Templenagalliagdoo (the 'church of the black nun'), Co. Mayo, as a nunnery chapel and anchorhold. Dating to the mid-thirteenth century, the structure has a small annex on its northern side that may have housed a female recluse. A rectangular pit in the floor may represent the site of an occupant's grave as it was customary for anchorites to be buried in their cells.[52]

Architectural features in a number of fifteenth-century mendicant foundations in the west of Ireland also suggest the presence of recluses, some of whom may have been female. The Franciscan tertiary foundations at Rosserk, Co. Mayo and Court, Co. Sligo and the Observant Franciscan house at Moyne, Co. Mayo have curious cells embedded in the walls of the transepts of the corresponding friary church. Each is equipped with a door frame, a squint looking onto the altar in the adjoining chapel and a narrow external window. Whereas their dimensions are extremely confined it is hard to envisage what function they could have fulfilled other than as an anchorhold.[53]

A fine example of a reclusorium has recently been identified by Con Manning at Kilkea chruch, Co. Kildare (Fig. 7.3).[54] Located in the demesne of Kilkea Castle, an important Fitzgerald residence in the later Middle Ages, it consists of a cell measuring 6.8 by 3.7 metres located on the north side of the chancel of the church. It represents a sixteenth-century extension to the building and when surveyed by Lord Walter Fitzgerald in 1892 was initially identified as a Lady chapel.[55] Manning argues that the

52 Collins, *Female monasticism*, p. 270.   **53** C. Ó Clabaigh, 'The hermits and anchorites of medieval Dublin' in S. Duffy (ed.), *Medieval Dublin X* (Dublin, 2010), pp 267–89 at pp 283–4. **54** Pers. comm. 22 October 2019.   **55** Lord W. FitzGerald, 'William FitzGerald of Castleroe

presence of an angled hagioscope in the north chancel wall and the remains of a fireplace within the cell itself are more indicative of it being an anchorhold. As noted above, the advowson of the church at Kilkea belonged to the Augustinian canonesses of Graney, who may have been predisposed to accommodate a female recluse like their colleagues at Grace Dieu and St Catherine's (Plate 6).

FRANCISCAN AND DOMINICAN TERTIARIES

The arrival of the Dominican and Franciscan friars in Ireland in the third decade of the thirteenth century led to a quickening of devotion among the laity and all orders attracted followers who wished to live more intense Christian lives inspired by mendicant ideals.[56] This lay association took a variety of forms, ranging from membership of confraternities to radical lifelong commitments undertaken by individuals living as vowesses and anchorites adjacent to friaries. It paralleled other forms of lay piety and confraternalism that emerged in the late medieval Irish church.[57] Of particular importance was the emergence in the early fifteenth century of the Franciscan and Dominican Third Orders. These organizations enabled lay men and women, called tertiaries, to practice a modified form of the religious life, while remaining in their secular occupations, marrying and rearing families, and the tertiary movement became one of the most important and widespread vehicles of lay piety in late medieval Ireland.

The 'tertiary' or 'Third Order' movement emerged from a pre-existing religious group, the 'Order of Penitents', in thirteenth-century Italy. The penitents consisted of laymen and women who had freely adopted the penitential lifestyle normally imposed by the church on public sinners. As the Franciscans and Dominicans spread through Italy and the rest of Europe, their preaching led to a revitalization of this movement. In consequence, some groups of penitents became more markedly 'Franciscan' or 'Dominican' in character and came to acknowledge St Francis or St Dominic as their founders and patrons. This process culminated in the emergence of groups associated with the friars and described as 'the Third Order of St Francis' or the 'Third Order of St Dominic'. In 1284, Friar Munio of Zamora, the master general of the Dominicans, formally gathered the Dominican tertiary groups into a Dominican order of penitents. In 1289, Pope Nicholas IV issued a formal rule for the Franciscan penitents, embodied in the bull *Supra montem*.

Little evidence survives to indicate that the friars in Ireland promoted the tertiary vocation among their lay followers in the thirteenth and fourteenth centuries. In 1326

and his tomb in the Kilkea churchyard', *JCKHAS*, 3 (1899–1902), 229–53 image at 244.   **56** This section summarizes C. Ó Clabaigh, *The Franciscans in Ireland, 1400–1534: from reform to Reformation* (Dublin, 2002), pp 80–105; ibid., *The friars in Ireland, 1224–1540* (Dublin, 2012), pp 285–317. For tertiary sisters in early modern Ireland see B.A. McShane, *Irish women in religious orders, 1530–1700: suppression, migration and reintegration* (Woodbridge, 2022) and her contribution to this volume. **57** C. Lennon, 'The confraternities and cultural duality in Ireland, 1450–1550' in C. Black and P. Gravestock (eds), *Early modern confraternities in Europe and the Americas* (Aldershot, 2006), 85–101.

the former mayor of Dublin, Robert de Moenes, left bequests to two women described as Minorite sisters (*sororibus minoribus*) in his will. This term was often used to describe Franciscan or Poor Clare nuns but it may also refer to tertiaries or even recluses attached to the city's Franciscan friary.[58] The earliest reliable reference to the Franciscan Third Order in Ireland occurs in 1425, when Pope Martin V granted a copy of the bull *Supra montem* to the Irish tertiaries. In the winter of 1426–7, a copy of the Dominican Third Order rule was issued to the Observant friars in Portumna, Co. Galway, indicating that they also promoted the tertiary vocation among their lay followers.

Membership of the Third Order entailed a commitment to an austere, ascetic regime that went far beyond what was expected of other lay Christians. The Franciscan tertiaries wore a simple grey habit, while the Dominicans wore a white tunic and black cloak. Female tertiaries in both orders wore veils. After profession of their vows, members could only leave the order if they were transferring to another religious order. Women were not allowed to join the Third Order without the permission of their husbands and male Franciscan tertiaries were forbidden to bear arms.

Franciscan tertiaries celebrated the Liturgy of the Hours by reading the Divine Office if they were literate, or by multiple recitations of the *Pater noster*, the Apostles' Creed and Psalm 50 at the appropriate times of the day. During Lent, they were expected to attend the morning hours of the Office in their parish churches. Given the haphazard nature of parochial structures in late medieval Ireland, it is likely that many secular tertiaries fulfilled this obligation by attending services in a friary church. Where possible, they attended daily Mass and confessed and received communion three times a year. They fasted from the feast of St Martin (11 November) until Christmas, and their Lenten fast began on Quinquagesima Sunday. They also fasted on Wednesdays from 1 November until the following Easter. Abstinence from meat was observed on Mondays, Wednesdays and Saturdays, and they were to be content with two meals a day. There were a number of exceptions to this regime: pregnant tertiaries were exempt until after they had been churched, as were travellers. Those engaged in physical work could take three meals a day and no one was required to fast for three days after being bled. The local superiors and the visitators could dispense from these requirements as circumstances demanded.

NURSING SISTERS

Another vocational option for medieval Irish women was as religious dedicated to nursing and healthcare. Approximately 210 hospitals and hospices are recorded in both Gaelic and Anglo-Norman territories but most are poorly documented with little evidence for the type of healthcare provided or the identity and lifestyle of those who ran them.[59] Medieval hospitals were primarily arenas for the worship of God and the

---

See also his contribution to this volume.   **58** Hall, *Women*, pp 186–7.   **59** *MRHI*, pp 344–57. See also T. Ivory, 'The medieval hospital in Ireland: a comment on the crusader connection' in E. Coleman, P. Duffy and T. O'Keeffe, *Ireland and the crusades* (Dublin, 2022), pp 129–35.

exercise of the corporal works of mercy. Here the sick were tended, the hungry fed and the naked received clothing while all residents, both patients and staff, followed a quasi-monastic regime, sharing a daily round of liturgical worship and individual prayer designed to evoke God's blessing on the hospital, its benefactors and the wider community.[60] Acute medical treatment was not the norm and care consisted primarily of the provision of good nourishment and shelter administered by the chaplains and nursing sisters and brothers.[61] The inmates of the hospital of St John at the New Gate in Dublin received donations of milk and salmon from their benefactors, while those resident in the institution established by Dean John Collyn in Waterford in 1478 were bound to rise during the night to pray for those who had given them 'meet or drynk clothis or fyr'.[62] It seems likely that the sisters were responsible for healthcare of the residents but that otherwise their regime of life would have differed little from that of their charges.

The best documented of these institutions was the hospital of St John the Baptist at the New Gate of Dublin which was established before 1188 by Aelred le Palmer and his wife. The couple took monastic vows and dedicated themselves and their resources to the care of the sick.[63] Others joined them and the community later adopted the lifestyle of the *Fratres Cruciferi* or Crutched friars, a body of religious men and women dedicated to health care that established foundations in Ireland, mostly in Anglo-Norman centres.[64] This order followed the Rule of St Augustine, the one most favoured by monastic hospital foundations on account of its adaptability.[65] Sometime around 1190, Robert de Aveney endowed the hospital with land near Tara, Co. Meath, in honour of his 'beloved relative Emeline' who 'God had called to his service in the said hospital'.[66] Although she is the only one known by name, a number of references to the sisters in the community occur in other thirteenth-century sources but later records, including the dissolution documents, only refer to the prior and brethren. Dianne Hall suggests that the female religious supervised the care of female inmates and oversaw the weaving work for which the hospital was noted.[67]

Women religious also helped staff the hospitals dedicated to St John the Baptist at Ardee and Drogheda (both houses of the *Fratres Cruciferi*) as well as at the hospital and priory of St Leonard at Dundalk.[68] In Wexford, the leper hospital of St Mary Magdalene established by Richard de Clare (Strongbow) before 1176 was staffed by male and female religious and references to both sisters and brothers occur as late as

60 N. Orme and M. Webster, *The English hospital, 1070–1570* (New Haven & London, 1995), pp 49–146.　**61** G. O'Keeffe, 'The hospital of St John the Baptist in medieval Dublin: functions and maintenance' in S. Duffy (ed.), *Medieval Dublin IX* (Dublin, 2009), pp 166–82, at pp 170–81.　**62** E. St John Brooks (ed.), *The register of the hospital of St John the Baptist without the New Gate, Dublin* (Dublin, 1936), pp 33, 40, 110, 164, 212, 236, 245; N. Byrne, *The register of St Saviour's chantry of Waterford* (Dublin, 2013), p. 76.　**63** M.P. Sheehy, *Pontificia Hibernica: medieval papal chancery records relating to Ireland, 640–1261*, 2 vols (Dublin, 1962–5), vol. I, pp 61–3.　**64** R.N. Hadcock, 'The Order of the Holy Cross in Ireland' in J.A. Watt, J.B. Morrall, F.X. Martin (eds), *Medieval studies presented to Aubrey Gwynn, SJ* (Dublin, 1961), pp 44–53.　**65** For the various forms of Augustinian canonical life in medieval Ireland see the contributions to Browne and Ó Clabaigh, *Households*.　**66** E. St John Brooks (ed.), *The register of the hospital of St John the Baptist without the New Gate, Dublin* (Dublin, 1936), pp 172–3.　**67** Hall, *Women*, p. 188.　**68** Ibid.,

1389 and 1408.[69] Another leper hospital, under the care of a certain Agnes, is recorded in Tipperary in 1312, though this may have been a short-lived foundation.[70]

Nursing sisters also helped staff the Benedictine hospital of St John the Evangelist at Waterford and its dependencies at Cork, Youghal and Legan.[71] The Waterford foundation was established sometime before 1190, when it was taken under the protection of Prince John, count of Mortain, who issued three charters guaranteeing its rights. It does not appear to have been a Benedictine foundation before 1204, when the community under their superior, Master Peter, agreed to submit to the authority of the Benedictine community of St Peter in Bath. In accepting them Prior Robert and the monastic chapter issued regulations governing the running of the Waterford priory and hospital. The prior or warden of Waterford was to be appointed by the prior of Bath, all male members of the community were to travel to Bath where they would make profession and promise obedience to the prior. The sick and infirm in the hospital were to be supported from the resources bequeathed for that purpose and any surplus income was to be devoted to the exercise of hospitality.

Despite the Benedictine connection, the day-to-day administration of the hospital devolved on a group of male and female religious known as the brethren and sisters of St Leonard. A document of 1299–1300 suggests that the community was then entirely male in composition, but the sisters are again mentioned in 1468. At the time of the Henrician Dissolution campaigns (late 1530s and 1540s), the community consisted of the prior, Sir Nicholas, who was a monk of Bath, together with four sisters and three brethren of St Leonard. The foundation was one of the oldest religious houses in Waterford and was well endowed with lands, rents, mills, docks and spiritualities, giving its name to a suburb of the medieval city. A measure of its importance was the appointment of two of the thirteenth-century priors as bishops of Waterford: Prior Walter in 1227 and Prior William in 1255. In 1536 the dissolved priory was granted to William Wyse, a prominent burgess, protégé of Henry VIII and twice mayor of the city, and its rights and properties transformed his fortunes and formed the basis of the Wyse estate, the Manor of St John.

The origin and history of the hospitals at Cork, Youghal and Monkstown in the county are even more obscure and confused than that of Waterford. Like the Waterford foundation the Cork house seems to have been in existence by the end of the twelfth century and its properties were also confirmed by Prince John. It is not clear what initial relationship existed between the Cork and Waterford foundations, but Waterford's submission to Bath in 1204 seems to have included Cork as well, perhaps indicating that the two properties were united from the beginning. The spiritual and charitable obligations of the Cork house were outlined in a document of 1330, which stated that it had been established for the 'sustenance of four chaplains performing divine service daily at Cork for the souls of the king's ancestors, and of all the faithful deceased yearly, and twelve beds for paupers, and sustenance for two brethren and two

pp 188–9. **69** *MRHI*, p. 357. **70** Hall, *Women*, p. 189. **71** For an account of these foundations see C. Ó Clabaigh, 'The Benedictines in medieval and early modern Ireland' in Browne and Ó Clabaigh, *Benedictines*, pp 79–121 at pp 113–16.

nursing sisters there, forever.' As in Waterford these religious were known as the brethren and sisters of St Leonard. Neglect of duties by the nursing staff precipitated a papal investigation in 1364, and again in 1484 at which time a complaint was made that the Benedictine monk in charge of the Cork hospital could not understand Irish. The monk in question had refused to appoint a chaplain linguistically competent to administer the sacraments and hear confessions. The earliest reference to the Youghal property occurs in 1306 when the prior of Bath ordered an investigation into its affairs and those of the other properties in Ireland. A late medieval building still extant in Youghal today is said to be the site of the hospital.

Less evidence survives for hospital activity in Gaelic Ireland but female religious again seem to have been at the forefront of providing healthcare. At Ballynagalliagh near Drumcliffe, Co. Sligo, a community of sisters was recorded as caring for the sick and poor in 1426 while the involvement of Sawe ingen Oconnolan with the hospital at Donoughmore, Co. Louth, in 1456 has already been noted above.[72]

In 1528, the Annals of Connacht recorded the death of Fionnuala Ní Bhriain at the Franciscan friary at Donegal. The daughter of Conor Ó Briain, lord of Thomond, her family had a long and close association with the friars. Her husband, Aodh Ruadh Ó Domhnaill (d. 1505), was likewise devoted to the order and, at the behest of his mother, had established the Donegal foundation in 1474 for its Observant reformed branch. After his death, his widow retired to the friary and spent the last twenty-one years of her life in the habit of a Franciscan tertiary, attending the liturgy, living chastely and 'practising piety and charity and good works towards God and the world'.[73] Like the women depicted in Sano di Pietro's painting, Fionnuala Ní Bhriain's search for sanctification took many forms in the course her lifetime and defies neat categorization. Despite this, and in common with the other devout women discussed in this volume, her sincerity in pursuing it and the impact it had on her contemporaries is undeniable.

72 Hall, *Women*, p. 189.   **73** Freeman, *Annals of Connacht*, p. 667.

Sisters of the priory confraternity of Christ Church, Dublin, in the late Middle Ages

COLM LENNON

INTRODUCTION

As elsewhere in Europe in the late Middle Ages, dozens of religious associations of laywomen and men had come into existence in towns and countryside throughout Ireland. Bound together in voluntary sister- and brotherhood, the members, who gathered together regularly to worship in chapels mostly in their parish churches, endowed not only the maintenance and ornamentation of ecclesiastical spaces for their ceremonials, but also the living expenses of their chosen chaplains, who ministered at fraternity altars, in chapel or nave, for the good of their souls. These priests, or chantry chaplains, had the key role of celebrating the obsequies of deceased members, and of remembering them on the anniversaries of their deaths through votive prayers and Masses, sung or spoken, for their salvation.[1] Underpinning these rituals was the belief that souls of the dead could be spared or have mitigated the temporal punishment due for sins in Purgatory through their full participation in the communion of saints.[2] As well as assuaging people's fears about the life to come, immersion in the earthly networks of association entailed a reaching out to the broader community beyond the ties of natural kinship. By forging social bonds with other men and women through fraternities, they were opting into a collaborative ethos of goodness through mutual friendship and charity.[3] Much of this lay-run confraternalism was expressed through the observing more intensively of the traditional religious rituals affiliated principally to parish institutions, but houses of male and female religious orders continued to hold the devotional allegiance of many.

As a counterpoint to the lay-run confraternities mainly in the towns and villages of the Englishry, another kind of fraternity and sorority characterized the church in the zone under major Irish influence. Here, in the century before the Reformation, up to fifty houses of secular or religious tertiaries were established under the influence mostly of the Observant branches of the mendicant orders.[4] This phenomenon fostered the

---

1 For the role of confraternities in late medieval Europe, see the essays in K. Eisenbichler (ed.), *A companion to medieval and early modern confraternities* (Leiden, 2019), and for the phenomenon in Ireland, see C. Lennon, 'Confraternities in late medieval Ireland: the evolution of chantry colleges', ibid., pp 194–211. **2** For general beliefs about purgatory, see E. Duffy, *The stripping of the altars: traditional religion in England, 1400–1580* (New Haven, 1992), pp 338–76, and in Ireland specifically, see C. Tait, *Death, burial and commemoration in Ireland, 1550–1650* (Basingstoke, 2002), pp 138–50. **3** See G. Rosser, *The art of solidarity in the Middle Ages: guilds in England, 1250–1550* (Oxford, 2015). **4** For the tertiary movement in the pre-Reformation period, see C. Ó Clabaigh,

bonding together of zealous laywomen and men to live either in community, or as devotees of the spirit of the founders in their domestic situations. The tertiary (or Third Order) movement was under the direction of the associated mendicant superiors across the mainly rural Irish *ecclesia* and was not normally connected to the parishes therein. Yet it may be mistaken to regard the tertiary movement as entirely *sui generis*, as there were suggestive convergences and interfaces between the differing kinds of confraternity to be found in the west and south of Ireland, as at Adare, Limerick and Galway, for example, and in the manor and town of Slane in the Pale.[5] That the brands of associationalism were not mutually exclusive but straddled ecclesiastical worlds is evidenced by the confraternity of the cathedral of Holy Trinity or Christ Church, Dublin, run by its priory of Augustinian canons.[6]

Cathedral confraternities that drew men and women into closer association with episcopal churches through patterns of endowment and fuller liturgical participation were known throughout Europe in the late Middle Ages.[7] Seville Cathedral, for instance, had a fraternity of up to 600 sisters and brothers who incorporated a charity for poor women without dowries in their annual round of celebration in the late Middle Ages.[8] In Dublin's other cathedral, St Patrick's, there was an association, dedicated to St Augustine, of female and male supporters who were benefactors of the collegiate clergy and buildings there, but little is known about its activity, apart from an admission roll of the 1360s.[9] The confraternity in Holy Trinity priory, on the other hand, is well documented, mainly through the late medieval 'book of obits' of Christ Church that records over 1,000 names of individuals whose souls were to be remembered on the anniversaries of their death in the sacred rituals of the prior and canons of the cathedral (Plate 13).[10] While a large number were religious and diocesan clerics, canons of the cathedral, nuns of convents in the Pale, and ecclesiastical dignitaries, over a third of those entered in calendarial order in the obits (the years of

The Franciscans in Ireland, 1400–1534: from reform to Reformation (Dublin, 2002), pp 80–105; idem, *The friars in Ireland, 1224–1540* (Dublin, 2021), pp 305–17 as well as his contribution to this volume. **5** See C. Lennon, 'The confraternities and cultural duality in Ireland, 1450–1550' in C. Black and P. Gravestock (eds), *Early modern confraternities in Europe and the Americas: international and interdisciplinary perspectives* (Aldershot, 2006), pp 35–52.   **6** For the socio-religious context, see J. Lydon, 'Christ Church in the later medieval Irish world' in K. Milne (ed.), *Christ Church Cathedral, Dublin: a history* (Dublin, 2000), p. 91.   **7** For the English background, see P. Dalton, C. Insley and L.J. Wilkinson (eds), *Cathedrals, communities and conflict in the Anglo-Norman world* (Woodbridge, 2011), pp 18–19, and for a later period, see many of the essays in D. Bullen Presciutti (ed.), *Space, place and motion: locating confraternities in the late medieval and early modern city* (Leiden, 2017).   **8** M.E. Perry, *Gender and disorder in early modern Seville* (Princeton, 1990), pp 66–7. **9** Women make up almost half of the enrolment: J. Crawford and R. Gillespie (eds), *St Patrick's Cathedral, Dublin: a history* (Dublin, 2009), pp 11, 137n, 145; M. Clark and R. Refaussé (eds), *Directory of historic Dublin guilds* (Dublin, 1993), pp 34–5.   **10** Originally edited by J.C. Crossthwaite, with an introduction by J.H. Todd, as *The book of obits and martyrology of the cathedral church of the Holy Trinity, commonly called Christ Church, Dublin* (Dublin, 1844), it was reprinted in R. Refaussé with C. Lennon (eds) *The registers of Christ Church Cathedral, Dublin* (Dublin, 1998). For the light it sheds on networks of commemoration among monastic communities in the Dublin region see C. Ó Clabaigh, 'Community, commemoration and confraternity: the chapter office and chapter books in Irish Augustinian foundations' in Browne and Ó Clabaigh, *Households,*

whose deaths are noted in many cases) are described as either '*soror*' or '*frater*' of 'our congregation' [confraternity]. Many of the brothers belonged to intersecting categories of laymen and clerics of differing standing, but the commemorated females were overwhelmingly laywomen, the body of sisters of the confraternity being more homogeneous, and including married and single women, or *femmes soles*.[11] It is principally upon this sisterhood associated with Christ Church in the cathedral records that this essay concentrates, with some reference to the broader context of obituarized females.

SOCIAL AND SPIRITUAL FUNCTIONS OF THE CONFRATERNITY

For women in the late Middle Ages attachment to an institution such as Christ Church provided an outlet beyond their domestic and neighbourhood spheres to a fuller measure of civic belonging. Like its prestigious counterpart of St Paul's in central London (to which Christ Church was known sometimes to compare itself), the Dublin cathedral had a history of chantry endowments by women such as Johanna FitzLeonis (in conjunction with her husband) since the thirteenth century.[12] As we shall see, the tradition of female generosity towards the church continued within the cathedral confraternity down to the early Reformation, with some sisters involved in giving to two or more religious institutions. Individual women might arrange for chantry chaplains to celebrate in memory of their immediate families, but their induction into a confraternity bonded them within a form of ritual kinship. Sharing the devotional and charitable aspirations of their fellow-members, women (and men) committed themselves to the reverential reception of the sacraments, most notably the Eucharist, and looked ultimately to their remembrance among the faithful departed as part of the communion of the saints.[13] And, as in the case of gifts by sisters to multiple religious institutions, membership of confraternities was not limited to that of Christ Church: Genet Stanihurst, a major donor to the cathedral, for example, had also gifted property to the religious fraternity of Corpus Christi in St Michael's parish, Dublin, in 1538,[14] as had Elena Clerk in 1489 in the form of a large house called Geneval's Inns.[15]

The integration of a monastery within the cathedral community at Christ Church, Dublin, made it a particularly attractive object of the philanthropy of pious women, no less than men. Bequests in fifteenth-century wills show the fidelity of female testators to religious houses in Dublin and its hinterland.[16] Monastic institutions and hospitals hosted confraternities, and also the guilds and altars of tradeswomen and men,

pp 235–51 at pp 249–50.   **11** For a useful discussion of the categories of associates and members of the confraternity, see Hall, *Women*, pp 24–6.   **12** M.J. McEnery and R. Refaussé (eds), *Christ Church deeds* (Dublin, 2001), pp 56–7 [nos 122, 123]; cf. M.-H. Rousseau, *Saving the souls of medieval London: perpetual chantries at St Paul's Cathedral, c.1200 –1548* (Aldershot, 2011), for the extent of women's endowment of chantries and chaplains.   **13** A.J. Fletcher, 'Liturgy in the late medieval cathedral priory' in Milne (ed.), *Christ Church Cathedral*, pp 137–8.   **14** Refaussé with Lennon (eds), *Registers of Christ Church*, pp 44, 89; *Christ Church deeds*, pp 111, 114, 227 [nos 405, 428, 1130]. **15** C. Lennon and J. Murray (eds), *The Dublin city franchise roll, 1468–1512* (Dublin, 1998), p. 64. **16** See H.F. Berry (ed.), *Register of wills and inventories of the diocese of Dublin in the time of Archbishops*

such as that of the Blessed Virgin for the carpenters, millers, masons and heliers of Dublin, in the Lady chapel of St Thomas's Abbey beside the city.[17] At Christ Church indeed, the powerful guild of merchants had its chantry in the chapel of Holy Trinity in the south aisle.[18] Besides the normal spiritual and social benefits of confraternity membership, sisters (and brothers) of Christ Church enjoyed the privileges of a quasi-monastic '*congregatio*', as it was termed (of Third Order standing), entailing the continuing prayers of the canons during life and after death, and association with the good works of the priory. Sisters and brothers could exhibit varying degrees of commitment to following the Rule of St Augustine, up to and including burial in the habit of a canon.[19] Administration was in the hands of the religious rather than the laity, but any diminution of responsibility for the latter was compensated for by the continuity of the monastic regime of the priors and canons, the stability of the ecclesiastical ecosystem and the ready supply of chaplains from among the ranks of the community.

To become a sister of the confraternity of Christ Church, a woman appears to have had to subscribe to a formulary of the Holy Trinity, as applied in the case of Joan Cusake, the lady of Killeen, Co. Meath, for example, who died in 1441. On or after her reception, Cusake gave to the high altar of the cathedral a gilded image of the Blessed Virgin, worth £10.[20] Donation of money, objects and lands was not uncommon among those who were female *commemoratae* of the cathedral, the gifts of a quarter of those listed being recorded. The link to qualification for membership of the confraternity by endowment, however, is unclear: it is possible that a small entry fine was payable on admission, as was customary in parish fraternities and guilds. A common amount bestowed by sisters of the confraternity on the works of the church was 3*s.* 4*d.*[21] Some sisters are mentioned in conjunction with their spouses or other relatives, as, for example, Anna Cusake, *uxor* or wife of Patrick Burnell, Rosina Clement, wife of Symon Fox, and Anna Fleming, *uxor* of Johannis Bellewe, who died in 1461, and shared with him in an office of nine lessons.[22] The recital of this liturgical office was normally reserved for major benefactors, including Sisters Cecilia Hegreve (d. 1470), Margaret Edward and Mariona Lerpoll, who gave 'many items', 10 marks of silver and 12*s.*, respectively.[23] The aforementioned Lady Joan Cusake was joined by some of her children on admission to the confraternity,[24] and there are several other such conjunctions between sisters and family members, including those commemorated on specific days and feasts in the cathedral calendar: these were grouped as men and women who were major benefactors, including the de Grauntsetes, Sueterbys and Fitzwilliam-Stanihursts.[25] On the whole, however, the impression given from a study of the obits is of women opting as independent agents into the system of spiritual benefits to be

Tregury and Walton, 1457–1483 (Dublin, 1898).   **17** Clark and Refaussé (eds), *Historic Dublin guilds*, pp 17–8.   **18** R. Stalley, 'The architecture of the cathedral and priory buildings' in Milne (ed.), *Christ Church Cathedral*, pp 105–6.   **19** Hall, *Women*, pp 24–6.   **20** Refaussé with Lennon (eds), *Registers of Christ Church*, pp 48, 68.   **21** Ibid., pp 46, 48, 51, 53, 67, 69, 72, 73, 77.   **22** Ibid., pp 49, 73, 76.   **23** Ibid., pp 57, 58, 82; *Christ Church deeds*, p. 86 [nos 268, 269].   **24** Refaussé with Lennon (eds), *Registers of Christ Church*, p. 68.   **25** Ibid., pp 44, 57, 59, 84, 89, 122; for John and Alice de Grauntsete's benefaction to the priory, see James Mills (ed.), *Account roll of the priory of Holy Trinity, Dublin, 1337–46* (Dublin, 1996 ed.), pp 148–51, 202–6.

garnered from close association with fellow-devotees in an institution serving as the ecclesiastical hub of Dublin.

COMPOSITION OF THE FEMALE COHORT OF THE CONFRATERNITY

An examination of the make-up of the female cohort in the book of obits reveals the complement of religious women as a small but significant subset.[26] Sisters Alicia Bron and Alice Cruce were nuns of Hogges Augustinian convent in Dublin: it is possible that the latter, who died in 1551, had turned to a religious way of life after her admission into the trade guilds of the city in 1493.[27] The abbess of that convent, Lady Matilda, and Katerina Hakket, superior of Grace Dieu convent in north Co. Dublin, likewise had their deaths remembered in the prayers of the priory on their anniversaries.[28] Two women of mere first-name appellation, Moroc and Eva, who were registered for remembrance in the obits, are described as '*conversae*', signifying that they were most likely lay sisters of the priory, perhaps accorded the privilege of burial in the appropriate robes or even the full Augustinian habit.[29] It has been posited that they may have held corrodies or pensions in the priory, although James Lydon suggests that the provision of facilities for the superannuated by the priory was unlikely.[30] Another woman, simply named Matilda, and referred to as 'soror' of the congregation, may also have been a lay sister, or '*conversa*'.[31] While there may have been differences in social ranking between the women of the Pale nunneries and the lay sisters of the priory, it is notable that both groups were represented *ex aequo* among the sorores. From among the communities of nuns in the convents of Hogges and Grace Dieu, moreover, ladies from leading gentry families such as Hacket, Cruise, Taylor, Preston and Darcy were attracted to membership of the sisterhood of Christ Church.[32]

Similar social gradations are evident among the lay sorores of the priory and cathedral. The presence among the sisters of Agneta Darsy (who became countess of Kildare before her death in 1430), and Elizabeth Fitzgerald (who was countess of Ormond until her demise in 1453) reinforced links between the great comital families of Ireland and the cathedral of Holy Trinity.[33] As well as that of Lady Joan Cusake of Killeen, donor of the gilded image of the Virgin to the high altar, the membership of chatelaines of gentry seats at Artane and Malahide, Katerina Preston and Elizabeth Bukley, broadened the context for ecclesiastical patronage beyond the walls of Christ Church out into the manorial hinterland of Dublin.[34] Marriage partnerships mentioned

---

26 See Hall, *Women*, pp 171–2; Ó Clabaigh, 'Community, commemoration and confraternity' pp 249–50.   **27** Hall, *Women*, p. 215; Refaussé with Lennon (eds), *Registers of Christ Church*, pp 78, 81, 82; an Alice Cruce was admitted in 1493 at the instance of Bailiff Henry Lawles (who may have been a brother of the confraternity): Lennon and Murray (eds), *Dublin city franchise roll, 1468–1512*, p. 29.   **28** Refaussé with Lennon (eds), *Registers of Christ Church*, pp 50, 71; Hall, *Women*, pp 213, 215.   **29** Refaussé with Lennon (eds), *Registers of Christ Church*, pp 54, 80. **30** Hall, *Women*, p. 26; J. Lydon, 'Introduction' in Mills (ed.), *Account roll of the priory of Holy Trinity*, p. xvii.   **31** Refaussé with Lennon (eds), *Registers of Christ Church*, p. 54.   **32** Berry (ed.), *Register of wills and inventories*, pp 174–5, 177.   **33** Refaussé with Lennon (eds), *Registers of Christ Church*, pp 66, 73.   **34** Ibid., pp 45, 49, 68.

between members of shire families and the merchant patriciate of Dublin, such as those of Eleanor Barby and Mayor Nicholas Handcock, and Rosina Holywood and Arland Ussher, were not only supportive of social bonding in Old English society.[35] Other benefits accrued too. Women such as Juliana Passavaunt and Johanna St Leger were to the fore through matrimony in facilitating the establishment of trusts for the transfer of lands to the cathedral's portfolio, for which their anniversaries were marked with special solemnity.[36] Also, in the sphere of provision for enhanced worship, women of the confraternity shared with men the zeal for intercessory Masses: Sisters Jenet Fynglas and Helena Strangwyche, both married (separately) to Thomas Plunket of Dunsoghly, were joined with him (and one Philippa Bermingham), in the prayers of a chaplain to be maintained in Christ Church by their donation of lands in north Co. Dublin in 1512.[37]

The category of freewomen of Dublin, to which almost one-sixth of the sisters belonged, covered the roles and privileges to which enfranchised women were entitled. Besides binding them more closely to civic life, free women could also transmit that status of freedom through marriage. Thus, for example, wedding a freewoman, Elizabeth Benet, probably was the means whereby her husband, Walter Ever or Evers, a lawyer, became free of the guilds in 1484.[38] The following year, Walter acted for the priory in a legal case concerning a disputed rental property.[39] Several women of the confraternity became free of the city through the special grace of sitting city magistrates, to whom they were sometimes related, as, for example, in the case of Sister Margaret Rochford and her sponsor, Bailiff John Rochford, in 1507.[40] Not only did Robert Caddell pass the freedom to his daughter, Margaret Walsh, in 1504, but he may have preceded her as a member of the congregation.[41] Through service to urban trades other women of the confraternity became free, including Sister Millana Harrold, who was apprenticed to Nicholas Harrold, a butcher, and Sisters Alicia Hassard and Elena Clarke, who completed their time under the merchants Stephen Harold and John Dansey.[42] Sister Margaret Lawless may have been in service to William Yonge, a cook, or else was admitted to the Dublin franchises by special grace.[43] A prominent benefactress of the cathedral, Genet Fitzwilliam, whose memory was specially solemnized, was herself a working merchant who inducted an apprentice, Maude Parrys, in 1500.[44] Among the women entered in the book of obits were some of an Irish

35 Ibid., pp 59, 60, 89, 127; *Christ Church deeds*, p. 247 (no. 1231); for the significance of gentry-patriciate marital bonds, see C. Lennon, *The lords of Dublin in the age of Reformation* (Dublin, 1989), pp 64–91.   **36** Refaussé with Lennon (eds), *Registers of Christ Church*, pp 47, 62; *Christ Church deeds*, pp 90–1, 111, 114, 227 (nos 298 405, 428, 1130); see also TCD, MS 1207, 'Miscellaneous deeds of the Passavaunt and Stanihurst families', 1246–1691.   **37** Refaussé with Lennon (eds), *Registers of Christ Church*, pp 41, 59; *Christ Church deeds*, p. 110 (no. 376).   **38** Lennon and Murray (eds), *Dublin city franchise roll*, p. 19; Refaussé with Lennon (eds), *Registers of Christ Church*, p. 68. **39** *Christ Church deeds*, p. 214 (no. 1055).   **40** Refaussé with Lennon (eds), *Registers of Christ Church*, p. 62; Lennon and Murray (eds), *Dublin city franchise roll*, p. 42.   **41** Refaussé with Lennon (eds), *Registers of Christ Church*, pp 47, 74; Lennon and Murray (eds), *Dublin city franchise roll*, p. 39. **42** Refaussé with Lennon (eds), *Registers of Christ Church*, pp 46, 70, 83; Lennon and Murray (eds), *Dublin city franchise roll*, pp 12, 13, 64.   **43** Refaussé with Lennon (eds), *Registers of Christ Church*, p. 64; Lennon and Murray (eds), *Dublin city franchise roll*, pp 15, 19.   **44** Refaussé with Lennon

ethnic background, whom Sparky Booker has examined, including Margaret Kelly and
Sister Anastasia Kennedy, both well integrated in civic life to judge by their anglicized
surnames.[45] Meanwhile, Johanna Doyn was registered in partnership with Lauglyn
Olaghrow, almost certainly a Gaelic newcomer, as donating five shillings and four
gallons of corn to the cathedral store.[46]

WOMEN'S ENDOWMENTS AND DEVOTIONAL LIFE IN THE CONFRATERNITY

Endowment of the priory and cathedral, whether modest or lavish, laid the foundations
for the confraternity's liturgical and obituarial round. A sizeable number of women
made donations or bequeathed items or property to the priory and for the maintenance
works of the church: these included monetary sums of from 2s. or 3s. to 10 silver marks
(left by Sister Margareta Edward); precious objects such as chalices, patens and cruets
in silver and gold, Sister Rosina Holywood's silver cup given to the common board of
vicars being twenty-seven ounces in weight; altar cloths and vestments, including a
gilded alb from Alicia Gernon; and even farms of land in Dublin and Meath (in the
cases of Elizabeth Bennet and Johanna Lamkyn, respectively).[47] While most of the gifts
were for the general benefit of maintaining the fabric and furnishing of the sacred
buildings and spaces, favoured shrines were the objects of specific patronage: Olive
Whyte left a chalice and 3s. 4d. for the altar of the chapel of the Blessed Virgin, Sisters
Christiana Gylagh and Margaret Holywood gave fine cloths to the altar of St Edmund's
chapel and the high altar respectively, and the lady of Killeen presented the gilded
image of the Virgin to the latter location.[48] In the context of a paucity of extant
women's wills in the late Middle Ages, the records of the Christ Church sisters'
bequests are all the more valuable, and may have represented only part of their legacies
to the ecclesiastical sector. Certainly in the case of Sister Johanna Cusake, 'who left us
many goods' on her death in 1441, her largesse was widely spread over the churches of
Dunsany and Rathmore, as well as Killeen, Co. Meath.[49]

   That the cathedral priory benefited by substantial endowment from confraternity
members and other sources is attested by the elaborateness of the liturgy that was
thereby facilitated. Sisters and brothers shared in the 'vigils, fasts, Masses, prayers, as
well as in all other spiritual matters' of the hebdomadal *round* of the canons,
experiencing the sacraments more intimately perhaps through the use of their own

(eds), *Registers of Christ Church*, p. 85; Lennon and Murray (eds), *Dublin city franchise roll*, p. 35;
Christ Church deeds, p. 219 (no. 1084). For a discussion of the context of late medieval civil society
in which women carried out public functions outside the household, such as working for wages
and participation in associational religious life, see K.A. Lynch, *Individuals, families and communities
in Europe, 1200–1800: the urban foundations of western society* (Cambridge, 2003), pp 18–21.
45 Refaussé with Lennon (eds), *Registers of Christ Church*, pp 51, 79; see S. Booker, *Cultural
exchange and identity in late medieval Ireland* (Cambridge, 2018), pp 53–4, 136.   **46** Refaussé with
Lennon (eds), *Registers of Christ Church*, p. 78.   **47** Refaussé with Lennon (eds), *Registers of Christ
Church*, pp 47, 58, 60, 68.   **48** Ibid., pp 65, 68, 72, 76.   **49** Ibid., pp 48, 68; M.A. Lyons, 'Lay
female piety in late medieval Ireland' in B. Bradshaw and D. Keogh (eds), *Christianity in Ireland:*

gifts of chalices, linens and vestments.[50] Some of the Masses and the chaplains became supplemental to the regular *cursus* of the canons, through private chantry foundations, such as that for the commemoration by two extra canons of Alicia Grauncet, her husband, John, and family; and Sister Helena Strangwych remembered with her husband, Thomas Plunket of Dunsoghly, a major donor, by a perpetual chaplain.[51] Patronage of chantries by wealthy members allowed for the refurbishment and enhancement of votive chapels in the cathedral in the fifteenth century, such as those of the Blessed Virgin and St Laurence O'Toole, and the establishment of the Kildare chantry by the eighth earl by 1512. According to Alan Fletcher, corporate liturgies devised for the confraternity of the cathedral priory as well as other guilds are reflected in an extant processional manuscript. This may have been associated at some stage with the Church of St John the Evangelist, Dublin, which was adjacent to the cathedral and served by its canons.[52]

One of the most important liturgical enhancements of the priory and confraternity in the late fifteenth century was the foundation in 1480 of a choral school for four boys or 'paraphonistas' to serve in the Lady chapel and main choir of the cathedral.[53] The founders were former mayor of Dublin, Thomas Bennet, a frater, and his wife, Elizabeth Bellew (specially remembered in the book of obits). Together they donated lands at Ballymore, Co. Dublin, to the priory for the support of the school, and in memory of his mother, Johanna Sueterby, who was also a *commemorata*.[54] The choristers were to be trained in plainsong and polyphonic music, which was becoming more popular in liturgical celebrations in England and Ireland. Already by 1485 provision was made by John Estrete, a senior state official and patron of the priory, for a Mass of the Holy Ghost sung by the choir in the chapel of St Laurence O'Toole every Thursday, using polyphony, or if not, plainsong. Eight years later the choir school was placed on a secure footing in a deed of the prior and convent of Holy Trinity providing for an appropriately-paid master to teach music, and for the care, feeding and clothing of the boys.[55]

Most prized among the benefits of association with the monastic community that accrued to the confraters of Christ Church in the late Middle Ages was that of the assisting of passage through death and interment to perpetual commemoration on one's anniversary. Members of the confraternity regularly requested burial within the precincts of the cathedral priory, some in favoured chapels, such as Holy Trinity and the Blessed Virgin, or in the cloister. Anne Plunkett oversaw the burial of her husband,

revisiting the story (Dublin, 2002), pp 67, 71.   **50** A. Fletcher, 'Liturgy in the late medieval priory' in Milne (ed.), *Christ Church Cathedral*, pp 130–1, 132–3.   **51** For the arrangements laid down for the commemoration of Alicia and John Grauncet (or de Grauntsete) in the cathedral, see Mills (ed.), *Account roll of the priory of Holy Trinity*, pp 148–51, 202–6; and of Helena and Thomas, see *Christ Church deeds*, p. 110 (no. 396).   **52** Fletcher, 'Liturgy in the late medieval priory', pp 132, 137–8; idem, *Drama, performance and polity in pre-Cromwellian Ireland* (Cork, 2000), pp 62–77, 281–301.   **53** Fletcher, 'Liturgy in the late medieval priory' in Milne (ed.), *Christ Church Cathedral*, pp 138–9.   **54** Refaussé with Lennon (eds), *Registers of Christ Church*, pp 68, 84, 122, 156.   **55** B. Boydell, 'The establishment of the choral tradition' in Milne (ed.), *Christ Church Cathedral*, pp 237–9; B. Boydell (ed.), *Music at Christ Church before 1800: documents and selected anthems*

John Goghe, in the chapel of Holy Trinity, in 1472 where she may have joined him after death.[56] Among the female donors who were definitely buried in various parts of the cathedral and whose obits were kept therein were Matilde Rosell, Joneta Sueterby, Elizabeth Bennet, Elizabeth Brytt, Agneta Whytt, Genet Fitzwilliam, Agnes Mareward and Jeneta Phillipp.[57] Sisters Katherine Boyse and Eleanor Barby, as well as Elizabeth Field and Genet Stanyhurst are included in the proctor's accounts of 1542 for payments for funerals and for month's and twelvemonths' minds.[58] As to the privilege of burial in the full Augustinian habit or the robes of a lay sister (or *conversa*), the records are silent, apart from the few examples above. There are no female examples of the practice of taking the habit in old age or illness in order to be cared for at the monastery until death ('*ad succurrendum*').

Described by James Murray as a 'great medieval chantry' down to the Reformation, Christ Church Cathedral and priory certainly played this role for wealthier female and male associates through their endowment of chaplains in perpetuity.[59] Although their earthly identity might fade over time, the bearing in the communal mind of deceased brothers and sisters in the months and years after death was extended through the memorial Masses and services of specially appointed chaplains. Alicia de Grauntsete profited spiritually by the ministrations of two chantry chaplains appointed from 1335 to say Mass for her, her husband and extended kin, including special collects or prayers. She was also commemorated annually on 6 June in the obits of the cathedral priory.[60] But guild membership was ultimately subversive of individual commemoration in its commitment to collective striving for salvation and shared participation in the intercessory rituals of their chaplains. As the immediacy of their worldly presence receded, the fraternity dead, who formed part of the vast communion of the saints, were not forgotten as they were held in the collective memory. As their souls were being purified in purgatory, they benefited not just by the prayers of these living supplicants but also through the mediation of the saints in heaven. Several who made substantial benefaction were commemorated in extended kin-groupings on Sundays or on days depending on moveable feasts in a more solemn manner with a special Mass with tolling bells and profusely lit by candles, while still being remembered in the ordinary series of obits. Sister Jenet Philipp was one such: her obit was fixed for 27 September but her more solemn commemorative Mass was held, in conjunction with that of her husband, John Savage, on the Sunday after the nativity of the Blessed Virgin.[61]

(Dublin, 1999), pp 238–43.   **56** Berry (ed.), *Registers of wills and inventories of the diocese of Dublin*, pp 39–41; Lydon, 'Introduction' in Mills (ed.), *Account roll of the priory of Holy Trinity*, p. xviii. **57** Refaussé with Lennon (eds), *Registers of Christ Church*, pp 84, 85.   **58** Ibid., p. 89.   **59** J. Murray, 'The Tudor diocese of Dublin: episcopal government, ecclesiastical politics and the enforcement of the Reformation, *c.*1534–1590' (PhD, University of Dublin, 1997), p. 373. **60** *Christ Church deeds*, p. 76 (no. 225); Refaussé with Lennon (eds), *Registers of Christ Church*, p. 59. **61** Refaussé with Lennon (eds), *Registers of Christ Church*, pp 72, 85.

FEMALE ASSOCIATIONALISM AND THE DEFENCE OF CHRIST CHURCH AT THE REFORMATION

In the decades immediately preceding the dissolution of the priory in 1540, there was no apparent diminution of devotion to the Christ Church confraternity on the part of women or men. An examination of the cohort of thirty-eight sorores in particular whose deaths are recorded as having occurred after 1500 reveals the close links between urban and county society and the cathedral, to the extent that the book of obits reads like a roll-call of civic and gentry families who were prominent in the Dublin area.[62] A phenomenon of membership on the male side was the high proportion of mayors of the city who became brothers of the congregation, and their wives were frequently sisters thereof. Sister Eleanor Barby (herself the daughter of Mayor James), who died in 1528, married Mayor Nicholas Hancock, whose obit was kept after his death in 1547;[63] Sister Johanna Colyer was daughter of Mayor Thomas Collyer who was a brother of the congregation;[64] and both Genet Stanyhurst and Mayor William Talbot, her husband, had been enrolled as members before their deaths in 1540 and 1528 respectively.[65] Not only did Sir Thomas Plunket of Dunsoghly follow his wife, Helena Strangwych, into the congregation of the cathedral priory, but she, as a freewoman, was instrumental in his being enfranchised as citizen in 1493.[66] Rosina Holywood, and her husband, Mayor Arland Ussher, who died in 1558 and 1557 respectively, were major donors to the cathedral priory, she having given a silver chalice of twenty-seven ounces to the vicars choral.[67] Matrimonial alliances of gentry and merchant patrician partners with close links to the cathedral could yield lucrative grants of lands to the cathedral property bank, such as the extensive Passavaunt lands in Co. Dublin, conferred by Genet Stanyhurst and William Talbot in 1517.[68]

During the first phase of the dissolution of the Irish monasteries in 1538, when its closure appeared to be imminent, the priory and cathedral of Christ Church were the subject of an appeal to Thomas Cromwell for its preservation on the part of the mayor and aldermen.[69] A comparison was drawn with St Paul's in London, not only in terms of its geographical centrality in the city but also of its secular significance as a 'verie station place' and administrative location for parliament, council and judiciary. Civic religion was also adduced in its support, the cathedral serving for assembly of processions, and notably for occasions of proclamations of royal births and triumphs, when 'Te Deum laudamus is songe'. Any dereliction of the site would, it was argued,

---

62 C. Lennon, 'Introduction' in Refaussé with Lennon (eds), *Registers of Christ Church*, pp 21–2; R. Gillespie, 'The coming of reform, 1500–58' in Milne (ed.), *Christ Church Cathedral*, pp 158–9. **63** Refaussé with Lennon (eds), *Registers of Christ Church*, pp 59, 74, 89; *Christ Church deeds*, p. 247 (no. 1231); Lennon and Murray (eds), *Dublin city franchise roll*, p. 35. **64** Refaussé with Lennon (eds), *Registers of Christ Church*, pp 44, 70; Lennon and Murray (eds), *Dublin city franchise roll*, p. 12. **65** Refaussé with Lennon (eds), *Registers of Christ Church*, pp 44, 65, 89; *Christ Church deeds*, p. 227 (no. 1130). **66** Refaussé with Lennon (eds), *Registers of Christ Church*, p. 41; Lennon and Murray (eds), *Dublin city franchise roll*, p. 29. **67** Refaussé with Lennon (eds), *Registers of Christ Church*, pp 42, 60. **68** *Christ Church deeds*, pp 89, 227 (nos 290, 1130); P. Crooks (ed.), *A calendar of Irish chancery letters, c.1244–1509*, Patent Roll 19 Edward IV, no. 3 [1479]. **69** *State Papers, Henry VIII*,

be a blight on the heart of the city, and a symbol of civic decay, to the comfort of 'the king's Irish enemies'. The petition for preservation was successful, the royal government authorizing that Christ Church be converted into a secular cathedral with a dean and chapter instead of a prior and convent, which were officially dissolved in 1540.[70] Then, in 1544, official policy questioned the continuation of two Dublin cathedrals in close proximity to one another, causing the mayor and his brethren to object once again, this time to what was termed 'the college' of Christ Church's being reduced to the status of parish church whereby the city would be 'totally defaced and disparaged'.[71] Strong civic backing for the maintenance of Christ Church as a cathedral, incorporating the close links between cathedral and community, not least those forged by the female and male members of the confraternity, prevented its being closed or diminished, and, in 1548, it was St Patrick's Cathedral that was reduced in status for a number of years.[72]

Despite the upheavals of the early 1540s, which saw Christ Church emerge as a secular cathedral with dean and chapter, continuity in the devotional regime of the priory ensured that the confraternity had an afterlife in the history of the institution, before being eased out of existence. Month's minds and twelvemonths' minds were still kept, according to the proctor's accounts of 1542, including those of Sisters Elizabeth Field, Eleanor Barby, Katerine Boyse, Johanna Collier, as well as Genet Stanyhurst.[73] Six new sisters were enrolled in the book of obits for commemoration after 1540, the final one being Rosina Holywood in 1558, the year of Queen Elizabeth I's accession.[74] At that time, the maintenance of chantries and fraternities, although not officially dissolved in Ireland, was becoming problematic, as the ecclesiastical buildings fell to the possession of the Protestant state church, in which intercessory rituals were discountenanced. Even though some obits continued to be kept in Christ Church until the mid-1560s, the notion of an association of prayers and Masses for the dead fell into official desuetude in the reform canon. Most of the other new entries in the register for the mid-Tudor period were of non-members of the confraternity, including public officials who were perhaps drawn to the re-constituted Christ Church as an institution not just for services in the state church but also for secular ceremonial such as the swearing-in of members of government.[75]

In conclusion, women in the congregation of the cathedral priory of Christ Church or Holy Trinity, Dublin, had enjoyed many of the benefits of their *sorores* in other predominantly lay religious associations. The confraternity offered a way of bridging social, ethnic and economic divisions through ritual kinship, and provided opportunities for involvement in civic religion and building social capital. Most highly prized were the outlets for devotional activity and the endowment of the church, with

part iii, pp 545–6. **70** Gillespie, 'The coming of reform, 1500–58' in Milne (ed.), *Christ Church Cathedral*, pp 165–6. **71** *Calendar of State Papers, Ireland, Tudor period 1509–47*, p. 368 [no. 658]. **72** J. Murray, *Enforcing the English Reformation in Ireland: clerical resistance and political conflict in the dioceses of Dublin, 1534–1590* (Cambridge, 2009), pp 194–7. **73** Refaussé with Lennon (eds), *Registers of Christ Church*, pp 89, 142. **74** Ibid., p. 60: the others were Katerina Boyse (d. 1541), p. 62; Alicia Byrsall (d. 1551), p. 78; Johanna Colyer (d. 1540), p. 44; Alicia Cruce (d. 1551), p. 78; and Elizabeth Felde (d. 1540), p. 41. **75** See Gillespie, 'The coming of reform, 1500–58' in Milne (ed.), *Christ Church Cathedral*, pp 170–1, 172–3.

a view to the securing of intercession with the saints on behalf of departed souls mainly through designated monastic priests. What was different about the priory sister- and brotherhood was that its continuation was undermined by the removal of the sheltering framework of priory and convent after their dissolution in 1540, and this appears to have happened also in the case of the secular and religious Third Orders or tertiaries. Other religious associations for laywomen and men, such as the confraternities of St Anne in Dublin and Drogheda, survived into the seventeenth century after their retreat from the public sphere of parish places of worship to the privacy of domestic residences or halls. And other forms of commemorative piety, such as charitable foundations or quasi-chantries, persisted into the early modern period with the active participation of laywomen.[76]

---

76 C. Lennon, 'The chantries in the Irish Reformation: the case of St Anne's guild, Dublin, 1550–1630' in R.V. Comerford, M. Cullen, J.R. Hill and C. Lennon (eds), *Religion, conflict and coexistence in Ireland: essays presented to Monsignor Patrick J. Corish* (Dublin, 1990), pp 6–25; Tait, *Death, burial and commemoration in Ireland*, pp 143–6.

Who were the nuns in early modern Ireland?

BRONAGH ANN McSHANE

INTRODUCTION

In the last twenty years, scholarship on women religious in late medieval and early modern Europe has flourished, expanding considerably our knowledge of the nature of female contemplative life. Themes such as the changing nature of female religious expression and women's spiritual work; institutional relations between convents and male clergy; the cultural production of religious communities; and the lived experiences of women housed in convents have all featured in studies of Italian, Spanish and, to a lesser extent, French and German nuns.[1] In the case of early modern English nuns, the work of the pioneering 'Who were the nuns?' project, led by Caroline Bowden (Queen Mary University of London) has made available an abundance of sources produced by and about members of English convents established in Europe. This has, in turn, led to a proliferation of scholarly publications on communities of English nuns on the Continent, expanding considerably our knowledge of the nature of contemplative life for women who left England to join convents established in Europe during the early modern period.[2]

Yet, despite these advances, the study of Irish women religious remains a neglected topic within the broader field of European female monasticism.[3] In recent years, several scholarly studies have advanced our understanding of the nature of female contemplative life in early modern Ireland, the challenges encountered by women who

---

1 S. Evangelisti, *Nuns: a history of convent life, 1450–1700* (Oxford, 2007); eadem, 'Wives, widows and brides of Christ: marriage and the convent in the historiography of early modern Italy', *Historical Journal*, 43 (2000), 233–47; M. Laven, *Virgins of Venice: broken vows and cloistered lives in the Renaissance convent* (London, 2003); E.A. Lehfeldt, *Religious women in Golden Age Spain: the permeable cloister* (Aldershot, 2005); B. Diefendorf, *From penitence to charity: pious women and the Catholic Reformation in Paris* (Oxford & New York, 2004); S.E. Dinan, *Women and poor relief in seventeenth-century France: the early history of the Daughters of Charity* (Aldershot, 2006); E. Rapley, *A social history of the cloister: daily life in the teaching monasteries of the Old Regime* (Montréal, 2001); eadem, *The Dévotes: women and the church in seventeenth-century France* (Montréal, 1993); L. Lux-Sterritt, *Redefining female religious life: French Ursulines and English Ladies in seventeenth-century Catholicism* (Aldershot, 2005); M. Wiesner-Hanks, *Convents confront the Reformation: Catholic and Protestant nuns in Germany* (Milwaukee, 1996); C. Woodford, *Nuns as historians in early modern Germany* (Oxford, 2002); S. Laqua-O'Donnell, *Women and the Counter-Reformation in early modern Münster* (Oxford, 2014); A.E. Leonard, *Nails in the wall: Catholic nuns in Reformation Germany* (Chicago, 2005); eadem, 'Female religious orders' in Ro Po-chia Hsia (ed.), *A companion to the Reformation world* (Oxford, 2004), pp 237–54.   2 For a general introduction see, C. Bowden and J.E. Kelly (eds), *The English convents in exile, 1600–1800: communities, culture and identity* (Burlington, VT, 2013) and J.E. Kelly, *English convents in Catholic Europe, c.1600–1800* (Cambridge, 2019).   3 Indeed one recent edited volume overlooks the Irish context entirely: C. Van Wyhe (ed.), *Female monasticism in early modern*

endeavoured to pursue religious lifestyles on the island, as well as their spiritual contribution to the European Counter-Reformation mission. In addition, the migrant experience of those who left Ireland to seek religious profession on the European continent has been explored, revealing the mobility of Irish nuns and the importance of their role within international religious orders.[4] This essay further expands our understanding of the lived experiences of women who undertook religious vocations in Ireland during the early modern era. It will begin by sketching out the landscape of female convents in seventeenth-century Ireland, establishing the number, order affiliation and geographical spread of female religious communities as well as identifying where possible the family backgrounds of those women who joined their ranks.[5]

FEMALE RELIGIOUS ORDERS IN SEVENTEENTH-CENTURY IRELAND

By the middle of the seventeenth century, on the eve of the Cromwellian campaigns in Ireland, no less than fourteen foundations for women religious, representing four distinct religious orders (Augustinians, Carmelites, Dominicans and Poor Clares), were active on the island. The geographical spread of the female foundations was wide but the majority were concentrated west of the Shannon, away from view of the Dublin

Europe (London, 2008). **4** The pioneer of the history of early modern Irish women religious was Helena Concannon (1878–1952), whose ground-breaking research in Irish convent archives at the beginning of the twentieth century resulted in the publication of two important books, *The Poor Clares in Ireland, 1629–1929* (Dublin, 1929) and *Irish nuns in penal days* (London, 1931). More recent studies include M.-L. Coolahan, *Women, writing and language in early modern Ireland* (Oxford, 2010), especially chapter one; eadem, 'Archipelagic identities in Europe: Irish nuns in English convents' in Bowden and Kelly (eds), *The English convents in exile*, pp 211–28; B. Cunningham, 'The Poor Clare Order in Ireland' in E. Bhreathnach, J. MacMahon and J. McCafferty (eds), *The Irish Franciscans*, pp 159–74; eadem, '"Bethlehem": The Dillons and the Poor Clare convent at Ballinacliffey, Co. Westmeath', *Áitreabh: Group for the Study of Irish Historic Settlement Newsletter* (hereafter *Áitreabh*), 17 (2012–13), 5–9; eadem, 'Nuns and their networks in early modern Galway' in S. Ryan and C. Tait (eds), *Religion and politics in urban Ireland, c.1500–c.1750: essays in honour of Colm Lennon* (Dublin, 2016), pp 156–72; J. Goodrich, 'The rare books of the Galway Poor Clares', *The Library*, 22:4 (2021), 498–522; A. Knox, 'The convent as cultural conduit: Irish matronage in early modern Spain', *Quidditas: The Journal of the Rocky Mountain Medieval and Renaissance Association*, 30 (2009), 128–40; eadem, 'Nuns on the periphery? Irish Dominican nuns and assimilation in Lisbon' in F. Sabate i Curull and L. Adno da Fonseca (eds), *Catalonia and Portugal: the Iberian peninsula from the periphery* (Berlin, 2015), pp 311–26; eadem, 'Her book-lined cell: Irish nuns and the development of texts, translation and literacy in late medieval Spain' in V. Blanton, V. O'Mara and P. Stoop (eds), *Nuns' literacies in medieval Europe: the Kansas City dialogue* (Turnhout, 2015), pp 67–86; *Irish women on the move: migration and mission in Spain, 1499–1700* (Bern, 2020); B.A. McShane, *Irish women in religious orders, 1530–1700: suppression, migration and reintegration* (Woodbridge, 2022); eadem, 'Negotiating religious change and conflict: female religious communities in early modern Ireland, c.1530–c.1641', *British Catholic History*, 33:3 (2017), 357–82; eadem, 'The pre-profession examination record of Sister Catherine Browne (in religion Sister Catherine of St Francis), Poor Clare convent, Bethlehem, Co. Westmeath, 1632', *AH*, 70 (2017), 284–93. **5** For the importance of family networks for earlier female religious in

Castle authorities. By far the most prolific of the orders for women in Ireland was the Poor Clares, reflecting the dominance of their male brethren, the Friars Minor or Franciscans, in seventeenth-century Ireland.[6] Founded in the thirteenth century by St Clare of Assisi (1194–1253), as the Order of the Poor Ladies, the order later became the Order of Poor Clares and spread rapidly across western Europe.[7] The first Irish house in the post-Reformation era was established in Dublin in 1629, when seven Irish Poor Clares, originally professed at the English Poor Clare convent in Gravelines, northern France, returned to the city.[8] Although this Dublin house was short-lived, being disbanded by government authorities, within a year the Poor Clares had re-emerged, this time establishing a convent named Bethlehem on the secluded banks of Lough Ree, near Athlone. During the two decades that followed, the number and size of Poor Clare foundations in Ireland expanded rapidly; houses were established at Lough Ree, Drogheda, Galway, Athlone, Loughrea, Wexford and Waterford (although not all of these houses were active simultaneously). At the same time, female houses of the Franciscan Third Order (or Regular Tertiaries) emerged, often in towns and cities where Poor Clare foundations were already present, as at Drogheda, Galway, Wexford and Waterford.[9] The expansion of these types of female communities in Ireland was part of a wider European phenomenon in which orders of female tertiaries flourished, particularly in France where, as Susan E. Dinan has shown, intense religious warfare and famine promoted their development.[10] Unlike the solemn vows undertaken by professed nuns, tertiaries did not observe formal religious vows that would have subjected them to the rules of the cloister. Instead, they practised what Silvia Evangelisti has described as 'a socially orientated form of commitment, fostering an active spirituality in direct contact with the world, rather than pure contemplation'.[11]

During the 1640s, as religious orders benefitted from the expanding power and protection of the Catholic Confederation (1642–9), foundations of Dominican (1643),

Ireland, see the contributions by Lyons and Lennon above.   **6** C. Ó Clabaigh, *The friars in Ireland, 1224–1540* (Dublin, 2012); idem, *The Franciscans in Ireland, 1400–1534: from reform to Reformation* (Dublin, 2002); E. Breathnach, J. Mac Mahon and J. McCafferty (eds), *The Irish Franciscans, 1534–1990* (Dublin, 2009).   **7** B. Roest, *Order and disorder: the Poor Clares between foundation and reform* (Lieden, 2013); idem, 'The Poor Clares during the era of Observant reforms: attempts at a typology', *Franciscan Studies*, 69 (2011), 343–86.   **8** As Bernadette Cunningham has shown, 'while there are tantalizing references to convents of Franciscan nuns in Ireland in the pre-Reformation period … there is no clear evidence of any Poor Clare foundations'. Cunningham, 'The Poor Clare Order in Ireland', p. 159.   **9** Female tertiary houses were also established at New Ross, Limerick and Kilkenny. See McShane, *Irish women in religious orders*, p. 197. For a discussion of Third Order Franciscan foundations in post-seventeenth century Ireland see Patrick Conlon, *Franciscan Ireland* (Dublin, 1978). On the Third Order in medieval Ireland see Ó Clabaigh, *Friars in Ireland*, pp 326–8 and his contribution to this volume.   **10** Dinan, *Women and poor relief in seventeenth-century France*, p. 31. There is a vast literature on tertiaries in late medieval and early modern Europe. See, for example, Marit Monteiro, 'Power in piety: inspiration, ambition and strategies of spiritual virgins in the northern Netherlands during the seventeenth century' in L. Lux-Sterritt and C.M. Mangion (eds), *Gender, Catholicism and spirituality: women and the Roman Catholic Church in Britain and Europe, 1200–1900* (New York, 2010), pp 115–30, and L. Lehtsalu, 'A welcome presence: the custodial activities of third order women religious in seventeenth- and eighteenth-century Italy', *Journal of Early Modern History*, 22 (2018), 49–66.   **11** Evangelisti, *Nuns:*

Augustinian (1646) and Discalced Carmelite (1646/7?) nuns emerged in Galway. But none of these orders expanded beyond the city.[12] The onset of the Cromwellian campaigns (1649–53) witnessed the widespread dispersal of these female communities. During the Interregnum (1649–60), when harsh sanctions were meted out against the Catholic community, some women religious remained in hiding in Ireland, while others went into exile, fleeing to destinations in France, Portugal and Spain. The Restoration of King Charles II witnessed the tentative re-emergence of religious orders, including houses of nuns across Ireland, although female religious communities did not recover to their pre-Cromwellian era levels either in number or geographical spread; communities of Poor Clare and Dominican nuns were re-established in Galway by the 1670s while two rival houses of Benedictine nuns were founded in Dublin during the 1680s. These later establishments were offshoots of the Irish Benedictine convent established in 1682 at Ypres, in Spanish Flanders; one of just two foundations of Irish nuns in Europe during the seventeenth century (the other being the Irish Dominican convent of Nossa Senhora do Bom Sucesso in Portugal established in 1639). Notably, foundations of Third Order Franciscan sisters did not re-appear. But the onset of the Williamite wars (1688–91) meant that these foundations were once again forced to disperse with many of their members seeking refuge on the Continent. Thus, the history of Irish female religious in seventeenth-century Ireland is one characterized by short-lived foundations, resettlement and exile. It is not surprising, therefore, that the extant archival material for Irish convents from this era is minimal; indeed the fact that anything at all survives is somewhat miraculous.

In the absence of detailed convent records, it is difficult to determine with any degree of certainty the family backgrounds of those who joined the Irish convents. Those which can be traced reveal strong links with families of Old English gentry and mercantile status and, in the case of the Poor Clare sisters, close relationships to the Franciscan friars, a trend that continued throughout the seventeenth century. The Irish women who joined the English Poor Clare Order at Gravelines in northern France during the 1620s are illustrative of this wider pattern. The first was Martha Cheevers (in religion Sister Martha Marianna), who was professed on Christmas day 1620, at the age of 21. According to the community's registers, her family originated from Co. Wexford, her father being one of the 'Chevers of Ballyhaly and Macetown'.[13] While details of her mother's background are not recorded, the Cheevers family had close links to the Franciscan Order; Martha's brother, Walter, a Franciscan friar, studied at the newly established (1607) Irish college of St Anthony's in Louvain and was a member of the Irish Franciscan province.[14]

a history of convent life, p. 201.   **12** T. Ó hAnnracháin, *Catholic reformation in Ireland: the mission of Rinuccini 1645–1649* (Oxford, 2002); M. Ó Siochrú, *Confederate Ireland, 1642–1649: a constitutional and political analysis* (Dublin, 1998).   **13** Her father was a relative of Edward Cheevers of Macetown, Co. Meath, created Viscount Mount-Leinster by King James II in 1689: see W.M. Hunnybun (ed.), 'Registers of the English Poor Clares at Gravelines, including those who founded filiations at Aire, Dunkirk and Rouen, 1608–1837', *Catholic Record Society*, Miscellanea 9:14 (London, 1914), 34–5. According to Mary Bonaventure Browne, Cheevers was a native of Co. Wexford.   **14** The family were related through marriage to the Nugents, earls of

By September 1622, two more Irish women had joined the community. These two sisters, Eleanor (in religion Sister Mary of St Joseph) and Cecily (in religion Sister Francis) Dillon, from another influential Old English family with close ties to the landed recusant elite of the Pale, were professed at the ages of 21 and 19 respectively.[15] Their parents were Sir Theobald Dillon (d. 1625), first Viscount Dillon of Costello-Gallen, and Eleanor (d. 1638), daughter of Sir Edward Tuite of Tuitestown, Co. Westmeath. The Dillon family had strong affinity with the Franciscan Order and Theobald and Eleanor fostered vocations for their sons as well as their daughters; Edward (d. 1641) and George Dillon entered the Irish college of Douai in 1616 and 1620 respectively and later became friars.[16] On 6 May 1625, two more girls of Irish origin were professed at the convent, both with connections to the Old English gentry of the Pale: Alice Nugent (in religion Sister Magdalen of St Clare), aged 24, the 'daughter of a prime gentleman of the Nugents', and Mary Dowdall (in religion Sister Mary Peter), aged 19, a Dublin native.[17]

Predominantly from elite Old English family backgrounds, the women who joined the English Poor Clare convent at Gravelines were most likely bilingual, speaking both English and Irish.[18] As young women already in their late teens and early twenties at the time of their profession, these Irish sisters would have likely already obtained a degree of education either in Ireland or elsewhere prior to entering the Gravelines house. Colm Lennon has identified the existence of unofficial grammar schools for boys throughout Ireland that acted as channels for entrants to the Irish male colleges established in Europe from the end of the sixteenth century.[19] While much less is known about the schooling and educational opportunities afforded girls in late sixteenth- and early seventeenth-century Ireland, some young women from wealthy Catholic backgrounds would have received educational instruction, usually at home by private tutors.[20] A smaller number were sent abroad to continental European convents for schooling not necessarily with the intention of undertaking a religious vocation afterwards. This was true in the case of Brigid and Mary Nugent, daughters of Sir Richard Nugent (1583–1642), fifteenth Baron Delvin and first earl of Westmeath. Together with their cousin, Elizabeth Nugent, the sisters were enrolled in a convent school run by French-speaking Sepulchrine canonesses in Charleville, northern France, where they resided for a period of four years between 1625 and 1629. There, in line with educational curriculums in convent schools elsewhere in France, the girls' education was heavily geared towards religious education with a focus on the

---

Westmeath; E. Curtis, 'Extracts out of Heralds' books in Trinity College, Dublin, relating to Ireland in the sixteenth century', *JRSAI*, ser. 7, 2 (1932), 43. On Walter Cheevers see H. Concannon, *The Poor Clares in Ireland, AD 1629–AD 1929* (Dublin, 1929), p. 7.   **15** Hunnybun (ed.), 'Registers of the English Poor Clares', pp 34–5.   **16** George Dillon was later guardian of the Franciscan friary at Killinure near Athlone and became superior of the Irish Franciscan residence in Paris. See C. Mooney, *Irish Franciscans and France* (Dublin, 1964), pp 27–8, 43, 118. **17** Hunnybun (ed.), 'Registers of the English Poor Clares', p. 35.   **18** The Nugents of Delvin were bilingual being fluent in both English and Irish. D. Casey, *The Nugents of Westmeath and Queen Elizabeth's Irish primer* (Dublin, 2016).   **19** C. Lennon, 'Education and religious identity in early modern Ireland', *Paedagogica Historica*, 35:1 (2015), 57–75.   **20** On educational opportunities

inculcation of Christian doctrine through the means of the catechism in addition to French language classes and instruction in writing.[21] Although none of the Nugent women opted for the religious life, their case illustrates the schooling options available to some women from elite social backgrounds in early seventeenth-century Ireland.

THE IRISH POOR CLARES: AUTHORSHIP AND TRANSLATION

The Irish sisters who professed at the English Poor Clares convent at Gravelines in the 1620s entered a vibrant community of women that, although enclosed, were themselves thoroughly engaged in the English Catholic mission and in the educational and literary endeavours associated with it. Established *c.*1608 by Yorkshire native, Mary Ward (1585–1645), members of the Gravelines house were responsible for the production of several key Clarissan texts in English, notably the 1621 English translation of the Rule of St Clare and the 1622 translation of the Colettine Rule, *The declarations and ordinances made upon the Rule of Our Holy Mother S[aint] Clare.*[22] As will be discussed below, the Irish Poor Clare sisters would later engage in their own translation project, translating the Rule of St Clare into Irish.

The pre-eminence of the Poor Clare Order in the history of female religious in seventeenth-century Ireland cannot be overstated. Not only was the order numerically and geographically dominant during this era, it is the only Irish female order to have its history preserved in the form of an extant chronicle written by one of its members. Mary Browne (in religion Sister Bonaventure) (d. *c.*1694), a native of Co. Galway, penned her history of the Irish Poor Clares while living in exile in the convent of El Cavallero de Garcia in Madrid (she was one of those forced to flee Ireland following the outbreak of the Cromwellian wars). Browne was the daughter of Andrew Browne, a merchant in Galway city with substantial landholdings across Co. Galway. She joined the Poor Clares at Bethlehem in 1632, alongside her sister, Catherine. They were also closely related to Valentine Browne, the Franciscan provincial in Ireland from 1629 to 1635.[23] An accomplished linguist, Browne was fluent in English, Irish and Spanish. Her chronicle, originally penned in Irish, charts the experiences of the Irish Poor Clare sisters from their time in the Gravelines convent during the late 1620s to their subsequent exile to Spain in the 1650s and 1660s.[24] Like chronicles written by nuns throughout early modern Europe, Browne's chronicle served a very particular purpose; in this case to preserve for posterity the collective history and spiritual endeavour of

for young women in sixteenth- and seventeenth-century Ireland, see M. O'Dowd, *A history of women in Ireland, 1500–1800* (Harlow, 2005), pp 206–10.   **21** The case of the Nugent girls in Charleville is discussed at length in McShane, *Irish women in religious orders*, pp 113–25. **22** J. Goodrich, 'A Poor Clare's legacy', *English Literary Renaissance*, 46:1 (Winter 2016), 3–28.   **23** M.-L. Coolahan, 'Browne, Mary (d. in or before 1694)', *Oxford dictionary of national biography.*   **24** The surviving manuscript, whose watermark dates from the late seventeenth century, is a contemporary translation into English; the original perished during the Williamite wars in 1691. See M.-L. Coolahan, *Women, writing and language in early modern Ireland* (Oxford, 2010), p. 81. For a modern edition of Browne's chronicle see C. O'Brien (ed.), *Recollections of an Irish Poor Clare in the seventeenth*

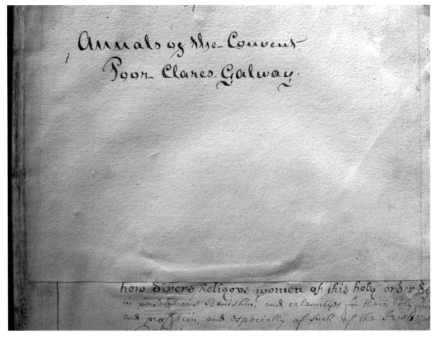

9.1 Image of the Browne Chronicle, courtesy of the Poor Clare Monastery Archive, Galway.

the Irish Poor Clare Order (Fig. 9.1).[25] Notwithstanding its retrospective nature and inherent bias, Browne's account is a valuable and unique source for the history of Irish women religious during the early modern period. It provides the only comprehensive account of the Irish Poor Clares' activities during this early phase of their history. Furthermore, it is the only known account of its kind composed by a female member of a religious order from Ireland during the seventeenth century.

As Marie-Louise Coolahan has contended in her ground-breaking study of Irish nuns' writing, Browne's reputation as a female author radiated far beyond the cloister walls. In 1732 Browne's chronicle was included in a bibliography of Franciscan publications collated by the Spanish Franciscan, Fr Joanne à. s. Antonio Salmantino. In Salmantino's bibliography, the chronicle was ascribed the title of 'The martyrdoms of certain Poor Clares and Tertiaries during the tyrannous cruelty of Ireland', while Browne herself was commemorated as 'a most famous Irishwoman from the Poor Clares of the monastery of the city of Galway' ['Hyberna clarissima, ex Clarissis Monasterij Civitatis Galvensis'] who was forced to withdraw to Spain 'because of risings and wars' ['ac bellorum causa'].[26] As Coolahan has argued, the inclusion of

Browne's chronicle in the Spanish friar's bibliographical list 'demonstrates that Browne's original text circulated far beyond its originally intended, cloistered female community'; rather it was read 'as an important Counter-Reformation document of national as well as transnational religious experience'.[27]

That Mary Browne was motivated to write her history of the Irish Poor Clares while living in exile in Spain demonstrates her desire for the stories of the early Irish sisters to be remembered for posterity. But it is also indicative of the wider literary culture in which her order was immersed. Far from living on the margins of political and religious developments, the Irish Poor Clares were firmly rooted within the wider Counter-Reformation nexus of seventeenth-century Europe. Since the early seventeenth century, prominent Irish Franciscan scholars such as Flaithrí Ó Maoil Chonaire (d. 1629), Bonaventure Ó hEodhasa (d. 1614) and Aodh Mac Aingil (d. 1626) had printed a series of Irish-language spiritual works at St Anthony's College, Louvain, designed to aid the Counter-Reformation mission in Ireland and abroad. In their endeavours the Irish friars spearheaded a highly politicized and religious linguistic project to establish a substantial corpus of religious and devotional texts.[28] In October 1636, the Bethlehem Poor Clares, under the direction of their abbess, joined this Irish Franciscan scholarly enterprise, commissioning the prominent Franciscan scholar and chief scribe of the 'Annals of the Four Masters', Mícheál Ó Cléirigh (d. 1643), to produce a transcript of the Irish version of the Rule of St Clare, the text recited at profession.[29] Ó Cléirigh visited the Bethlehem convent over a period of about three days. During that time, he completed the Irish transcription, which he signed and dated 19 and 21 October 1636 (Fig. 9.2). In his dedication Ó Cléirigh wrote:

> For the love of Jesus and his sweet Mother, the Virgin holy Mary, for the love of St Francis and St Clare and her Rule which is here begun, remember, Sisters, in your prayers each day your poor brother Michel O Cleirigh.

> Ar Ghrádh Íosa Críost agus a naomhmathar milsi an Óg Naomh Muire, ar ghrádh San Frainseis, agus San Clara, sa riaghail tionnsgaintear annso, bíodh cuimhne agaibh a dheirbhseathra in bhar nurnuighe go laitheamhail ar bhar ndearbhrathair bocht Michel Ó Cleirigh.[30]

The nuns' recruitment of Ó Cléirigh gave them added legitimacy by situating them within the wider sphere of Franciscan scholarly enterprise and connecting them with

'Transnational reception and early modern women's "lost" texts', *Early Modern Women: An Interdisciplinary Journal*, 7 (2012), 261–70. **27** Coolahan, 'Transnational reception and early modern women's "lost" texts', 268. **28** M.A. Lyons, 'The role of St Anthony's College, Louvain in establishing the Irish Franciscan college network' in E. Bhreathnach, J. MacMahon and J. McCafferty (eds), *The Irish Franciscans, 1534–1990* (Dublin, 2009), pp 27–44. **29** The initial translation had been made by two priests, Aodh Ó Raghallaigh and Séamus Ó Siaghail, both relatively obscure characters. RIA, MS D i 2, 'The Rule of St Clare', pp xvii. The manuscript can be viewed on the Irish Script on Screen website (www.isos.dias.ie). For an edition see E. Knott (ed.), 'An Irish seventeenth-century translation of the Rule of St Clare', *Éiru*, 15 (1948), 1–187. **30** RIA, MS D i 2, 'The Rule of St Clare',

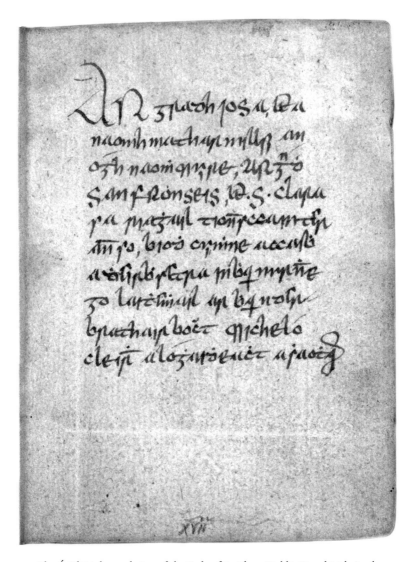

9.2 The Ó Cléirigh translation of the Rule of St Clare, Dublin Royal Irish Academy, MS D i 2, p. xvii. Image © Royal Irish Academy, 2002.

a network of scholars and patrons.[31] As Coolahan has highlighted, the Poor Clares' production of an Irish version of the Rule of St Clare aligned the community with the broader Counter-Reformation movement to 'fashion a national, Catholic Irish identity'.[32] Their production of foundation documents in the vernacular was also consistent with the activities of enclosed communities elsewhere on the Continent, including the English Poor Clares at Gravelines, who undertook to translate St Clare's

p. xvii.   **31** Cunningham, 'The Poor Clare Order in Ireland', p. 162.   **32** Coolahan, *Women, writing and language*, p. 67.

9.3 1647 document and nuns' signatures.
Image courtesy of the Poor Clare Monastery Archive, Galway.

thirteenth-century rule into English in 1621.[33] On a domestic level, the Irish Poor Clares were addressing the needs of their own community. As Coolahan contends, the community's translation project may have been part of a targeted recruitment drive since the provision of an Irish version of the Rule of St Clare enabled the recruitment of women from Gaelic-Irish speaking backgrounds.[34] It also highlights the growing 'cooperation between Old English and Gaelic ethnic groups on the basis of shared religion'.[35] This position was to be reinforced six years later following the establishment of the Catholic Confederation of Kilkenny in 1642 (discussed below). As Raymond Gillespie has shown, the Confederacy redefined the political 'nation' in religious rather than ethnic terms, by resolving to avoid 'national distinctions between the subjects of His Majesty's dominions'.[36]

Mary Bonaventure Browne is arguably the best-known Irish nun of the seventeenth century. As well as serving as the order's chronicler, Browne also served as abbess of

33 Ibid., pp 61–2.   **34** Ibid., p. 66.   **35** Ibid., p. 78.   **36** R. Gillespie. *Seventeenth-century Ireland: making Ireland modern* (Dublin, 2006), p. 156. As Pádraig Lenihan argues, increasingly assertive anti-Catholic policies blurred any residual political differences between Old English and Irish by the 1620s while according to Ó Siochrú intermarriage and a common interest in land meant that by the 1640s ethnicity was less important than social status in determining an individual's outlook: see P. Lenihan, *Confederate Catholics at war, 1642–49* (Cork, 2001), p. 8; M. Ó Siochrú, *Confederate Ireland, 1642–1649: a constitutional and political analysis* (Dublin, 1998), p. 17.

the Galway Poor Clare convent for a three year term beginning in 1647. The Galway house was originally established in January 1642 as an offshoot of the Bethlehem foundation.[37] It flourished from the outset, aided as it was by strong support from the local Catholic elite and connections with the friars at nearby Kilconnell friary.[38] Initially the Galway sisters rented a small premises in the centre of the town.[39] There, within two years of their arrival, they attracted as many as twenty-three postulants who were 'brought up and educated in their regular observance, not omitting in the least any of the great religion and good education they received in Bethlehem'.[40] But on taking up her position as abbess in 1647, Bonaventure Browne set her sights on further expansion, spearheading a project to establish a daughter convent at Loughrea, a town about forty kilometres south-east of the town of Galway. However, in doing so, Browne also sought to safeguard the financial security of both the Galway and Bethlehem houses. Thus, an agreement signed by Browne and eight other Galway Poor Clare sisters (Fig. 9.3) was concerned with keeping intact the dowries of those who had professed in Bethlehem and Galway but who now intended to join the new foundation. In addition, the Galway house was to provide vestments and furnishings for the new foundation while the costs incurred from the construction of the Loughrea cloister were to be shared between both communities.[41]

In addition to overseeing the physical expansion of the Poor Clares in Galway, Abbess Browne continued the earlier project of commissioning the translation of key foundation texts into Irish. In 1647, she employed the renowned Gaelic scholar Dubhaltach Óg Mac Firbhisigh (*c.*1600–71) to translate from English into Irish the constitutions of St Colette and other documents elucidating the Rule of St Clare, presumably with a view to recruiting more Gaelic Irishwomen into what was up to that point an order dominated by an Old English membership.[42]

FEMALE RELIGIOUS AND THE IMPACT OF WARFARE

The Irish Poor Clares' focus on translation projects was interrupted by the ongoing Confederate wars (1642–9) and the economic hardships that ensued. The difficulties experienced by the female order are reflected in a series of petitions for aid made by

---

37 'Licence to found in Galway', 30 Jan. 1642 (Poor Clare monastery, Galway, MS A2). The document is signed by Fr Anthony Mac Geoghegan, a native of Westmeath and one of the first superiors of the Athlone friary at Killinure, Co. Westmeath.   **38** See, for example, the donation of a silver monstrance to Kilconnell friary by Sister Mary O'Kelly. Sister O'Kelly was one of two novices who had travelled from Bethlehem to begin the new foundation in Galway in January 1642. Her family had long standing connections with the friars at Kilconnell dating back to the fourteenth century. For a discussion, see McShane, *Irish women in religious orders*, pp 188–9.   **39** The exact location of the community's first premises in Galway is not known, however, it is thought to have been off the present St Augustine Street and close to the town wall. See P. Walsh, *Renaissance Galway: delineating the seventeenth century city* (Dublin, 2019), p. 91.   **40** Quoted in Concannon, *Poor Clares in Ireland*, p. 44. See also C. O'Brien (ed.), *Recollections of an Irish Poor Clare in the seventeenth century* (Galway, 1993), pp 6–7.   **41** 'An agreement between the sisters in Galway and those founding in Loughrea' (Poor Clare monastery, Galway, MS A6).   **42** For an

Poor Clare abbesses to the Catholic Confederacy throughout the 1640s. In May 1645, for example, Sister Clare Nugent, abbess of the Waterford community, compelled by 'urgent extreamety', solicited help from General Thomas Preston, a leading member of the Catholic Confederation.[43] Abbess Nugent's targeting of Preston was deliberate since at least one of his daughters was a member of the order and he presumably would be favourably disposed to her requests.[44] In a petition presented to the supreme council of the Catholic Confederation on 5 May 1647, Abbess Cecily Dillon of the Athlone house implored the council to assist the sisters who were 'poor damosells' and 'afflicted handmaydes' then residing in the 'ruinous' town of Athlone.[45] In her lengthy supplication, Dillon set out her case for support. She began by drawing attention to her community's continental origins, asserting that they were 'the first of their profession who ever came into Ireland out of Flanders'. She highlighted the sisters' influential connections, 'both spiritual and temporal', and their recent suffering including the destruction of their convent at Bethlehem, an event which had inured them to 'betake them into islands, woods and bogs'.[46] The abbess explained that whereas the previous council had instructed the vicar general of Clonmacnoise, Fr Anthony Mac Geoghegan, to pay £80 annually out of diocesan funds towards the upkeep of her community, to date only £10 had been forthcoming.[47] In addition, since their chief benefactors in the 'Counties and City of Dublin, Meath, Kildare, Westmeath' were no longer in a position to support them, the sisters could not continue to pay their rent.[48] In a revealing insight into the precarious position of the community, the abbess explained that building supplies which they had procured to construct a new convent, including 'forty poundes [worth] of Breekes', had been stolen from them by one 'Capt[ai]n Tibbott MaGawley'.[49]

On account of these hardships, the abbess requested that an annual payment of £200 procured from church and municipal taxes, and from the estate profits of Lord Ranelagh who, according to Dillon, was responsible for the destruction of their former foundation at Lough Ree.[50] One week later the council granted the abbess's request.[51] However, indicative of the straitened economic circumstances, the sum awarded was far below the amount requested.[52] The sisters were to receive just £60 per annum; if

extended discussion Coolahan, *Women, writing and language*, pp 66–7.   **43** *The calendar of the State Papers, Ireland, 1633–1647* (London, 1901), pp 662–3. The petition is printed in Concanon, *Poor Clares in Ireland*, pp 28–9 and Gilbert, *Irish Confederation*, iv, 242.   **44** 'The humble petition of the Mother Abbesse and poore Sisters of St Clare of ye Convent of Bethlehem in Athlone', 5 May 1647 (TNA SP 63/264, ff 144–6).   **45** (TNA SP 63/264, ff 144–6).   **46** (TNA SP 63/264, ff 144–6).   **47** (TNA SP 63/264, ff 144–6).   **48** (TNA SP 63/264, ff 144–6).   **49** (TNA SP 63/264, ff 144–6). See deposition of Thomas Fleetwood of Co. Westmeath, 22 Mar. 1643 (TCD MS 817, f. 37r), 'ffurther he sajth that the lord President of Connaghts steward mr Booth rydeing one morning towards the English army on westmeath side, was slaine, by one Tibbott Magawly a notorious Rebell & late servant to mr Thomas mc Talbot Dillon'.   **50** (TNA SP 63/264, ff 144–6).   **51** (TNA SP 63/264, ff 144–6).   **52** By 1647, Ranelagh had died and been succeeded by his son, Arthur (d. 1669), 2nd Viscount. At the outbreak of the 1641 rebellion, Ranelagh was one of the largest landholders in Ireland, with property held across Cos Sligo, Roscommon, Longford, Meath, Dublin and Wicklow. For an overview, see J. Ohlmeyer, *Making Ireland English: the Irish aristocracy in the seventeenth century* (New Haven and London, 2012), pp 91, 97, 306, 572.

this sum could not be paid from municipal taxes, the ecclesiastical authorities were to supply the balance.[53] There was no reference to the recovery of losses from Ranelagh's estate.

In 1649, the Galway Poor Clares petitioned the city's corporation for relief, owing to the inability of their former benefactors to support them. The petition, signed 'Mary Bonaventure, unworthy abbesse', outlined the particular hardships faced by the community, including the threat of imminent eviction. Browne explained that:

> through necessity by reason of the tymes their parents and friends are unable to furnish their wants as in peacable tymes they have intended, and that your poore petitioners doe suffer much by the exorbitant rent they pay, and notwithstanding their due payment, are to be thrust out of their dwelling next May, their lease being ended.

Because of their imminent eviction, the nuns' requested 'sufficient room for building a monastery and rooms convenient thereunto, a garden and orchard, in the next island adjoining the bridge of Illanltenagh'. Highlighting the unique function of female contemplative life, the petition outlined the benefits that would accrue to the town in the future from the presence of a convent of devout 'religious women' who would support the town through their prayers, and whose presence would be the honour of the town.[54]

> The premises considered and taken to your consideracion the inconveniencie of religious women whoe want habitacion, the conveniencie of their residence [to] this place, the preferment of your children though poore shallbe reveeled by God's assistance in our Convent, the everlasting prayers to made for yow, the glory of God, the preservacion of the towne by your petitioners and their successors their intercessions, the honour of Galway to be founders of such a monasterie.[55]

The corporation acceded to their request, and the sisters proceeded with construction of a 'good large and spacious house with other conveniences' on the designated island. The structure was built from timber and other materials at a cost of £200, paid for out of the nuns' dowries.[56] On a seventeenth-century pictorial map of Galway city the sisters' convent building is clearly visible and depicts a substantial church with Gothic-style windows.[57] In consequence of their presence, this island would become known as Nuns' Island (Fig 9.4).

The actions of the Irish Poor Clare abbesses during the turbulent era of the 1640s reveals a self-assured and highly articulate leadership intent on securing their place in

---

53 (TNA SP 63/264, ff 144–6).   **54** Copy of the petition from the congregation to the municipality of Galway, signed 'Mary Bonaventure, unworthy abbess', asking for permission to establish a monastery on Islannallenny, and reply in the affirmative signed by Mayor William Blake, recorder John Blake, of 1 and 10 July 1649, printed in HMC, *10th Rep.*, App. 5, p. 498. **55** HMC, *10th Rep.*, App. 5, p. 498.   **56** Ibid.   **57** Walsh, *Renaissance Galway*, p. 91.

9.4 Poor Clare monastery, Nuns' Island, Galway, mid-seventeenth century.
Image © Trinity College Dublin, reproduced by kind permission of the Board.

the broader Counter-Reformation mission and safeguarding the long-term viability of
their communities. However, despite these efforts, the onset of the Cromwellian
campaigns (1649–53) resulted in the complete dispersal of the network of Irish female
religious houses that had been established over the previous twenty years. In a 1656
report sent to the *Congregation de Propaganda Fide* in Rome, the Irish Franciscan friar, Fr
Anthony Gearnon, described the decimation experienced by the Catholic Church in
Ireland as a result of the recent Cromwellian military campaigns.[58] A former student
at St Anthony's College in Louvain, Gearnon was among those friars who left Ireland
in the aftermath of the 1653 banishment act.[59] Writing from his exiled abode in Paris,
he lamented the ruinous condition of the kingdom's 'churches, monasteries and
convents' which:

> were erected for religious men and women or were recently restored through
> Catholic piety, all of these buildings which the zeal of our ancestors and the
> work of charity had sanctified are now either demolished or converted to
> profane uses such as homes for heretics or stables for beasts. Among the ruins
> that have been produced by this heresy are sixty-two monasteries of St Francis,
> which were not long ago full of devotés, and ten of St Clare, now not offering
> sacrifice or invoking God.[60]

58 Gearnon later served as chaplain to the queen-mother, Henrietta Maria. See A. Faulkner,
'Anthony Gearnon, O.F.M. (*c.*1610–80) and the Irish Remonstrance', *CLAHJ*, 17 (1971), 141–9.
59 'Ordered, that it be, and is hereby referred to ye Lord Chief Justice Pepys to give order for
ye transporting unto France on(e) Anthony Gernon a popish Priest lately apprehended and now
under custody of Philip Peak Marshall to ye four courts in Dublin. Dated at ye Councel
Chamber in Dublin, 30 July 1656. T.H.C.C.' (quoted in Faulkner, 'Anthony Gearnon', p. 146).
60 The report was entitled '*Brevis relation conditionis praesentis regni Hiberniae*'. See B. Millett, *The*

The ten monasteries of 'St Clare' referred to by Gearnon comprised both Second Order and Third Order houses. Their members had been widely dispersed as the parliamentarian army advanced across the island during the early 1650s. The houses of Dominican, Carmelite and Augustinian nuns in Galway were likewise dispersed in the aftermath of the campaigns.

DISPERSAL AND EXILE

The fate of these dispersed communities was addressed in the 1653 banishment act which ordered the immediate expulsion from Ireland of all 'Jesuits, seminary priests, and persons in popish orders'; those found to be in contravention of the decree were to be sentenced to death.[61] Female religious were included within this wider expulsion campaign since the act was promptly followed by an additional directive 'commanding all nuns, of whatsoever condition, to marry or quit the kingdom'.[62] A large-scale exodus of Irish clergy and religious to Catholic Europe ensued. Although some individuals remained in Ireland even after the proclamation of the 1653 act, it was a risky undertaking, since authorities actively sought out those who defied the directives.[63] We know that the majority of nuns who left Ireland after 1653 travelled to Spain aboard vessels bound for Galician ports. From there, the women were widely dispersed to towns and cities across the Spanish mainland from Bilbao and Orduña, in the north, to the southern port town of Málaga (or Maqueda), where they were subsequently admitted to local convents. Spain was a particularly attractive destination, since King Philip IV offered generous financial assistance to Irish religious migrants, including nuns.[64] But despite the financial resources on offer to Irish sisters, assimilation within

Irish Franciscans, 1651–65 (Rome, 1964), p. 280. The original Latin text is printed in P.F. Moran (ed.), *Spicilegium Ossoriense: being a collection of original letters and papers illustrative of the history of the Irish church*, 3 vols (Dublin, 1874), i, p. 415. I am grateful to Colm Lennon for this translation. **61** The 1653 proclamation evoked the 1584 Elizabethan 'Act against Jesuits, seminary priests, and such other like disobedient persons', also known as the 'Jesuits Act' (27 Eliz. 1, c. 2). J.P. Prendergast, *The Cromwellian settlement of Ireland* (2nd ed., London, 1870), p. 319; 'order for Banishing all priests', 6 Jan. 1653, and order of 19 Feb. 1653 (King's Inns, Prendergast papers, vol. 2, ff 65–6, ff 99–100. A Latin copy is printed in T. Burke, *Hibernia Dominicana: sive, Historia provinciæ Hiberniæ Ordinis Prædicatorum: ex antiquis manuscriptis* (1762), pp 704–5). As Micheál Ó Siochrú has discussed, a handful of sick and elderly clergy were granted licences to remain in the country as long as they made no attempt to minister. During the latter stages of the Interregnum the government operated a de facto policy of toleration of clergy. See M. Ó Siochrú, *God's executioner: Oliver Cromwell and the conquest of Ireland* (London, 2008), pp 233–4. **62** Quoted in Concannon, *The Poor Clares in Ireland*, p. 50. See Fr Quin, 'State and condition of the Catholics of Ireland from 1652 to 1656', printed as an appendix in John Lynch, *Cambrensis Eversus, seu potius historica fides in Rebus Hibernicis*, ed. M. Kelly, 3 vols (Dublin, 1848–52), i, p. 81. **63** The government offered a reward for their capture, fixed at £5 in 1653. Ó Siochru, *God's executioner*, p. 233; B. Millett, 'Survival and reorganization, 1650–95' in P.J. Corish (ed.), *A history of Irish Catholicism*, 3 vols (Dublin, 1967–), 3:7, pp 1–12.   **64** M. Begoña Villar García, 'Irish migration and exile patterns in Spain: refugees, soldiers, traders and statesmen' in Thomas O'Connor and Mary Ann Lyons (eds), *Irish communities in early modern Europe* (Dublin, 2006),

Spanish convents was challenging. Language was undoubtedly a major barrier to integration. The acquisition of language skills would have been further complicated by variations in dialect since Basque was spoken in convents across northern Spain where several Irish nuns were resident.[65] However, linguistic barriers were clearly surmountable and for some migrant nuns the attainment of high levels of linguistic proficiency was a possibility. This was true in the case of Sister Mary O'Halloran, a member of the Galway Dominicans who joined the convent of the Blessed Virgin Mary at Zamora, north-western Spain.[66] O'Halloran's linguistic proficiency was commended by the Dominican priest and historian, Fr John O'Heyne, who remarked that 'never was there a woman known to me of stronger intellect. She had a more accurate acquaintance with the Spanish tongue than the Spanish themselves'.[67] In the case of the Poor Clares, Sister Mary Bonaventure Browne, who found refuge in the Conceptionist convent of Cavallero de Gracia in Madrid, was lauded for being 'well spoken in English, Irish and Spanish'.[68] Drawing on her Spanish-language skills, Browne personally visited several convents across Spain in order to obtain material which she later used to pen her chronicle of the Irish Poor Clares. Thus, she explained in the chronicle that 'dureing my banishment heare in Spaine, I have seene severall convents, in some of which I lodged some nights, and heard true relations of many'.[69] Her account was therefore based largely on eyewitness testimony from the convents in which the nuns had resided, something that would not have been possible without her language proficiency.

REVIVAL

Mary Browne never returned to Ireland. She died in Madrid *c.*1694, by which time she would probably have been in her eighties.[70] But others made the journey home encouraged by the environment of Catholic advancement initiated following the 1685 accession of James II to the throne. Among them were two Galway-born Dominican sisters, Julian Nolan (d. 1701) and Mary Lynch, who had been residing in Bilbao in northern Spain since the 1650s. In November 1686 the pair boarded a vessel at Bilbao and eight days later arrived in Galway where, according to their confessor, Fr John O'Heyne, they were 'received by all with great joy' ['ubi receptae sunt ab omnibus cum

p. 189. For a recent analysis of Irish religious migration to Spain, see Cristina Bravo Lozano, *Spain and the Irish mission, 1609–1707* (London, 2018).   **65** Nere Jone Intxaustegi Jauregi, *La mujer religiosa en Bizkaia durante los siglos XVI–XVIII* (Bilbao, 2018), pp 201–8.   **66** Sister Mary O'Halloran, a Galway native, was one of the first members to profess at the Galway Dominican house following its establishment in 1644.   **67** J. O'Heyne, *The Irish Dominicans of the seventeenth century* (Dundalk, 1902), p. 167.   **68** A chronicle preserved in the Galway Poor Clare monastery describes Mary Bonaventure Browne as 'a very good, holy and perfect religious Sister … endowed with many rare vertues as obedience, poverty, chastity, humility and charetie, she was prudent and wise, well spoken in English, Irish and Spanish' (quoted in O'Brien (ed.), *Recollections of an Irish Poor Clare*, foreword [unpaginated]).   **69** Galway chronicle, f. 15. The contemplative order of the Immaculate Conception had been founded by St Beatrice da Silva in 1484. O'Brien, *A short history of the Poor Clares*, p. 28.   **70** Browne joined the Poor Clares in 1632 at an unknown

summo gaudio'].[71] The women received support from Sir John Kirwan, the Catholic mayor of the town, who granted them use of a substantial stone premises in Kirwan's Lane. Nolan was appointed prioress while Lynch served as sub-prioress and mistress of novices. Together, the women established a house 'favourable to a solitary and religious life' ['habitaculo congruenti ad solitariam et religiosam vitam'], and soon received their first novice, Agnes Browne, a local woman, who was professed on 7 May 1688.[72] Under the leadership of Prioress Nolan the fledgling community expanded, admitting several new novices who were 'educated with the utmost care in the greatest piety' ['quas educavit cura impensissima in summa pietate'].[73]

But the Dominicans were not the first community of nuns to reappear in Galway post-Cromwell. As early as 1673, the Poor Clares were once again in residence in the town when Abbess Elizabeth Skerrett travelled to London to petition no less a person than King Charles II for her community's rights to their former premises in Nuns' Island. Professed in Galway in 1644, Skerrett was among those Poor Clares who left Ireland for Spain in the aftermath of the Cromwellian banishment act. She resided for a time in Madrid and Bilbao before returning to Ireland at an unknown date (she was in Bilbao until at least 1667 and had returned to Ireland by 1673 when she travelled to London).[74] Appearing at the royal court in London before Queen Catherine of Braganza dressed in full habit, the abbess's petition was favourably received and the nuns reoccupied their former premises in Galway. There, under Skerrett's direction, the community expanded, admitting several 'well-born virgins inspired by God to embrace the Gospel life'.[75]

The re-emergence of the Dominican and Poor Clare communities in Galway represented an important element of continuity with the pre-Cromwellian era and were a testament to the resilience of these female religious orders and their membership. Their presence was sustained and remarkably both communities retain a presence in Galway today; the Poor Clares on their original Nuns' Island site, and the Dominicans in Taylor's Hill. The survival of several items, including chalices, vestments, reliquaries, statues and other devotional objects dating to the seventeenth and early eighteenth centuries points to the rich material culture of these communities. These include a silver ciborium gifted to the Galway Poor Clares in 1644 by Sister Mary Kelly, a member of that community. Sister Kelly's family had long-standing

age but was probably younger than 20.   **71** O'Heyne, *Irish Dominicans*, p. 163.   **72** 'Profession document of Sister Agnes Browne', 7 May 1688 (Archives of the Galway Dominican sisters, Taylor's Hill, Galway).   **73** O'Heyne, *Irish Dominicans*, p. 163.   **74** As Jone Intxaustegi Jauregi has shown, Sister Elizabeth Skerrett (Sister Isabel de San Francisco Escorret) entered a convent in Bilbao in 1664 and remained there until 1667. She had previously resided at the Cavallero de Gracia in Madrid, where Mary Bonaventure Browne resided. See Jone Intxaustegi Jauregi, *La mujer religiosa en Bizkaia*, p. 206. For a discussion of Abbess Elizabeth Skerrett's petition at the royal court see McShane, *Irish women in religious orders*, p. 229.   **75** 'Letter to Mother Elizabeth Skerrett, Mother Abbess, giving the faculty of admitting to the habit "two well-born virgins". Signed Fr Anthony De Burgo', 30 July 1683 (Poor Clare monastery, Galway, MS A8). The Portuguese house of Braganza were supporters of the community of Irish Dominican sisters of Nossa Senhora do Bom Sucesso, established at Lisbon in 1639. See H. McCabe, OP, *A light undimmed: the story of the convent of Our Lady of Bom Sucesso Lisbon, 1639–2006* (Dublin, 2007)

9.5 The Kirwan chalice veil. Image courtesy of Galway City Museum.

connections with the friars at Kilconnell dating back to the medieval era: William Buide O'Kelly, king of Uí Maine (*c.*1349–81), was founder of the friary in the fourteenth century. The ciborium, inscribed 'Sr. Maria Killy procuravit pro Convento, S. Clare Gallway L. Dupont 1644', remains in the possession of the Galway Poor Clare sisters today.[76] In the case of the Dominicans, a chalice veil made in 1683 by Bridget Kirwan is the earliest of a collection of Dominican chalice veils dating from the seventeenth and early eighteenth centuries and now preserved in Galway City Museum (Fig. 9.5).[77] Indicative of the importance of convents as centres of embroidery and

and McShane, *Irish women in religious orders*, pp 127–62. **76** According to Kurt Ticher, the Kelly ciborium is 'the most remarkable' piece of silver among the convent's collection and may very well have been made in France. See K. Ticher, 'The silver in the St Clare's Monastery, Galway', *Journal of the Galway Archaeological Society*, 37 (1979/80), 1. **77** The chalice veil is initialled 'B.K.' (Bridget Kirwan) and dated 1683 in Roman numerals. Galway City Museum (https://galway citymuseum.ie/ collection/kirwan-veil/).

VIDA,
VIRTVDES, Y
MILAGROS, DE LA
BIENAVENTVRADA VIRGEN

Teresa de Iesus, Madre y Fundadora de la
nueua Reformacion de la Orden de los
Descalços, y Descalças de nuestra
Señora del Carmen.

*Por Fray Diego de Yepes, Religioso de la Orden de san Gerony-
mo, Obispo de Taraçona, y Confessor del Rey de España
Don Felipe II. y de la Santa Madre.*

A nuestro Santissimo Padre Paulo Papa V.

Año de   1616.

En Lisboa, Con licencia: En la Officina de Pedro Crasbeeck.

Está taixado na mesa Real a trezentos & sesenta reis em papel.

9.6 Life of St Teresa of Ávila in the Dominican collections. Image © Convent of Jesus & Mary
Dominican Collection, Special Collections, University of Galway Library.

textile production, the so-called Kirwan chalice veil comprises a single panel of silk satin appliquéd to a linen mix fabric backing with hand sewn intricate detail.[78] According to Ultan Lally, Bridget Kirwan was likely a member of the Third Order Dominican community in Galway.[79]

In addition to a vibrant material culture, the Poor Clare and Dominican communities in Galway have preserved an equally rich literary culture in the form of substantial library collections. The Dominican library collection, which comprises more than 2,000 volumes, accumulated over five centuries, was recently donated to the library at the University of Galway. The collection, which has since been catalogued, is thematically, linguistically and chronologically diverse and includes a range of literary, devotional, liturgical, biographical and historical works in English, Irish, French, German and Italian as well as bibles, primers, dictionaries and thesauri.[80] The collection represents the oldest continuously used library in Galway city today and contains a selection of significant seventeenth-century religious publications, including a 1617 edition of St Thomas Aquinas' *Summae Theologicae* and a 1616 edition of the life of the Spanish Carmelite and mystic Teresa of Ávila (1515–82), one of the bestsellers in all languages in the early modern period (Fig. 9.6).[81] Jaime Goodrich's pioneering analysis of the seventeenth- and eighteenth-century rare books of the Galway Poor Clares – the 'most comprehensive single collection of early-modern Clarissan material in English in the world' – has revealed how 'textual consumption and production' played an important role in the 'cultivation of communal spirituality' within early modern Irish female religious foundations.[82] Goodrich has also produced an extensive catalogue of this unique book collection, which will undoubtedly act as a boon to further research in this promising field of scholarship.[83]

BENEDICTINE FOUNDATIONS IN DUBLIN

The prevailing atmosphere of toleration under James II sparked the emergence of two entirely new religious foundations for women in Ireland. Both were Benedictine

---

78 A. Brannigan and F. Bradley, 'Dominican altar frontal: sewing spangles in the face of adversity', National Museum of Ireland website (https://www.ouririshheritage.org/content/archive/place/mo-ghaillimh-fein-my-own-galway/galway-in-30-objects/dominican-altar-frontal) [accessed 25 October 2022].   **79** U. Lally, 'Hora Determinata: Dominican nuns and Catholic identity among Galway city's elite in the seventeenth and eighteenth centuries', unpublished paper delivered at the Fifth Glenstal History Conference, 'Brides of Christ: women and monasticism in medieval and early modern Ireland', online, July 2021.   **80** B.A. McShane, 'Three seventeenth-century books from the Galway Dominican convent library collection' (https://recirc.universityofgalway.ie/2017/05/three-seventeenth-century-books-galway-dominican-convent-library-collection); eadem, 'Inscriptions in the Galway Dominican convent library collection' (https://recirc.universityofgalway.ie/2017/08/inscriptions-galway-dominican-convent-library-collection).   **81** D. de Yepes, *Vida, virtudes, y Milagros, de la bienaventurada virgin Teresa de Jesus* (Lisbon, 1616).   **82** Goodrich, 'The rare books of the Galway Poor Clares', p. 499.   **83** The catalogue is produced as an appendix, 'Catalogue of books in Galway, Poor Clare convent, Special Collections' in Goodrich, 'The rare books of the Galway Poor Clares',

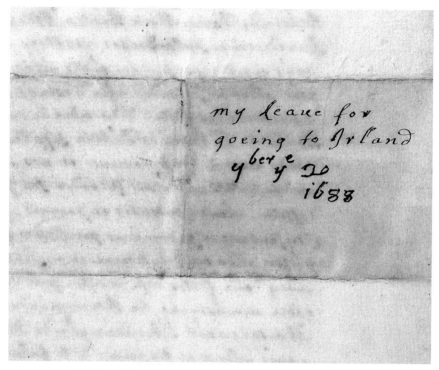

9.7 Mary Butler's 'leave for goeing to Irland'. Image courtesy of the Benedictine Monastery Archive, Kylemore Abbey, Co. Galway.

establishments located in the heart of Dublin city. Unlike the Dominican and Poor Clare foundations in Galway, which were revivals of earlier seventeenth-century houses, the convents in Dublin were an entirely new articulation of female religious life on the island as there had been no Benedictine foundations for women in Ireland since the Reformation.[84] In addition, both Benedictine houses had an adjoining school, and offered education services to the daughters of the country's Old English elite. As such, the order spearheaded the first official convent schools in Ireland.[85] The first, at Channel Row, led by Sister Mary Joseph Ryan (d. 1718), a Dublin-born woman, was in operation by 1687, while the second, at Great Ship Street, adjacent to Dublin Castle, was established in 1688 and directed by Kilkenny-native, Sister Mary Joseph Butler (1641–1723), a relation of the first earl of Ormond. Both Ryan and Butler had begun their religious careers in English Benedictine foundations in Europe. After the death

pp 514–22.   **84** For the history of the Irish Benedictine nuns see P. Nolan, *The Irish dames of Ypres: being a history of the Royal Irish Abbey of Ypres founded A.D. 1665 and still flourishing* (Dublin, 1908); K. Villiers-Tuthill, 'The Irish Benedictine nuns: from Kylemore to Ypres' in Browne and Ó Clabaigh, *Benedictines*, pp 122–39; C. Ó Clabaigh, 'The Benedictines in medieval and early modern Ireland' in Browne and Ó Clabaigh, *Benedictines*, pp 79–121; D. Raftery and C. Kilbride, *The Benedictine nuns and Kylemore Abbey: a history* (Dublin, 2020), pp 133–203.   **85** On convent schooling in late seventeenth- and eighteenth-century Ireland see O'Dowd, *Women in Ireland,*

of her father in 1649, Mary Butler was sent to be educated at the Benedictine convent in Ghent, where her aunt Dame Mary Knatchbull was abbess (Fig. 9.7).[86] She was professed at the convent in Boulogne in the winter of 1657 at the age of 16 and the following year moved with the English community to Pontoise.[87] She became abbess of the Irish Benedictine convent at Ypres in 1686, a position she retained until her death in 1723 (Plate 14).[88] Ryan came to her religious vocation later in life; she joined the English Benedictine convent at Dunkirk where she was professed in 1670 at the age of 40.[89]

The establishment of the Benedictine schools in Dublin clearly attracted the support of the Catholic elite. The school managed by Abbess Butler soon welcomed over thirty students while according to Sister Ryan's own report her pupils comprised the offspring of 'the first [of the] nobility of the country'.[90] Among those entrusted to Ryan's care were two sisters, Margaret and Honora Burke, daughters of William Burke (d. 1687), seventh earl of Clanricarde and his wife Helen (née MacCarthy).[91] The Clanricarde family were one of Ireland's leading Catholic noble families. Their estate, situated at Portumna in Co. Galway, had recently been restored by Charles II and the earl was a significant patron of the Catholic Church in Ireland throughout the 1670s and 1680s.[92] However, the work of these two foundations was marred in controversy since their leaders were engaged in a bitter rivalry. While the root cause of the acrimony between Ryan and Butler is unclear, the conflict escalated quickly. In a series of letters sent to the vicars of Ypres in autumn 1687, Butler alleged that Ryan had disseminated unfavourable reports about the school attached to the Irish Benedictine convent at Ypres.[93]

The outbreak of the Williamite wars in 1688 dealt yet another blow to the enterprise of female religious orders in Ireland and precipitated the collapse of an already fragile convent network. The Benedictine foundations at Dublin were immediately wound up and their leadership returned to the Continent where they remained until their deaths. In the case of the Poor Clares and Dominicans in Galway, the onset of the wars

pp 195–205.   **86** On the relationship between Abbess Mary Knatchbull and the Stuart monarchy see C. Walker, 'Prayer, patronage, and political conspiracy: English nuns and the Restoration', *Historical Journal*, 43 (2000), pp 1–23.   **87** Mary Jane Butler's mother, Anne Audley, was the daughter of Catherine Audley (1607–72) of Essex from her first marriage. Anne Audley married her stepbrother, Toby Butler of Callan, Co. Kilkenny, son of Piers Butler of Callan Castle, her mother's second husband. See 'Registers of the English Benedictine nuns of Pontoise', *Miscellanea X*, *Catholic Record Society*, 17 (1915), pp 283–4.   **88** F. Clarke, 'Butler, Dame Mary Joseph (1641–1723), Benedictine abbess' in J. McGuire and J. Quinn (eds), *Dictionary of Irish biography*, dib.cambridge.org.   **89** Sister Mary Joseph Ryan professed at Dunkirk on 10 Feb. 1670, aged 43 ('Mary Ryan, in religion Mary Joseph', 'Who were the nuns?' online database, ID DB144).   **90** Mary Ryan to Mary Caryll, Abbess of Dunkirk [23 Aug. 1687] printed in Nolan, *Irish dames of Ypres*, p. 190.   **91** Margaret married Bryan Magennis, 5th Viscount Iveagh, and later Thomas Butler, with whom she had eight children, including John Butler, 15th earl of Ormond. Honora first married Patrick Sarsfield and then James II's illegitimate son, James FitzJames, 1st duke of Berwick; see Nolan, *Irish dames of Ypres*, p. 189; A. Creighton, 'Burke, William (d. 1687), 7th earl of Clanricard', *DIB*.   **92** Creighton, 'Burke, William', *DIB*.   **93** For an extended discussion see McShane, *Irish women in religious orders*, pp 237–8.

precipitated yet another phase of uncertainty for the sisters. While some opted to depart Ireland in search of relative peace and stability abroad, others remained in Ireland, finding refuge in the homes of family members and friends. Others adopted alternative strategies for survival. For example, by 1698 the Galway Poor Clares had established a house in Market Street, where, under the direction of Abbess Mary Gabriel Skerrett (d. 1750), they lived as a community under the pretence of running a boarding house.[94]

The outbreak of the Williamite wars in 1689 initiated a period of instability and clandestine survival for communities of women religious in Ireland. The immediate consequences were nowhere near as traumatic as those of the Cromwellian conflict. Unlike the upheavals of the 1650s, within a decade of cessation of the Williamite campaigns in 1691, both the Poor Clare and Dominican foundations in Galway were once again functioning and admitting new members to their ranks. The early years of the eighteenth century would prove challenging but these communities persevered so that by the 1710s they were in a position to turn their attention towards expansion. Thus in 1712, the Galway Poor Clares established a filiation in Dublin where they resided for a time in the former residence of the Benedictine community once led by Sister Mary Ryan at Channel Row.[95] Five years later, the Galway Dominicans followed suit with the foundation of a Dublin house; in 1722, a third Dominican convent, dedicated to St Catherine of Siena, was established in Drogheda, Co. Louth.[96] The success and expansion of these eighteenth-century foundations was predicated on the resilience of individuals such as Abbess Elizabeth Skerrett, Abbess Mary Gabriel Skerrett and Prioress Julian Nolan, who led their communities through the turbulence of the previous decades and survived to tell the tale.

94 A memorial inscription in the Franciscan cemetery in Galway records the death of Abbess Mary Gabriel on 29 April 1750 (Cunningham, 'Poor Clare Order in Ireland', p. 168). Sister Mary Gabriel Skerrett was professed in 1677.   **95** Cunningham, 'Poor Clare Order in Ireland', p. 168. **96** Six Dominican sisters from Galway settled first in Fisher's Lane and then relocated to the Channel Row premises formerly occupied by the Poor Clares and Benedictines. The Dominicans remained at the Channel Row location until the nineteenth century. See R. O'Neill, *A rich inheritance: Galway Dominican nuns, 1644–1994* (Galway, 1994), pp 20–1; M.M. Kealy, *From Channel Row to Cabra: Dominican nuns and their times, 1717–1820* (Dublin, 2010). According to Hugh Fenning, there was an Irish Dominican convent in Drogheda from at least as early as 1671 until 1690, but I have been unable to locate any other references to this foundation. See H. Fenning, 'Dominican nuns of Meath, 1671–1713', *Ríocht na Midhe*, 3 (1965), 201–3.

Brides of Christ: 'ladies of fame and women worthy of praise'[*]

BISHOP ANNE DYER

My interest in the history of the women in the church, including female religious, is both amateur and professional. I am not an academic, but like many who joined in the Glenstal conference *Brides of Christ* from around the world, I am drawn by the desire to understand the origins and shaping of the Christian tradition in Ireland. On the other hand, I serve God day by day with women (and men) who explore and understand their present vocation through referencing and drawing on the past, however inaccessible and hidden this might seem at times. We know we stand in continuity with women and men who have been caught up into the things of Christ and the church since the first centuries, even if the threads of that continuity through some periods and in some places have been lost to us. We know we are people of faith today in some way because of them.

For example, my own diocese of Aberdeen and Orkney covers the north-east corner of mainland Scotland and the northern island groups of Orkney and Shetland. Historically the mainland was Pictish, and the islands Norse.

As far as we can tell, Christianity first came to all of these lands and islands from Ireland. The mission to the Picts came across the mountains into what is now Aberdeenshire led by Moluag, out of Lismore, in the sixth century. Christianity first came to Orkney and Shetland through the movement of Irish missionary monks through the northern seas, settling in places of quiet, if stormy, beauty on the edge of the world, probably in the late seventh century. These monks were called 'papar' by the pre-Christian Norse, and across the islands their presence is remembered through the naming of islands, churches, and small inland lakes, for example, Papa Westray, Papa Stronsay, in Orkney and Papa Stour and Papil in Burra in Shetland.

On Fetlar, Shetland, the monks came ashore on the long sandy beach at Tresta. The fresh water lake close to the beach retains the name Papil Water. This was the place of their monastic home. It was remote and quiet then, and it remains so today. All that marks the presence of the Irish monks is the placename. However, there is a continuity in Christian presence and worship here through to the present day.

At Papil in Burra (Shetland) a shrine panel was found (Fig. 10.1). It depicts the arrival of the Irish monks from across the sea. They walk across the waves towards a standing cross. There is lots that is interesting about this panel that is not for this chapter, save

[*] Christine de Pizan, *The Book of the City of Ladies* (1405), part 1, section 3.

10.1 The shrine panel, Papil, Burra, Shetland. Image © Didier Piquer.

that it might suggest to us that Irish monastics walk on water! These Irish monks have been in my mind as I have considered the material in this book, particularly that concerned with early religious communities in Ireland. I look at a stone like this and ask 'how were the women of Ireland, particularly the religious women, part of this mission'? There is nothing to suggest that religious women were missionaries at this time, but that does not mean they did not participate in some way.

In these northern islands, in the past but continuing to the present day to some extent, the relationships and relative roles of women and men were less binary and more complementary than elsewhere. In places where survival is a pressing issue, then everyone's contribution to the common cause is vital. A major contribution of women was in textile manufacture, the making of clothes and sails. So I look at a panel like this and wonder, who made the cloth for the habits? And, knowing that the monks did not actually walk across the sea from Ireland, who made the cloth for the sails? If the cloth was made by women, then Cathy Swift has found no evidence that it was woman religious. There are textual references to St Bridgit making vestments, and aristocratic women engaged in embroidery, clear indicators of how women through their gifts participated in, and made themselves essential to, what happened at the celebration of the Eucharist. How tantalizing the single spindle weight (so essential for weaving) shown us by Tracy Collins. Is this evidence of groups of female religious producing the more prosaic yet essential resources for everyday life and mission for monks and clerics? On the one hand we must be restrained, and not suppose things for which there is no evidence, while at the same time remembering that so much has been lost.

Concerning early Christianity in Ireland we are reminded again and again that there is continuity with other areas in the West. So we might wonder, were there Irish women involved in the learning that preceded and accompanied early Christian missions, as there were in England (Leoba) and in Frankish land (Radegund)? Or, might it be that some of the monks involved in the mission to Orkney and Shetland were spiritually mothered in some way, following the model of St Íte mothering Brendan?

What we might say is that the religious life, rooted in prayer, connected women to the missionary movement, but that all that remains to be seen in the northern isles is indeed the continuing place names that connect my diocese to Ireland.

Christian lives, religious lives, have internal and external dimensions. The internal is mostly often hidden, but not entirely so. For an integrated and holy person that which is seen will relate to that which is unseen, hidden within. Those things that can be seen are usually acts of charity and love, or maybe an observed life shaped around regular prayer, but these do not leave much of a historical record. In every generation there are those who shape the lives of others through their love and care. This affect was often associated with the roles of women, secular and religious. That which survives does not relate to the many but to the few, to the cults around women saints who were considered 'foster-mothers' and to the actions of elite and well-connected women, those with powerful political or economic connections.

What has been offered through the research of the contributors to this book is a mapping of the different dimensions of identity, those things which were in the mix from the beginning but changed in relative significance over time. If in receiving this research we are too quick to categorize, then we can become handicapped when considering reality. Understandings of what it means to be Christian, religious, indeed Irish or a woman, change through time. Indeed for a single woman, particularly in the early period considered in these chapters, roles change through life alongside changing relationships, especially for those connected to significant men (spouses, sons) whose own status and roles in the church changed through their lifetime. Alongside this we note the enduring effect of patriarchy on the lives of women, particularly the limiting of options and opportunities. However, in fluid societies, where violence is a present reality, what patriarchy did offer was the provision of essential protection for women's bodies. It must be clear to all what St Íte is referring to as 'demons that beguile our sex' (Swift's chapter above) when describing the necessity of needing the protection of a bishop in order to make a safe journey. As with a geographical journey, so too in the journey of life, protection of the body through the provision of oversight, and even enclosure, was seen as essential for many women in order to be able to live safely. Through the church's history women have not fared well in their religious and faith development when they have been unsafe, maybe suggesting a good reason why male and female religious houses were founded in proximity to each other, close enough for support, but not too close in case of 'weakness'. From our viewpoint we might ask how much women bought into the cultural assumptions about gender identity and sexuality of their days? Did the women agree with the patristic understanding that they were more prone to sexual sin, and so take more than their fair share of responsibility? Or, did they acquiesce for the sake of a safe abode and a relatively peaceful and protected community life?

While in the early medieval period the issue of safety might arise from tribal quarrels and gendered threats, in the later periods danger came from a different source. The nuns of Galway offer us a story of women supported by the benefaction of powerful local families, who come under threat in the growing Protestant context of the seventeenth century. The issue here is not being a woman, but a religious woman. The leaving of Ireland, an ongoing diaspora, enabled the nuns first of all to be safe, and then to be able to live the religious life openly once again in Spain and Portugal. Here too they needed men to care for them and be their benefactors and advocates. Friars, bishops, and well-resourced men supported them. The argument used to persuade was that these women were Irish and in flight, learned, and that they lived devout religious lives. Theirs is a story of turmoil and loss, regrouping and return, re-establishment and further abandonment of their foundations. In the end they persevere, sisters are added to their number, they live quietly and survive. The story runs through several generations, they do not seem to shake the world, and yet they remain steadfast, which through such times was a victory in itself.

We have been helped to consider what it meant for women when the culture of Ireland became Christianized, to think about what might have had continuity with earlier structures of familial and tribal society, and the roles that were carried. It will be good to consider further how the arrival of Christianity, and its impact on the receiving culture, differentiated over time to produce a variety of vocations, shaped to some extent by context and pre-existing gender relations. This is part of a wider exploration of what happens when Christianity encounters cultures, very relevant in the world today.

If in the early period structures and relationships were more fluid, 'porous' and 'permeable', less binary, then there comes the possibility of changing or malleable gender roles, and the coming together of men and women for a common mission and purpose, as seen in and through the shared life of double houses, and later in confraternities. This again is the past encouraging possibilities in the present, where gender roles and boundaries are changing in society, and latterly even in churches. That which has seemed set for so long really need not be so.

Alongside this the anxiety around the control of women, not least their bodies, that became so common in later times through enclosure and understandings of virginity and chastity, is the understanding that women were commonly commodities. Woman religious have variously been described as 'spare' or 'excess' women. They were significant in negotiating family allegiances and negotiations of power, both through marriage and the control of lands. Marrying women 'to Christ' in these contexts does not sit well with modern sensibilities, but again we do not know what the women themselves thought of this. If we remove the possibility of vocation, the rewards of personal devotion, and the real blessings of living a life configured around charity and love, then what is left can seem abusive and reductionist. Once faith is in play, then the value system, and our judgments of it, are changed. And more than this, we have been reminded of the importance of supplication in prayer, that is the work that religious do for others. Again, this is something of which there is often no trace. St Íte's example of military victories ensured through her prayers is a rarity.

Elva Johnston describes in her contribution the possibility of investing in female foundations as a way of giving kin-groups extra status. The challenges for women of expanding estates to secure sufficient resources for survival made it more likely than for male establishments that the foundation would not long survive the death of the foundress outside of high-status locations such as Kildare. Although the memory of some of these holy women might be retained in martyrologies, in reality this would mean a repeating experience of women beginning again, with all of the loss of learning that is a consequence. One result here is that female foundations might appear small or feeble in comparison to male establishments, an accident of circumstances rather than of female capability. The research referenced in these articles points to a different story, one where female establishments were as vital as those of men, revealed through the careful reading and interpretation of primary source material.

A continuing theme has been the importance of place and kin, the sovereignty of the lands where a church or community was located. The actions of religious women are understood as political because they always sat within this context, where economic boundaries and the exercise of power are co-terminus with an extended family or kin group who are all Christian. Considered in these articles are the consequences for these women when they become collateral damage in a tribal or political conflict. We might note, for example, how often the existence of sexual relationships are used as an indicator of loss of control of a foundation, or of the 'secularization' of an abbess or prioress. Rather, the removal or diminishment of the abbess could be part of the out-playing of political or social turmoil in the locality or between family power groups.

We can see in the material presented in these chapters that for elite women, and maybe those with particular abilities, the role of an abbess or senior member of a community would bring the opportunity to live a life of independence and status, exercising a satisfying and rewarding control over land and material goods.

It might be then that for many religious women, the role became more secular, with less and less attention given to the spiritual content of life. Even so, we must be wary of projecting back in time modern internal constructions of the person. Spiritual, material and political power have always been closely connected, and remain so today.

And we must be wary of assuming that a woman who is seeking intellectual fulfilment through the management of an estate say, or political involvement, could not at the same time have a vocation to pray and be contemplative, that is to be religious. In fact such a woman might consider a religious life essential to doing these other things well.

The contributors to this book have reminded us again and again that we know practically nothing about what the women thought, how belief sat within their persons, whether they thought primarily in community or individual terms. There are few surviving writings, poems or hymns, letters even, to help us. We don't know how they felt about their bodies, or how these affected how they prayed, especially as they aged. These things are very important for women of faith today; it is difficult to imagine that it was not always so. A door is opened a little on this through the consideration of women's literacy generally, and of women religious.

What remains for me is a question about how the life of a religious woman in Ireland in the past relates to those living the religious life today. If the past has no words, can the present help us? Well, maybe, if we are careful.

To return to the context of my own diocese. In the early 1980s, a woman religious arrived alone on Fetlar, Shetland, at the same place the Irish monks had arrived thirteen centuries before. Sr Agnes, as she was then, went to the top of the world to live as a hermit. She restored a croft house, and built herself a chapel, and there a community sprang up around her. These are her words:

> I unhitch the bell rope and hold it in my right hand, tugging it to and fro, carefully yet firmly. The clapper falls heavily against the bell's great belly and so reverberates a peal of hopefulness over the isle. Three times three I ring, with a pause for prayer at the end of each triplet. I listen to the murmur of voices through the open byre/chapel door and I too move my lips, saying the familiar words. Now, as I prepare to ring out the last long toll of the final Collect, my eyes automatically peer, as they always do, across the potato rig and on, up, over the fields into the distance.[1]

We may not know what religious women in the past thought, how they understood themselves or their shared vocation, but we do know what they prayed, because these are the same prayers that we say today, day after day.

We know, roughly speaking, how much time they gave to this. We don't know what their voices sounded like when they sang – were they high and frail, were they deeper, with substance? But we know what they sang, the psalms, canticles, and ancient hymns which are the backbone of our liturgies today.

And those that do these things day after day – pray and sing – who live to a rhythm of life including fasting and feast, know that very gradually they are changed. Today we call this formation. Where once vocation might have been weak, in this way over time it can deepen. And doing these things in community, that is in the company of others, living to a rule, reshapes a woman (or man) as they serve God – they are 'converted' as we describe it. They learn to bend their bodies and their wills to something they believe to be greater. These things lie behind all the glimpses of holy and religious women from the past – nuns, virgins, mothers, foster-mothers, wives, sisters, vowesses, tertiaries (and this is just a start!) – that we have been offered in these wonderful chapters.

Our thanks are due to all those who search for signs of these women's lives in the earth, in documents, in libraries, in artefacts, and in architecture. In the greater part the names of these religious women are not known, but the remaining effect of those who have gone before us is seen in and through how women and men of faith live in the world today.

---

1 Mother Mary Agnes SOLI, *The song of the lark* (SPCK, 1992), p. 121.

Bibliography

MANUSCRIPTS

England
The National Archives, Kew
SP 63/264, ff 144–6: 'The humble petition of the Mother Abbesse and poore Sisters of St Clare of ye Convent of Bethlehem in Athlone', 1647.

Cambridge, Corpus Christ College, Parker Library
MS 79: Illustrated pontifical, England, early fifteenth century.

France
Archives départementales de l'Oise
H 6009.

Bibliothèque municipale, Ville de Soissons
MS 7.

Ireland
National Library of Ireland, Dublin
NLI MS D 1978: 'Will of Renalda Ní Bhrian', 1510.

Royal Irish Academy, Dublin
MS D i 2: 'The Rule of St Clare'.

Trinity College Dublin
MS 1207/85-26.
MS 97.
MS 576, 'Book of obits and martyrology of the Cathedral Church of Holy Trinity'.
MS 1207, 'Miscellaneous deeds of the Passavaunt and Stanihurst families', 1246–1691.

Monastery of the Poor Clares, Galway
MS A2: 'Licence to found in Galway'.
MS A6: 'An agreement between the sisters in Galway and those founding in Loughrea'.
MS A8: 'Letter to Mother Elizabeth Skerrett, Mother Abbess, giving the faculty of admitting to the habit "two well-born virgins"', 1683.

Archives of the Galway Dominican sisters, Taylor's Hill, Galway
'Profession document of Sister Agnes Browne', 1688.

Archives of the Irish Benedictine Sisters, Kylemore Abbey, Galway
MS KYAA1/1/1: Mary Butler's 'leave for goeing to Irland', 1688.

Russell Library, St Patrick's College, Maynooth
MS RB 201, ff 233–40.

PRINTED SOURCES

Primary sources indicated with★

[Anonymous], 'Registers of the English Benedictine nuns of Pontoise', *Catholic Record Society,* Miscellanea 10:17 (London, 1915).★

Africa, Dorothy C., 'Life of the holy virgin Samthann' in Thomas Head (ed.), *Medieval hagiography: an anthology* (London, 2000), pp 97–110.★

—, 'The chronology of the Life of St Íte and the architecture of theft', *Eolas: The Journal of the American Society of Irish Medieval Studies,* 12 (2019), 2–25.

Alcock, Olive, Kathy De hÓra, and Paul Gosling, *Archaeological inventory of County Galway: vol. II: North Galway* (Dublin, 1999).

Ambrose, St, *Ambrose: Select works and letters,* trans H. de Romestin and H.T.F. Duckworth, Nicene and Post–Nicene Fathers, Series II volume x (second printing, Massachusetts, 1995).★

Andrieu, Michel (ed.), *Le Pontifical Romain au Moyen-Age,* III: *Le Pontifical de Guillaume Durand* (Vatican City, 1940).★

Antry, Theodore J., and Neel, Carol (eds), *Norbert and early Norbertine spirituality* (New York, 2007).

Ardura, Bernard, *Prémontrés histoire et spiritualité,* 7 (Saint-Etienne, 1995).

Auslander, Dianne Peters, 'Gendering the *Vita Prima*: an examination of Brigit's role as "Mary of the Gael"', *Proceedings of the Harvard Celtic Colloquium,* 20–1 (2000/1), 187–202.

Backmund, Norbert, *Monasticon Praemonstratense, id est historia circariarum atque canoniarum candidi et canonici ordinis Praemonstratensis,* 3 vols (Straubing, 1952).

—, 'Sainte Marguerite de La Rochelle, un couvent de moniales prémontrées', *Bulletin de la Société des Antiquaires de l'Ouest et des Musées de Poitiers,* 2 (1956), 441–5.

Barnhouse, Lucy, 'Disordered women? The hospital sisters of Mainz and their late medieval identities', *Medieval Feminist Forum: A Journal of Gender and Sexuality,* 552 (2020), 60–97.

Baumann, Franz Ludwig (ed.), *Necrologium monasterii inferioris Ratisbonensis,* MGH Necrologia Germaniae 3 (Berlin, 1905).★

—, *Necrologium monasterii superioris Ratisbonensis,* MGH Necrologia Germaniae 3 (Berlin, 1905).★

Beach, Alison I., and Andra Juganaru, 'The double monastery as a historiographical problem (fourth to twelfth century)' in Beach and Cochelin, *CHMMLW,* pp 561–78.

Begley, John, *The diocese of Limerick ancient and modern* (Dublin 1906, repr. Limerick, 1993).

Berman, Constance H., 'Were there twelfth-century Cistercian nuns?', *Church History,* 68:4 (1999), 824–64.

—, *The white nuns: Cistercian abbeys for women in medieval France* (Philadelphia, 2018).

Bernard, J.H., and Atkinson, R., *The Irish Liber Hymnorum,* HBS 13, 2 vols (London, 1898).★

Berry, Henry F. (ed.), *Register of wills and inventories of the diocese of Dublin in the time of Archbishops Tregury and Walton, 1457–1483* (Dublin, 1898).★

Best, R.I., and H.J. Lawler (eds), *The martyrology of Tallaght from the Book of Leinster and MS 5100–4 in the Royal Library, Brussels*, HBS, 68 (London, 1931, repr. Woodbridge, 2010).★

Bhreathnach, Edel, 'Abbesses, minor dynasties and kings *in clericatu*: perspectives of Ireland 700–850' in Michelle Brown and Carol Ann Farr (eds), *Mercia: an Anglo-Saxon kingdom in Europe* (Leicester, 2001), pp 113–25.

—, 'The genealogies of Leinster as a source for local cults in Leinster' in John Carey, Máire Herbert and Pádraig Ó Riain (eds), *Studies in Irish hagiography: saints and scholars* (Dublin, 2001), pp 250–67.

—, *Ireland in the medieval world AD 400–1000: landscape, kingship and religion* (Dublin, 2014).

—, 'The *Vita Apostolica* and the origin of the Augustinian canons and canonesses in medieval Ireland' in Browne and Ó Clabaigh (eds), *Households*, pp 1–27.

Bieler, Ludwig (ed. and trans.), *The Patrician texts in the Book of Armagh*, Scriptores Latini Hiberniae 10 (Dublin, 1979).★

Binchy, Daniel A., '*Bretha Crólige*', *Ériu*, 12 (1938), 1–77.★

Binchy, Daniel A., *Corpus Iuris Hiberniae*, 5 vols (Dublin, 1979).

Bitel, Lisa, 'Women's donations to the churches in early Ireland', *JRSAI*, 114 (1984), 5–23

—, 'Women's monastic enclosures in early Ireland: a study of female spirituality and male monastic mentalities', *Journal of Medieval History*, 12 (1986), 15–36.

—, *Land of women: tales of sex and gender from early Ireland* (Ithaca and London, 1996).

—, *Landscape with two saints: how Genovfa of Paris and Brigit of Kildare built Christianity in Barbarian Europe* (Oxford, 2009).

—, 'Monastic identity in early medieval Ireland' in Beach and Cochelin, *CHMMLW*, pp 297–316.

Bledsoe, Jenny C., 'St Íte of Killeedy and spiritual motherhood in the Irish hagiographical tradition', *Proceedings of the Harvard Celtic Colloquium*, 32 (2012), 1–29.

Bleier, Roman, 'Re-examining the function of St Patrick's writings in the early medieval tradition', *PRIA*, 116C, (2016), 95–117.

Bliss, W.H. (ed.), *Calendar of entries in the papal registers relating to Great Britain and Ireland*, 17 vols (London, 1896).★

Bliss, W.H. and J.A., Twemlow (eds), *Calendar of papal registers relating to Great Britain and Ireland*, 17 vols (London, 1902).★

Boazman, Gillian, 'The material culture of self-promotion: the Conaille Muirthemne kings and the ecclesiastical site of Faughart, County Louth', *CLAHJ*, 28 (2015), 327–50.

Bodarwé, Katrinette, 'Immer Ärger mit den Stiftsdamen: Reform in Regensburg' in Eva Schlothuber, Helmut Flachenecker and Ingrid Gardill (eds), *Nonnen, Kanonissen und Mystikerinnen. Religiöse Frauengemeinschaften in Süddeutschland* (Studien zur Germania Sacra Band 3, Göttingen, 2008), pp 79–102.

Bolger, Teresa, 'Status inheritance and land tenure: some thoughts on early medieval settlement in the light of recent archaeological excavations' in Christian Corlett and Michael Potterton (eds), *Settlement in early medieval Ireland in the light of recent archaeological excavations* (Dublin, 2011), pp 1–10.

Bolster, Evelyn, *A history of the diocese of Cork from the earliest times to the Reformation* (Shannon, 1972).

Bond, C.J., 'The Premonstratensian Order: a preliminary survey of its growth and distribution in medieval Europe' in Martin Carver (ed.), *In search of cult: archaeological investigations in honour of Philip Rahtz* (Woodbridge, 1993), pp 153–85.

Booker, Sparky, *Cultural exchange and identity in late medieval Ireland* (Cambridge, 2018).

Bowden, Caroline, and James E. Kelly (eds), *The English convents in exile, 1600–1800: communities, culture and identity* (Burlington, VT, 2013).

Boyd, Matthew, 'On not eating dog' in Matthew Boyd (ed.), *Ollam: studies in Gaelic and related traditions in honour of Tomás Ó Cathasaigh* (Madison, NJ, 2016), pp 35–46.

Boydell, Barra (ed.), *Music at Christ Church before 1800: documents and selected anthems* (Dublin, 1999).★

—, 'The establishment of the choral tradition' in Kenneth Milne (ed.), *Christ Church Cathedral, Dublin, a history* (Dublin, 2000), pp 237–54.

Bradshaw, Brendan, *The dissolution of the religious orders in Ireland under Henry VIII* (Cambridge, 1974).

Brady, John, 'The nunnery of Clonard', *Ríocht na Midhe*, 2:2 (1960), 4–7.

Bray, Dorothy Ann, 'Secunda Brigida: St Íta of Killeedy and Brigidine tradition' in C.J. Byrne et al., *Proceedings of the Second North American Congress of Celtic Studies* (Halifax 1989), pp 27–38.

—, 'The *Vita Prima* of St Brigit: a preliminary analysis of its composition' in Joseph Eska (ed.), *Narrative in Celtic tradition: essays in honor of Edgar M. Slotkin, Celtic Studies Association of North America Yearbook 8–9,* (New York, 2011), pp 1–15.

Breatnach, Liam, 'An edition of *Amra Senáin*' in Donnchadh Ó Corráin, Liam Breatnach and Kim McCone (eds), *Sages, saints and storytellers: Celtic studies in honour of Professor James Carney* (Maynooth, 1989), pp 7–31.

—, 'Poets and poetry' in Kim McCone and Katherine Simms (eds), *Progress in medieval Irish studies* (Maynooth, 1996), pp 65–77.

—(ed.), *Córus Bésgnai: an old Irish law tract on the church and society,* Early Irish Law Series 7 (Dublin, 2017).★

Breatnach, Pádraig, *Die Regensburger Schottenlegende-Libellus de fundacione ecclesiae consecrati Petri. Untersuchung und Textausgabe* (Munich, 1977).★

Brown, Karen T., *Mary of Mercy in medieval and renaissance Italian art: devotional image and civic emblem* (Routledge, 2017).

Brown, Peter, *The body and society: men, women and sexual renunciation in early Christianity* (New York, 1988).

Browne, Martin, OSB, and Colmán Ó Clabaigh OSB (eds), *Households of God: the regular canons and canonesses of Saint Augustine and of Prémontré in medieval Ireland* (Dublin, 2019).

Buckley, Ann, 'Music and musicians in medieval Irish society', *Early Music*, 28:2 (2000), 165–90.

Burgess, Clive, *The right ordering of souls: the parish of All Saints, Bristol on the eve of the Reformation* (Woodbridge, 2018).

Burke, Thomas, *Hibernia Dominicana: sive, historia provinciæ Hiberniæ Ordinis Prædicatorum: ex antiquis manuscriptis* (1762).★

Burton, Janet, 'Looking for medieval nuns' in Janet Burton and Karen Stöber (eds), *Monasteries and society in the British Isles in the later Middle Ages* (Woodbridge, 2008), pp 113–23.

— and Julie Kerr, *The Cistercians in the Middle Ages*, Monastic Orders Series (Woodbridge, 2011).

— and Karen Stöber (eds), *The regular canons in the medieval British Isles*, Medieval Church Studies, 19 (Turnhout, 2011).

— and Karen Stöber (eds), *Women in the medieval monastic world* (Turnhout, 2015).

Callan, Maeve, 'Líadáin's *Lament*, Darerca's *Life*, and Íte's *Ísucán*: evidence for nuns' literacies in early Ireland' in Victoria Blanton, Veronica O'Mara and Patricia Stoop (eds), *Nuns' literacies in medieval Europe* (Turnhout, 2015), pp 209–27.

—, *Sacred sisters: gender, sanctity and power in medieval Ireland* (Amsterdam, 2019).

Carey, Vincent, 'Neither good English nor good Irish': bi-lingualism and identity formation in sixteenth-century Ireland' in Hiram Morgan (ed.), *Political ideology in Ireland, 1541–1641* (Dublin, 1999), pp 45–61

Carville, Geraldine, 'Cistercian nuns in medieval Ireland: Plary Abbey, Ballymore, County Westmeath' in John A. Nichols and Lillian Thomas Shank (eds), *Hidden springs: Cistercian monastic women*, 3 vols (Kalamazoo, MI, 1995), 3, Part 1, pp 62–84.

—, *The impact of the Cistercians on the landscape of Ireland, 1142–1541* (Wicklow, 2002).

Casey, Denis, *The Nugents of Westmeath and Queen Elizabeth's Irish primer* (Dublin, 2016).

Charles-Edwards, Thomas M., *Early Irish and Welsh kinship* (Oxford, 1993).

—, *Early Christian Ireland* (Cambridge, 2000).

—, 'Early Irish saints' cults and their constituencies', *Ériu*, 54, (2004), 79–102.

—, 'Early Irish law' in D. Ó Cróinín (ed.), *A new history of Ireland*: i, *Prehistoric and early Ireland* (Oxford, 2005), pp 331–70.

Clancy, Thomas Owen, 'Women poets in early medieval Ireland: stating the case' in Christine Meek and Katharine Simms (eds), *The fragility of her sex: medieval Irish women in their European context* (Dublin 1996), pp 43–72.

Clark, Mary and Raymond Refaussé (eds), *Directory of historic Dublin guilds* (Dublin, 1993).

Clarke, Elizabeth A., 'The celibate bridegroom and his virginal brides: metaphor and the marriage of Jesus in early Christian exegesis', *Church History*, 77:1 (2008), 1–25.

Clyne, Miriam, 'The founders and patrons of the Premonstratensian houses in Ireland' in Janet Burton and Karen Stöber (eds), *The regular canons in the medieval British Isles*, Medieval Church Studies, 19 (Turnhout, 2011), pp 145–72.

—, 'Premonstratensian settlement in the Czech lands and Ireland, 1142–1250', *JMMS*, 7 (2018), 127–52.

—, 'The monasteries of the canons of *Prémontré*, *c.*1180–*c.*1607' in Browne and Ó Clabaigh (eds), *Households*, pp 62–86.

Cohen, Adam, 'Abbess Uta of Regensburg: patterns of patronage around 1000', *Aurora: The Journal of History of Art*, 4 (2003), 39–49.

Coleman, Ambrose (ed.), 'Regestum monasterii Fratrum Praedicatorum de Athenry', *AH*, 1 (1912), 201–21.★

Colker, Marvin L., *Trinity College Library Dublin: Descriptive catalogue of the mediaeval and renaissance Latin manuscripts*, (2 vols, Aldershot, 1991).

Collins, Tracy, 'Timolin: a case study of a nunnery estate in later medieval Ireland', *Anuario de Estudios Medievales*, 44:1 (2014), 51–80.

—, 'An archaeological perspective on female monasticism in the Middle Ages in Ireland' in Janet Burton and Karin Stöber (eds), *Women in the medieval monastic world* (Turnout, 2015), pp 229–51.

—, 'An archaeology of Augustinian nuns in later medieval Ireland' in Browne and Ó Clabaigh (eds), *Households,* pp 87–102.

—, 'Unveiling female monasticism in later medieval Ireland: survey and excavation at St Catherine's, Shanagolden, Co. Limerick', *PRIA* 119C (2019), 103–71.

—, 'Transforming women religious? Church reform and the archaeology of female monasticism in Ireland' in Edel Bhreathnach, Kevin Smith and Malgorzata Krasnodebska-D'Aughton (eds) *Monastic Europe: medieval communities, landscapes, and settlement*, Medieval Monastic Studies, 4 (Turnhout, 2019), pp 277–301.

—, *Female monasticism in medieval Ireland: an archaeology* (Cork, 2021).

Concannon, Helena, *The Poor Clares in Ireland, AD 1629–AD 1929* (Dublin, 1929).

—, *Irish nuns in the penal days* (London, 1931).

—, 'Historic Galway convents', *Studies: An Irish Quarterly Review*, 38:152 (1949), 439–46.

—, 'Historic Galway convents II: the Dominican nuns', *Studies: An Irish Quarterly Review*, 39:153 (1950), 65–71.

Conchubranus, 'The Life of St Monenna by Conchubranus Part I', ed. Ulster Society for Medieval Latin Studies, *Seanchas ArdMhacha*, 9:2 (1979), 250–73.★

Conlon, Patrick, *Franciscan Ireland* (Dublin, 1978).

Connolly, Philomena (ed.), *Irish Exchequer payments*, 2 vols (Dublin, 1998).★

Connolly, Seán, 'Vitae Primae Sanctae Brigitae: background and historical value', *JRSAI*, 119 (1989), 5–49.

— and Jean-Michel Picard, 'Cogitosus' Life of St Brigit: content and value', *JRSAI*, 117 (1987), 5–27.

Constable, Giles, *Three studies in medieval, religious and social thought: the interpretation of Mary and Martha, the ideal of the Imitation of Christ, the orders of society* (Cambridge, 1995).

Coolahan, Marie-Louise, *Women, writing and language in early modern Ireland* (Oxford, 2010).

—, 'Transnational reception and early modern women's "lost" texts', *Early Modern Women: An Interdisciplinary Journal*, 7 (2012), 261–70.

—, 'Archipelagic identities in Europe: Irish nuns in English convents' in Caroline Bowden and James Kelly (eds), *The English convents in exile, 1600–1800: communities, culture and identity* (Burlington, 2013), pp 211–28.

Costello, Michael A., Ambrose Coleman, William H. Grattan Flood (eds), *De Annatis Hiberniæ: a calendar of the first fruits' fees levied on papal appointments to benefices in Ireland, AD 1400 to 1535* (Dundalk, 1909).★

Crawford, Henry S. 'A descriptive list of early cross slabs and pillars [3 parts]', *JRSAI*, 43 (1913), 151–69, 261–65, 326–34.

Crawford, John, and Raymond Gillespie (eds), *St Patrick's Cathedral, Dublin: a history* (Dublin, 2009).

Crossthwaite, John Clarke (ed.), *The book of obits and martyrology of the Cathedral Church of the Holy Trinity, commonly called Christ Church, Dublin* (Dublin, 1844).★

Crusius, Irene, 'Sanctimoniales quae se canonicas vocant. Das Kanonissenstift als Forschungsproblem' in Irene Crusius (ed.), *Studien zum Kanonissenstift* (Göttingen, 2001), pp 9–38.

Cullum, Patricia H., 'Vowesses and female lay piety in the province of York, 1300–1500', *Northern History*, 32 (1996), 21–41.

Cunningham, Bernadette, 'The Poor Clare Order in Ireland' in Edel Bhreathnach, Joseph Mac Mahon and John McCafferty (eds), *The Irish Franciscans, 1534–1990* (Dublin, 2009), pp 159–74.

—, '"Bethlehem": the Dillons and the Poor Clare convent at Ballinacliffey, County Westmeath', *Áitreabh*, 17 (2012–13), 5–9.

—, 'Nuns and their networks in early modern Galway' in Salvador Ryan and Clodagh Tait (eds), *Religion and politics in urban Ireland, c.1500–c.1750: essays in honour of Colm Lennon* (Dublin, 2016), pp 156–72.

—, *Medieval Irish pilgrims to Santiago de Compostela* (Dublin, 2018).

Curran, Kimm, and Janet Burton (eds), *Medieval women religious, c.800–c.1500: new perspectives* (Woodbridge, 2023).

Curtis, Edmund, 'Extracts out of Heralds' books in Trinity College, Dublin, relating to Ireland in the sixteenth century', *JRSAI*, 7:2 (1932), 28–49.★

Dallmeier, Lutz-Michael, Harald Giess and Kurt Schnieringer, *Stadt Regensburg Ensembles – Baudenkmäler Archäologische Denkmäler* (Regensburg, 1997).

Dalton, Paul, Charles Insley and Louise J. Wilkinson (eds), *Cathedrals, communities and conflict in the Anglo-Norman world* (Woodbridge, 2011).

Dauzet, Dominique-Marie, *L'ordre de Prémontré: Neuf cent ans d'histoire* (Paris, 2021).

Diefendorf, Barbara, *From penitence to charity: pious women and the Catholic Reformation in Paris* (Oxford & New York, 2004).

Dinan, Susan E., *Women and poor relief in seventeenth-century France: the early history of the Daughters of Charity* (Aldershot, 2006).

Dirmeier, Artur, 'Regensburg – ein "Idealtypus der Urbanität". Klöster, Stifte und Spitäler einer mittelalterlichen Stadt' in Helmut Flachenecker and Rolf Kiessling (eds), *Urbanisierung und Urbanität. Der Beitrag der kirchlichen Institutionen zur Stadtentwicklung in Bayern* (*Zeitschrift für Bayerische Landesgeschichte* Beiheft 36) (Munich, 2008), pp 101–26.

Doherty, Charles, Linda Doran and Mary Kelly (eds), *Glendalough: city of God* (Dublin, 2011).

Doran, Linda, 'Medieval communication routes through Longford and Roscommon and their associated settlements', *PRIA*, 104:3C (2004), 57–80.

Dubois, Jacques, *Les martyrologues du moyen âge Latin* (Turnhout, 1978).

—, *Martyrologes: d'Usuard au Martryologe romain* (Abbeville, 1990).

Duffy, Damien, *Aristocratic women in Ireland, 1450–1660: the Ormond family, power and politics* (Woodbridge, 2021).

Duffy, Eamon, *The stripping of the altars: traditional religion in England, 1400–1580* (New Haven, 1992).

Dumville, David, '*Félire Óengusso*: problems of dating a monument of Old Irish', *Éigse*, 33 (2001), 19–48.

Dunning, P.J., 'The Arroasian Order in medieval Ireland', *IHS*, 4:16 (1945), 297–315.

Dunstan, G.R. (ed.), *Register of Edmund Lacy, Bishop of Exeter 1420–145*, Canterbury and York Society 60–3 (1963–71).★

Edwards, Nancy, 'The archaeology of early medieval Ireland, *c*.400–1169: settlement and economy' in Dáibhí Ó Cróinín (ed.), *A new history of Ireland*: i, *Prehistoric and early Ireland* (Oxford, 2005), pp 235–300.

Eisenbichler, Konrad (ed.), *A companion to medieval and early modern confraternities* (Leiden, 2019).

Elliott, Dyan, *Spiritual marriage: sexual abstinence in medieval marriage* (Princeton, 1993).

Ellis, Steven, and James Murray (eds), *Calendar of State Papers, Ireland, Tudor period, 1509–47* (Dublin, 2017).★

Emerton, Ephraim (trans.), *The letters of Saint Boniface* (New York 1940, new edition 2000).★

Erler, Mary C., 'Three fifteenth-century vowesses' in Caroline M. Barron and Anne F. Sutton (eds), *Medieval London widows, 1300–1500* (London and Rio Grande, 1994), pp 165–81.

Eska, Charlene M. (ed.), *Cáin Lánamna – an Old Irish tract on marriage and divorce law* (Leiden, 2010).★

Etchingham, Colmán, 'Bishops in the early Irish church: a reassessment', *Studia Hibernica*, 28 (1994), 35–62.

—, *Church organization in Ireland AD 650 to 1000* (Maynooth, 1999).

Evangelisti, Silvia, 'Wives, widows and brides of Christ: marriage and the convent in the historiography of early modern Italy', *Historical Journal*, 43 (2000), 233–47.

—, *Nuns: a history of convent life, 1450–1700* (Oxford, 2007).

Fahy, E.M., 'Inishleena Abbey and other sites in the Lee Valley', *JCHAS*, 62, (1957), 65–76.

Farmer, David, *The Oxford dictionary of saints* (5th edition, 2011).

Faulkner, Anselm, 'Anthony Gearnon, OFM (*c*.1610–80) and the Irish Remonstrance', *CLAHJ*, 17:3 (1971), 141–9.

Feistner, Edith, 'Das spätmittelalterliche Regensburg als Literaturstadt: Werke, Sammlungen, Fragmente' in Peter Schmid (ed.), *Regensburg im Spätmittelalter. Bestandsaufnahme und Impulse* (Regensburg, 2007), pp 125–36.

Fenning, Hugh, 'Dominican nuns of Meath, 1671–1713', *Ríocht na Midhe*, 3:3 (1965), 201–3.

Fitzgerald, Lord Walter, 'William FitzGerald of Castleroe and his tomb in the Kilkea churchyard', *JCKAHS*, 3 (1899–1902), 229–53.

FitzPatrick, Elizabeth, 'Rethinking settlement values in Gaelic society: the case of cathedral centres', *PRIA*, 119C, (2019), 69–102.

—, and Caimin O'Brien, *The medieval churches of County Offaly* (Dublin, 1988).

Flachenecker, Helmut, *Schottenklöster. Irische Benediktinerkonvente im hochmittelalterlichen Deutschland* (Paderborn-Munich-Vienna-Zurich, 1995).

—, 'Irische Stützpunkte in Regensburg – Weih Sankt Peter und Sankt Jakob im Mittelalter' in Stephan Acht and Paul Mai (eds), *Scoti Peregrini in Sankt Jakob. 800 Jahre irisch-schottische Kultur in Regensburg* (Bischöfliches Zentralarchiv und Bischöfliche Zentralbibliothek Regensburg Kataloge und Schriften 21), (Regensburg, 2005), pp 13–24.

Flanagan, Marie Therese, *Irish royal charters: texts and contexts* (Oxford, 2005).

—, *The transformation of the Irish church in the twelfth century* (Woodbridge, 2010).

Flechner, Roy, *The Hibernensis* (Washington, 2019).

Fletcher, Alan J., 'Liturgy in the late medieval cathedral priory' in Kenneth Milne (ed.), *Christ Church Cathedral Dublin: a history* (Dublin, 2000), pp 129–41.

—, *Drama, performance and polity in pre-Cromwellian Ireland* (Cork, 2000).

Follett, Westley, *Céli Dé in Ireland: monastic writing and identity in the early Middle Ages* (Woodbridge, 2006).

Foot, Sarah, *Veiled women: the disappearance of nuns from Anglo-Saxon England*, 2 vols (Aldershot, 2000).

Freeman, A. Martin (ed.), *Annála Connacht: the annals of Connacht (AD 1224–1544)* (Dublin, 1944).★

Freise, Eckhad, Dieter Geuenich and Joachim Wollasch (eds), *Das Martyrolog–Necrolog von St Emmeram zu Regensburg*, MGH *Libri memoriales et necrologia, Nova series* 3 (Hannover, 1986).★

Gallwey, H., 'The Cusack family of county Meath and Dublin', *Irish Genealogist*, 5 (1974–9), 591–8.

García, María Begoňa Villar, 'Irish migration and exile patterns in Spain: refugees, soldiers, traders and statesmen' in Thomas O'Connor and Mary Ann Lyons (eds), *Irish communities in early modern Europe* (Dublin, 2006), pp 172–99.

Gardiner, Eileen, 'The vision of Tnugdal' in Richard Matthew Pollard (ed.), *Imagining the medieval afterlife* (Cambridge, 2020), pp 247–63.

Geier, Johann, 'Das Traditionsbuch des Klosters St Paul in Regensburg', *Verhandlungen des Historischen Vereins für Oberpfalz und Regensburg*, 111 (1971), 169–71.

Gilbert, John T., *History of the Irish confederation and war in Ireland, 1641–1649. Containing a narrative of affairs in Ireland,* 7 vols (Dublin, 1882–91).

— (ed.), *Chartularies of St Mary's Abbey, Dublin: with the register of its house at Dunbrody, and annals of Ireland*, 2 vols (London, 1884).★

Gilchrist, Roberta, *Gender and material culture: the archaeology of religious women* (London, 1994).

—, *Contemplation and action: the other monasticism* (London, 1995).

Gillespie, Raymond, 'The coming of reform, 1500–58' in Kenneth Milne (ed.), *Christ Church Cathedral, Dublin: a history* (Dublin, 2000), pp 151–73.

—, *Seventeenth-century Ireland: making Ireland modern* (Dublin, 2006).

—, 'The Irish Franciscans, 1600–1700' in Edel Bhreathnach, Joseph Mac Mahon and John McCafferty (eds), *The Irish Franciscans, 1534–1990* (Dublin, 2009), pp 45–76.

Gil-Mastalerczyk, Joanna, 'Premonstratensian convent complex in the Polish lands: Imbramowice in the past and today', *IOP Conference Series: Materials Science and Engineering*, 603:5 (2019), DOI: 10.1088/1757-899X/603/5/052089, 52089.

Gilomen-Schenkel, Elsanne, 'Double monasteries in the south-western empire (1100–1230) and their women's communities in Swiss regions' in Fiona J. Griffiths and Julie Hotchin (eds), *Partners in spirit: women, men, and religious life in Germany, 1100–1500*, Medieval Women: Texts and Contexts, 24 (2014), pp 47–74.

Golding, Brian, *Gilbert of Sempringham and the Gilbertine Order, c.1130–c.1300* (Oxford, 1995).

Goodrich, Jaime, 'A Poor Clare's legacy', *English Literary Renaissance*, 46:1 (2016), 3–28.

—, 'The rare books of the Galway Poor Clares', *The Library*, 22:4 (2021), 498–522.

Gougaud, Louis, 'The Isle of Saints', *Studies*, 13 (1924), 363–80.

Graham, B.J., 'Medieval settlement in County Roscommon', *PRIA*, 88C (1988), 9–38.

Greene, David, and Frank O'Connor (eds), *A golden treasury of Irish poetry AD 600–1200* (2nd ed., Dingle 1990).★

Greene, Sharon, 'Killeen Cormac Colbinstown: an ecclesiastical site on the Kildare-Wicklow border', *County Kildare Online Electronic History Journal* (2011). http://www.kildare.ie/library/ehistory/2011/03/killeen_cormac_colbinstown_an.asp (accessed 23 April 2022).

Griffiths, Fiona J., 'Women and reform in the central Middle Ages' in Judith M. Bennett and Ruth Mazo Karras (eds), *The Oxford handbook of women and gender in medieval Europe* (Oxford, 2013), pp 447–63.

—, *Nuns' priests' tales: men and salvation in medieval women's monastic life*, The Middle Ages Series (Philadelphia, 2018).

Gruber, Johannes, 'Geschichte des Stiftes Obermünster in Regensburg' in Paul Mai (ed.), *Obermünster Regensburg. Von den Anfängen bis heute* (Ausstellung in der Bischöflichen Zentralbibliothek Regensburg St Petersweg 11–13, 18. Juli bis 8. Oktober 2008) (Regensburg, 2008), 10–11.

Gundacker, Claudia, 'Die Viten Irischen Heiliger im Magnum Legendarium Austriacum' (M.Phil., University of Vienna, 2008).

Gwynn, Aubrey, 'The early history of St Thomas's Abbey, Dublin', *JRSAI*, 84 (1954), 1–35.

— and Dermot Gleeson, *A history of the diocese of Killaloe* (Dublin, 1962).

— and R. Neville Hadcock, *Medieval religious houses: Ireland* (Dublin, 1970 [reprint, 1988]).

Gwynn, E.J., and W.J. Purton (eds and trans.), 'The monastery of Tallaght', *PRIA*, 29C (1911–12), 115–79.★

Hadcock, R. Neville, 'The Order of the Holy Cross in Ireland' in J.A. Watt, J.B. Morrall, F.X. Martin (eds), *Medieval studies presented to Aubrey Gwynn, SJ* (Dublin, 1961), pp 44–53.

Hall, Dianne, 'Towards a prosopography of nuns in medieval Ireland', *AH*, 53 (1999), 3–15.

—, 'The nuns of the medieval convent of Lismullin, County Meath, and their secular connections', *Ríocht na Midhe*, 10 (1999), 58–70.

—, *Women and the church in medieval Ireland, c.1140–1540* (Dublin, 2003).

Hamlin, Ann, and Claire Foley, 'A women's graveyard at Carrickmore, County Tyrone, and the separate burial of women', *UJA*, 46 (1983), 41–6.

Hammermayer, Ludwig, 'Die irischen Benediktiner-„Schottenklöster" in Deutschland und ihr institutioneller Zusammenschluss vom 12.–16. Jahrhundert', *Studien und Mitteilungen zur Geschichte des Benediktinerordens* 86 (1976), 249–339.

Hardy, Thomas Duffus (ed.), *Rotuli chartarum in turri Londinensi asservati* (London, 1837).★

Harrington, Christina, *Women in a Celtic church Ireland, 450–1150* (Oxford, 2002).

Hennessey, W.M., and B. MacCarthy (eds), *Annála Uladh, Annals of Ulster; otherwise Annála Senait: a chronicle of Irish affairs, 431–1131, 1155–1541*, 4 vols (Dublin, 1887–1901).★

Hennig, John, 'Ireland's contribution to the devotion to Old Testament saints', *Irish Ecclesiastical Record*, 104 (1965), 333–48.

—, 'Studies in the Latin texts of the *Martyrology of Tallaght*, of *Félire Óengusso* and of *Félire hÚi Gormáin*', *PRIA*, 69:4C (1970), 45–112.

Hepplethwaite, Margaret, 'Woman of fire', *The Tablet* (19 March 2022), 8–10.

Herbert, Máire, *Iona, Kells and Derry: the history and hagiography of the monastic* familia *of Columba* (Oxford, 1988, repr. Dublin, 1996).

Herbert McAvoy, Liz, (ed.), *Anchoritic traditions of medieval Europe* (Woodbridge, 2010).

Herbert, Jane, 'The transformation of hermitages into Augustinian priories in twelfth-century England' in W.J. Shiels (ed.), *Monks, hermits and the ascetic tradition*, Studies in Church History 22 (Padstow, 1985), pp 131–46.

Heist, W.W. (ed.), *Vitae Sanctorum Hiberniae ex Codice olim Salmanticensi, nunc Bruxellensi* (Brussels, 1965).★

Herity, Michael, Dorothy Kelly and Ursula Mattenberger, 'List of early Christian cross slabs in seven north-western counties', *JRSAI*, 127 (1997), 80–124.

— (ed.), *Ordnance Survey letters Kildare: letters containing information relative to the antiquities of the county of Kildare collected during the progress of the OS in 1837–1839* (Dublin, 2002).

Hillaby, Joe, 'Colonization, crisis-management and debt: Walter de Lacy and the lordship of Meath, 1189–1241', *Ríocht Na Midhe*, 8:4 (1993), 1–50.

Hoffmann, Hartmut, 'Irische Schreiber in Deutschland im 11. Jahrhundert', *Deutsches Archiv für Erforschung des Mittelalters*, 59 (2003), 97–120.

Hogan, Edmund, *Onomasticon Goedelicum* (Dublin, 1910).

Houston, Robert A., *Literacy in early modern Europe: culture and education* (London, 1988).

Howlett, David, 'Vita I Sanctae Brigitae', *Peritia*, 12 (1998), 1–23.

Hull, Graham, *N18 Ennis bypass and N85 western relief road Clare Abbey, Co. Clare. Final archaeological excavation report for Clare County Council national monument consent: C020. Record Number: E2021 (NGR Job J04/01 (NGR 134700 175730)* https://www.clare library.ie/eolas/coclare/archaeology/n18_n85/A025.pdf (accessed 7 March 2022).

—, and Sébastien Joubert, 'Medieval monastic occupation and post-medieval military activity at Clare Abbey, Co. Clare', *The Other Clare: Journal of the Shannon Archaeological and Historical Society*, 32 (2008), 21–6.

Hunnybun, William Martin (ed.), 'Registers of the English Poor Clares at Gravelines, including those who founded filiations at Aire, Dunkirk and Rouen, 1608–1837', *Catholic Record Society*, Miscellanea, 9:14 (London, 1914), 25–173.★

Hunt, John, *Irish medieval figure sculpture, 1200–1600,* 2 vols (Dublin, 1974).

Ivory, Thomas, 'The medieval hospital in Ireland: a comment on the crusader connection' in Edward Coleman, Paul Duffy and Tadhg O'Keeffe (eds), *Ireland and the crusades* (Dublin, 2022), pp 129–35.

Jamroziak, Emilia, *Survival and success on medieval borders: Cistercian houses in medieval Scotland and Pomerania from the twelfth to the late fourteenth century*, Medieval Texts and Cultures of Northern Europe, 24 (Turnhout, 2011).

Jasper, Kathryn, and John Howe, 'Hermitism in the eleventh and twelfth centuries' in Beach and Cochelin, *CHMMLW*, pp 684–96.

Jauregi, Nere Jone Intxaustegi, *La mujer religiosa en Bizkaia durante los siglos XVI–XVIII* (Bilbao, 2018).

John Chrysostom, St, *Commentary on the Epistle to the Galatians and homilies on the Epistle to the Ephesians*, trans. Anon. (Oxford, 1840).★

John Paul II, Pope, *The theology of marriage and celibacy* (Boston, 1986).

Johnston, Elva, 'Transforming women in Irish hagiography', *Peritia*, 9, (1995), 197–220.

—, 'Íte: patron of her people?' *Peritia*, 14 (2000), 421–8.

—, 'Powerful women or patriarchal weapons? Two medieval Irish saints', *Peritia*, 15 (2001), 302–10.

—, 'The "pagan" and "Christian" identities of the Irish female saint' in Mark Atherton (ed.), *Celts and Christians: new approaches to the religious traditions of Britain and Ireland* (Cardiff, 2002), pp 60–78.

—, 'Review of *Women in a Celtic church: Ireland, 450–1150,* by Christina Harrington', *The English Historical Review*, 119:483 (2004), 1025–6.

—, *Literacy and identity in early medieval Ireland* (Suffolk, 2013).

—, 'Exiles from the edge? The Irish contexts of *peregrinatio*' in Roy Flechner and Sven Meeder (eds), *The Irish in early medieval Europe: identity, culture and religion* (Basingstoke, 2016), pp 38–52.

—, 'Movers and shakers? How women shaped the career of Columbanus' in Alexander O'Hara (ed.), *Columbanus and the peoples of post-Roman Europe* (Oxford, 2018), pp 69–89.

—, 'A woman's voice? The cult of St Canir of Bantry in the early Middle Ages', *Journal of the Bantry Historical and Archaeological Society*, 4 (2022), 124–36.

Jones, David (ed.), *Friars' tales: thirteenth-century exempla from the British Isles* (Manchester, 2011).★

Jones, E.A., 'Ceremonies of enclosure: rite, rhetoric and reality' in Liz Herbert McAvoy (ed.), *Rhetoric of the anchorhold: space, place and body within the discourses of enclosure* (Cardiff, 2008), pp 34–49.

Jordan, Erin, *Women, power and religious patronage in the Middle Ages*, The New Middle Ages (New York, 2006).

Kealy, Máire M., *From Channel Row to Cabra: Dominican nuns and their times, 1717–1820* (Dublin, 2010).

Kelly, Fergus, *A guide to early Irish law* (Dublin, 1988).

Kelly, James E., *English convents in Catholic Europe, c.1600–1800* (Cambridge, 2019).

Kenney, J.F., *The sources for the early history of Ireland (ecclesiastical): an introduction and guide* (New York, 1929, repr. Dublin, 1979).★

Kenny, Gillian, *Anglo-Irish and Gaelic women in Ireland, c.1170–1540* (Dublin, 2007).

Killanin, Lord, and Michael V. Duignan, *The Shell guide to Ireland*, (2nd ed., London, 1967).

King, Heather (ed.), *Clonmacnoise studies, volume 1* (Dublin, 1998).

— (ed.), *Clonmacnoise studies, volume 2* (Dublin, 2003).

Kirakosian, Racha, *The Life of Christina of Hane* (New Haven, CT, 2020).★

Kissane, Noel, *Saint Brigid of Kildare: life, legend and cult* (Dublin, 2017).

Klingshirn, William E., *Caesarius of Arles: life, testament, letters* (Liverpool, 1994).★

Knott, Eleanor (ed.), 'An Irish seventeenth-century translation of the Rule of St Clare', *Éiru*, 15 (1948), 1–187.★

Knox, Andrea, 'The convent as cultural conduit: Irish matronage in early modern Spain', *Quidditas: The Journal of the Rocky Mountain Medieval and Renaissance Association*, 30 (2009), 128–40.

—, 'Nuns on the periphery?: Irish Dominican nuns and assimilation in Lisbon' in F. Sabate i Curull and L. Adno da Fonseca (eds), *Catalonia and Portugal: the Iberian peninsula from the periphery* (Berlin, 2015), pp 311–26.

—, 'Her book-lined cell: Irish nuns and the development of texts, translation and literacy in late medieval Spain' in V. Blanton, V. O'Mara and P. Stoop (eds), *Nuns' literacies in medieval Europe: the Kansas city dialogue* (Turnhout, 2015), pp 67–86.

—, *Irish women on the move: migration and mission in Spain, 1499–1700* (Bern, 2020).

Kolmer, Lothar, 'Regensburg in der Salierzeit' in Stefan Weinfurter (ed.), *Die Salier und das Reich*, Band 3 (Sigmaringen, 1991), pp 191–213.

Koschwitz, Gisela, *Der hl. Bischof Erhard von Regensburg. Legende-Kult-Ikonographie*, Studien und Mitteilungen zur Geschichte des Benediktinerordens 86 (1975), 481–644.

Kraus, Andreas, *Civitas Regia. Das Bild Regensburgs in der deutschen Geschichtsschreibung des Mittelalters* (Kallmünz, 1972).

Krings, Bruno, 'Die Prämonstratenser und ihr weiblicher Zweig' in Irene Crusius and Helmut Flachenecker (eds), *Studien zum Prämonstratenserorden*, (Göttingen, 2003), pp 73–106.

Krusch, Bruno (ed.), *Ionae Vitae Sanctorum Columbani, Vedestis, Johannis*, MGH Scriptores Rerum Germanicarum in usum scholarum 37 (Hannover & Leipzig, 1905), pp 144–294.★

Lacey, Brian, *Medieval and monastic Derry: sixth century to 1600* (Dublin, 2013).

Laqua-O'Donnell, Simone, *Women and the Counter-Reformation in early modern Münster* (Oxford, 2014).

Laven, Mary, *Virgins of Venice: broken vows and cloistered lives in the Renaissance convent* (London, 2003).

Lawlor, H.J., 'A fresh authority for the synod of Kells', *PRIA*, 36C (1921–4), 16–22.

Lehfeldt, Elizabeth A., *Religious women in Golden Age Spain: the permeable cloister* (Aldershot, 2005).

Leidinger, Georg, 'Bruchstücke einer verlorenen Chronik eines unbekannten Regensburger Verfasser des 12. Jahrhunderts', *Sitzungesberichte der Bayerischen Akademie der Wissenschaften Philosophisch-historische Abteilung* Jahrgang 33 Heft I (Munich, 1933), 3–72.

Leigh Fry, Susan, *Burial in medieval Ireland, 900–1500* (Dublin, 1999).

Leinsle, Ulrich G., *Die Prämonstratenser* (Stuttgart, 2020).

Lenihan, Pádraig, *Confederate Catholics at war, 1642–49* (Cork, 2001).

Lennon, Colm, *The lords of Dublin in the age of Reformation* (Dublin, 1989).

—, 'The chantries in the Irish Reformation: the case of St Anne's guild, Dublin, 1550–1630' in R.V. Comerford, Mary Cullen, J.R. Hill and Colm Lennon (eds), *Religion, conflict and coexistence in Ireland: essays presented to Monsignor Patrick J. Corish* (Dublin, 1990), pp 6–25.

—, 'The confraternities and cultural duality in Ireland, 1450–1550' in Christopher Black and Pamela Gravestock (eds), *Early modern confraternities in Europe and the Americas: international and interdisciplinary perspectives* (Aldershot, 2006), pp 35–52.

—, 'Education and religious identity in early modern Ireland', *Paedagogica Historica*, 35:1 (2015), 57–75.

—, 'Confraternities in late medieval Ireland: the evolution of chantry colleges' in Konrad Eisenbichler (ed.), *A companion to medieval and early modern confraternities* (Leiden, 2019), pp 194–211.

— and James Murray (eds), *The Dublin city franchise roll, 1468–1512* (Dublin, 1998).★

Leonard, Amy E., 'Female religious orders' in Ro Po-chia Hsia (ed.), *A companion to the Reformation world* (Oxford, 2004), pp 237–54.

—, *Nails in the wall: Catholic nuns in Reformation Germany* (Chicago, 2005).

Lester, Anne E., *Creating Cistercian nuns: the women's religious movement and its reform in thirteenth-century Champagne* (Ithaca, 2011).

Levison, Wilhelm (ed.), *Vita Erhardi episcopi Bavarici auctore Paulo*, MGH Scriptores Rerum Merovingicarum VI (Hannover & Leipzig, 1913), pp 1–21.★

— (ed.), *Vita Sti Albarti archiepiscopi Casselensis*, MGH Scriptores Rerum Merovingicarum VI (Hannover & Leipzig, 1913), pp 21–3.★

— (ed.), *Vita Odiliae abbatissae Hohenburgensis*, MGH Scriptores Rerum Merovingicarum VI (Hannover & Leipzig, 1913), pp 24–50.★

Lewis, Samuel, *A topographical dictionary of Ireland: comprising the several counties; cities; boroughs; corporate, market and post towns; parishes; and villages, with historical and statistical descriptions*, 2 vols (London, 1837).

L'Hermite-Leclercq, Paulette, 'Reclusion in the Middle Ages' in Beach and Cochelin (eds), *CHMMLW*, pp 747–65.

Licence, Tom, *Hermits and recluses in English society, 950–1250* (Cambridge, 2011).

Lifshitz, Felice, *The name of the saint: the martyrology of Jerome and access to the sacred in Francia, 627–827* (Notre Dame, 2006).

Lionard, Pádraig, 'Early Irish grave slabs', *PRIA*, 61C (1961), 95–169.

Little, A.G. (ed.), *Liber exemplorum ad usum praedicantium saeculo xiii compositus a quondam fratre minore Anglico de provincial Hiberniae* (Aberdeen, 1918).★

Lozano, Cristina Bravo, *Spain and the Irish mission, 1609–1707* (London, 2018).

Luecke, Janemarie, 'The unique experience of Anglo-Saxon nuns' in John Nichols and Lillian Thomas Shank (eds), *Peace weavers: medieval religious women, volume 2* (Kalamazoo, 1987), pp 55–66.

Lux-Sterritt, Laurence, *Redefining female religious life: French Ursulines and English Ladies in seventeenth-century Catholicism* (Aldershot, 2005).

Lydon, James, 'Christ Church in the later medieval Irish world' in Kenneth Milne (ed.), *Christ Church Cathedral, Dublin: a history* (Dublin, 2000), pp 75–94.

Lynch, John, *Cambrensis Eversus, seu potius historica fides in Rebus Hibernicis*, ed. Matthew Kelly, 3 vols (Dublin, 1848–52).★

Lynch, Katherine A., *Individuals, families and communities in Europe, 1200–1800: the urban foundations of western society* (Cambridge, 2003).

Lynn, Chris, 'Excavations in 46–48 Scotch Street, Armagh, 1979–80', *UJA*, 51 (1988), 69–84.

Lyons, Mary Ann, *Church and society in County Kildare, c.1470–1547* (Dublin, 2000).

—, 'Lay female piety in late medieval Ireland' in Brendan Bradshaw and Dáire Keogh (eds), *Christianity in Ireland: revisiting the story* (Dublin, 2002), pp 57–75.

—, 'The role of St Anthony's College, Louvain in establishing the Irish Franciscan college network' in Edel Bhreathnach, Joseph Mac Mahon and John McCafferty (eds), *The Irish Franciscans, 1534–1990* (Dublin, 2009), pp 27–44.

Macalister, Robert A.S., *The memorial slabs of Clonmacnoise, King's County* (Dublin, 1909).

—, 'Some cross-slabs in the neighbourhood of Athlone', *JRSAI*, 42 (1912), 27–31.

—, *Corpus inscriptionum insularum Celticarum*, 2 vols (Dublin, 1945).

Mac Airt, Seán (ed.), *The Annals of Inisfallen: MS Rawlinson B.503* (Dublin, 1951).★

MacCotter, Paul, *Medieval Ireland: territorial, political and economic divisions* (Dublin, 2008).

MacCurtain, Margaret, Mary O'Dowd and Maria Luddy, 'An agenda for women's history in Ireland, 1500–1900', *IHS*, 28 (1992), 1–37.

MacDermott, Máire, 'The crosiers of St Dympna and St Mel and tenth-century Irish metal-work', *PRIA*, 58C (1957), 167–95.

Mac Eoin, Gearóid, 'The Life of Cumaine Fota', *Béaloideas*, 39/41 (1971–3), 192–205.★

MacNeill, Charles, and A.J. Otway-Ruthven (eds), *Dowdall deeds* (Dublin, 1960).★

Madigan, Kevin, *Medieval Christianity: a new history* (New Haven, CT, 2015).

Magnani, Eliana, 'Female house ascetics from the fourth to the twelfth century' in Beach and Cochelin, *CHMMLW,* pp 213–31.

Mai, Paul (ed.), *100 Jahre Stift St Paul (Mittelmünster) in Regensburg Jubiläumsausstellung* (Regensburg, 1983).

Makowski, Elizabeth, *A pernicious type of woman: quasi-religious women and canon lawyers in the later Middle Ages* (Washington, DC, 2005).

Malvielle, Guy, 'Le prieuré d'Aubeterre, ses prieures et prieurs', *Bulletin de la Société d'émulation du Bourbonnais: lettres, sciences et arts* (1951), 111–17.

Maney, Laurance, 'The date and provenance of Vita Prima Sanctae Brigitae', *Proceedings of the Harvard Celtic Colloquium* 23 (2003), 200–18.

Manning, Conleth, 'Excavation at Kilteel church, Co. Kildare', *JCKAHS*, 16 (1982), 173–229.

—, 'Some early masonry churches and the round tower at Clonmacnoise' in Heather King (ed.), *Clonmacnoise studies, volume 2* (Dublin, 2003), pp 63–95.

—, 'A suggested typology for pre-Romanesque stone churches in Ireland' in Nancy Edwards (ed.), *The archaeology of the early medieval Celtic churches* (Leeds, 2009), pp 265–79.

Märtl, Claudia, 'Regensburg in den geistigen Auseinandersetzungen des Investiturstreits', *Deutsches Archiv für Erforschung des Mittelalters*, 42 (1986), 145–91.

—, 'Die Damenstifte Obermünster, Niedermünster, St Paul' in Peter Schmid (ed.), *Geschichte der Stadt Regensburg*, 2 (2000), pp 745–63.

Masterson, Rory, *Medieval Fore, County Westmeath*, Maynooth Studies in Local History, 112 (Dublin, 2014).

McCabe, Honor, OP, *A light undimmed: the story of the convent of Our Lady of Bom Sucesso, Lisbon, 1639–2006* (Dublin, 2007).

McCarthy, Daniel, 'The chronology of St Brigit of Kildare,' *Peritia*, 14 (2000), 255–81.

McClintock, H.F., 'The mantle of St Brigid at Bruges', *JRSAI*, 6:1 (1936), 32–40.

McCone, Kim, '*Aided Cheltchair maic Uthechair*: hounds, heroes and hospitallers in early Irish myth and story', *Ériu*, 35 (1984), 1–30.

—, 'Brigit in the seventh century: a saint with three lives?', *Peritia*, 1 (1982), 107–45.

McCullough, Catherine, and W.H. Crawford, *Irish historic towns atlas, no. 18: Armagh* (Dublin, 2007).

McEnery, M.J., and Raymond Refaussé (eds), *Christ Church deeds* (Dublin, 2001).★

McInerney, Luke, 'A 1555 papal bulla for Clare Abbey', *JRSAI*, 141 (2011), 128–48.

—, *Clerical and learned lineages of medieval Co. Clare: a survey of the fifteenth-century papal registers* (Dublin, 2014).

—, 'Was *Caithréim Thoirdhealbhaigh* written at Clare Abbey in the mid-fourteenth century?', *The Other Clare: Journal of the Shannon Archaeological and Historical Society*, 45 (2021), 26–32.

McNamara, Jo Ann Kay, *Sisters in arms. Catholic nuns through two millennia* (Harvard, 1996).

McShane, Bronagh Ann, 'The roles and representations of women in religious change and conflict in Leinster and south-east Munster, *c*.1560–*c*.1641' (PhD, Maynooth University, 2015).

—, 'Negotiating religious change and conflict: female religious communities in early modern Ireland, *c*.1530–*c*.1641', *British Catholic History*, 33:3 (2017), 357–82.

—, 'The pre-profession record of Sister Catherine Browne ("in religion" Sister Catherine of St Francis), Poor Clare convent, Bethlehem, County Westmeath, 1632', *AH*, 70 (2017), 284–93.

—, 'Visualising the reception and circulation of early modern nuns' letters', *Journal of Historical Network Research*, 2:1 (2018), 1–25.

—, *Irish women in religious orders, 1530–1700: suppression, migration and reintegration* (Woodbridge, 2022).

— and Frances Nolan (eds), 'A new agenda for women's and gender history in Ireland', Special Issue, *IHS*, 46:170 (2022), 207–355.

Melville, Gert, 'The institutionalization of religious orders (twelfth and thirteenth centuries)' in Beach and Cochelin, *CHMMLW* (Cambridge, 2020), pp 783–802.

Meyer, Kuno, *The Triads of Ireland*, Royal Irish Academy Todd Lecture Series 13 (Dublin, 1906).

—, *Hail Brigit: An Old-Irish poem on the Hill of Allen* (Dublin, 1912).★

Millett, Benignus, *The Irish Franciscans, 1651–65* (Rome, 1964).

—, 'Survival and reorganization, 1650–95' in Patrick J. Corish (ed.), *A history of Irish Catholicism*, 3 vols (Dublin, 1967), 3:7, pp 1–12.

Milne, Kenneth (ed.), *Christ Church Cathedral, Dublin: a history* (Dublin, 2000).

Migne, Jacques-Paul (ed.), *Patrologiae Cursus Completus. Series Latina*, 221 vols (Paris, 1879).★

Mills, James (ed.), *Account roll of the priory of Holy Trinity, Dublin, 1337–46* (Dublin, 1996).★

— (ed.), *Calendar of the Justiciary Rolls: Ireland, 1295–1303* (Dublin, 1905).★

Moody, T.W., F.X. Martin and F.J. Byrne (eds), *A new history of Ireland*; iii, *Early modern Ireland 1534–1691* (Oxford, 1976).

Mooney, Canice, *Irish Franciscan relations with France, 1224–1850* (Dublin, 1951).

Mooney, Catherine M., *Clare of Assisi and the thirteenth-century church: religious women, rules, and resistance*, The Middle Ages Series (Philadelphia, 2016).

Moran, Patrick F. (ed.), *Monasticon Hibernicum, or, A history of the abbeys, priories and other religious houses in Ireland, by Mervyn Archdall*, 2 vols (Dublin, 1873, 1876).★

—, *Spicilegium Ossoriense: being a collection of original letters and papers illustrative of the history of the Irish church*, 3 vols (Dublin, 1874).★

More, Alison, *Fictive orders and feminine religious identities, 1200–1600* (Oxford, 2018).

Morrin, James (ed.), *Calendar of the Patent and Close Rolls of Chancery in Ireland in the reigns of Henry VIII, Edward VI, Mary and Elizabeth*, 3 vols (Dublin, 1861–3).★

Morsbach, Peter, *Das Mittelmünster in Regensburg – Nur ein Straßenschild ist geblieben*, Haus der Bayerischen Geschicht, Klöster in Bayern: https://www.hdbg.eu/kloster/index.php/pdf?id=KS0337 (accessed 7 March 2022).

Mulchrone, Kathleen, *Bethu Phátraic: the Tripartite Life of Patrick* (Dublin, 1939).★

Mulholland, John, 'The trial of Alice Butler, abbess of Kilculiheen, 1532', *Decies*, 25 (1984), 45–6.

Mulder-Bakker, Anneke, 'The reclusorium as an informal centre of learning' in J.W. Drijvers and A.A. MacDonald (eds), *Centres of learning: learning and location in pre-modern Europe and the near East* (Leiden, 1995), pp 246–54.

—, *Lives of the anchoresses: the rise of the urban recluse in medieval Europe* (Philadelphia, 2005).

Murphy, Donald, 'Excavation of an early monastic enclosure at Clonmacnoise' in Heather King (ed.), *Clonmacnoise studies, volume 2* (Dublin, 2003) pp 1–33.

Murphy, Emilie K.M., 'Language and power in an English convent in exile, *c.*1621–*c.*1631', *Historical Journal*, 62:1 (2019), 101–25.

—, 'Exile and linguistic encounter: early modern English convents in the Low Countries and France', *Renaissance Quarterly*, 73 (2020), 147–8.

Murphy, Gerard, *Early Irish lyrics: eighth to twelfth centuries* (Dublin, 1998).★

Murphy, Margaret, 'Rural settlement in Meath 1170–1660: the documentary evidence' in Mary Deevy and Donald Murphy (eds), *Places along the way: first findings on the M3* (Bray, 2009), pp 153–68.

Murray, James, 'The Tudor diocese of Dublin: episcopal government, ecclesiastical politics and the enforcement of the Reformation, *c.*1534–1590' (PhD, University of Dublin, 1997).

—, *Enforcing the English Reformation in Ireland: clerical resistance and political conflict in the dioceses of Dublin, 1534–1590* (Cambridge, 2009).

Mytum, Harold, 'Surface and geophysical survey at Clonmacnoise: defining the extent of intensive monastic settlement' in Heather King (ed.), *Clonmacnoise studies, volume 2* (Dublin, 2003), pp 35–58.

Nicholls, Kenneth, 'Towards a new *Monasticon Hibernicum*', *Peritia*, 3 (1984), 330–3.

Ní Chonaill, Bronagh, 'Child-centred law in medieval Ireland' in R. Davis and T. Dunne (eds), *The empty throne: childhood and the crisis of modernity* (Cambridge, 2008), pp 1–31.

Ní Dhonnchada, Máirín, '*Caillech* and other terms for veiled women in medieval Irish texts', *Éigse*, 26 (1994–5), 71–96.

—, 'Mary, Eve and the church *c.*600–1800' in Angela Bourke et al. (eds), *The Field-Day anthology of Irish writing,* vol. IV: *Irish women's writing and traditions* (Cork, 2002), pp 45–165.★

Ní Ghrádaigh, Jennifer, '"But what exactly did she give?": Derbforgaill and the Nuns' Church at Clonmacnoise' in Heather King (ed.), *Clonmacnoise studies, volume 2* (Dublin, 2003), pp 175–207.

—, 'Mere embroiderers? Women and art in early medieval Ireland' in Therese Martin (ed.), *Reassessing the roles of women as 'makers' of medieval art and architecture* (Leiden/Boston, 2012), pp 93–128.

Ní Mhaonaigh, Máire, 'Tales of three Gormlaiths in medieval Irish literature', *Ériu*, 52 (2002), 1–24.

Nolan, Patrick, *The Irish dames of Ypres: being a history of the Royal Irish Abbey of Ypres founded AD 1665 and still flourishing* (Dublin, 1908).

Ó Baoill, Ruairí, 'Excavations at Aghavea, Co. Fermanagh' in Christian Corlett and Michael Potterton (eds), *The church in early medieval Ireland, in the light of recent archaeological excavations* (Dublin, 2014), pp 159–72.

O'Brien, Celsus, *A short history of the Poor Clares, Galway* (Galway, 1992).

— (ed.), *Recollections of an Irish Poor Clare in the seventeenth century* (Galway, 1993).★

—, *The story of the Poor Clares* (Limerick, 1996).

O'Brien, Elizabeth, *Mapping death: burial in late Iron Age and early medieval Ireland* (Dublin, 2020).

Ó Carragáin, Tomás, 'A landscape converted: archaeology and early church organisation on Iveragh and Dingle, Ireland' in Martin Carver (ed.), *The cross goes north: processes of conversion in northern Europe AD 300–1300* (Woodbridge, 2003), pp 127–52.

—, 'Habitual masonry styles and the local organisation of church building in early medieval Ireland', *PRIA,* 105C (2005), 99–149.

—, 'Church buildings and pastoral care in early medieval Ireland' in Elizabeth FitzPatrick and Raymond Gillespie (eds), *The parish in medieval and early modern Ireland: community, territory and building* (Dublin, 2006), pp 91–123.

—, 'The architectural setting of the Mass in early medieval Ireland', *Medieval Archaeology*, 53 (2009), 119–54.

—, *Churches in early medieval Ireland: architecture, ritual, and memory* (New Haven, 2010).

—, 'From family cemeteries to community cemeteries in Viking Age Ireland?' in Christian Corlett and Michael Potterton (eds), *Death and burial in early medieval Ireland in the light of recent archaeological excavations* (Dublin, 2010), pp 217–26.

—, 'Patterns of patronage: churches, round towers and the Dál Cais kings of Munster (*c*.950–1050)' in Roger Stalley (ed.), *Medieval art and architecture in Limerick and south-west Ireland. British Archaeological Association Conference Transactions Series,* 34 (Leeds, 2011), pp 23–41.

—, 'The view from the shore: perceiving island monasteries in early medieval Ireland, *Hortus Artium Medievalium*, 19 (2013), 21–33.

—, 'The archaeology of ecclesiastical estates in early medieval Ireland: a case study of the kingdom of Fir Maige', *Peritia*, 24/5 (2014), 266–312.

—, 'Is there an archaeology of lay people at early Irish monasteries?' *Bulletin du Centre D'études Médiévales d'Auxerre BUCEMA*, 8 (2015), 2–17.

—, *Churches in the Irish landscape, AD 400–1100* (Cork, 2021).

Ó Clabaigh, Colmán, *The Franciscans in Ireland, 1400–1534: from reform to Reformation* (Dublin, 2002).

—, 'The Benedictines in medieval and early modern Ireland' in Martin Browne and Colmán Ó Clabaigh OSB (eds), *The Irish Benedictines: a history* (Dublin, 2005), pp 79–121.

—, 'Anchorites in late medieval Ireland' in McAvoy (ed.) *Anchoritic traditions*, pp 153–77.

—, 'The hermits and anchorites of medieval Dublin' in Seán Duffy (ed.), *Medieval Dublin X* (Dublin, 2010), pp 267–89.

—, *The friars in Ireland, 1224–1540* (Dublin, 2012).

—, 'The church, 1050–1460' in Brendan Smith (ed.), *The Cambridge history of Ireland, Volume 1, 600–1550* (Cambridge, 2018), pp 364–75.

— 'Community, commemoration and confraternity: the chapter office and chapter books in Irish Augustinian foundations' in Browne and Ó Clabaigh, *Households*, pp 235–51.

—, 'Monasticism, colonization, and ethnic tension in late medieval Ireland' in Beach and Cochelin, *CHMMLW*, pp 908–12.

O'Connor, Lil, 'Faughart investigation 1966,' *CLAHS*, 17 (1966), 125–9.

Ó Corráin, Donnchadh, 'Dál Cais-church and dynasty', *Ériu*, 24 (1973), 52–63.

—, 'Foreign connections and domestic politics: Killaloe and the Uí Bhriain in twelfth-century hagiography' in Dorothy Whitelock, Rosamund McKitterick, David Dumville (eds), *Ireland in early medieval Europe* (Cambridge, 1982), pp 213–31.

—, *The Irish church, its reform and the English invasion* (Dublin, 2017).

Ó Crónín, Dáibhí, *Early medieval Ireland* (London, 1995).

Ó Dálaigh, Brian, 'Mistress, mother and abbess: Renalda Ní Bhriain *c.*1447–1510', *NMAJ*, 32 (1990), 50–63.

O'Dowd, Mary, *A history of women in Ireland, 1500–1800* (Harlow, 2005).

Ó Floinn, Raghnall, *Irish shrines and reliquaries of the Middle Ages* (Dublin, 1994).

—, '"The market cross" at Glendalough' in Charles Doherty et al., *Glendalough: city of God* (Dublin, 2011), pp 80–111.

Ó hAnnracháin, Tadhg, *Catholic Reformation in Ireland: the mission of Rinuccini, 1645–1649* (Oxford, 2002).

Ó hAodha, Donncha, *Bethu Brigte* (Dublin 1978).★

O'Hara, Alexander, and Ian Wood (trans.), *Jonas of Bobbio: Life of Columbanus, Life of John of Réomé and Life of Vedast* (Liverpool, 2017).★

Ó hEaluighthe, Donnchadha, 'St Gobnet of Ballyvourney', *JCHAS*, 57 (1952), 43–61.

O'Heyne, John, *The Irish Dominicans of the seventeenth century* (Dundalk, 1902).

Ó hInnse, Séamus (ed.), *Miscellaneous Irish Annals (AD 1114–1437)* (Dublin, 1947).★

Ohlmeyer, Jane, *Making Ireland English: the Irish aristocracy in the seventeenth century* (New Haven and London, 2012).

O'Keeffe, Grace, 'The hospital of St John the Baptist in medieval Dublin: functions and maintenance' in Seán Duffy (ed.), *Medieval Dublin IX* (Dublin, 2009), pp 166–82.

O'Kelly, Michael J., 'St Gobnet's house, Ballyvourney, Co. Cork', *JCHAS*, 57 (1952), 18–40.

—, 'Church Island near Valentia, Co. Kerry', *PRIA*, 59C (1958), 57–136.

Oliger, Livarius (ed.), 'Regulae tres reclusorum et eremitarum Angliae saec. XIII–XIV', *Antonianum*, 3 (1928), 151–90.★

Ó Néill, Pádraig, 'The Old-Irish glosses of the *prima manus* in Würzburg m.p.thf.12 – text and context reconsidered' in Michael Richter and Jean-Michel Picard (eds), *Ogma: essays in Celtic studies in honour of Próinséas Ní Chatháin* (Dublin, 2002), pp 230–42.

O'Neill, Rose, *A rich inheritance: Galway Dominican nuns, 1644–1994* (Galway, 1994).

Ó Riain, Diarmuid, 'New light on the history of St Mary's priory, Rosscarbery', *JCHAS*, 113 (2008), 56–68.

—, 'The *Magnum Legendarium Austriacum*: a new investigation of one of medieval Europe's richest hagiographical collections', *Analecta Bollandiana*, 133 (2015), 87–165.

—, 'The *Schottenklöster* in the world: identity, independence and integration' in Eirik Hovden, Christina Lutter, Walter Pohl (eds), *Meanings of community across medieval Eurasia: comparative approaches* (Leiden, 2016), pp 388–416.

— 'The *Schottenklöster* and the legacy of the Irish *sancti peregrini*' in Wolfram R. Keller and Dagmar Schlüter (eds), *'A fantastic and abstruse Latinity': Hiberno-Continental cultural and literary interactions in the Middle Ages* (Münster, 2017), pp 141–64.

—, '*Monachi peregrini*. The mobile monks of the Irish Benedictine houses in medieval Germany and Austria' in Olivier Delouis, Maria Mossakovska-Gaubert and Annick Peters-Custot (eds), *Les mobilités monastiques en Orient et en Occident de l'Antiquité tardive au Moyen Âge (ive–xve siècle)* (Rome, 2019), pp 337–52.

Ó Riain, Pádraig, *The making of a saint: Finnbarr of Cork, 600–1200* (Dublin, 1997).

—, *Feastdays of the saints: a history of Irish martyrologies*, Subsida Hagiographica, 6 (Brussels, 2006).

—, *A dictionary of Irish saints* (Dublin, 2011).

—, *The martyrology of the Regensburg Schottenkloster* (London, 2019).★

Ó Riain-Raedel, Dagmar, 'Irish kings and bishops in the memoria of the German Schottenklöster' in Prionsias Ní Chatháin and Michael Richter (eds), *Irland und Europa: die Kirche im Frühmittelalter* (Stuttgart, 1984), pp 390–404.

—, 'Das Nekrolog der irischen Schottenklöster. Edition der Handschrift Vat. lat. 10 100 mit einer Untersuchung der hagiographischen und liturgischen Handschriften der Schottenklöster', *Beiträge zur Geschichte des Bistums Regensburg*, 26 (1992), 1–119.★

—, 'Patrician documents in medieval Germany', *Zeitschrift für celtische Philologie*, 49–50 (1997/8), 712–24.

—, 'The question of the "pre-Patrician" saints of Munster' in Michael A. Monk and John Sheehan (eds), *Early medieval Munster. Archaeology, history and society* (Cork, 1998), pp 17–22.

— 'The travels of Irish manuscripts: from the Continent to Ireland' in Toby Barnard, Dáibhí Ó Croinín and Katharine Simms (eds), *A miracle of learning: studies in manuscripts and Irish learning* (Aldershot, 1998), pp 52–67.

—, 'German influence on Munster church and kings in the twelfth century' in Alfred Smyth (ed.), *Seanchas: studies in early and medieval Irish archaeology, history and literature in honour of Francis J. Byrne* (Dublin, 2000), pp 323–30.

—, 'Irish Benedictine monasteries on the Continent' in Martin Browne and Colmán Ó Clabaigh (eds), *The Irish Benedictines: a history* (Dublin, 2005), pp 25–63.

—, 'Cashel and Germany: the documentary evidence' in Damien Bracken and Dagmar Ó Riain-Raedel (eds), *Ireland and Europe in the twelfth century: reform and renewal* (Dublin, 2006), pp 176–217.

—, '„Wie der deutsche Kaiser" Sakraltopographie und Krönungskirche in Cashel/Irland' in Caspar Ehlers (ed.), *Places of power – Orte der Herrschaft – Lieux du Pouvoir. Deutsche Königspfalzen. Beiträge zu ihrer historischen und archäologischen Erforschung 8* (Göttingen, 2007), pp 313–71.

—, '"Wide-reaching connections": the list of abbots from Iona in the *Liber confraternitatum ecclesiae S. Petri* in Salzburg' in Elizabeth Mullins and Diarmuid Scully (eds), *Listen, O Isles, unto me: studies in medieval word and image in honour of Jennifer O'Reilly* (Cork, 2011), pp 60–72.

—, *Vita Sti Cóemgeni*: an edition of the earliest manuscript version' in Charles Doherty, Linda Doran and Mary Kelly (eds), *Glendalough: city of God* (Dublin, 2011), pp 145–64.★

—, 'The other paradise: perceptions of Ireland in the Middle Ages' in Rudolf Simek and Asya Ivanova (eds), *Between the islands – and the Continent. Papers on Hiberno-Scandinavian-Continental contacts in the early Middle Ages* (Vienna 2013), pp 167–92.

—, 'St Koloman: ein irischer Pilger?' in Meta Niederkorn-Bruck (ed.), *Ein Heiliger unterwegs in Europa. Tausend Jahre Koloman-Verehrung in Melk (1014–2014)* (Vienna/Cologne/Weimar, 2014), pp 219–38.

—, 'St Kilian and the Irish network in early Carolingian Europe' in Wolfram R. Keller and Dagmar Schlüter (eds), *'A fantastic and abstruse Latinity?' Hiberno-Continental cultural and literary interactions in the Middle Ages*, Studien und Texte zur Keltologie 12 (Münster, 2017), pp 31–53.

—, 'New light on the beginnings of Christ Church Cathedral, Dublin' in Seán Duffy (ed.), *Medieval Dublin XIII* (Dublin, 2019), pp 63–80.

Ó Riain-Raedel, Dagmar, and Pádraig Ó Riain, 'Weitreichende Verbindungen: Köln und Irland im 11. Jahrhundert' in Harald Horst (ed.), *Mittelalterliche Handschriften der Kölner Dombibliothek* (Achtes Symposium der Diözesan- und Dombibliothek Köln zu den Dom-Manuskripten (30. November und 1. Dezember 2018), *Libelli Rhenani* 24 (Cologne, 2019), pp 113–52.

Orme, Nicholas, and Margaret Webster, *The English hospital, 1070–1570* (New Haven & London, 1995).

Ó Siochrú, Micheál, *Confederate Ireland, 1642–1649: a constitutional and political analysis* (Dublin, 1998).

—, *God's executioner: Oliver Cromwell and the conquest of Ireland* (London, 2008).

O'Sullivan, Aidan, Finbar McCormick, Thomas Kerr and Lorcan Harney (eds), *Early medieval Ireland AD 400–1100: the evidence from archaeological excavations* (Dublin, 2014).

O'Sullivan, Jerry, and Tomás Ó Carragáin, *Inishmurray: monks and pilgrims in an Atlantic landscape*, vol. 1: *Archaeological survey and excavations 1997–2000* (Cork, 2008).

Oxenham, Helen, *Perceptions of femininity in early Irish society* (Woodbridge, 2016).

Paige, Jean Le, *Bibliotheca Praemonstratensis ordinis*, 2 vols (Paris, 1633).★

Paricius, Johannes Carl, *Allerneueste und bewährte Historische Nachricht Von Allen in denen Ring-Mauren der Stadt Regensburg gelegenen Reichs-Stifftern, Haupt-Kirchen und Clöstern Catholischer Religion* (Regensburg, 1753).

Perry, Mary Elizabeth, *Gender and disorder in early modern Seville* (Princeton, 1990).

Petersen, Joan M. (trans.), *Handmaids of the Lord* (Kalamazoo, 1996).★

Pfeil, Brigitte, *Die ‚Vision des Tnugdalus' Albers von Windberg. Literatur- und Frömmigkeitsgeschichte im ausgehenden 12. Jahrhundert. Mit einer Edition der lateinischen "Visio Tnugdali" aus Clm 22254* (Frankfurt a. M. – Berlin, 1999).

Phelan, Margaret M., 'An unidentified tomb in St Canice's Cathedral, Kilkenny', *Old Kilkenny Review,* 48 (1996), 40–4.

Picard, Jean Michel, 'L'exégèse irlandaise des Épîtres de Saint Paul: les gloses latines et gaéliques de Würzburg', *Recherches augustiniennes et patristiques*, 33 (2003), 155–67.

—, and Yolande de Pontfarcy, *The vision of Tnugdal* (Dublin, 1989).★

Piper, John, 'A vision of biblical complementarity: manhood and womanhood defined according to the Bible' in John Piper and Wayne Gruden (eds), *Recovering biblical manhood and womanhood* (Wheaton, 1991), pp 25–55.

Plummer, Charles (ed.), *Vitae Sanctorum Hiberniae*, 2 vols (Oxford, 1910).★

Poncelet, Albert (ed.), 'Vita S. Mochullei episcopi', *Analecta Bollandiana*, 17 (1898), 135–54.★

Prendergast, J.P., *The Cromwellian settlement of Ireland* (2nd ed., London, 1870).

Presciutti, Diana Bullen (ed.), *Space, place and motion: locating confraternities in the late medieval and early modern city* (Leiden, 2017).

Quigley, W.H.G., and E.F.D. Roberts (eds), *Registrum Iohannis Mey: the register of John Mey, archbishop of Armagh* (Belfast, 1972).★

Quin, E.G., 'The Early Irish poem Isucán', *Cambridge Medieval Celtic Studies*, 1 (1981), 39–52.★

Quinlan, Margaret, and Rachel Moss, *Lemanaghan, County Offaly conservation plan* (Kilkenny, 2007).

Radner, Joan Newlon, *Fragmentary annals of Ireland* (Dublin, 1978).★

Rapley, Elizabeth, *The Dévotes: women and the church in seventeenth-century France* (Montréal, 1993).

—, *A social history of the cloister: daily life in the teaching monasteries of the Old Regime* (Montréal, 2001).

Raftery, Deirdre, and Catherine KilBride, *The Benedictine nuns and Kylemore Abbey: a history* (Dublin, 2020).

Refaussé, Raymond, with Colm Lennon (eds), *The registers of Christ Church Cathedral, Dublin* (Dublin, 1998).★

Reynolds, Roger, 'Virgines subintroductae in Celtic Christianity', *Harvard Theological Review*, 61:4 (1968), 547–66.

Risse, Alexandra, *Niedermünster in Regensburg. Eine Frauenkommunität in Mittelalter und Neuzeit* (Beiträge zur Geschichte des Bistums Regensburg Beiband 24), (Regensburg, 2014).

Ritari, Katja, 'The image of Brigit as a saint: reading the Latin Lives', *Peritia*, 21 (2010), 191–207.

Roest, Bert, 'Regionalism and locality as factors in the study of religious orders' in Gert Melville and Anne Müller (eds), *Mittelalterliche Orden Und Klöster Im Vergleich. Methodische Ansätze Und Perspektiven*, Vita Regularis. Abhandlungen, 34 (Berlin, 2007), pp 243–68.

—, *Order and disorder: the Poor Clares between foundation and reform* (Leiden, 2013).

Röhrkasten, Jens, 'The Poor Clares during the era of Observant reforms: attempts at a typology' in *Franciscan Studies*, 69 (2011), 343–86.

Rosser, Gervase, *The art of solidarity in the Middle Ages: guilds in England, 1250–1550* (Oxford, 2015).

Rousseau, Marie-Hélène, *Saving the souls of medieval London: perpetual chantries at St Paul's Cathedral, c.1200–1548* (Aldershot, 2011).

Russell, Paul, 'Patterns of hypocorism in early Irish hagiography' in John Carey, Máire Herbert and Pádraig Ó Riain (eds), *Studies in Irish hagiography: saints and scholars* (Dublin, 2001), pp 237–49.

Salisbury, Joyce, *Church Fathers, independent virgins* (London, 1991).

Salmantino, Joanne à s. Antonio, *Bibliotheca universa franciscana*, 3 vols (Madrid, 1732; repr. Farnborough, 1966).★

Sanderlin, Sarah, 'The monastery of Lismore, AD 638–1111' in William Nolan and Thomas P. Power (eds), *Waterford history and society* (Dublin, 1992), pp 27–48.

Sauer, Michelle M., 'The meaning of russet: a note on vowesses and clothing', *Early Middle English*, 2:2 (2020), 91–7.

Schmid, Peter, 'Die Bischöfe und die Hauptstadt: Residenzen der bayerischen Bischöfe in Regensburg' in Peter Morsbach (ed.), *Ratisbona sacra. Das Bistum Regensburg im Mittelalter* (Ausstellung anläßlich des 1250jährigen Jubiläums der kanonischen Errichtung des Bistums Regensburg durch Bonifatius 739–1989) (Munich and Zurich, 1989), pp 93–5.

Schwaiger, Georg, 'Bischof Wolfgang von Regensburg (ca. 924–994). Geschichte, Legende, Verehrung' in Georg Schwaiger and Paul Mai (eds), *Wallfahrten im Bistum Regensburg. Zur Tausendjahrfeier des Todes des hl. Bischofs Wolfgang* (Regensburg, 1994), pp 7–36.

Scott, Brendan, *Religion and reformation in the Tudor diocese of Meath* (Dublin, 2006).

Seale, Yvonne, '"Ten thousand women": gender, affinity, and the development of the Premonstratensian Order in medieval France' (PhD, University of Iowa, 2016).

—, '*De Monasterio Desolato*: patronage and politics in a frontier Irish convent', *JMMS*, 4 (2015), 21–45.

Seaver, Matthew, Conor McDermott and Graeme Warren, 'A monastery among the glens', *Archaeology Ireland*, 32:2 (2018), 19–23.

Sensi, Mario, 'Anchorites in the Italian tradition' in Liz Herbert-McAvoy (ed.), *Anchoritic traditions of medieval Europe* (Woodbridge, 2010), pp 62–90.

Seymour, St John, 'Studies in the Vision of Tundal', *PRIA*, 37C (1926), 87–106.

Sharpe, Richard, 'Vita S Brigitae: the oldest texts,' *Peritia*, 1 (1982), 81–106.

—, *Medieval Irish saints' Lives* (Oxford, 1991).

—, 'Churches and communities in early Ireland: towards a pastoral model' in John Blair and Richard Sharpe (eds), *Pastoral care before the parish* (Leicester, 1992), pp 81–109.

—, *A handlist of the Latin writers of Great Britain and Ireland before 1540* (Turnhout, 1997).

Sheehan, Sarah, 'Loving Medb' in Sarah Sheehan, Joanne Findon and Westley Follett (eds), *Gablánacht in Scélaigecht: Celtic studies in honour of Ann Dooley* (Dublin, 2013), pp 171–86.

Sheehy, Maurice P., *Pontificia Hibernica: medieval papal chancery records relating to Ireland 640–1261* (2 vols, Dublin, 1962–65).★

Silvas, Anna M., *The Rule of St Basil in Latin and English* (Collegeville, 2013).★

Smith, Brendan, *Conquest and colonization in medieval Ireland: the English in Louth, 1170–1330* (Cambridge, 1999).

Southern, Richard W., *Western society and the church in the Middle Ages* (London, 1970).

Sperber, Ingrid, 'The Life of St Monenna or Darerca of Killevy' in A.J. Hughes and William Nolan (eds), *Armagh: history and society* (Dublin, 2001), pp 63–97.

Spilling, Herrad, *Die Visio Tnugdali: Eigenart und Stellung in der mittelalterlichen Visionsliteratur bis zum Ende des 12 Jahrhunderts* (Munich, 1975).

Stalley, Roger, 'The architecture of the cathedral and priory buildings' in Kenneth Milne (ed.), *Christ Church Cathedral, Dublin: a history* (Dublin, 2000), pp 95–129.

Stam, Nike, *Typology of code-switching in the commentary to the Félire Óengusso* (Utrecht, 2017).

—, '"Hij Die Niet Leest Is Een Dweil": Nieuw Licht Op de Commentaartraditie van de *Félire Óengusso*', *Kelten*, 81 (2020), 4–10.

Stancliffe, Clare, 'The miracle stories in seventh-century Irish saints' Lives' in Jacques Fontaine and J. N. Hillgarth (eds), *The seventh century: change and continuity* (London, 1992), pp 87–115.

Stephen of Lexington, *Letters from Ireland: 1228–1229*, trans. by Barry W. O'Dwyer (Kalamazoo, MI, 1982).★

St John Brooks, Eric (ed.), *The register of the hospital of St John the Baptist without the New Gate, Dublin* (Dublin, 1936).★

Stokes, Whitley, *Three Middle Irish homilies on the Lives of St Patrick, St Brigit and St Columba* (Calcutta, 1877).★

— (ed.), *Lives of the saints from the Book of Lismore* (Oxford, 1890).★

— (ed.), *Félire Húi Gormáin: The martyrology of Gorman* (London, 1895).★

— (ed.), *Félire Óengusso Céli Dé: The martyrology of Oengus the Culdee* (London, 1905; repr. Dublin, 1984).★

— and John Strachan (eds), *Thesaurus Palaeohibernicus – a collection of Old Irish glosses, scholia, prose and verse*, 2 vols (Dublin 1903).★

Stout, Geraldine, 'De Bello Beco: a French foundation in the Boyne Valley', *CLAHSJ*, 29:2 (2018), 194–204.

— and Matthew Stout, *The Bective Abbey project, Co. Meath: excavations, 2009–12* (Dublin, 2016).

Stout, Matthew, *Early medieval Ireland, 431–1169* (Dublin, 2017).

Swift, Catherine, 'The social and ecclesiastical background to the treatment of the Connachta in Tírechán's seventh-century *Collectanea*' (D.Phil., University of Oxford, 1994).

—, 'Tírechán's motives in compiling the *Collectanea*: an alternative interpretation', *Ériu*, 45 (1994), 53–84.

—, *Ogham stones and the earliest Irish Christians* (Maynooth, 1997).

—, 'Sculptors and their customers: a study of Clonmacnoise grave slabs' in Heather King (ed.), *Clonmacnoise studies, volume 2* (Dublin, 2003), pp 105–23.

—, 'Brigid, Patrick and the kings of Kildare, AD 640–850' in William Nolan and Thomas McGrath (eds), *Kildare: history and society* (Dublin, 2006), pp 97–128.

—, 'Early Irish priests in their own locality' in Fiona Edwards and Paul Russell (eds), *Tome: studies in medieval Celtic history and law in honour of Thomas Charles-Edwards* (Woodbridge, 2011), pp 29–40.

—, 'Lands that time forgot: the early Cistercian settlement of Monasternenagh, Co. Limerick', *Proceedings of the Harvard Celtic Colloquium*, 38 (2018), 259–304.

Sykes, Katharine, *Inventing Sempringham: Gilbert of Sempringham and the origins of the role of the master*, Vita Regularis. Abhandlungen, 46 (Münster, 2011).

Tait, Clodagh, *Death, burial and commemoration in Ireland, 1550–1650* (Basingstoke, 2002).

Thomas, Charles, *Christianity in Roman Britain to* AD *500* (Berkeley, 1981).

—, *Christian Celts: messages and images* (Stroud, 1998).

Thomas, Gabor, 'Life before the minster: the social dynamics of monastic foundation at Anglo-Saxon Lyminge, Kent', *The Antiquaries Journal*, 93 (2013), 109–45.

Thompson, Sally, 'The problem of the Cistercian nuns in the twelfth and early thirteenth centuries' in Derek Baker (ed.), *Medieval women* (Oxford, 1978), pp 227–52.

Thurneysen, Rudolf, 'Die Abfassung des *Félire* von Oengus', *Zeitschrift für celtische Philologie* 6 (1908), 6–8.

—, *Irisches Recht: Díre. Ein altirischer Rechtstext* (Berlin, 1931).★

Ticher, Kurt, 'The silver in the St Clare's Monastery, Galway', *JGAHS*, 37 (1979/80), 62–77.

Tiersonnier, Philippe, 'La chapelle de l'ancien prieuré d'Aubeterre', *Bulletin de la Societé d'émulation et des beaux-arts du Bourbonnais*, 10 (1902), 80–2.

Twemlow, J.A., *Calendar of entries in the papal registers relating to Great Britain and Ireland*, 17 vols (London, 1906).★

Van Waefelghem, Raphaël, *L'Obituaire de l'abbaye de Prémontré (XIIe s., ms. 9 de Soissons)* (Louvain, 1913).

Van Wyhe, Cordula (ed.), *Female monasticism in early modern Europe* (London, 2008).

Veach, Colin, *Lordship in four realms: the Lacy family, 1166–1241*, Manchester Medieval Studies, 12 (Manchester, 2014).

Venarde, Bruce L., *Women's monasticism and medieval society: nunneries in France and England, 890–1215* (Ithaca, NY, 1997).

Villiers-Tuthill, Kathleen, 'The Irish Benedictine nuns: from Kylemore to Ypres' in Martin Browne and Colmán Ó Clabaigh (eds), *The Irish Benedictines: a history* (Dublin, 2005), pp 122–39.

Vita S Disibodi episcopi et confessoris, Acta Sanctorum Jul. II (Antwerp, 1721), pp 581–97.★

Vogüé, Adalbert de, and Joël Courreau, *Césaire d'Arles: Oeuvres Monastiques Tome I: Oeuvres pour les moniales*, Sources Chrétiennes 345 (Paris, 1988).★

Von Vaupel Klein, Lisette C., 'The Lives and times of St Íte of Killeedy' (MA, Mediëvistiek and Keltische Taal- en Letterkunde, Utrecht University, July 2003).

Waefelghem, Raphaël van, 'Les premiers statuts de l'Ordre de Prémontré. Le Clm. 17. 174 (XIIe siècle)', *Analectes de l'Ordre de Prémontré*, 9 (1913), 1–74.★

Waitz, Georg (ed.), *Othloni Vita sti Wolfkangi epi*, MGH Scriptores (in folio) 4 (Hannover, 1841), pp 521–42.★

Walker, Claire, 'Prayer, patronage, and political conspiracy: English nuns and the Restoration', *The Historical Journal*, 43:1 (2000), pp 1–23.

—, '"Doe not supose me a well mortifyed nun dead to the world": Letter writing in early modern English convents' in James Daybell (ed.), *Early modern women's letter writing, 1450–1700* (Basingstoke, 2001), pp 159–76.

—, *Gender and politics in early modern Europe: English convents in France and the Low Countries* (Basingstoke, 2003).

Walker Bynum, Caroline, 'Jesus as mother and abbot as mother: some themes in twelfth-century Cistercian writing', *Harvard Theological Review*, 70:3–4 (1977), 257–84.

—, *Jesus as mother: studies in the spirituality of the high Middle Ages* (Berkeley, 1982).

Walsh, Paul, 'The topography of the town of Galway in the medieval and early modern period' in Gerard P. Moran and Raymond Gillespie (eds), *Galway history and society: interdisciplinary essays on the history of an Irish county* (Dublin, 1996), pp 27–96.

—, *Renaissance Galway: delineating the seventeenth-century city* (Dublin, 2019).

Wardell, John, 'The history and antiquities of St Catherine's, Old Abbey, County Limerick' (with a description of the conventual buildings by T.J. Westropp), *JRSAI*, 14 (1904), 41–64.

Ware, James, *De Hibernia et antiquitatibus ejus, disquisitiones* (2nd ed., London, 1658).★

Warren, Anne K., *Anchorites and their patrons in medieval England* (Berkeley, 1985).

Watt, John A., *The church in medieval Ireland* (Dublin, 1972).

Weber, Stefan, *Iren auf dem Kontinent. Das Leben des Marianus Scottus von Regensburg und die Anfänge der irischen ‚Schottenklöster'* (Heidelberg, 2010).

—, 'Die Konstruktion eines fabulösen „irischen" Heiligenlebens? Der heilige Albert, Regensburg und die Iren' in Dorothea Walz and Jakobus Kaffanke OSB (eds), *Irische Mönche in Süddeutschland. Literarisches und kulturelles Wirken der Iren im Mittalalter* (Heidelberg, 2009), pp 229–304.

Weisgerber, Leo, 'Eine Irenwelle an Maas, Mosel und Rhein in ottonischer Zeit?' in *Aus Geschichte und Landeskunde. Forschungen und Darstellungen. Franz Steinbach zum 65. Geburtstag gewidmet von seinen Freunden und Schülern* (Bonn, 1960), pp 727–50.

Westropp, Thomas. J., 'The antiquities of the northern portion of the county of Clare', *JRSAI*, 30 (1900), 126–33.

—, 'The Augustinian houses of the County Clare: Clare, Killone and Inchicronan', *JRSAI*, 30 (1900), 118–135.

—, 'A survey of the ancient churches in the County of Limerick', *PRIA*, 25 (1905), 325–480.

—, 'The churches of County Clare and the origin of the ecclesiastical divisions in that county', *PRIA*, 6 (1900–1902), 100–80.

White, Newport B. (ed.) *Irish monastic and episcopal deeds, 1200–1600* (Dublin, 1936).★

—, *Extents of Irish monastic possessions, 1540–41. Manuscripts held in the Public Record Office London* (Dublin, 1943). ★

Wiesner–Hanks, Merry, *Convents confront the Reformation: Catholic and Protestant nuns in Germany* (Milwaukee, 1996).

Wiethaus, Ulrike, 'Bride of Christ imagery' in Margaret C. Schaus (ed.), *Women and gender in medieval Europe: an encyclopaedia* (London, 2006), pp 94–5.

Wolbrink, Shelley Amiste, 'Women in the Premonstratensian Order of northwestern Germany, 1120–1250', *The Catholic Historical Review*, 89:3 (2003), 387–408.

—, 'Necessary priests and brothers: male-female cooperation in the Premonstratensian women's monasteries of Füssenich and Meer, 1140–1260' in Fiona J. Griffiths and Julie Hotchin (eds), *Partners in spirit: women, men, and religious life in Germany, 1100–1500*, Medieval Women: Texts and Contexts, 24 (Turnhout, 2014), pp 171–212.

Wood, Michael K., and Malcolm G. Underwood, *The king's mother: Lady Margaret Beaufort, Countess of Richmond and Derby* (Cambridge, 1992).

Woodford, Charlotte, *Nuns as historians in early modern Germany* (Oxford, 2002).

Wycherley, Niamh, *The cult of relics in early medieval Ireland* (Turnhout, 2015).

Yepes, Diego de, *Vida, virtudes, y Milagros, de la bienavenrurada virgin Teresa de Jesus* (Lisbon, 1616).★

WEBSITES

https://arts.st-andrews.ac.uk/monasticmatrix/home; Monastic Matrix, accessed 15 September 2022.

www.isos.dias.ie. Monastic Matrix, Irish Script on Screen website.

https://monasticon.celt.dias.ie/, accessed 23 April 2022.

https://confessio.ie/#, accessed 23 April 2022.

https://aschresources.org/who-were-the-nuns-a-prosopographical-study-of-the-english-convents-in-exile-1600-1800/, accessed 23 October 2022.

www.irish-annals.cs.tcd.ie, accessed 23 April 2022.

https://chancery.tcd.ie/content/welcome-circle, CIRCLE accessed 15 September 2022.

www.dil.ie 2019, *An electronic dictionary of the Irish language, based on the contributions to a Dictionary of the Irish language* (Dublin, 1913–76), accessed 29 November 2021.

https//www.dib.it/biography/Fedelmid-feidhlimid-a3034, accessed 14 March, 2022.

Index

References in *italics* indicate illustrations